W9-CCC-622

MARVEL
ENCYCLOPEDIA

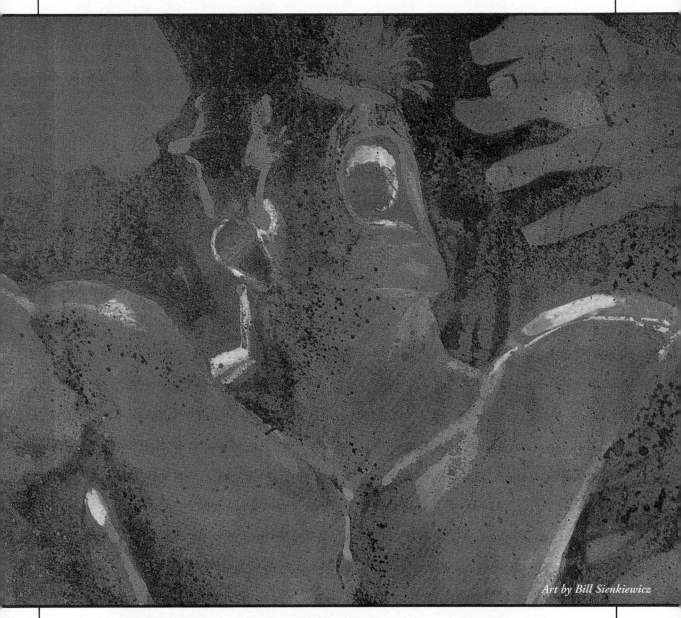

Art by Bill Sienkiewicz

THE INCREDIBLE NULK

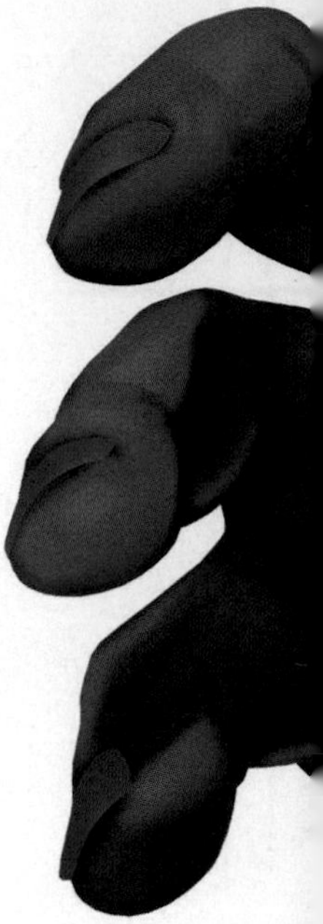

Art by Dale Keown

MARVEL
ENCYCLOPEDIA

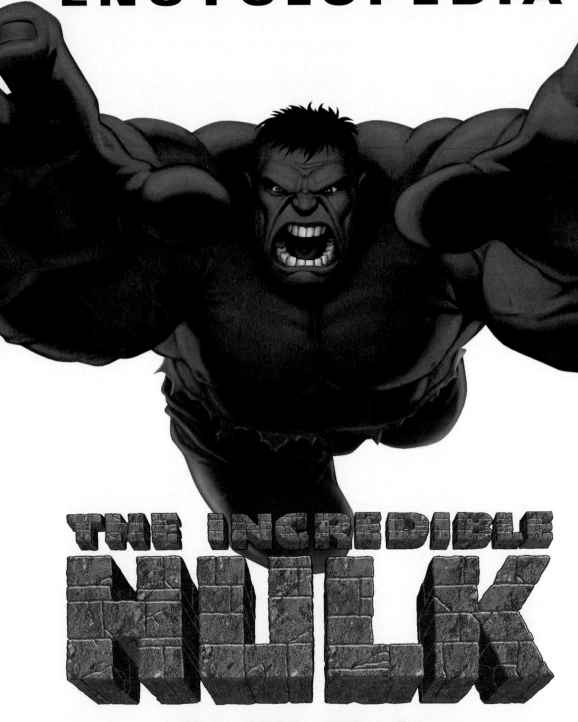

THE INCREDIBLE HULK

By Kit Kiefer

MARVEL ENTERPRISES, INC.

CEO & GENERAL COUNSEL	Allen Lipson
CHIEF CREATIVE OFFICER	Avi Arad
PRESIDENT & CEO, TOY BIZ	Alan Fine
EVP OPERATIONS AND CIO	Gui Karyo
CHIEF FINANCIAL OFFICER	Ken West
EVP SALES, TOY BIZ	Ralph Lancelotti
V.P.-HUMAN RESOURCES	Mary Sprowls

ADVERTISING — PROMOTION — RETAIL SALES

EXEC. VICE PRESIDENT CONSUMER PRODUCTS, PROMOTIONS, AND MEDIA SALES	Russell A. Brown
TRADE BOOK SALES MANAGER	Jennifer Beemish
ADVERTISING SALES	Sara Beth Schrager

PUBLISHING GROUP

PRESIDENT AND COO PUBLISHING, CONSUMER PRODUCTS & NEW MEDIA	Bill Jemas
EDITOR IN CHIEF	Joe Quesada
MANAGING EDITOR	David Bogart
DIRECTOR OF OPERATIONS	Sangho Byun
PRODUCTION DIRECTOR	Dan Carr
DIRECTOR OF MARKETING	Peter Mathews
MARKETING COMMUNICATIONS MANAGER	Michael Doran
SENIOR MANUFACTURING MANAGER	Fred Pagan
MANUFACTURING MANAGER	Christine Slusarz
MANUFACTURING REPRESENTATIVE	Stefano Perrone, Jr.
EDITOR	Jeff Youngquist
ART DIRECTOR/BOOK DESIGNER	Matty Ryan
FRONT DUST JACKET ART	Dale Keown
BACK DUST JACKET ART	Joe Jusko
COVER ART	Adam Kubert
COPY EDITOR	Jake Kornegay

SPECIAL THANKS: Axel Alonso, Judy Bass, Mark D. Beazley, Seth Biederman, Tom Brevoort, Chris Fondacaro, Johnny Greene, Jennifer Grünwald, Gamal Hennessy, Tom Marvelli, Sean Ryan, Cory Sedlmeier, Joshua Silverman, Jeff Suter and *Wizard: The Comics Magazine*.

Toy images courtesy the personal collection of Mr. Stephen Yarish. Used with permission.

MARVEL ENCYCLOPEDIA VOL. 3: HULK. Contains material originally published in magazine form as HULK #1, INCREDIBLE HULK #34 and THE ULTIMATES #5. First printing 2003. ISBN# 0-7851-1164-6. Published by MARVEL COMICS, a division of MARVEL ENTERTAINMENT GROUP, INC. OFFICE OF PUBLICATION: 10 East 40th Street, New York, NY 10016. THE HULK Movie: © 2003 Universal Studios. Licensed by Marvel Characters, Inc. THE INCREDIBLE HULK and All Related Comic Book Characters: TM & © 1962, 2001, 2002 and 2003 Marvel Characters, Inc. All Rights Reserved. $19.99 per copy in the U.S. and $32.00 in Canada (GST #R127032852); Canadian Agreement #40668537. All characters featured in this publication and the distinctive names and likenesses thereof, and all related indicia are trademarks of Marvel Characters, Inc. No similarity between any of the names, characters, persons, and/or institutions in this publication with those of any living or dead person or institution is intended, and any such similarity which may exist is purely coincidental. **Printed in the U.S.A.** STAN LEE, Chairman Emeritus. For information regarding advertising in Marvel Comics or on Marvel.com, please contact Russell Brown, Executive Vice President, Consumer Products, Promotions and Media Sales at 212-576-8561 or rbrown@marvel.com

10 9 8 7 6 5 4 3 2 1

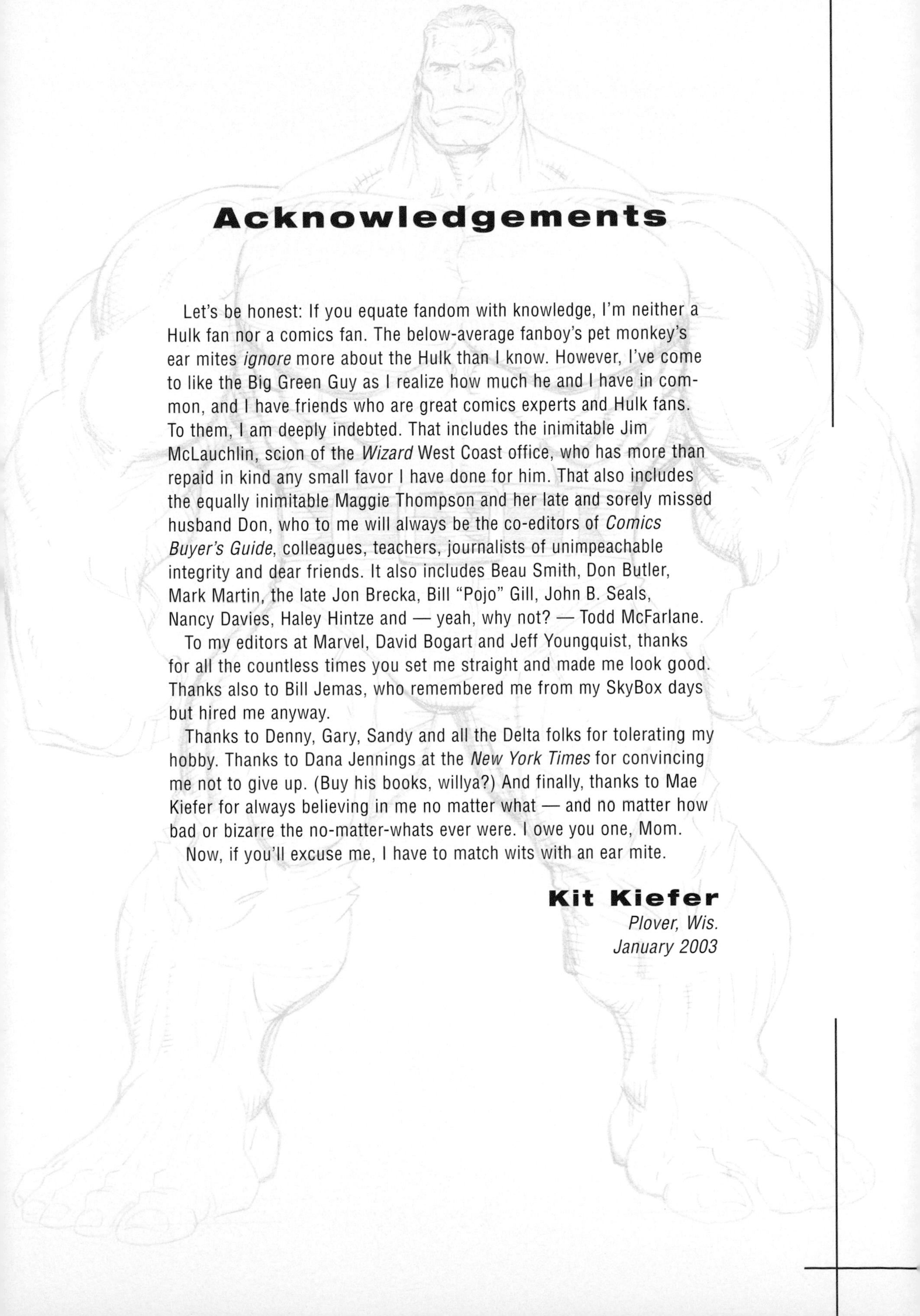

Acknowledgements

Let's be honest: If you equate fandom with knowledge, I'm neither a Hulk fan nor a comics fan. The below-average fanboy's pet monkey's ear mites *ignore* more about the Hulk than I know. However, I've come to like the Big Green Guy as I realize how much he and I have in common, and I have friends who are great comics experts and Hulk fans. To them, I am deeply indebted. That includes the inimitable Jim McLauchlin, scion of the *Wizard* West Coast office, who has more than repaid in kind any small favor I have done for him. That also includes the equally inimitable Maggie Thompson and her late and sorely missed husband Don, who to me will always be the co-editors of *Comics Buyer's Guide*, colleagues, teachers, journalists of unimpeachable integrity and dear friends. It also includes Beau Smith, Don Butler, Mark Martin, the late Jon Brecka, Bill "Pojo" Gill, John B. Seals, Nancy Davies, Haley Hintze and — yeah, why not? — Todd McFarlane.

To my editors at Marvel, David Bogart and Jeff Youngquist, thanks for all the countless times you set me straight and made me look good. Thanks also to Bill Jemas, who remembered me from my SkyBox days but hired me anyway.

Thanks to Denny, Gary, Sandy and all the Delta folks for tolerating my hobby. Thanks to Dana Jennings at the *New York Times* for convincing me not to give up. (Buy his books, willya?) And finally, thanks to Mae Kiefer for always believing in me no matter what — and no matter how bad or bizarre the no-matter-whats ever were. I owe you one, Mom.

Now, if you'll excuse me, I have to match wits with an ear mite.

Kit Kiefer
Plover, Wis.
January 2003

Dedication

To my lovely Ann, Molly, Andy and Danny, who
know I get a little green sometimes, and understand.

-KK

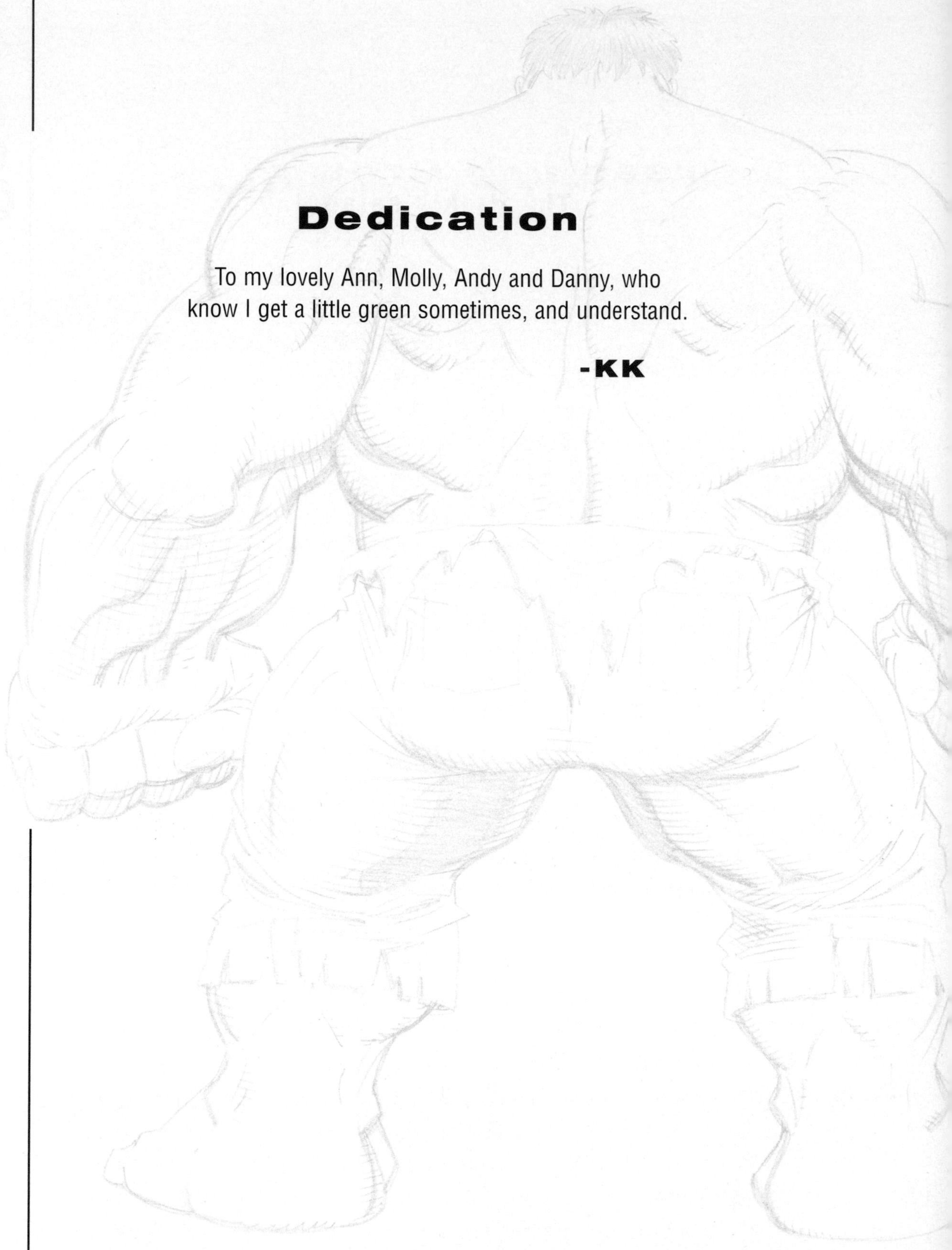

Contents

Chapter One   11
Bleedin' Green
Why the Hulk matters

Chapter Two   25
Green and Growin'
The Hulk's salad days

Hulk #1   49

Chapter Three   75
Hulk, as in Bulk
From Flying Fists to Fun Putty, and back again

Chapter Four   89
Big Hulk, Small Screen
The Hulk on TV

Chapter Five   107
The Hulk Reborn
This ain't your Daddy's Hulk

Incredible Hulk #34   127

Chapter Six   153
Big Hulk, Big Screen
The Hulk at the movies

Chapter Seven   173
Green Day
The Hulk commands the spotlight—again!

The Ultimates #5   182

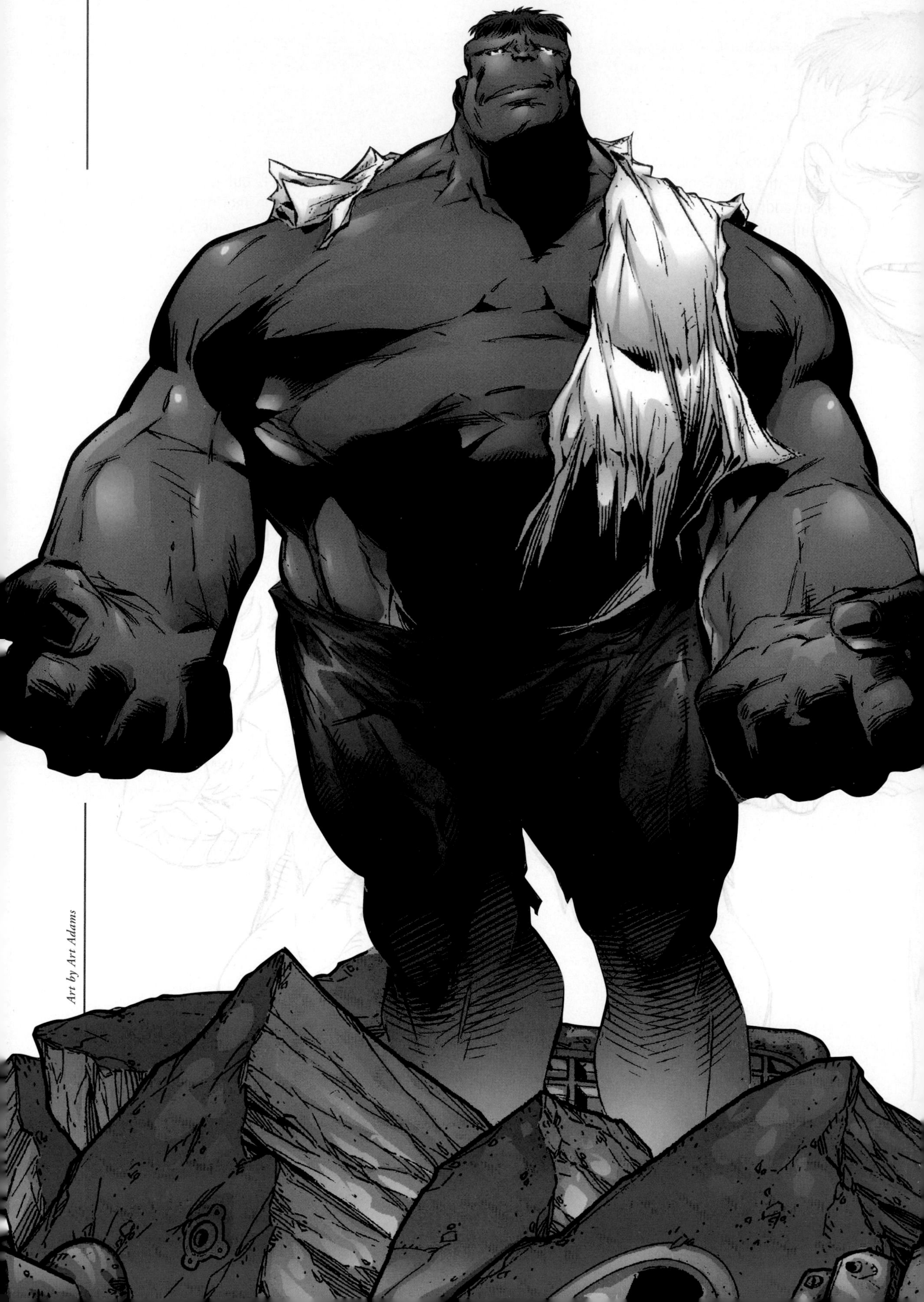

Art by Art Adams

Introduction

"Hi-Ho, Silver" ...
"Go ahead, make my day" ...
"A long time ago, in a galaxy far, far away" ...

It's a rare, rare thing in popular fiction to find such a combination of words that instantly, vividly and effortlessly explains the "high concept," stirs emotions, and sets the stage for eager audiences to witness the fantastic events about to unfold before them.

Marvel Comics has had its share ... "With great power, there must also come great responsibility," for example, succinctly but eloquently describes what makes the Amazing Spider-Man the most popular superhero in the world. But when it comes to eloquence and the art of brevity, there are two simple words — famous for their lack of articulation but bold in their clarity of meaning — that have come to define a character that arguably could give Spidey a run for his money.

"HULK SMASH!"

No two words, ever in the history of American pop culture, have been able to incite a more visceral reaction. It's the call of the wild, the release of the spoiled child, the id in all of us allowed out to run free.

Stan Lee and Jack Kirby's mean, green walking engine of destruction first uttered those two infamous words more than forty years ago, and the Incredible Hulk hasn't stopped since — smashing his way into popular cultural iconography.

This brilliantly uncomplicated nuclear-age melding of Dr. Jeykll and Mr. Hyde with Frankenstein's Monster has appealed to readers of all ages and walks of life. Fans have either marveled at his awesome feats of strength, or identified and sympathized with the primal, raw emotions and urges seething inside the seemingly "mild-mannered" exterior of Dr. Bruce Banner, ready to burst out in times of extreme stress. A character ripe for the likes of Freudian analysis but simple enough to take us all on wild flights of heroic fantasy.

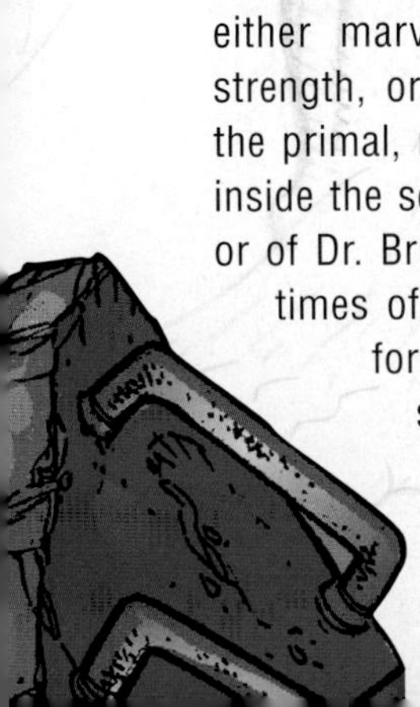

Who among us hasn't wanted to "Hulk-out" at one time in our lives? Demanding parents, torturous school bullies, lousy relationship, a terrible boss, screaming kids, nothing on TV? How many of us wish we could just turn a bright shade of green and throw a super-powered tantrum, and then get back to our lives as if it never happened? We can't, but it sure is fun watching Hulk do it. That in fact has been the greatest appeal of the Hulk through the years: He is what we all know lurks deep inside all of us yet have been brought up to suppress.

Despite being the most untraditional of "superheroes," the Hulk's simple and universal appeal has struck a resonant chord with fans in every single decade since his creation. In the '60s, '80s and '90s, he was brought to life in several hit animated series — but it was in the '70s that the Hulk really made his mark. Unless you've been living under a rock — most likely thrown on you by the Hulk — we've all seen the wonderful Bill Bixby Hulk TV show. Translated into countless languages and syndicated worldwide since it first aired on American television, this show has made the Hulk quite possibly even more popular than Spider-Man on an international level.

And now, finally in 2003, four decades after Dr. Banner's Gamma Ray Bomb first exploded in the pages of Marvel Comics, technology has finally caught up to Lee and Kirby's amazing vision and found a new way to do it justice. So for you new fans who may have just discovered the Hulk through director Ang Lee's tour-de-force film — or for you old-timers who have thrilled to his comic book, cartoon and TV adventures for years — this book is for you. A detailed history of why, even after the world has changed over and over again, the two words "HULK SMASH!" get our blood pumping, touch something in our hearts and sometimes bring a knowing green glint to our eyes ...

See ya in the funnybooks!

'03

JQ
EEK

Chapter One

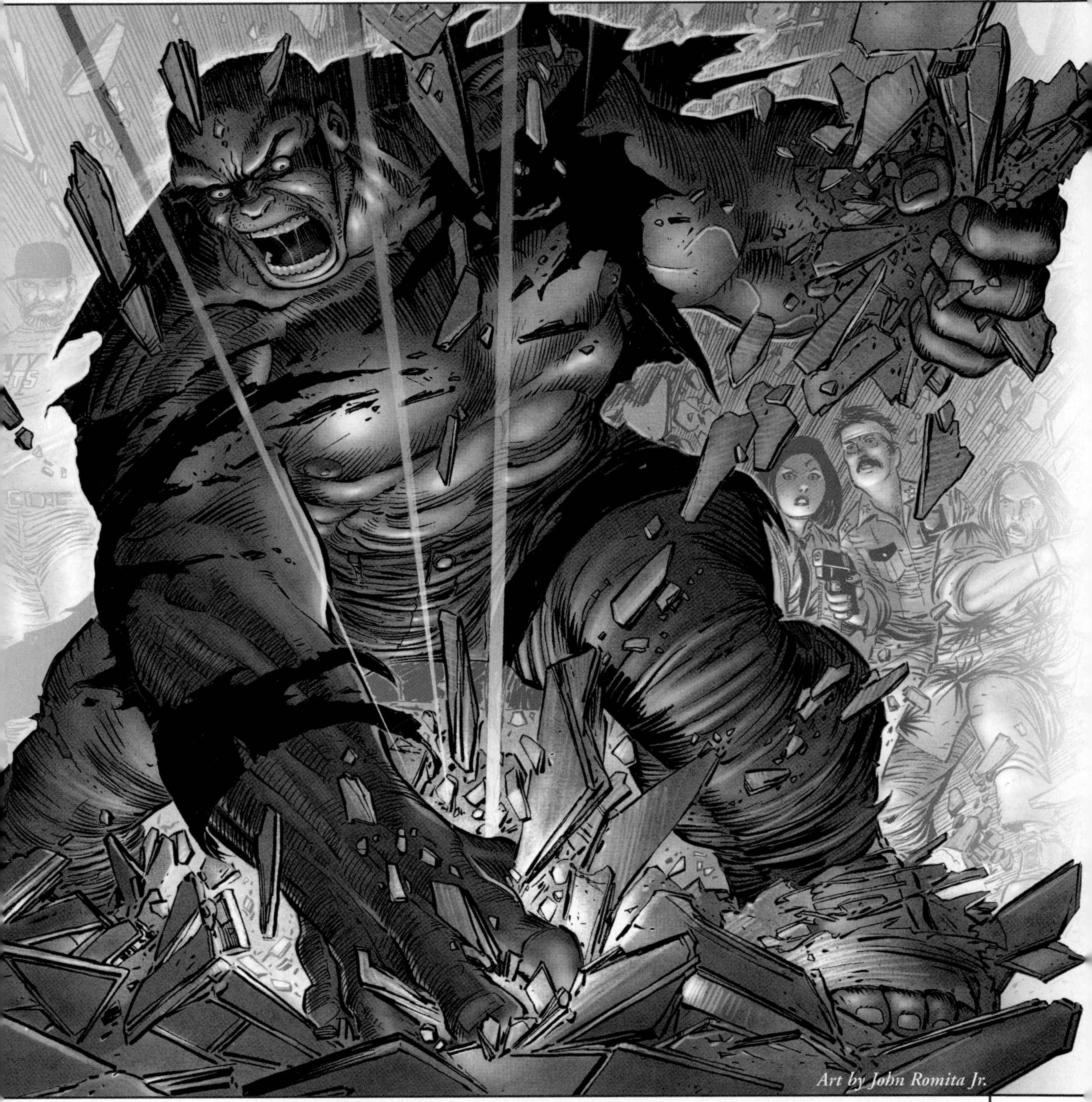

Art by John Romita Jr.

BLEEDIN' GREEN

Why the Hulk matters

Eminem.

Saddam Hussein.

Attack dogs.

Sept. 11, 2001.

Professional wrestlers.

And you ask whether the Hulk still matters. Of course the Hulk still matters. The Hulk has never stopped mattering. There is still rage in the world. It's Sept 11, 2002, as this is being written in a Chicago hotel room, and the rage is everywhere, in the city and in the little place where I live.

The Hulk not relevant? How can someone who deals with stress in the most satisfying way imaginable — by pounding on it until it goes away — not be relevant? Wouldn't it be great to turn into a super-muscle-bound, atomic-powered green guy *right now*, be in Baghdad in a couple of leaps and pound on the monkey skull of the aforementioned Mr. Hussein until it rings like a Chinese gong?

That is what the Hulk is all about.

Just *thinking* about doing what the Hulk does is satisfying. And sitting in a 50-speaker, sub-woofer-equipped, stadium-style theater and *seeing* the Hulk makes thinking about the Hulk seem like ... uh, thinking. If watching the Hulk make library paste out of a couple G-dogs in Ang Lee's movie doesn't make you want to stand and cheer, better check your pulse. Make sure you still have one. If you do and still don't feel like pumping your fist, punching your popcorn, screaming "Yeah!" and embarrassing your girlfriend, you're in the wrong theater. The Meg Ryan movie is next door.

The best superheroes are the ones who are most obvious to six-year-old boys: a guy from another planet who can split trains with his nose, see through drywall, fly through the air with the greatest of ease and grab bullets like they were french fries; a kid who can shoot webs and crawl up walls like a spider; a super-bendy guy who can hit a home run simply by having his pinky circle the bases; and best of all, a guy who gets mad and wrecks stuff — gets really mad and wrecks really big stuff. Ain't no hammer can do what the Hulk can, and that's not a desirable personality trait unless you're a six-year-old boy. And then it's perfect.

There's some six-year-old boy in most of us, so at this point we have to tip our hats west to Mr. Stan Lee, who recognized that fact nearly half a century ago and created most of the aforementioned characters. There's probably some pseudo-Freudian explanation for what Lee did, the superego overcoming the id in overtime and going on to win the Super Bowl, but what he really did is take the inhabitants of a six-year-old boy's brain and move 'em on up to the East Side.

The characters never go away, either. You can be a family guy, pillar of the community, upright and well-respected, and you can still put yourself to sleep at night trashing the home office of the customer who switched to the other guy's piston rings. Someone starts making nice to the one girl who makes the party bearable, the one possibility in a sea of impossibility, and you take the can of Mello Yello in your hand and make a coaster out of it, thinking all the time, "This could be his head," and wishing for a nanosecond you could be Bruce Banner and have the power to get really out of control *right now*. It's nothing personal. He just hurt you, and the thing that makes sense is hurting him back. Just like the Hulk.

You bet the Hulk matters.

Is it proper? Of course not. Who said anything about propriety? This is anti-propriety. Being a superhero, any super-hero, even a stiff like Superman, isn't proper. Tights are not proper. Bare chests aren't proper. Climbing up the sides of walls isn't proper. X-ray vision is definitely not proper. And changing into an

> **How can someone who deals with *stress* in the most satisfying way *imaginable* — by pounding on it until it goes away — not be *relevant*?**

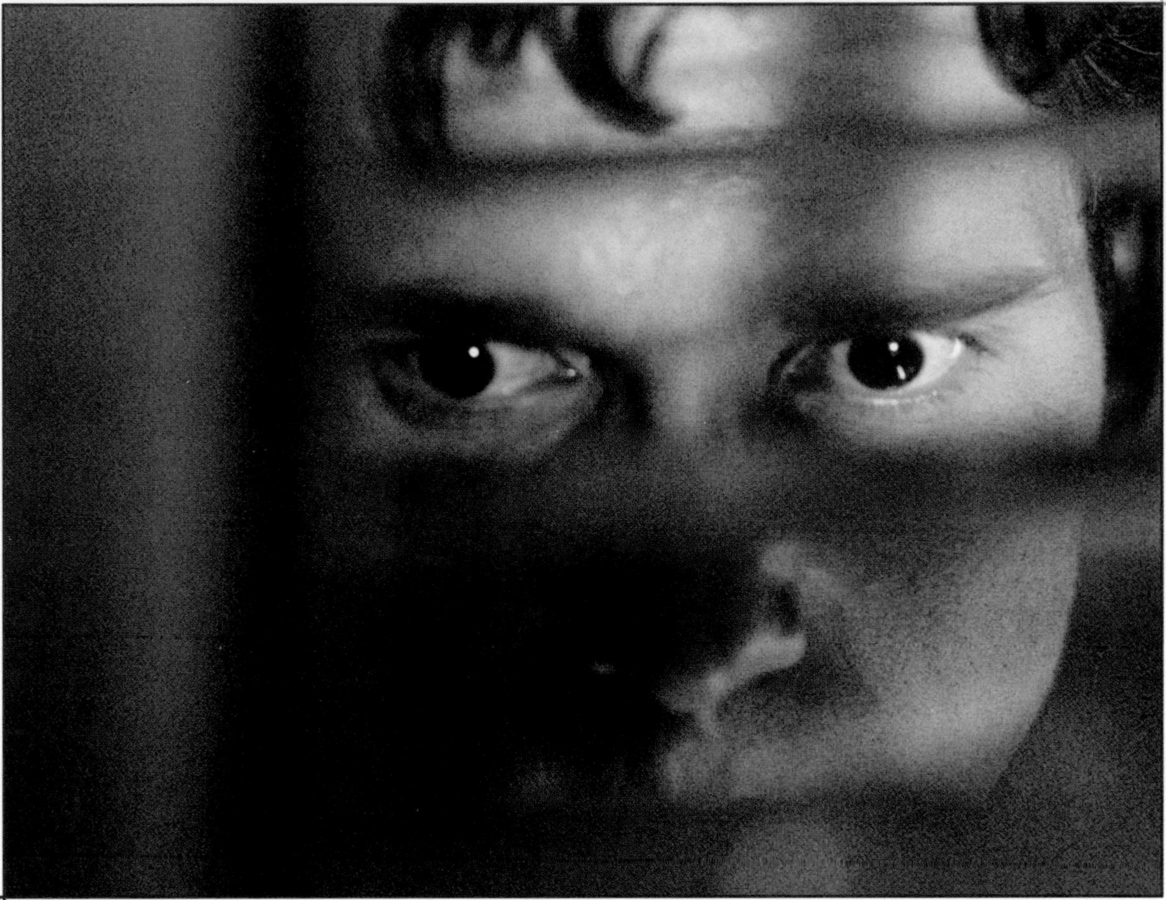

Get a large pot. Toss in irrepressible rage, confusion, fear, anger, self-doubt, self-loathing and maybe a little indigestion, chopped fine. Add one bay leaf. Bring to a rolling boil. What do you get? A look like Eric Bana displays in Hulk.

eight-foot-tall hunka-hunka burning rage is way off the propriety meter.

Besides, if you're looking for propriety in first, a classic superhero and second, in the Incredible Hulk, you just ain't getting it. Watch the movie. Soak up the message, which is basically that there is no message. The proper people are wrong. The outcast is right, and he's being punished for it. And when they hit him he hits back harder.

Sounds like something out of the Marshall Mathers files. Also sounds like *Rebel Without a Cause.* And a little like *The Odyssey* and *The Bible.* This stuff isn't new. There are about a dozen classic themes in literature, and the Hulk uses the persecuted-outcast theme. And it sure makes for a better comic than the I'm-in-love-with-my-mother theme.

The Hulk is pop culture, though. And though the theme might be classic, the beats are different. Pop culture has to play on a Victoria or a Philco radio or a Zenith home-entertainment center or a cassette deck or a VCR or a CD player or a DVD/MP3 combo. It can't stop at the printed page.

Pop culture swelled like a Banzai Pipeline wave through most of the 20th century and crested in the '60s. The Hulk first shot the curl in 1962, making him a child of the '60s — but not the flower-power, Jefferson Airplane, Summer of Love '60s. The Hulk was a creation of the Botany 500 '60s, the Frankie Valli and the Four Seasons '60s, the Brylcreem and Vitalis '60s, the uptight '60s where being successful meant having an analyst and wearing Florsheims ... and being paranoid.

People who couldn't even spell "paranoia" in 1960 knew all about it by 1969, and the Hulk helped. The Hulk had the Army chasing him, the police on his tail, the TV networks reporting on his whereabouts, the Russkies anxious to crack his secrets, the Red Chinese slapping mind-controlling remotes on his neck, and even freelance villains from the center of the earth and outer space trying to sway him to their side. Hulk paranoia was a different brand from the they're-dropping-acid-in-my-Metrecal-and-shipping-me-to-Da-Nang variety that grew wild through the decade — but paranoia, like punk, is all about feeling. And the Hulk had the feeling.

Except for a six-issue run in 1962, the Hulk didn't get his own comic book until 1968, which coincidentally *was* the Summer of Love. The timing's no accident, and neither was the comic's tremendous popularity from that point forward. The 10-year-old reading a copy in the barber shop and waiting his turn for a flattop couldn't grow his hair like the kids he saw on TV, couldn't march in the streets, couldn't stick flowers down gun barrels, couldn't burn his draft card, couldn't go to Vietnam, couldn't play rock-'n'-roll — but he could still tune in to that station and show how darn dissatisfied he was with the state of the world. He could read the Hulk. And just to show he was really with-it, he wouldn't order any Amazing Sea Monkeys or Revolutionary War soldiers, and he absolutely would not sell flower seeds door to door.

A 17-year-old friend said the other day, "Aw, all the cool stuff happened in the '70s." Want to reconsider? In 1977, the No. 1 song for the year was "You Light Up My Life." In 1979, a radio station asked its listeners to name the 500 greatest rock songs of all time. Know what won? "Keep On Lovin' You" by REO Speedwagon. In the '70s, what were vices became habits, the counterculture and the underground became mainstream, and where's the fun in that? Bing Crosby and David Bowie sang Christmas carols together, Bob Hope grew sideburns, and the Hulk came to the surface along with Bob and Bowie and Bing. And TV did most of the work in a way that only TV, the Great Universal Sandpaper of pop culture, can.

Mention the Hulk in casual conversation, and you hear, "Yeah, I used to watch that" — not, "Yeah, I used to read that." Just as it's no coincidence the Hulk got his first big book in 1968, it's also no coincidence the first *Incredible Hulk* TV movie aired in 1977, the year of "You Light Up My Life," with the TV series premiering a year later.

The series, like hit TV series do, reached millions more people than ever read the comic, which is good and bad. It built brand loyalty for the Hulk — but the *TV* Hulk. The TV show appealed to everyone from five to 95, star Bill Bixby said, but

Puny humans! When will they learn dressing in helmets and fatigues, and firing pop guns at the Hulk, is not the best way to earn his trust? Not in this movie, obviously.

that's not the comic Hulk's audience. Wasn't then, isn't now. TV-show fans who picked up the comic book in the late '70s expecting Stan Lee's creation to blow a head gasket and turn into Lou Ferrigno were disappointed. Sales of the Hulk comic after the series' run were less than they were before. So as far as the long-term success and survival of the Hulk was concerned, the TV series was a wash.

One of the best things about the new *Hulk* movie is that it's not the TV show turned into a movie; it's the comic book turned into a movie. That's a new one. The real Hulk, the comic-book Hulk, can leap across Manhattan in a couple jumps, and the movie brings that as close to real as you can get. The former Mr. Universe who played the TV Hulk might be able to squat 700 pounds, but he could never do the things a CGI Hulk can. And to the TV show's eternal credit, they never had him try.

The TV Hulk was a small-screen Hulk who lived (relatively) small and did small things. The movie Hulk is a big-screen Hulk all the way, with specs (and pecs) and performance to match. It's about time.

Still, the TV Hulk gets props for being better than Wonder Woman and beating up on the Greatest American Hero, even if he could never reach the rarified heights of the Dukes of Hazzard.

And, oh, yeah, he mattered.

The '80s and '90s spawned new heroes and spun off different manifestations of the Hulk and that anger-management issue of his, with most occurring way beyond the confines of comic books: road rage, soccer riots, Stone Cold and the Rock. It seemed like everyone was trying to muscle in on the Hulk's territory. The Hulk responded to the

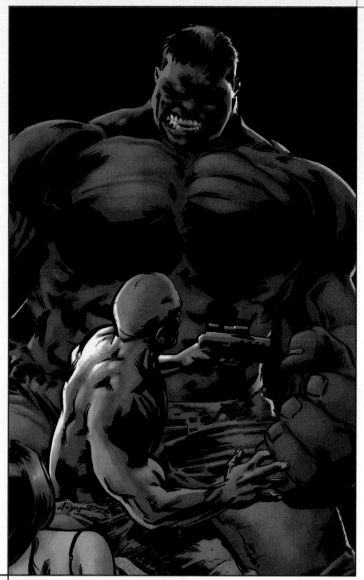

Take the word of countless guffs who have gone down before the Hulk: The gun ain't gonna cut it. Art by Stuart Immonen

competition not the way you'd expect the Hulk to answer competition and threats — by squashing them like bugs — but by getting analytical. By thinking about a situation. By being put in perspective with all his superhero mates.

Silly. The Scarecrow didn't really need a brain in *The Wizard of Oz*, and the Hulk doesn't need one to do that voodoo he do. He doesn't even need a diploma. Nothing has to be put in perspective for the Hulk. The perspective is this: Hulk smash. There's nothing to analyze. His blood pressure rises, he goes off, someone tries to catch him, and he runs away. See you next episode. Even John Madden is speechless.

So in the '70s and '80s, it wasn't that the Hulk didn't matter. He mattered more than ever. But fewer people realized it.

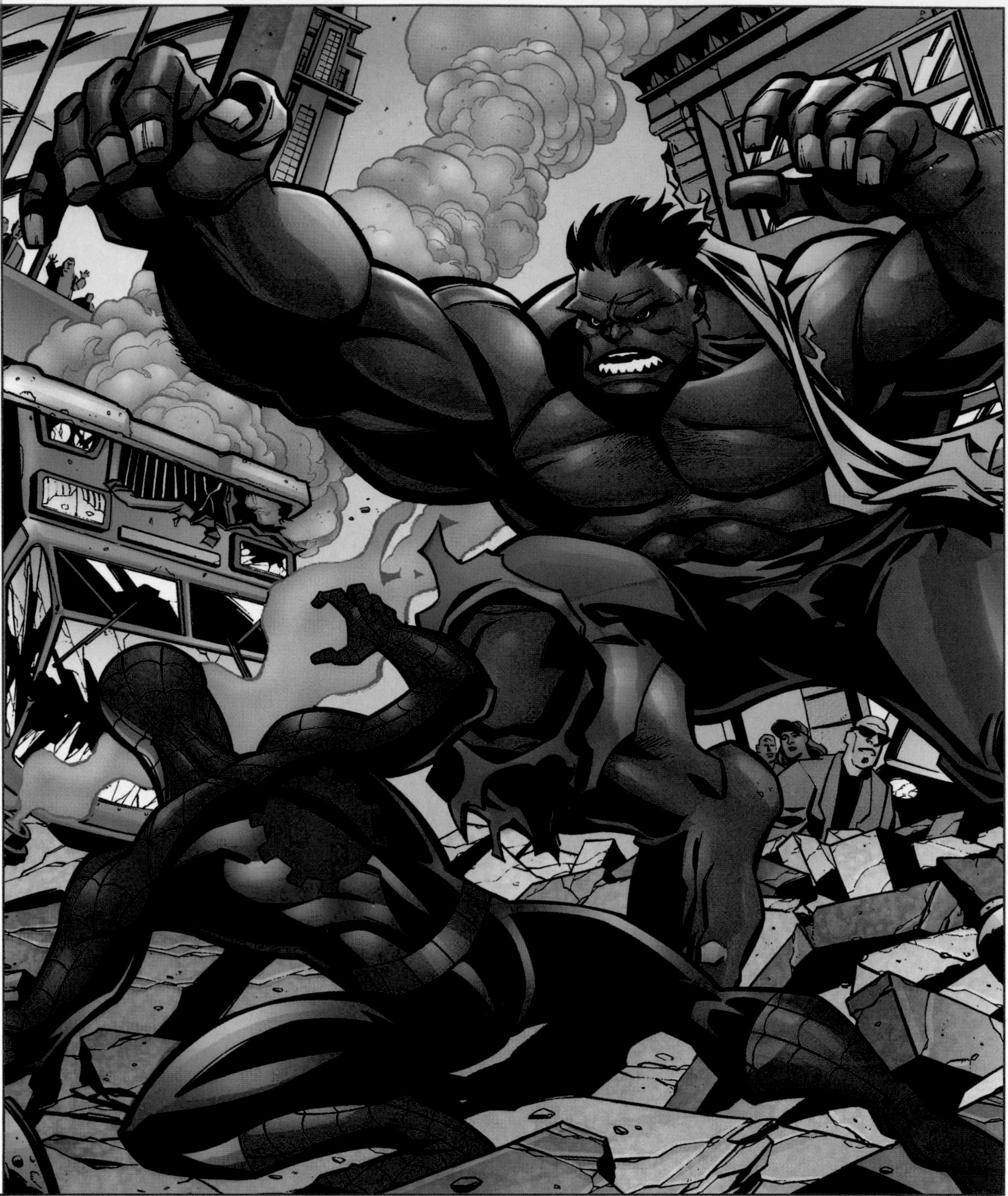

The Hulk doesn't play favorites. If Spider-Man ticks off the Hulk, the Hulk takes on Spidey. Just for fun, compare Phil Hester's post-modern Hulk above to Stuart Immonen's Hulk on the previous page — and then compare both to Jack Kirby's original Hulk on page 18. You've come a long way, baby.

These days, the Hulk is as good as he's ever been. The jingoism of the early books is gone, but the biff-pow and the swift, simple plots remain. Marvel's Ultimate line takes a fresh turn at the primal theme and employs team-ups that make sense. (The Hulk, being a loner, a fugitive and a human, has never been a great crossover character. Put the Hulk and Spider-Man together, and what can they do? Play pinochle until the Hulk loses? Plots do not come naturally.) The *Incredible Hulk* title mines the classic territory for its themes, and that's the way it should be. The mine's nowhere near played out. Yet the look at feel of this 40-year-old title is very much 21st-century.

Whatever, whenever, the Hulk matters because rage is eternal and ever-present. We all get a little green sometimes. And because we do and don't always know how to handle it, we need to have the Hulk around. He can handle it for us.

The Hulk in comics history:
Why this outcast lasted

This isn't a history book, and it's not meant to be about anyone else but the Hulk — but to appreciate the Hulk's role in comics history, it's good to know a little comics history.

Comics have ages, like dinosaurs and hand tools. The Golden Age ran from the late '30s through World War II, and belonged to Batman, Superman and a couple of the Hulk's future stablemates — Captain America, the Human Torch and Namor the Sub-Mariner. For the most part, these Golden Age superheroes were perfect beings who wouldn't belch if you poured a dump-truck load of bicarbonate down their gullets and chased it with a gallon of Mountain Dew. They had to be perfect to fight their arch-enemies: gangsters and Nazis. Comics were simple. The art was in color, but the plots were black-and-white all the way.

The Silver Age began in the late '50s, and belonged to Marvel Comics and its immensely talented creators, artist Jack Kirby and writer/editor Stan Lee. From Summer 1961 through Fall 1964, Kirby and Lee introduced the comic books and characters that would change the world: the Fantastic Four, the Amazing Spider-Man, the Mighty Thor, the Uncanny X-Men, the Avengers and the Incredible Hulk — not to mention Iron Man, Ant-Man, Sgt. Fury and Daredevil. Not bad for a few months' work.

The comics were the perfect synthesis of Lee's wise-cracking realism and Kirby's barrier-breaking art, and they had something Golden Age superheroes never had: depth. They got cranky. They had attitude. They got married. While none of these characters were human, they had human attributes, personalities that readers could relate to. And relate they did.

You can ponder for hours why almost all the greatest comic characters of the last half-century were created in a single 30-month span — but in the end, it's more a Kirby-Lee thing than a societal thing. These characters had been bumping around in one form or another for a decade or more. It took a little bit of success and a big demand for "fantasy" comics (which is what superhero comics were called) to bring them into print.

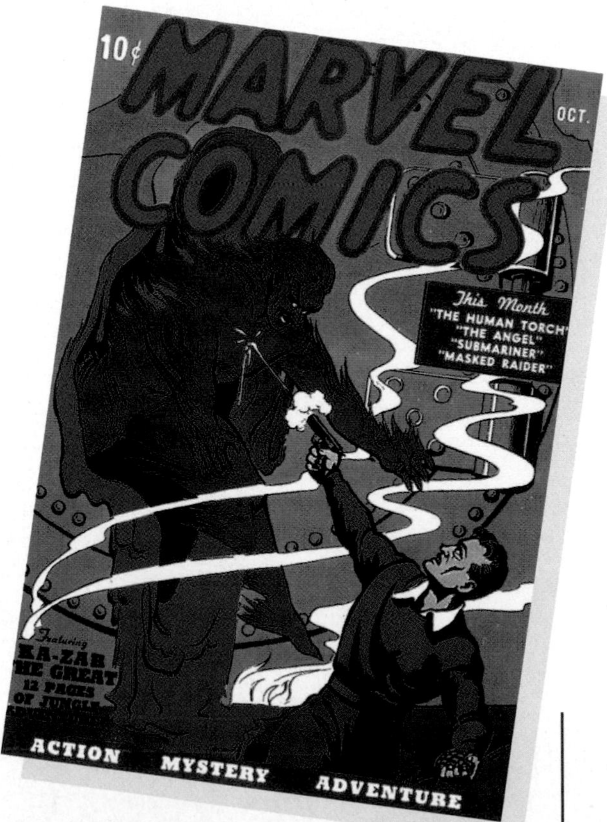
10¢
MARVEL COMICS
OCT.
This Month
"THE HUMAN TORCH"
"THE ANGEL"
"SUBMARINER"
"MASKED RAIDER"
Featuring
KA-ZAR THE GREAT
12 PAGES
ACTION
MYSTERY
ADVENTURE

Marvel Comics #1, October 1939

But being a comics icon takes more than being born at the right time, and it takes more than longevity. The Sub-Mariner is 30 years older than the Hulk, and Sgt. Fury is a contemporary, but there's no talk of the soon-to-be-released Sub-Mariner movie or the new Sgt. Fury flick, great as those comics and characters may be. Both characters were alienated from society like the Hulk; both had tempers; both dealt with problems by getting mad and beating up stuff, more or less — but they lacked the Hulk's simplicity and directness. (They had other problems, too. Sgt. Fury couldn't make it through Vietnam and the war at home, and underwater comics, like underwater movies, are just plain difficult.)

The comics were the perfect synthesis of Lee's wise-cracking realism and Kirby's barrier-breaking art, and they had something Golden Age superheroes never had: depth.

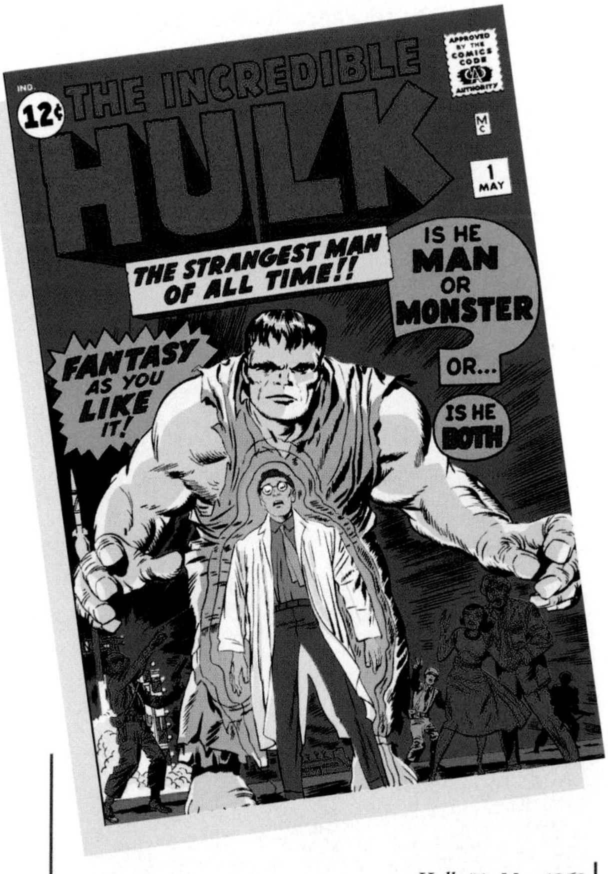
IND.
12¢
THE INCREDIBLE HULK
APPROVED BY THE COMICS CODE AUTHORITY
1 MAY
THE STRANGEST MAN OF ALL TIME!!
IS HE MAN OR MONSTER ?
OR...
IS HE BOTH
FANTASY AS YOU LIKE IT!

Hulk #1, May 1962

Simplicity is comics' most oft-forgotten virtue. Can you pick up a comic book in a barber shop while you're waiting for a flat-top, start reading and not feel like you've missed something? That's the secret to Archie's enduring popularity (What? It's not the intricate storylines?), and it works for the Hulk, too. You can pick up a copy of *Incredible Hulk* and just get going, the same way you can watch any episode of *The Fugitive* but can't with *The Prisoner*, or more recently, *Alias* or *The X-Files.* (It's no wonder *The Prisoner* is available on video only as a boxed set. That's the only way it makes sense.)

You can buy a compilation of early Hulk comics and read it start to finish, but there's no reason to unless you have a Commie-bashing itch that needs to be scratched. Early Hulk titles are more to admire for what they represent than read for what they contain. Still, there's plenty to admire. The Hulk's compact story line and easily understood motivations mean anyone could pick it up and within a few panels be right up to breakneck speed: A fugitive is on the run and oh, yeah — he changes into the world's strongest man when he's mad. If you neglected to read a few issues, there was "Scornful Stan" looking over your shoulder and saying, "See what you've missed if you dallied with Brand Echh these past few months?" — but truth be told, you didn't miss anything you couldn't figure out in half a page.

It wasn't all fun and games. The wisecracks pretty much got left at the door with the Hulk (unlike his counterpart in big-guydom, the cigar-smoking Thing from the Fantastic Four, who went to war bellowing, "It's clobberin' time!"). At one point, *Incredible Hulk* branded itself as "The only super-hero soap opera in all of comicdom," which aren't words that ring the bells of comic-book fans, not to mention eight-year-old boys. But it might be more honesty than anything else. Same with the line that appeared on the inside splash page of the first issue of *Tales to Astonish* that had the Hulk as a regular feature: "Starring the world's strongest mortal, who dares to ask the burning question, 'Can a man with green skin and a petulant personality find happiness in today's status-seeking society?'" Honest and more than a little tongue-in-cheek — just the way we like it.

Funny thing about soap operas, though: They're built to last. Look at *The Guiding Light,* which was first seen by people watching TVs hewn from granite blocks with stone tools, like the ones on *The Flintstones.* Look at professional wrestling, which allows Hulk Hogan more face time than any peroxided 60-year-old deserves. Soap operas last a long time because they show people we can relate to in predicaments more sticky than anything we'd ever get into. While the Hulk isn't exactly a normal human, he is human, and a lot easier to relate to than Batman or Superman. And his wickets are definitely sticky.

Still, it's a long way from soap opera to icon. No one touts *General Hospital* as one of the pop-culture milestones of the age. And comics? If seriality was all it took to make a great comic, we'd all be gearing up for the *Prince Valiant* movie. It takes more, and the Hulk's got it.

Actually, the Hulk has less — and that's how he gets to be an icon. He's a great character, period. He's the embodiment of primal rage and makes no bones about it. He's a fugitive, an underdog despite his immense size and strength, and we all love to root for the underdog. And unlike many of his comics counterparts, the Hulk has pretty much done it by himself.

When you ask comics fans what makes the Hulk memorable, the answer is ... the Hulk. It's not his supporting cast. Thunderbolt Ross is all bluff and bluster and scrambled eggs on the shoulders. He's Spider-Man's Jonah Jameson with the believability knocked off. Rick Jones is as distinctive as a Quarter Pounder, a plot device thrown in to keep the kids happy.

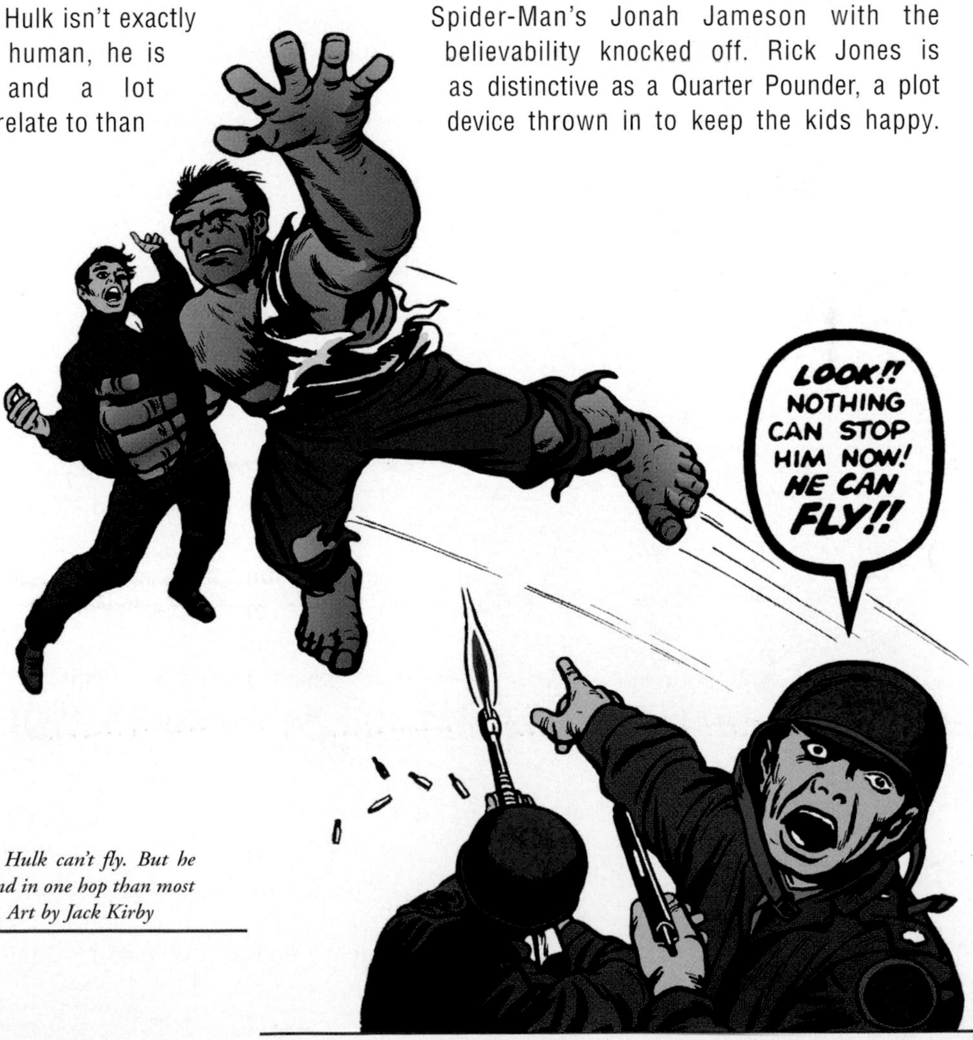
LOOK!! NOTHING CAN STOP HIM NOW! HE CAN FLY!!

No, guys — the Hulk can't fly. But he covers more ground in one hop than most commuter flights. Art by Jack Kirby

(Lord knows there's nothing for kids in Bruce Banner.) Thank goodness he ran off to help start the Avengers. Glenn Talbot is the Ronald Colman character from a thousand '30s war movies and hardly believable as a rival love interest for Betty Ross — who, come to think of it, isn't much more than a hairdo and a tailored suit. And Bruce Banner alternates between being a schlep and a nerd, only he has a reason: He has to, in order to make his transformation into the Hulk that much more believable.

There's not a Mary Jane Watson, an Aunt May or a Professor X in the bunch. The movie makes characters out of these caricatures, but it has to work at it.

The villains are hardly more memorable. If you're hoping for a Dr. Doom or Magneto, you're in the wrong comic. The No. 1 baddie is the Leader, a one-time janitor who got a dose of the same gamma radiation that causes Bruce Banner to transform into the Hulk. Instead of turning green and getting really strong when he becomes enraged, the Leader is green all the time and thinks really hard. (A former toilet cleaner turned evil genius? What will they think of next?) It's not exactly the archetypal battle between brains and brawn, but it has its moments.

For almost 40 years, the Hulk hasn't had a strong supporting cast, unforgettable villains, powerful team-ups or a dynamic love interest. He also hasn't spun off any characters except the She-Hulk, who is to the Hulk what Goldmember is to Goldfinger. But the Hulk has the Hulk, which is more than enough to overcome everything else. Of all the characters Stan Lee created, the Hulk may be the strongest — literally and figuratively.

Almost all the great artists in Marvel's Bullpen have taken a shot at the Hulk. In this panel, Adam Kubert (from the Kubert family of fine comic artists) takes on Big Green showing off for Thunderbolt Ross.

The Hulk
in the pop-culture landscape

It ain't easy being green. Kermit the Frog knows, and so does the Hulk.

It's that old color thing again. Who can relate to a green pop-culture icon? Can you imagine if Dorothy in *The Wizard of Oz* had been green, and not the Wicked Witch of the West? What if Elvis had been green? Would he have sung rhythm 'n' blues the way he did?

A green James Bond? A green Britney Spears? The entire cast of *Star Trek* in varying shades of olive and chartreuse? Never in a million years.

The Hulk is green, which is a tough color when you're in the biz. The Jolly Green Giant can get away with it, but he's selling brussels sprouts. Michigan J. Frog (the occasionally singing frog in the classic Chuck Jones cartoon *One Froggy Evening*) had potential, but he was a one-toon wonder. The Hulk manages, but the funny thing about the Hulk is he was originally gray.

Sure enough: The first issue of *Hulk*, way back in 1962, portrayed the Hulk as gray instead of green. The Hulk was the product of an atomic test gone bad, remember, and it was easier to imagine radiation turning someone's skin gray instead of green. (When was the last time your barbecue grill cooked your burgers a deep, rich *green?*) Besides, back then, the Hulk only came out when Bruce Banner was asleep —

something like a big, bad dream.

By the time the Hulk appeared regularly in *Tales to Astonish,* he was bigger, bolder and *greener* than ever. He stood out in a crowd even more. And that was when he started on the road to becoming a pop icon.

The pop-icon biz is tough. The only actual human beings who spring to mind as pop icons are Elvis and Princess Diana, and they had to die to get there. You need to be larger than life to be a pop icon, which means you have to be fictitious or dead. Or both.

The Hulk is definitely larger than life and unarguably a pop icon, and the *Hulk* movie only makes him more of an icon. How he got there takes some explaining.

The Hulk has been a comics mainstay since 1962. The Hulk TV show ran from 1978-82 and has been in worldwide syndication ever since. If you want to get exposed to the Hulk, you don't have far to go — even if you're in Glykbryczistan.

During his salad days, the Hulk was a licensing giant, spinning off more action figures than you can shake an endcap at, trading cards, die-cast cars, board games, comb-and-brush sets, Halloween costumes, coloring books, toothbrushes — you name it.

About the toys: They play good. The Hulk is an action-oriented superhero turned up to 11. He spends zero time with his chin in his hands pondering. He hits the ground at

> He's **big** and **green,** good to some and evil to others, adept at **scaring** the bejabbers out of a population and **saving** it at the same time.

Say what you will about the goofy good looks of Megos and the charm of older action figures. Fact is, the new stuff (like this 14-inch ToyBiz figure) absolutely rocks.

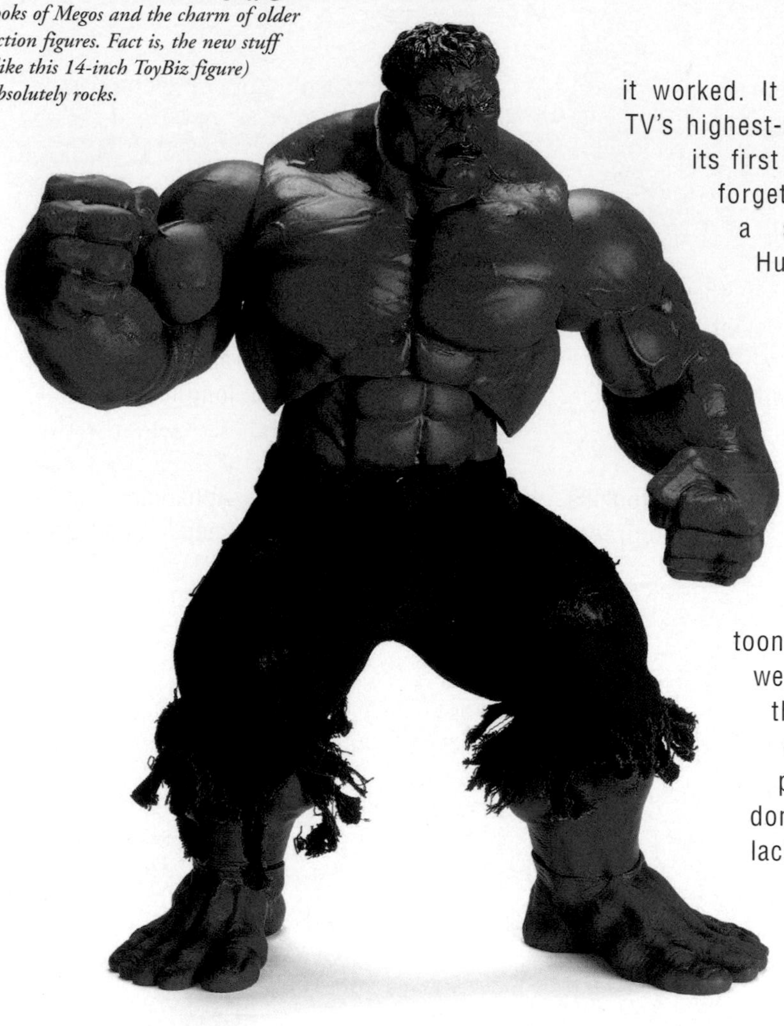

it worked. It won an Emmy; it was TV's highest-rated show for much of its first two seasons. And don't forget: The fact that there was a successful live-action Hulk TV series must have made the *Hulk* movie that much easier to green-light.

The comics have been around 40 years, the toys play good, the TV series is remembered and still plays on, the cartoons were decent when they were around ... is that all there is? Pretty much, outside of the earlier point that the Hulk has done it on his own. The lack of a strong supporting cast or memorable villains has kept the focus on the Hulk this whole time, and that's been like an anabolic steroid to the Hulk's pop-icon physique. That's why there's Hulk candy at the dollar store, and not Daredevil candy. While Double-D has been thrilling comics fans for years with his beautifully plotted, intricate story arcs with multiple main characters, fantastic team-ups and great adversaries, the Hulk just strolls in, whomps on Galactus and collects his money at the bar. And next issue it's someone else.

In the comics these days, not too many characters have a 40-year run at anything, and certainly not one where the character gets off without toting around an annoying 12-year-old sidekick or being put through seven different time warps and five parallel universes. The Hulk has missed out on most of that, and he's all the better for it. He's the original keep-it-simple-stupid character, and he works.

Before the pop-icon thing is given a drink of water and tucked in bed, there's one pop

full speed and hits hard. Spend a couple hours with an eight-year-old boy, and you'll realize he and the Hulk are soulmates — at least in the hit-the-ground-running department. Give him a Hulk toy, and it'll be airborne within 30 seconds. It'll be dive-bombing, rock-piling, thunder-clapping, doin' the earthquake stomp and taking on every T-Rex in the yard. Maybe Spider-Man swings better, but the Hulk aces the rest of the playtime tests. Can't vouch for how the Hulk toothbrush performs, though.

Don't underestimate the power of play and toys. When kids grow up, they remember the toys they play with a whole lot more than the toys they didn't. And kids have played with Hulk toys since there have been Hulk toys to play with.

Don't underestimate the TV show, either. It's a '70s action show all the way — with lots of Ford Torinos, shirts and sportcoats without ties, and California backlots — but

icon who hasn't yet been discussed who deserves to be mentioned in the same breath as the Hulk. He's big and green, good to some and evil to others, adept at scaring the bejabbers out of a population and saving it at the same time. He's Godzilla, and while he's had the benefit of some great adversaries — just think where the Hulk could have gone if he had had Mothra to bump heads with every election year — he also hasn't had Bill Bixby and Lou Ferrigno, or Stan Lee and Jack Kirby.

Every time they think they have Godzilla killed off, he comes back, bigger and greener and scalier — and more popular — than ever. Fifty years from now, when movies are replaced by holograms that flash inside people's eyeballs, Godzilla will still be knocking over Plasticville replicas of Tokyo and acting darn peeved about it. And you can bet the Hulk will be right there on the double feature.

We do love our monsters, that's for sure — and if they're anything approaching good, we'll love 'em for a long, long time. We don't even mind if they're not ripe yet. The Hulk, Godzilla, Frankenstein — it almost seems like the greener, the better. Apparently, on the monster side, you can't keep a good green pop icon down. Never could, never will.

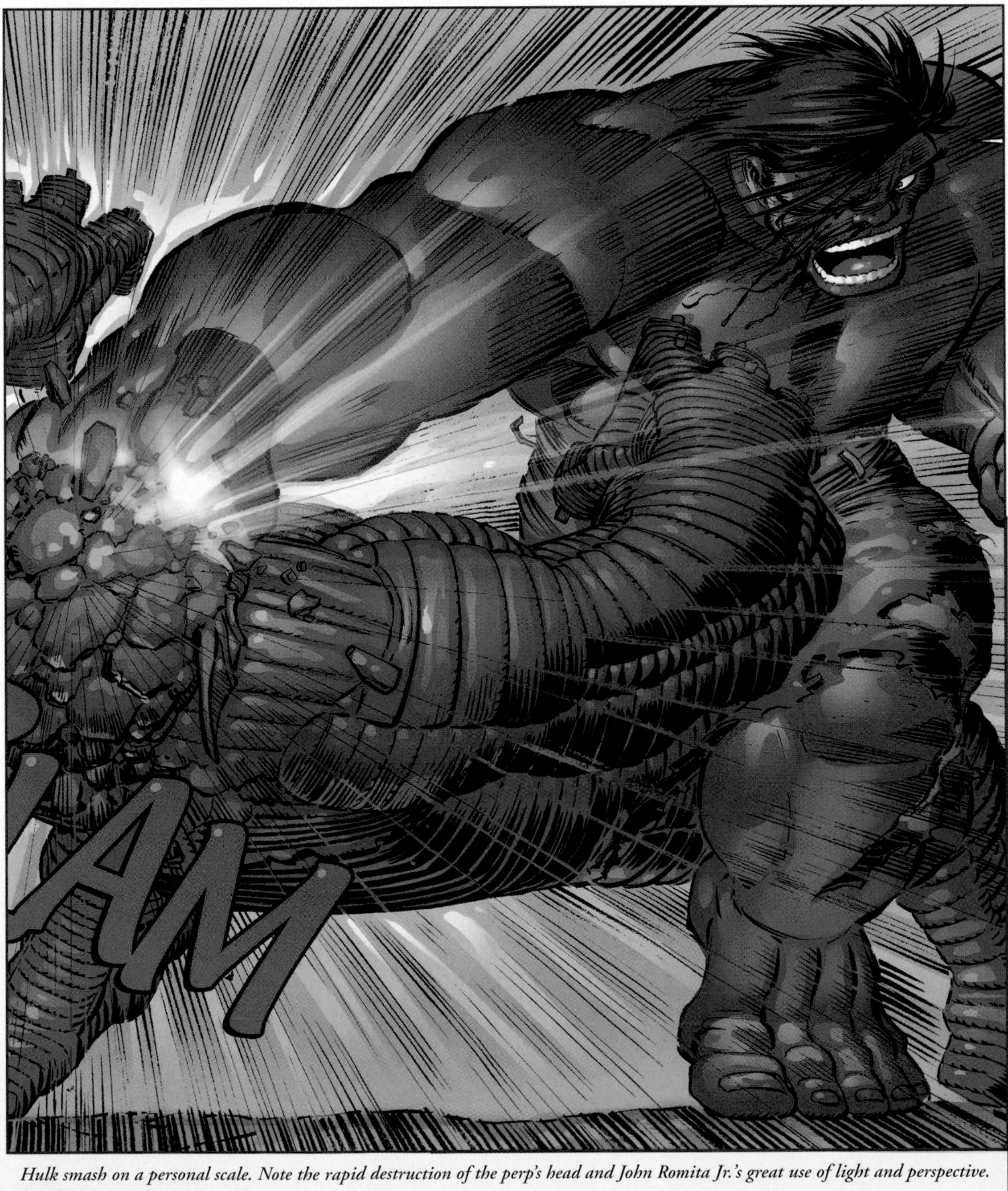

Hulk smash on a personal scale. Note the rapid destruction of the perp's head and John Romita Jr.'s great use of light and perspective.

Chapter Two

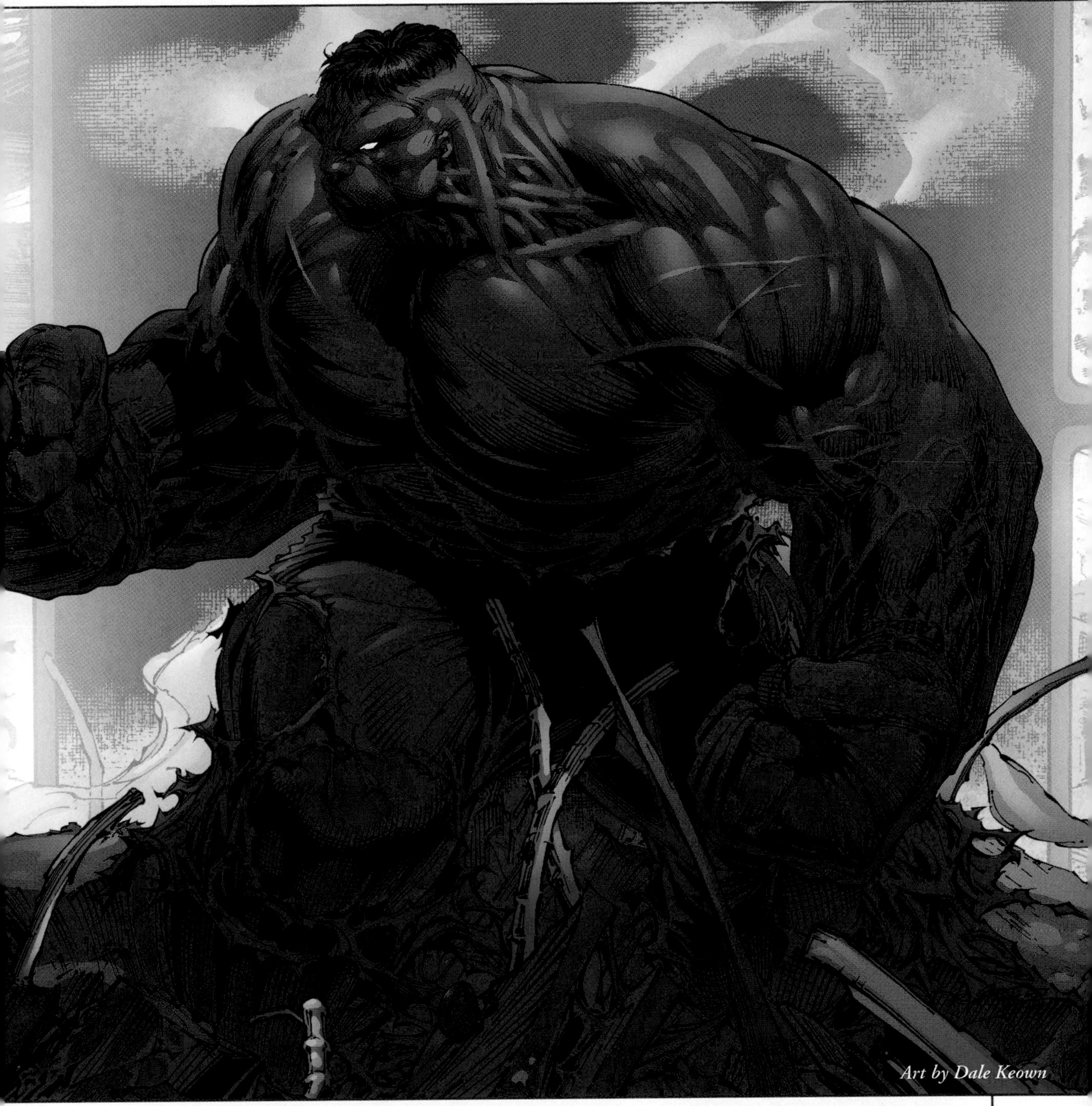

Art by Dale Keown

GREEN AND GROWIN'

The Hulk's salad days

It was one of the most amazing transformations in pop-culture history. What Marvel Comics did in the early '60s makes Ozzy Osbourne look like a cross-dressing amateur.

In 1960, Marvel's big titles were *A Date with Millie, Kathy, Teen-Age Romance, Patsy and Hedy, Gunsmoke Western* and a handful of what were then called "fantasy" titles: *Amazing Adult Fantasy, Amazing Adventures, Tales of Suspense* and *Tales to Astonish*. By the end of 1964, all the girl comics were gone except for *Patsy and Hedy*, which somehow hung on until the end of 1965. (It's a good thing they left, too. Can you imagine the world getting worked up over the *A Date with Millie* big-screen extravganza?)

Replacing them were a brash series of comics, tough-minded and slangy in a new way. Pulpy Raymond Chandler film-noir stuff was out. In its place was science fiction played like British blues, with characters spun fully into three dimensions and given the so-whaddya-gonna-do-kick-me-out-of-school? tone of a second-semester senior on double-secret detention.

The characters were the cornerstones on which virtually the entire comics world is built: The Amazing Spider-Man. The Fantastic Four. The Uncanny X-Men. Sgt. Fury and His Howling Commandos. The Mighty Thor. Daredevil, the Man Without Fear. The Incredible Hulk.

They are the creations of a former office boy at Timely-nee-Atlas-nee-Marvel Comics: Stanley Lieber, a.k.a. Stan Lee. He got to be office boy because he was the nephew of the publisher, pulp-magazine scion Martin Goodman. He stuck around because World War II took everyone else into the service, and because he was good at what he did — not so good that he didn't suffer through the '50s like everyone else in the comics biz before finding the formula at Marvel, but good enough to come up big when the time and the temperament were right.

The art that brought them to life sprung

Kirby's superheroes churned out *lightning bolts* like Reddy Kilowatt at a Las Vegas bachelor party.

mostly from the pen and pencils of Jack Kirby. For most of his first two decades in comics, Kirby (born Jacob Kutzberg) was a bigger, brighter and more successful star than Lee. Kirby drew so much you couldn't claim everything he drew turned to gold, but he entered the '60s with at least three stars on his shoulders. He and partner Joe Simon created the most successful comic of the war years, *Captain America*. (People forget Captain American whupped up on Superman during the war years. Superman was so '30s. When the war ignited and patriotism reigned, Captain America was *way* bigger than Superman.) After the war, Kirby and Simon created the teenage-girl comics and westerns (like the delightful *Boys' Ranch*) that would keep the comics business afloat for the next decade.

Kirby drew ingenues and cowpokes, enlisted men and animals — but when given the chance to draw anything he wanted, Kirby drew superheroes. His superheroes had dimensions — three to be exact, or one more than Superman and Batman. They churned out lightning bolts like Reddy Kilowatt at a Las Vegas bachelor party. They burst through the square panels that had ruled comics since the '30s like they were made of paper (which they were, but you understand). Along with Will Eisner's *Spirit*, Jack Kirby's comics were literally state-of-the-art for the next 60 years. His contributions to comics art are at least as great as Stan Lee's contributions to comics characters.

In fact, when Jack Kirby hooked up with Stan Lee and Marvel in the late '50s, Lee needed Kirby a whole lot more than Kirby needed Lee. There are stories that Stan Lee was about to give Marvel Comics the old heave-ho when Jack Kirby came strolling through the door. It makes a good Stan Lee story — and Stan Lee has always been the best with stories. But there's likely a grain of truth to it. Marvel couldn't have kept the doors open with the artists they had doing *Linda Carter, Student Nurse*.

Meet the Family

You can too tell the players without a program. The Hulk is the Big Green Thing (but not the Thing. That's a different comic.). Betty Ross is the girl. Bruce Banner is the guy with the glasses, at least some of the time. Major Glenn Talbot and General Thunderbolt Ross are the antagonists, if not the out-and-out villains. What more do you need to know?

A little wouldn't hurt. So here it is.

Bruce Banner: Brilliant scientist. Abused child. Fugitive from justice. Loving husband with a not-so-secret secret. Nerd. While he's never been so far down that the bottom looks like up to him, Bruce Banner's path to scientific fame and fortune has been anything but straight and narrow. When he's in the government's good graces, he's like the atomic Emeril. No one can do more with a couple grams of enriched plutonium, some olive oil and a clove of garlic. He's been accused of being a traitor, turned into a fugitive, reduced to sleeping in fleabag motels, thrown in the klink more times than Robert Downey Jr., poked and prodded by a used-car lot full of mad scientists, dropped from an airplane, cast into a whirlpool, catapulted into outer space, transported back in time, divorced-slash-widowed, and transformed into Bill Bixby. Yeah, sure, Albert Schweitzer used to do the same thing, but change into the Hulk, too? Only one person is capable of all that. So whatever you do, don't make him angry. You won't like him when he's angry.

First Appearance: *He's been in it from the start.* Incredible Hulk *without Bruce Banner would be like a car without wheels or oatmeal without brown sugar. It just can't take you very far.*

Betty Ross Banner: Ever notice how close "Betty Ross" is to "Betsy Ross"? That's no accident. The strong-willed-by-'60s-standards daughter of General Thunderbolt Ross was raised to be as patriotic as her dad; too bad love intervened in the bipolar form of Bruce Banner. And when we say love, we mean blind-as-Ray-Charles love. Bruce Banner can run away from her, vanish entirely when the Hulk shows up, ignore her in favor of his books and formulas, court her with the schooled grace of an ostrich on Nyquil, alienate her father, and generally do everything he can to disgrace himself in her eyes, and still she loves the lug. Madly. Their relationship is fraught with roadblocks to happiness — hey, what relationship isn't? — like dysfunctional extended families, dark secrets and both parties occasionally transforming into super-powered, irrational beings that can destroy the universe in less time than it takes to warm up leftovers. (She was called the Harpy, and she was one nasty mamma-jamma badly in need of some Midol or Tic-Tacs or *something*.) It would be nice to say that all this ends happily, with Betty and Bruce snuggling up on the couch and watching *Ya-Ya Sisterhood* while the little atomic-powered younguns roll on the floor, but it's not to be. (This is the only superhero soap opera in all of comicdom, remember.) Depending on which

Continued on page 29

Kirby's turbocharged art let Lee unleash the superhero-with-an-attitude stories that had been kicking around his head for the entire blasted decade of the '50s. With Kirby to play Lennon to Lee's McCartney, the hits started flowing and wouldn't stop.

The parallels between Kirby and Lee and the Beatles are, to steal a phrase from Smilin' Stan, uncanny. Both associations fused together great but disparate talents. Both took a stale scene and turned it on its ear. Both had a staggering string of hits in a mere handful of months — hits that have new generations copping their licks 40 years on. And both set the tone for the decade to follow.

The Beatles blew away almost a decade of Percy Faith and white-boy doo-wop with the first chords of "She Loves You." Stan Lee buried *Gunsmoke Western* forever with one blow from the Incredible Hulk's mighty fists.

Look at the first Kirby-Lee Hulk comic today, and the first thing that comes to mind is … how square. Literally and figuratively. Kirby's art broke out of the box, but the box wasn't banished by any means. There are rectangles galore on the pages of the first Hulk comics, and they're so pervasive that you think for a minute you're reading *Retentive Man* instead of one of the barrier-breaking comics of the age. Only the "splash" pages (the scene-setting first page of a comics story) and the fight scenes give hints of the free-form stuff to come.

Not only is the art square, but in *Hulk #1*, the Hulk is gray. It flies in the face of reason today (how can you not have a green Hulk?), though it makes sense when you realize that people back then were atom-conscious the way people today are Al-Qaida-conscious. Bruce Banner was nailed with a dose of gamma radiation, and radiation turns things gray. Microwave a pork chop, and you'll understand. And if radiation turned things green, Bikini Atoll would be one of the earth's garden spots.

The Hulk in these early issues (and the handful of Kirby-drawn issues that show him as a member of the Avengers) retained all of Bruce Banner's faculties. When Bruce Banner becomes the Hulk in these issues, he's just a bigger, meaner Bruce Banner — not the man-child we love. It makes for some interesting byplay, but it's like being able to read a hyena's mind and finding Billy Crystal inside. Way too Disney; way too scary. It's infinitely more satisfying to have the Hulk react first and save the pondering for that schlep Bruce Banner.

On top of everything else, the original Hulk only emerged while Bruce Banner slept. It's Freudian all right, but try sustaining that plot device for 40 years. Banner would be sucking

Captain America has survived 60 years with minimal alterations to his looks. You can do that when A) you've been frozen in an iceberg for 59 of those 60 years, and B) you wear a costume and a mask. Art by Jack Kirby

Continued from page 27

continuity you're in, Betty is either estranged from Bruce and swingin' with Freddie Prinze Jr. (*The Ultimates*) or dead, killed by the Abomination. The path of true love is never straight. It's just not usually this crooked.

First appearance: *She's been in it from the start, too. What? You expected Glenn Talbot to wear a flip hairdo and dab at his eyes with a hankie at the slightest inkling of trouble?*

General Thunderbolt Ross: Well, if it isn't ol' Blunderbuss Ross himself. Thunderbolt Ross comes from the old, *old* school of military leaders, the type that won dubya-dubya-two, wasn't allowed to win Korea and subscribed to the noble-cause/parking-lot theory in Vietnam (i.e., it *was* a noble cause, and the only way to prove it was to bomb the whole bloody subcontinent until it resembled a parking lot). Generals like these were ill-equipped to handle the new realities of the atomic age, and Thunderbolt Ross was no exception. In manner and temperament, he makes *Dr. Strangelove*'s Jack Tripper look like John Lennon. As a well-rounded character, he's just this side of trapezoidal. Once he gets an idea in his Alaska-sized craw, nothing's going to stop him until it's taken care of. Usually, that takes only a couple of trips to the bathroom, but it's different with Bruce Banner. Thunderbolt can't get used to a brainy scientist running the show — especially *this* particular brainy scientist running *his* show. And there's something about Banner — like he's hiding something. And that blankety-blank Hulk always shows up when Banner's around — but you never see Banner at the same time as the Hulk. What gives? Thunderbolt Ross doesn't know, but by God he's going to find out. (Incidentally, Ross goes crazy at the thought of his daughter marrying Bruce Banner — can you blame him? — and tries to stop the wedding the only way his straight-line brain will allow: by blasting Bruce Banner to kingdom come at the altar. The only thing he forgot was to pack the Sidewinder missile launcher instead of the .38 special.) In a stroke of inspired casting right up there with Jerry Mathers as the Beaver, Sam Elliot lands the movie role and gives Ross *way* more than the character deserves. Somewhere, George C. Scott is smiling — or scowling mightily, which to George C. was practically the same thing.

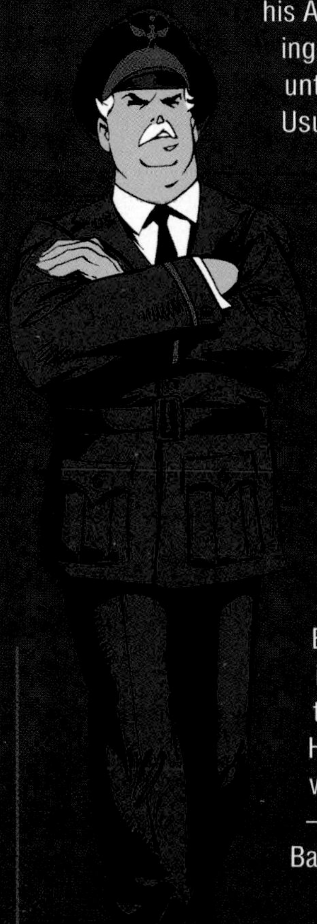

First appearance: *Thunderbolt's been muttering about Banner since day one. And don't forget: None of this would have happened if Banner had been an Army scientist, dagnabbit.*

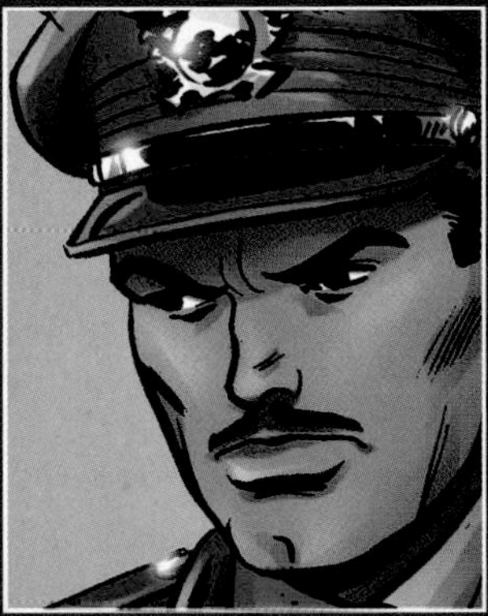

Major Glenn Talbot: When Jimmy Buffett sang, "Wish I had a pencil-thin mustache," the mustache he was referring to did not belong to Maj. Glenn Talbot. Jimmy Buffett has no desire to become Maj. Glenn Talbot, and neither does anyone else whose profession is something other than professional roller-coaster rider. This is because Glenn Talbot's job was more thankless than Saddam Hussein's food taster. Talbot was that oldest of all dramatic schleps, the would-be beau. He loved Betty Ross and wanted Betty to love him back, but even when he intercepted a boulder meant for her or took a ray-gun dose strong enough to sizzle his Vitalis, it was never going to happen for more than a couple of panels. His job was to yearn for the heroine and vex the hero, and he did both about as well as any mustachioed six-foot plank could. In the comics, Major Talbot met his end after being captured by the Russkies and returned with a

Continued on page 31

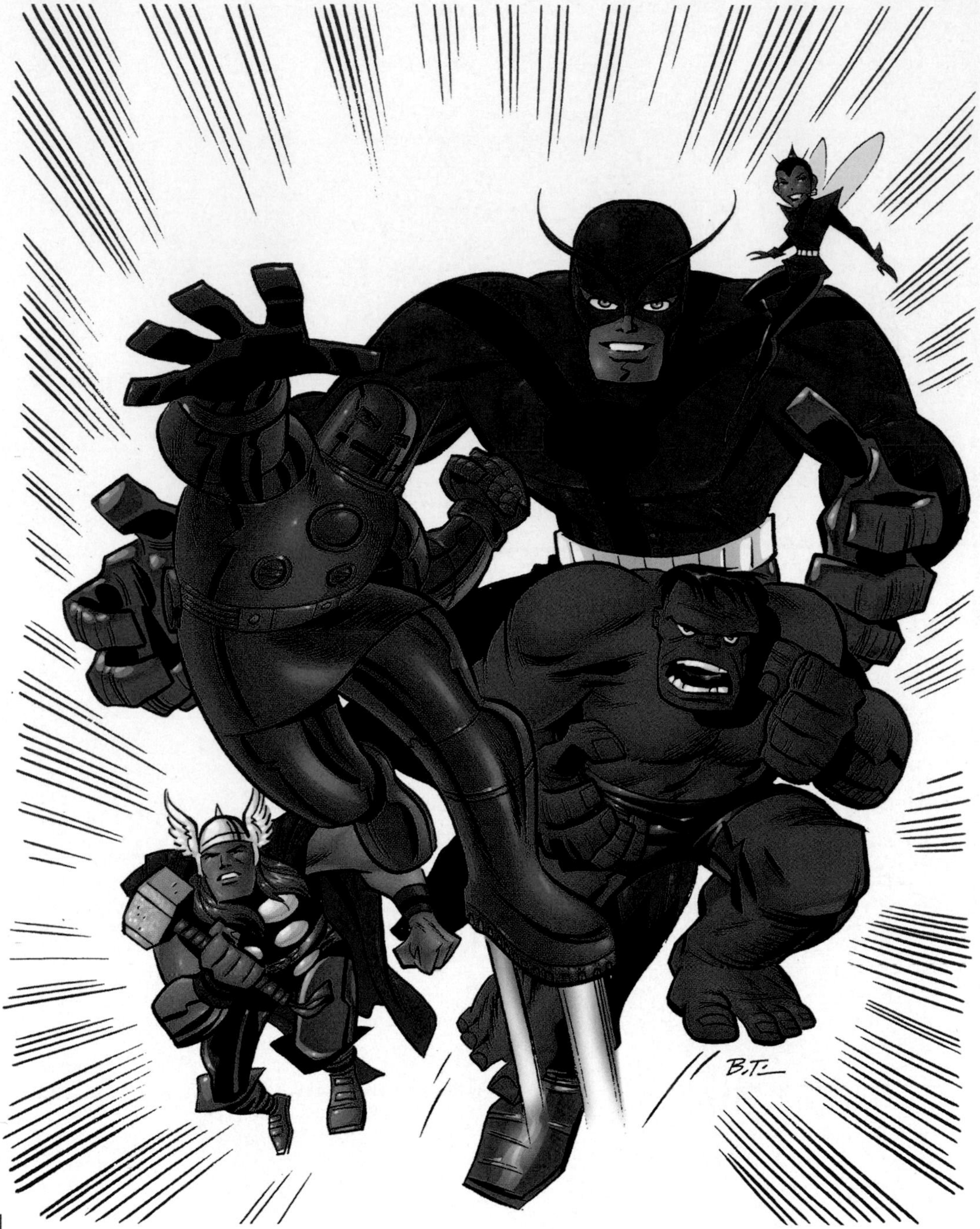
B.T.

Talk about your unwillingness to commit. The Hulk has never been able to join the Avengers and stay joined. As a team, though, the Avengers put the '27 Yankees to shame. Art by Bruce Timm

Sominex like they were Altoids just so the stories could get going.

Otherwise, the original rendition of the Hulk is certainly Hulk-like. He may be a far cry from the bipolar gray Hulk of the '80s and '90s, but trust us: This is not a bad thing.

Speaking of things, the entity the early Hulk most closely resembles in physique and attitude is Frankenstein. The skin color may have been off at first, but everything else suggests the original misunderstood monster. Seeing as the Hulk was a misunderstood monster, too, and Marvel comics of the early '60s were not paragons of subtlety and eagerly wore their influences on their sleeves, this isn't a stretch. (Both the Hulk and the monster were invariably kind to children, and the Hulk probably would have been sweet to Jean Hersholt if the old coot hadn't kicked the bucket decades earlier.)

And if the Hulk's brow and hairline were more human, along the lines of Mr. Hyde

Continued from page 29

bomb in his chest, which the Hulk was more than willing to detonate for him. In the movie, Major Talbot is infinitely better shaded and better played (by Josh Lucas, who's no more capable of bad acting than a three-year-old is of sitting still for longer than, say, a millisecond). He's also meaner, on purpose. Not-really-bad guys never have cut it.

First appearance: *Thunderbolt Ross had Maj. Glenn Talbot to kick around stating in* Tales to Astonish #61. *That's what majors are for.*

Rick Jones: Rick really deserves a knuckle sandwich for joyriding into a nuclear-blast zone, forcing Bruce Banner to risk his life to save him and triggering the chain of atomic events that caused Banner to become the Hulk, but instead he gets the most coveted of bit parts: occasional sidekick to Bruce Banner and the first keeper of his big, green secret. Jones soon ran off to help found Marvel's first superhero all-star team, the Avengers, where one of the first recruits was — you guessed it — the Hulk. But as a team player, the Hulk falls somewhere between Randy Moss and J.R. Rider; within two issues, he had bolted the Avengers, never to return to the fold unless the entire civilized world hung in the balance and newsstand sales really needed a shot in the shorts. The Hulk really doesn't need a sidekick, anyhow. Just ask him.

First appearance: *How soon we forget — Jones was the guy that got Banner into this, way back in ish #1.*

Doc Samson: Dr. Leonard Samson accidentally blasts himself with some leftover gamma radiation from his encounter with the Hulk and voila! He becomes Doc Samson, a sort of green Glenn Talbot with a whole lot more atti-

tude. Think Ted Nugent without the guitar and with crème de menthe in his hair. Samson helps the Army capture the Hulk so they can restore a mutated Betty Ross to her prim-'n'-proper self, and in the process causes Betty's heart to skip a beat or three. Over time, the Hulk and the Doc find lots of occasions to duke it out — chance meetings, not-so-chance meetings, anniversaries, Arbor Day, children's parties — and the one who wins the battle doesn't always leave with the girl. The battles can stick in your memory like the left hook before the lights go out. Who else but the good doctor would tell the Hulk to "hit me with your best shot" the way he does in the vastly entertaining *Banner* comic-book mini-series? With cajones like those, sometimes you even find yourself rooting for the rational-thinking Doc over the smash-first-and-ask-questions-later Hulk. (On second thought: nah.) One thing's for sure: With Doc Samson around, there's no need to resurrect Glenn Talbot — and for that, Doc Samson deserves our eternal thanks.

First appearance: Finally, someone who *wasn't* in it from the start. The Doc hit the pulps in *Incredible Hulk #141*, back in the Herb Trimpe days.

The She-Hulk: Hey, she's gotta go somewhere. Jennifer Walters is Bruce Banner's first cousin and the daughter of Morris Walters, sheriff of Los Angeles County, Commissioner Gordon having been taken by a different comic. Jennifer grows up all normal and becomes a successful lawyer (unsuccessful lawyers having a hard time getting work in the comics), still connecting with her successful atomic-scientist cousin from time to time. During one of those connections, a crucial one

Continued on page 33

(as in "Dr. Jekyll and ..."), that's no stretch either. A scientist willing to take his experimentation to whatever lengths necessary, regardless of the consequences, is as much Bruce Banner (and his movie father, David Banner) as he is Robert Louis Stevenson's creation.

The sort of horror that spawned Frankenstein and Mr. Hyde is more psychological than physical, despite all the transformations and grotesqueries, and that's where the Hulk shines above all other Marvel creations. No Marvel character has such a psychological element to his being — and if you didn't believe it before the movie, you surely must believe it now. Spider-Man is the kid next door turned crimefighter; Thor deals in issues of sibling rivalry; the X-Men make a case for tolerance. The Hulk is all about the repressed dark physical side taking over and doing what repressed dark physical sides do: making life miserable for the side that wants everything tidy. No wonder the Hulk's villains scarcely get a paragraph's worth of mention in any history of the Marvel Universe (and why the movie borrows the Absorbing Man concept of the villain-father from Thor).

Of course, all this stuff that goes into the Hulk — the kindly monster, the bipolar personality, the fugitive, the soap opera (at times reading like it was lifted straight from the pages of *Teen-Age Romance*) — took some time to come together. It didn't gel during the early days. You get the feeling that Lee and Kirby knew they were on to something, but they weren't sure what. It didn't really come together in the soap-opera era that followed. Sometimes, the comics couldn't decide if they wanted to be *Tales to Astonish* or *Sherry the Showgirl*. The inbetween setting didn't work. The lopsided machine that is the Incredible Hulk didn't get going until the late '60s and early '70s – ironically, when Jack

Kirby was long gone from the comic, and Stan Lee was on his way out.

The Incredible Hulk's best days start in the late '60s at the very end of his run as a member of the troupe in *Tales to Astonish*. Artists Herb Trimpe and Marie Severin owed much of their style to Jack Kirby, but what artist didn't? They managed to give some definition and dimension to what had been a pretty square character. And if his dimensions weren't always consistent from issue to issue, big deal. As long as he was powerful enough to play Frisbee with Sherman tanks, the rest was gravy. And besides, who was going to tell him he was the wrong size?

If you're looking for a Hulk comic that shows just how much can be done with the character, start with *Incredible Hulk #47,* from 1972. This classic story was written by Roy Thomas but comes straight out of the Ray Bradbury lexicon: The Hulk finds himself in a land where people respect him, are nice to him, don't run from him, treat him like a normal human being despite his Cro-Magnon-esque appearance. Of course, the land is a figment of the Hulk's imagination. The final panel is as poignant a cry of rage as you'll find.

No Marvel character has such a **psychological element** *to his being — and if you didn't believe it before the movie, you surely* **must** *believe it now.*

Speaking of Ray Bradbury and people like him, science-fiction scion Harlan Ellison jumped back into comics to pen an issue of *Incredible Hulk* in 1971. Ellison made the Hulk ant-sized and plopped him in the kingdom of K'ai, where everyone is ant-sized and has green skin. There, the Hulk was the noble warrior incarnate. He even got the girl, the lovely Princess Jarella. It's a story that makes for some great reading, even if it was responsible for spawning some later Hulk trends (the smart Hulk, for one) that didn't always read so great.

In the hands of good writers, the Hulk was a beast of a character — maybe the deepest and most complex in the deep, complex

Continued from page 31

where Bruce Banner was going to tell his cousin just what a drag it is to be the Hulk, Jennifer is shot in a sort of gangland-double-cross/ *Sopranos* outtake. The only way she lives is if Bruce gives her a do-it-yourself blood transfusion. He does, and before long Jennifer is springing out of her hospital bed and taking down the thugs that plugged her. From that point on, a second career is born. Considering the She-Hulk and the Hulk literally sprung from the same blood, they don't hang out together — which is more the Hulk's fault than hers. Jennifer Walters knows what she's doing when she becomes the She-Hulk, and keeps knowing it all through her adventures. She doesn't try to hide her identity, and spends no time at all running from the law. As a result, she's a far less complex character, but a lot more fun on college-football Saturdays (especially if your team is the Green Wave of Tulane). Gamma radiation also didn't wreck her looks: The She-Hulk is 6'7" and 650 pounds of pure pulchritude. And how many other women do you know who can withstand temperatures from 3,000° Fah-renheit to -190°F and take a Toma-hawk missile like it's a flu shot? The She-Hulk is an integral part of the Avengers, and though she's not in the movie, don't lose hope. There's always the sequel.

First Appearance: *Where else?* She-Hulk #1.

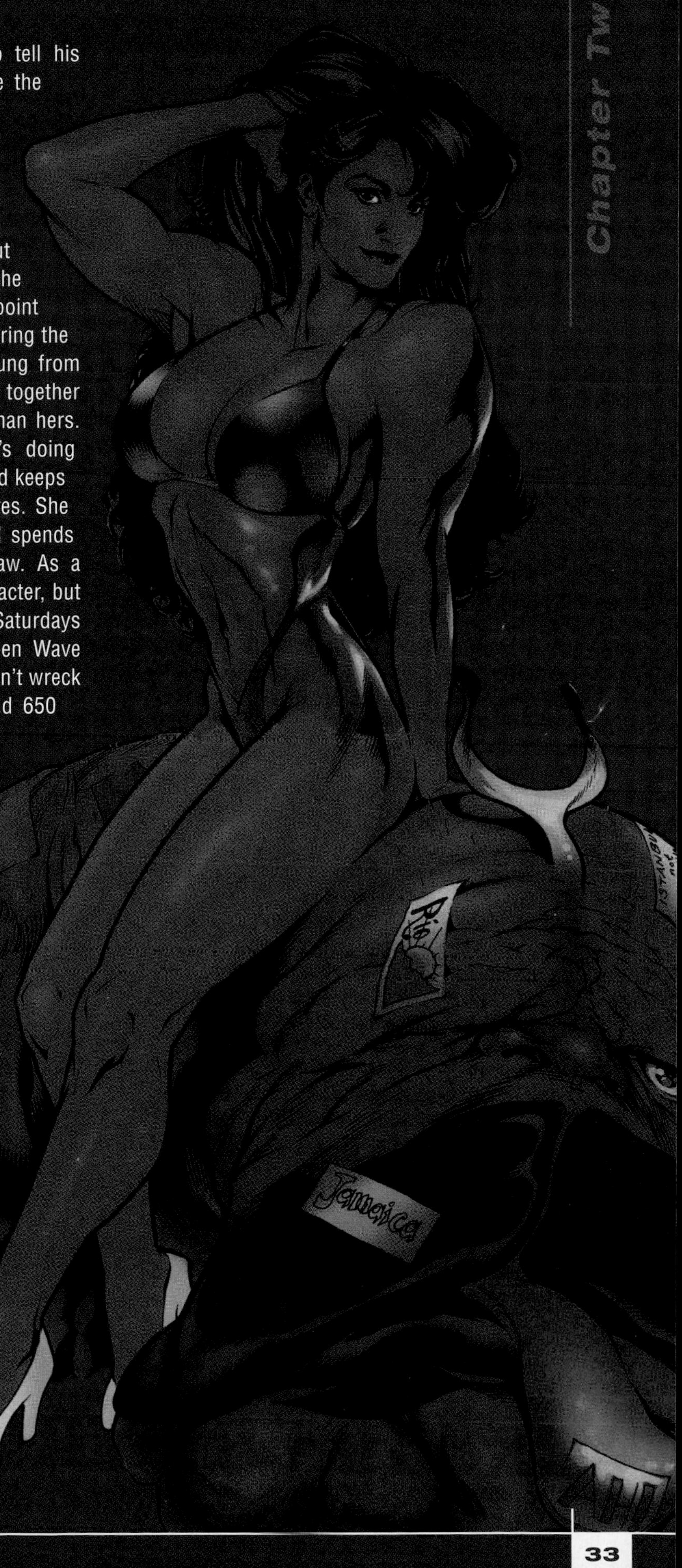
Rio
Jamaica

Art by Adam Hughes

Doc Samson and the Hulk chancing into a pretty-as-you-please roadside diner and sitting down to a couple plates of noodles? Sure, that'd happen. But it makes for an awesome Kaare Andrews cover. Note the issue date and the Norman Rockwell-esque appearance of the counter boy.

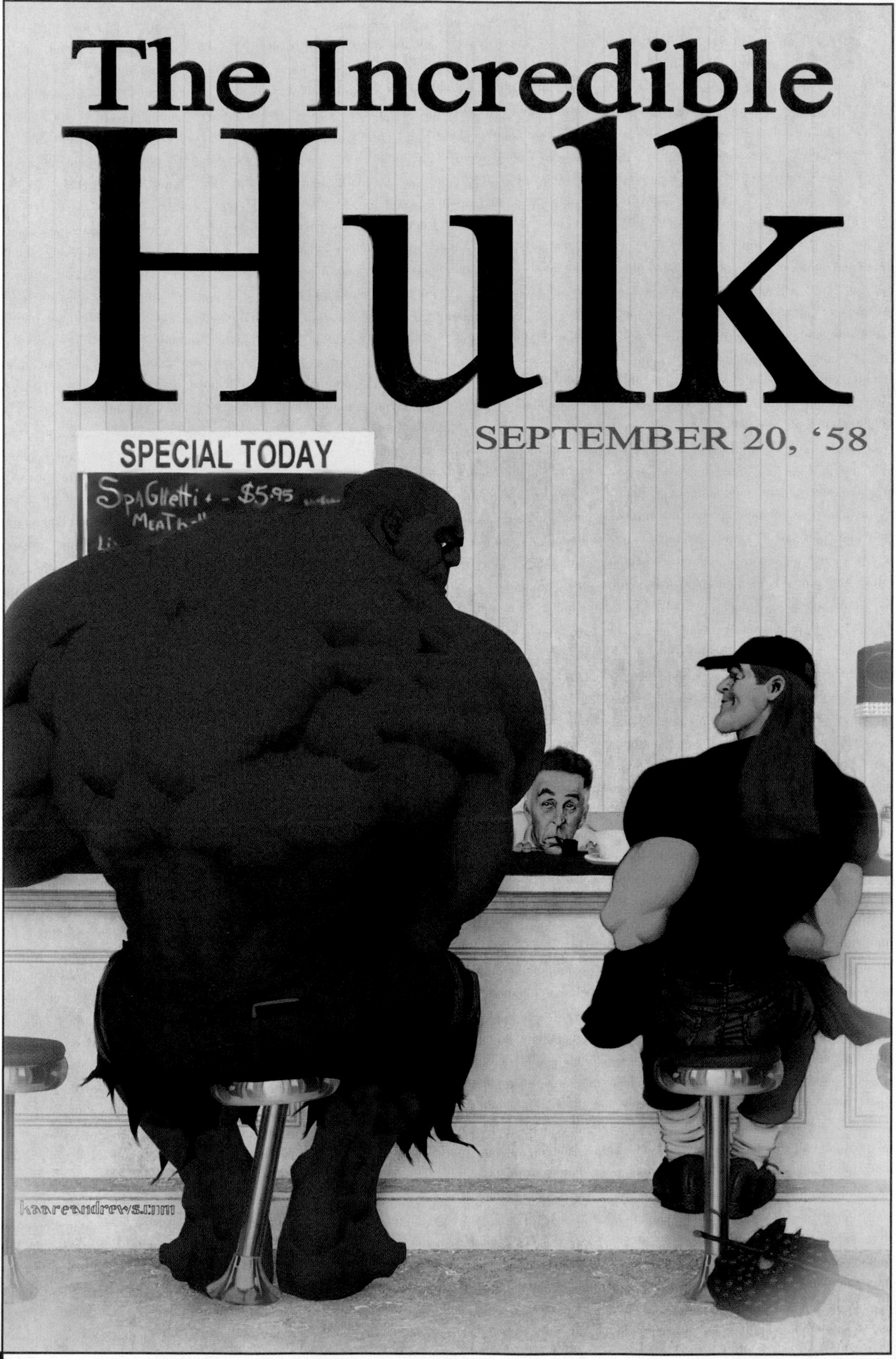

The Incredible
Hulk
SEPTEMBER 20, '58
SPECIAL TODAY
kaareandrews.com

Marvel Universe — laden with more ways of getting your blood racing than the coffee menu at Starbucks. But in the hands of less-skilled writers, these things are neither poignant nor brilliant, though they do incite rage among Hulk fans who like their super-hero psychodrama straight with chaser.

Hulk comics of the '80s and '90s played up the "psycho" in the psychodrama, sending the Hulk through incarnation after incarnation as though he was Shirley MacLaine played on 78. These comics, like a lot of Marvel comics from that era, drifted a little too far afield. They were guilty of only one thing: They weren't the Hulk.

Well, that's changed. With the new millennium, the Hulk is back to being the Hulk. He gets out his fair share, but down deep, he's just one big can o' rage — which is just how we like him.

There's an irresistable comic undercurrent to some of today's Hulk titles. For instance, a recent Hulk cover by Kaare Andrews borrows liberally — okay, steals — from that great comic artist Norman Rockwell without disclosing the taut drama inside. Somewhere, Smilin' Stan is ... well, smilin'.

Just so you know the players in the current Hulk arena, there's *Incredible Hulk,* which is still about as pure and simple as it gets. Lots of people want to get Bruce Banner for lots of different reasons, but one thing stays the same: Once they get him, they always get more than they bargained for. Bruce Jones' stories zip along like a police cruiser in a Fox docudrama; the art of John Romita Jr., Lee Weeks and Stuart Immonen is dead-solid-perfect comics art — nothing fancy, just right.

The Ultimates is another matter entirely. Think *Ocean's Eleven* where everyone has a super-power and Samuel L. Jackson drives the truck. This is a superstar comic book, gentlemen, but with an attitude. The Hulk gets pushed over the edge by the thought of Betty Ross having dinner with Freddie Prinze Jr. Thor is a street person until President Bush makes a cameo and pledges to double the foreign-aid budget. Captain America is thawed out of an ice floe. Giant Man pops Prozac. The Wasp distracts the Hulk by open-

Even if transforming into the Hulk doesn't mean going against a lifetime of orthodontia and brushing after meals, as Tim Sale's rendering suggests, it still makes for a heck of a Hulk.

ing her outfit at a crucial moment in the proceedings. (She also has a prehensile nest she sneaks off to and a craving for caterpillars, but so does everyone on *Fear Factor.*)

The Ultimates goes way beyond a comic book. Mark Millar's story jumps like the Brian Setzer Orchestra. To quote Fred Astaire, *that's* entertainment.

And then there's *Hulk: Gray.* This upcoming title will pay homage to Jack Kirby and Steve Ditko's original conceptualization of the Big Green Guy, using the Hulk's origin as a jumping-off point for some diverting excursions down Silver Age sideroads.

(Incidentally, the gray Hulk is going through something of a renaissance. Dynamic Forces, which makes busts and sculptures of comics characters great and small, recently brought out an eight-inch Gray Hulk bust. The anti-Banner is shown reading a copy of *Dr. Jekyll and Mr. Hyde* — upside-down. Only 1,963 were made at a $89.99 issue price. Better check out eBay now.)

Everything you want the Hulk to be and everything he's always been — an outcast, a seething mass of primal rage, the world's strongest human, the barely repressed dark side of a brilliant scientist — is in *Incredible Hulk* and its cohorts today. So whaddya waiting for?

Hulk Stats & Specs

So just how big is the Hulk, anyway? Depends on who you're asking and who's doing the measuring. And when.

The goal from the start was to have the Hulk be about the size and shape of a normal human, only bigger in all dimensions — thicker chest, longer arms, more powerful thighs, bigger neck. He's a human being even when he's the Hulk, remember — but he's the world's *most powerful* human being. Whatever alterations it takes to make him so, without making him into Godzilla in the process, are the alterations that are done.

The Hulk's dimensions go a long ways toward explaining how he can do what he does. He can knock down buildings, for instance, but he doesn't make it look effortless. He's not supposed to. Geometry gets in the way. On the other hand, geometry has nothing to explain how the Hulk can go from Tucson to Tucumcari in a single bound. But being a superhero in the '60s meant traveling through the air one way (Spider-Man's webs) or another (Thor's hammer), so the Hulk had to fly. The way he flies, by long-jumping from place to place, is the most human means of soaring Stan Lee could concoct (though in the process, the Hulk commits some felony infractions against the gravity statutes).

Within the loose definition of whatever-it-takes-to-be-human, the Hulk has found plenty of wiggle room to change his size as the situation demands, sometimes within the course of a single comic. In some issues, his head is big as a three-bedroom apartment; in other issues, it's merely studio-sized; and in some issues, it could fit in the hall closet with room left over for a tennis racket.

These days, the Hulk tends to run large. The trend in comics is to crank the contrast, make what's big BIGGER, and the Hulk is the perfect candidate

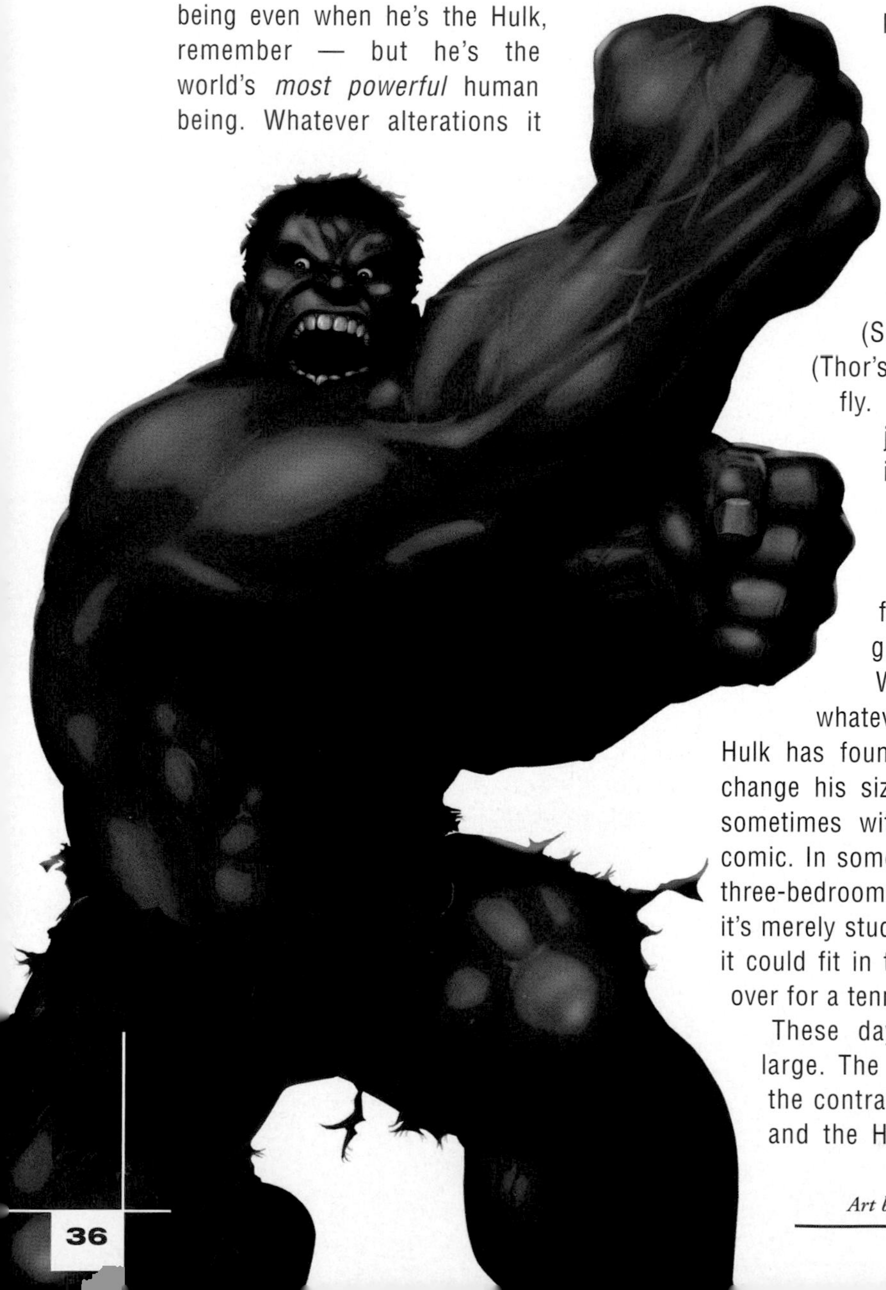

Art by Dale Keown

for super-sizing. And the movie Hulk is the biggest Hulk of all — not Godzilla-sized, but not some former weightlifter in fright makeup, either.

Speaking of which, the TV Hulk stuck close to the most-powerful-human-being concept. It had no choice. The Hulk TV series had enough trouble getting the little things taken care of on its shoestring budget — like making sure the viewers don't see the mattress the stunt men jump into, for instance — to technologically pump up Lou Ferrigno into something other than a six-foot-tall former Mr. Universe. The implications of a smaller Hulk were smaller plots and less drastic powers, but also more emphasis on the Hulk-as-fugitive storyline. And the Hulk is just as much *The Fugitive* with a seriously bipolar title character as it is a superhero fable.

If you had to come up with numbers, here's the tale of the tape on the various Hulks:

Comic-Book Hulk: Given dimensions of 10 feet tall and 1,000 pounds. But he's added weight since his debut, and those dimensions depend on who's drawing him and how the Hulk feels about his current predicament. In the hands of the old masters like Jack Kirby and Herb Trimpe, the Hulk ran smaller; when it's Sam Kieth or Dale Keown doing the drawing, anything this size of Godzilla is fair game.

TV Hulk: Around six feet and 270 pounds, meant to look seven feet and 330.

Movie Hulk: At least a good 15 feet of computer-generated green rage.

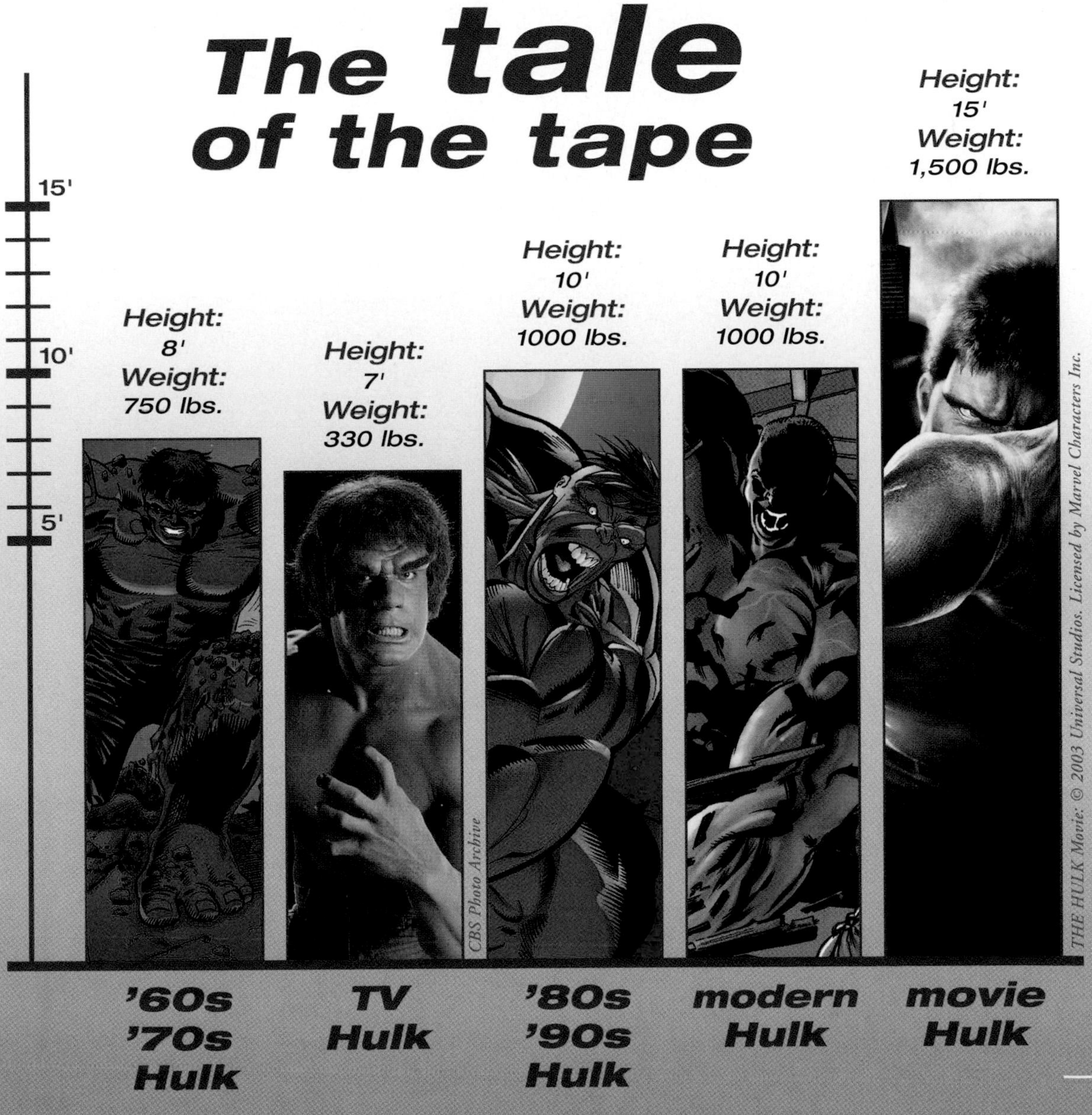

The tale of the tape
15'
10'
5'
Height: 8' Weight: 750 lbs.
Height: 7' Weight: 330 lbs.
Height: 10' Weight: 1000 lbs.
Height: 10' Weight: 1000 lbs.
Height: 15' Weight: 1,500 lbs.
'60s '70s Hulk
TV Hulk
'80s '90s Hulk
modern Hulk
movie Hulk

Big heads & leather pants:
Great Hulk villians

The Hulk has found himself on the other side of the ball from about as motley a crew of villains as ever crawled from beneath the drawing table and prostrated themselves on the pages of Marvel comics. The reason for that's pretty obvious: The Hulk doesn't need villains. He's on the run from the ostensible good guys, the high-ranking representatives of the United-bloody-States-bloody-Army and their various welcoming committees, most of which pack some serious heat. He doesn't need villains to muck things up — does he?

Evidently, someone thought so, because as if the Hulk didn't have enough troubles — what with the whole repressed-rage thing and the child-abuse thing and the hots-for-his-chief-adversary's-daughter thing — he got villains to vanquish.

None of the Hulk's villains ever generated the fear Dr. Doom, Galactus, the Green Goblin or the Red Skull instilled in their adversaries. Gut-busting laughter was the most reasoned response.

Of the lot, the most developed, literally and figuratively, was the ex-janitor known as the Leader. After accidentally being exposed to ... heck, let him tell it (in *Tales to Astonish #63)*: "An ordinary laborer was moving a load of waste in the sub-cellar of a chemical research plant. Suddenly, a one-in-a-million freak accident occurred, as an experimental GAMMA RAY CYLINDER exploded! The trapped laborer was caught in the blast without warning ... with no place to turn! For a period of almost a full minute his entire body was bombarded by the mysterious gamma rays, one of the strongest forces known to man!

"Although a fraction of the dosage he received would have been enough to kill a dozen men, for some inexplicable reason the laborer SURVIVED the uncanny ordeal! Medical science was baffled! He seemed com-

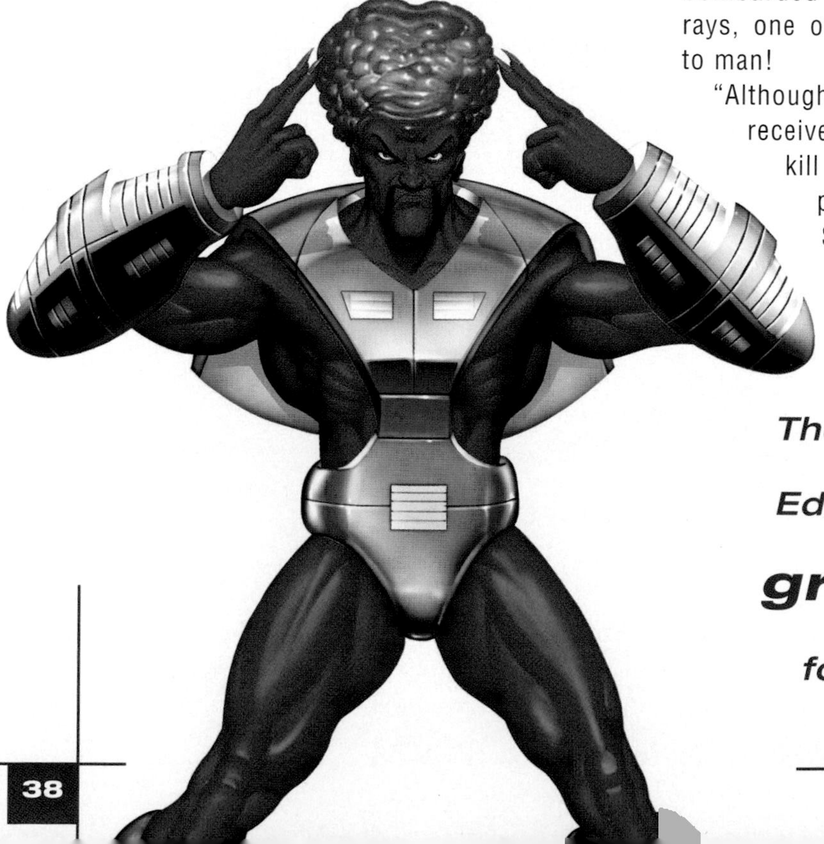

The Leader looked like Edmund O'Brien in D.O.A. with green skin and a Harvestore for a skull.

Art by Tom Marvelli

pletely unharmed ... although in one way, he was different ...

"Even after leaving the observation ward, he devoured every book he could find! He studied like a man possessed ... and he remembered everything he read! His mind absorbed knowledge like a sponge! But then, one day a new CHANGE came over him!

"Although he hadn't known it at the time,

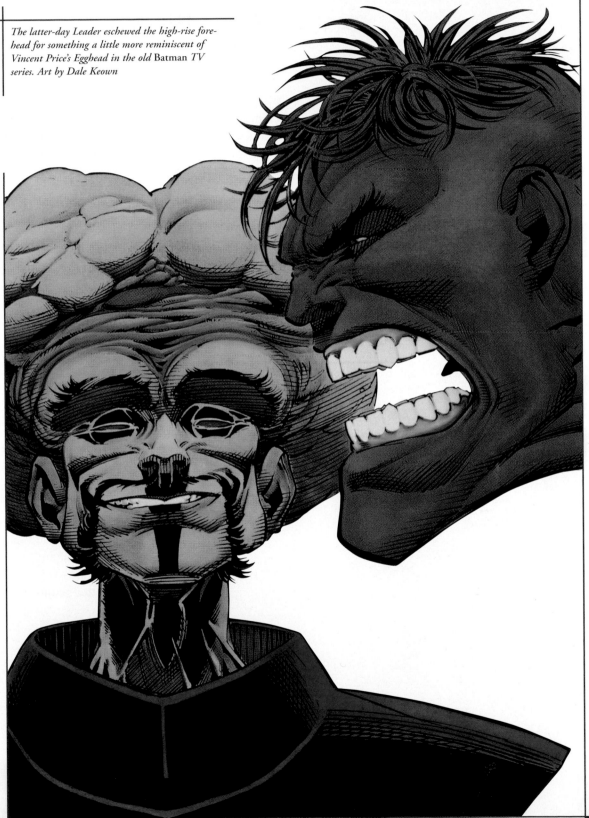

The latter-day Leader eschewed the high-rise forehead for something a little more reminiscent of Vincent Price's Egghead in the old Batman *TV series. Art by Dale Keown*

it had taken THIS LONG for the effects of the GAMMA RAYS to finally be felt! And, as he lay on the floor, unconscious, the TRANSFORMATION took place ...

"Slowly, consciousness returned. Weakly, he began to lift himself from the floor ... still not dreaming, not suspecting what had HAPPENED to him! It was not until he looked into the mirror that he knew ...! 'I've become something MORE than human!'

"'I am that once unskilled laborer! That man has been transformed by the gamma rays into one of the greatest BRAINS that ever lived! My former name is meaningless now! I choose to be known simply as ... THE LEADER!'"

The Leader looked like Edmund O'Brien in *D.O.A.* with green skin and a Harvestore for a skull. It's never made clear why he didn't use his superior knowledge to do good, and why he persisted in thinking big clanking robots were the best way to destroy the Hulk (except that in the early '60s, big clanking robots — and missiles — were the best way to destroy *everything*).

His taste for robots aside, the Leader was formidable as Hulk villains go. The usual plot device was for Thunderbolt Ross to employ the Leader as an alternative brilliant scientist to Bruce Banner, let him showcase his latest breakthrough weapon (usually a big clanking robot), and then fall over sideways as the Leader takes over the base and turns it into his launching pad for world domination.

The first Hulk-Leader meeting is the best, particularly if you like to snort Mountain Dew out of your nose while you read comics. The Leader's humanoid is battling the Hulk on top of a train carrying Bruce Banner's latest nuclear invention. The Leader commands the humanoid to give the Hulk a shock, which throws the "grim, green goliath" off his game just enough for the humanoid to push the Hulk from the train and into the path of a highway overpass.

The Abomination has been the Hulk's toughest enemy down through time. It's not hard to see why. Art by Carlos Pacheco

How do you capture a Hulk anyway?

So if you're a megabaddie and the Hulk is the only thing that stands between you and the conquest of an Army base/America/earth/our solar system/the universe, *plus* 48 million-billion dollars, *plus* a new washer and dryer, what's your goal? Wipe out the Hulk, obviously. And how do you plan go about doing that? Ah, there's the rub.

See, the Hulk is about as close to inde-structible — in the comics, anyway — as a human being can get. Shoot bullets at him, and the bullets bounce off. Fire missiles at him, and they detonate on his chest without causing so much as a powder burn. Drop him from an airplane, and he makes a crater, dusts himself off and growls something about puny weaklings thinking they can defeat Hulk. Topple a building on him, and he bursts through the wreckage like Vixen VaVoom popping out of a birthday cake. Catapult him into outer space, and he does just fine. Doesn't even have to breathe if he doesn't feel like it. So how can you subjugate the human race with something like that hanging around?

In answering that question, the assort-ment of baked goods that is his rogues gallery have put their evil creativity to the ultimate test. And the majority of their answers have been: gas and plastic.

Hard to believe knockout gas can topple the Hulk if he can hang in outer space with the Silver Surfer and not have any side effects other than an urge to use highfalutin' language, but that's apparently the case. The Leader in particular was fond of gas as a Hulk-bustin' measure, but it's like this: The same gas the Leader used put the Hulk to sleep acted as an anti-toxin for Bruce Banner, and doubling the quantity used on the Hulk caused Banner to transform and destroy the absorbatron and rescue the little kitten up a tree, and no one won the washer and dryer. Can you imagine that?

Plastic was another favorite Hulk-trapping ploy. The selfsame Leader more than once shot the Hulk with a goo-spouting pistol. The goo congealed around the Hulk like Spam juice around that tasty blend of pork shoulder and ham, forming a barrier that simply reflected back the Hulk's attempts to break free. But silly Leader! No goo can hold the Hulk forever, and with one titanic blow, the Hulk disintegrated the silly-putty straitjacket and made a beeline for Mr. Big Head.

Along the same lines as the plastic prison, the Sandman, among others, used anti-matter beams to keep the Hulk holed up. They weren't as creative as King Arkham's concentrated gravity (love that), but they worked just the same. The only thing was, all these villains had to turn off the beams sometime so they could process with their evil conquest du jour, and that's when the Hulk would strike.

Maybe the most fitting — literally — way to keep down the Hulk was devised by the Chameleon, who in the guise of Bruce Banner imprisoned the Hulk in special chains manu-factured by Tony Stark — Iron Man to you — based on designs invented by Bruce Banner!

Even then, the Hulk had a way out. After several hours of imprisonment as the Hulk, he fell asleep, changed back to Bruce Banner, and slipped through the chains as easily as a three-year-old slips through a babysitter's hands. Hey, it ain't *all* about brute force.

Art by Adam Kubert

"But the Incredible HULK is not so easily defeated! Possessing the mightiest muscles of any living mortal, he performs a seemingly impossible feat! By sheer brute power alone, by actual muscle control, he forces his flying body to lift itself UP, over the solid stone trestle! (NOTE: The man driving under the Hulk will soon become known as the biggest LIAR in his entire neighborhood!)

"Only the HULK could have attempted it! Only the HULK would have been capable of it! Only the HULK could have done it!"

So was it brute power or actual muscle control? And shoot, any superhero that can fly can fall up off a train instead of

Black Bolt & the Inhumans

Art by Jae Lee

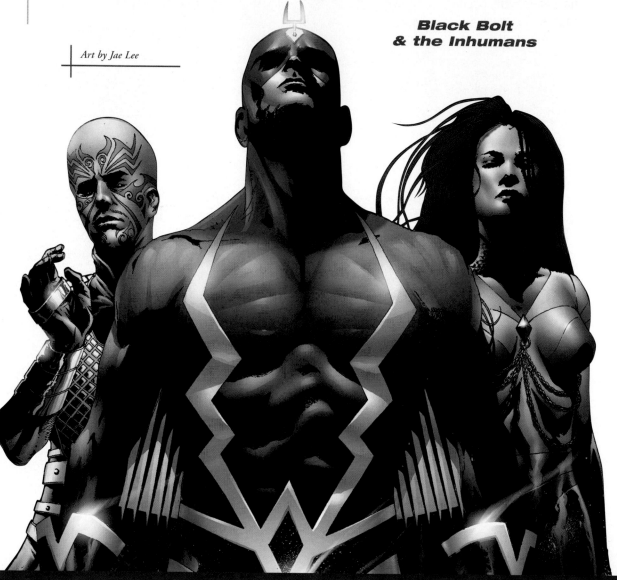

Puppet Master

Sandman

Hercules

Boomerang

down. But that was the Hulk in those days: 110 percent of the minimum daily adult requirement of suspended disbelief.

The Leader's humanoids kept multiplying and getting bigger, but the Hulk always found a way to get the better of them, whether it was a bottomless pit or an exploding volcano. But since the Hulk never directly fought the Leader, Ol' Green Noggin was always free to make a dash for the nearest rocket ship and make a break for it — and he always got away clean.

Besides the Leader, the most constant source of trouble for the Hulk — besides himself, of course, because this guy defines being one's own worst enemy — is the Abomination. Bigger and uglier than the Hulk, he even succeeds in beating down the Big Green Guy — temporarily. As adversaries go, he's about as adversarial as they get. He doesn't carry the cloak of menace around his shoulders with the power and style of a great Marvel villain like Dr.

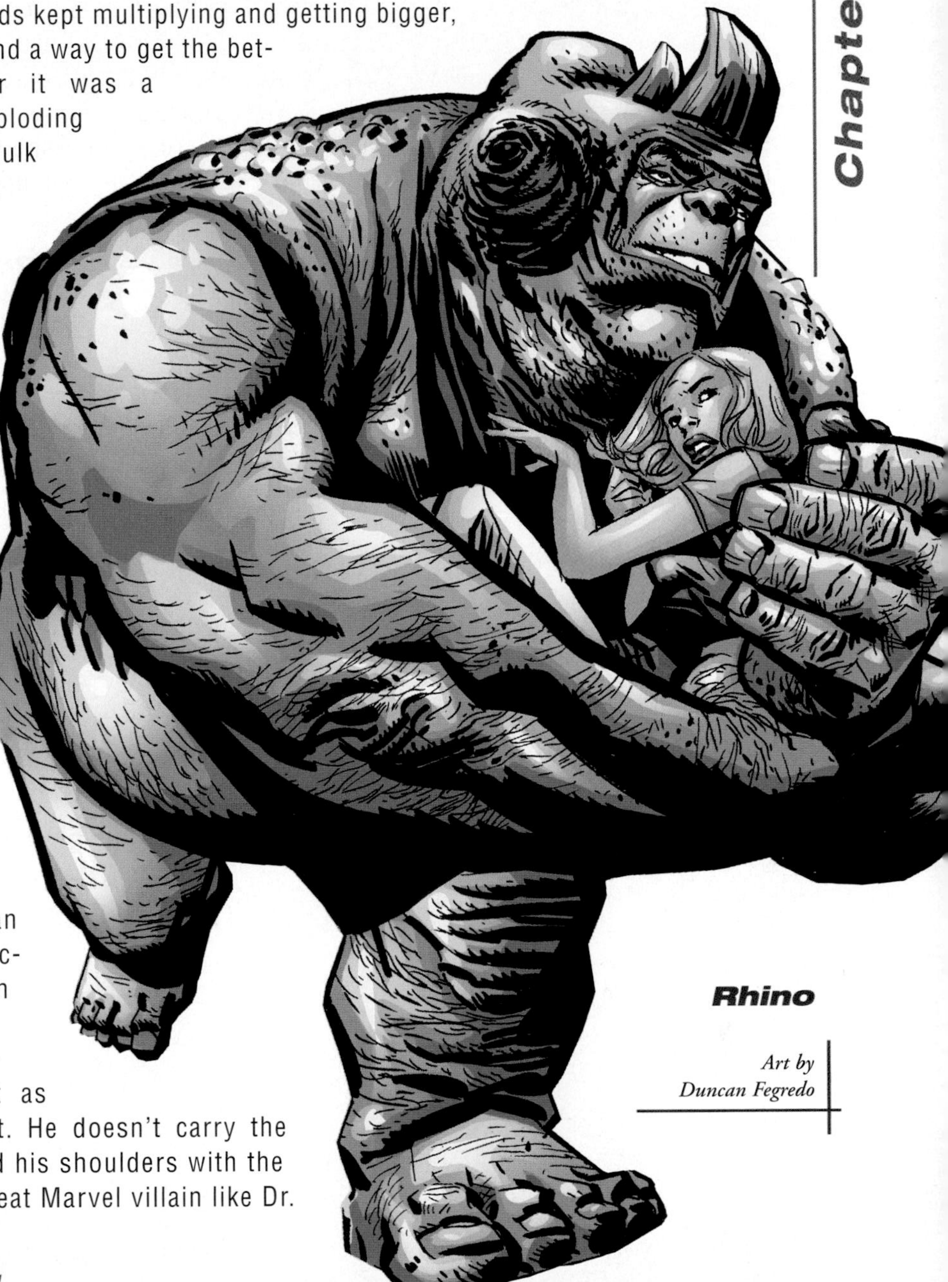

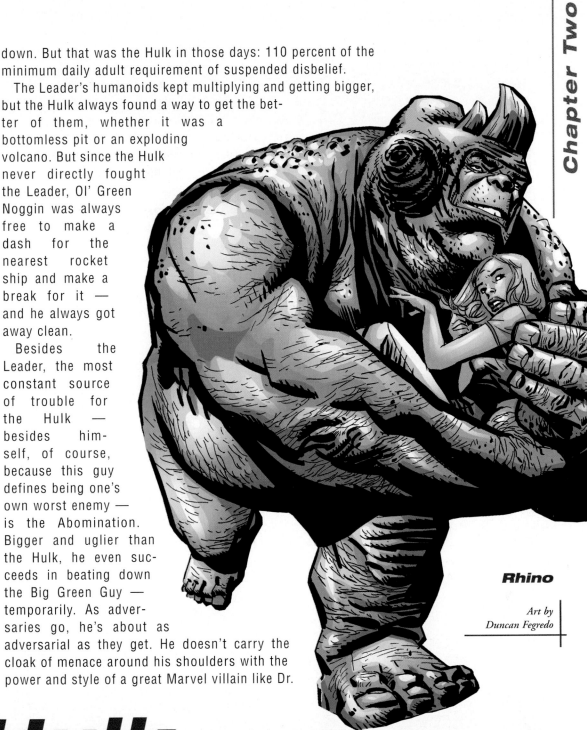

Rhino

Art by Duncan Fegredo

Hulk ROGUES GALLERY

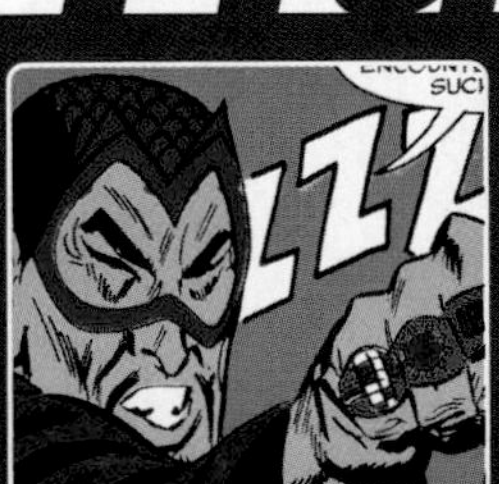

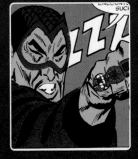

Mandarin

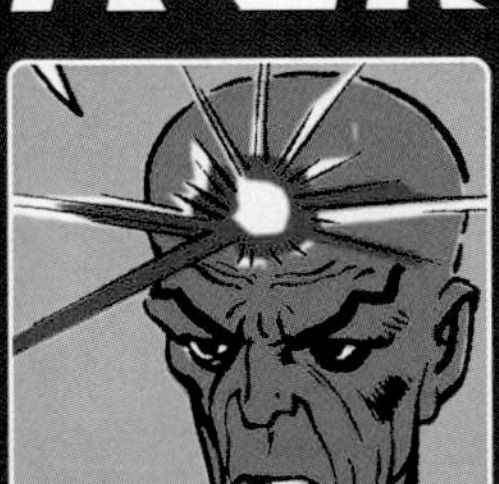

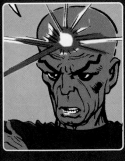

Metal Master

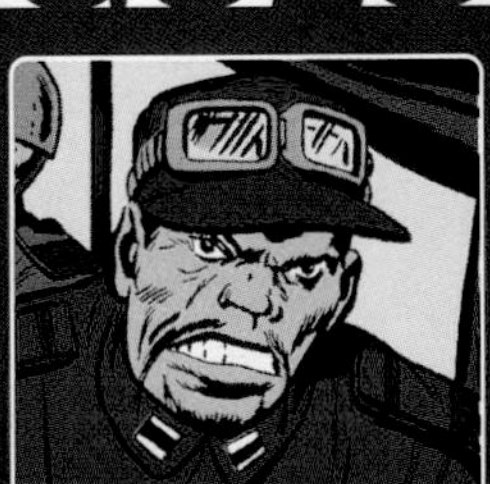

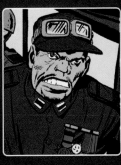

General Fang

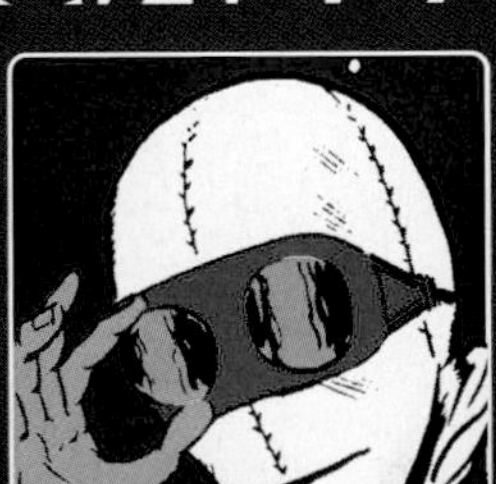

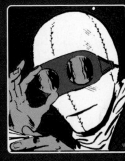

Chameleon

Doom, but he beats everyone but Hanna-Barbera when it comes to rubble creation. The Big A also gets some kind of props for taking out Betty Ross Banner, proving once again that the biggest danger in the workplace isn't paper cuts but being married to a superhero. The Abomination's triumphs are short-lived, though. They'd better be, or else we're wasting a ton of really slick paper here. You can't keep a good Hulk down, but the Abomination gives it his best shot.

Those are the best of the Hulk's villains. The rest fall into two categories: semi-serious guest villains from other Marvel titles (where they were usually used to greater effect) and what the naughty-'n'-nice comics magazine *Wizard* calls "Morts" – characters unworthy of the situations into which they're placed.

The two categories should sort themselves out pretty clearly as the names roll on. If they don't, maybe another Mort needs to be added to the list.

Tyrannus

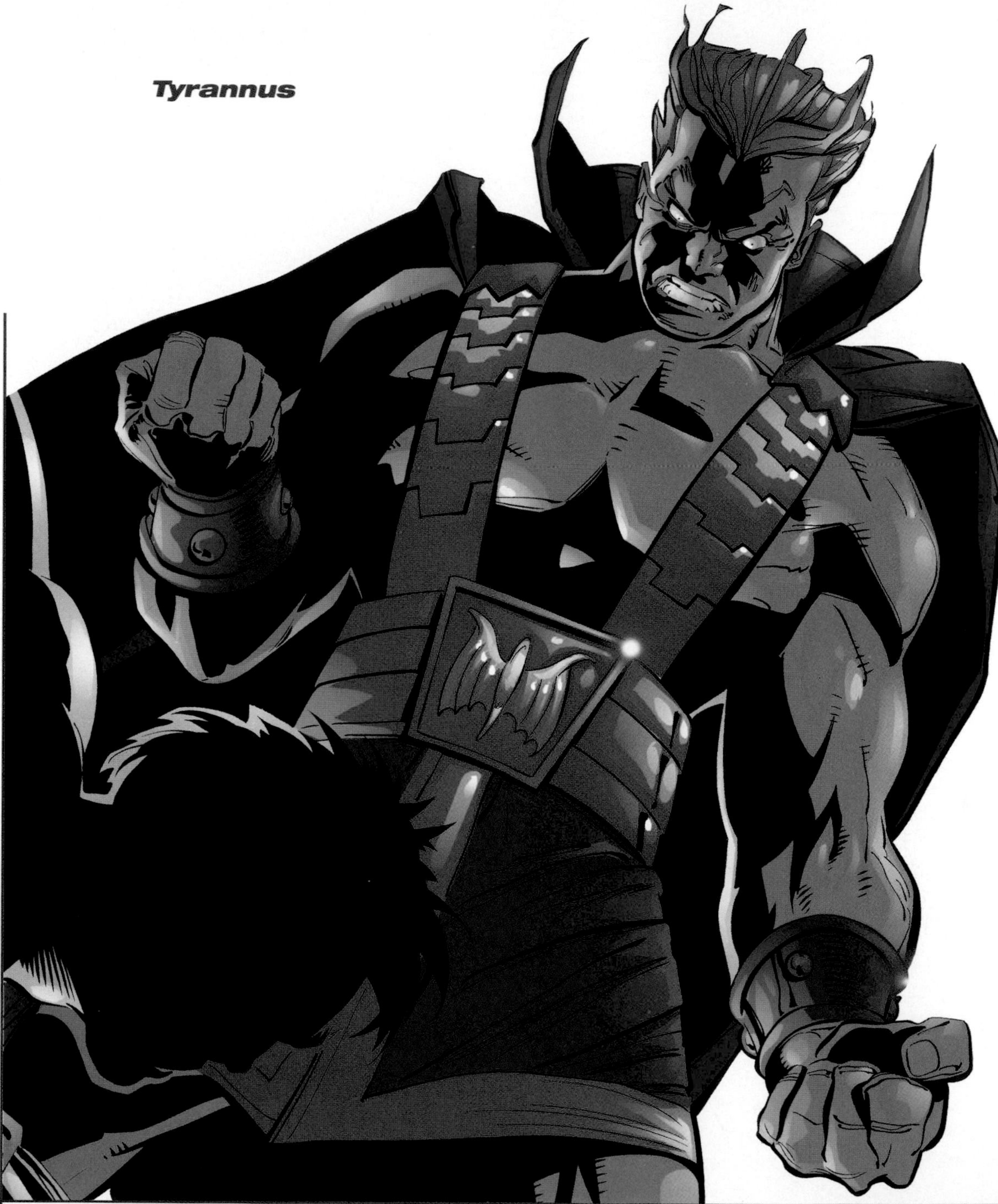

Art by Ron Garney

The High Evolutionary: In turning into the most evolved creature in the universe, he did what any sensible evolved creature would do: vanish into thin air without receiving so much as a bang on the ear from the Hulk. And where's the fun in that?

Lord of the Living Lightning: A cross between Reddy Kilowatt and Toby Keith. A mini-Mort who also paid a call on the Mighty Thor, where he was voted Most Likely to Get His Skull Bashed Wide Open by the Hammer Mjolnir.

The Puppet Master: Controls creatures by making sculptures of them from radioactive clay. A dead ringer for Dr. Evil. Also pushed around by the Fantastic Four.

Beast-Man: Described as "a walking atomic pile." That about sums it up. A mega-Mort.

The Mandarin: Ming the Merciless without the depth of character. His magic rings are straight out of a '30s pulp serial. On the other hand, the Mandarin's android has a career on WWE anytime he wants it. Most of the Mandarin's time and energy is spent pounding away on Iron Man, who evidently doesn't have any better luck with villains than the Hulk.

Absorbing Man: Of all the Mort superheroes — and there have been plenty, from the Golden Age on up — the Mortiest are Zan and Jayna, the Wonder Twins. The Wonder Twins have that essential crime-fighting capability of being able to change into any animal (Jayna) and any form or water (Zan). Oh, and they also carry around a monkey named Gleek. The Absorbing Man is sort of the dark side of the Wonder Twins without the monkey. He was given the ability to absorb the properties of his opponent by the Norse god Loki, which should tell you whose comics he mostly hangs around. When he's not getting dunked on by Thor, he tries to absorb the Hulk's power, only to get caught in a change back to Bruce Banner or inadvertently take on the properties of glass. He's a straight-line super-villain in a complicated world; naturally he's going to get dunked on. But at least he knows enough never to go near anyone named Gleek.

Black Bolt: Not really a villain and not really exclusive to the Hulk, this deaf, dumb and blind kid (dumb, anyway) sure plays a mean pinball. Pretty interesting, as Hulk protagonists go.

The Galaxy Master: The High Evolutionary with a pretty niece and no fighting cats.

The Sandman: Kinda bizarre and kinda interesting, but he ought to be: He's a refugee from the Fantastic Four and Spider-Man. In

Absorbing Man

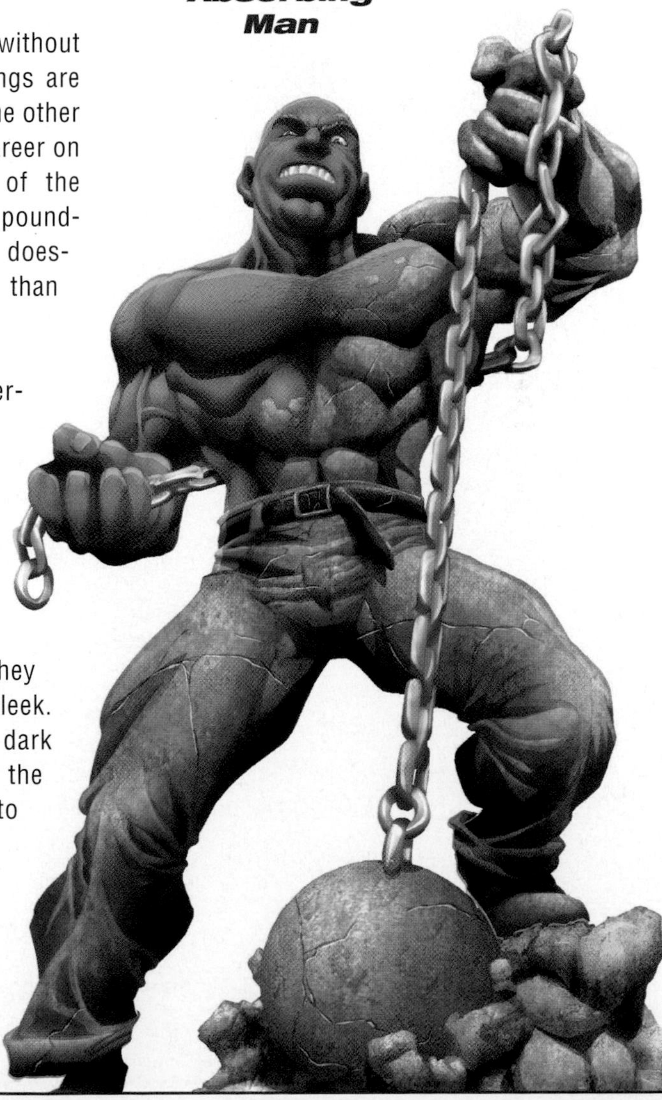

Art by Carlos Pacheco

fact, he's guest-starred as the villain more times than Orson Welles played a fat guy. And that's a lot.

The Metal Master: Can make any item of metal do his bidding. That made him a mean foe against the likes of Ray Nitschke and the steel plate in his skull, but left him vulnerable to the flesh-and-blood Hulk and the cardboard cannon the Hulk used to subdue him. (Oh, yeah: What did the Metal Master want? Good question. He was a space alien who wanted to conquer Earth by bending railroad tracks. Uri Geller had the same idea, and look where it got him.) The Hulk also does his best Rocky Marciano impersonation at the end of his encounter with the Metal Master, telling a

group of kids, "If you hadn't rounded up all the junk I needed to make the gun, it woulda been too late" — to which the kids reply, "Gosh! Imagine the Hulk complementing us! Wowee!" You've come a long way, baby.

The Chameleon: Guess. Just guess what the Chameleon can do. We double-dog dare you.

General Fang: Your basic heartless, gutless Red Chinese commie pinko apeman leading his hordes of heartless, gutless Red Chinese commie pinko apemen against the Hulk. Stereotype? Whaddya mean, stereotype?

Tyrannus: An immortal Roman dictator from the center of the earth, of course. A mega-Mort if only for the legions of mole people who follow him.

Dr. Konrad Zaxon: As mad a scientist as Bruce Banner, only evil. How can you tell? The cheekbones, mustache and name give him away. They always do. Can you in your wildest dreams conceive of a good guy named Dr. Konrad Zaxon? We rest our case.

Boomerang: A former baseball pitcher who throws explosive discs ... only they don't come back. So if they don't come back, then why is he called Boomerang? Eat your broccoli.

Hercules: Yeah, that Hercules. In town for a movie shoot, he and the Hulk have a little rock fight — with big pieces of a mountain. Great fight scenes, but they forgot to put film in the camera! Don't you hate it when that happens?

The Rhino: You, too, could be the Rhino. All you do is take one of those pickup-truck bed-liners that claim to be able to withstand a direct hit from an Al-Samoud missile, peel it gently from the pickup-truck bed, wrap it around your body, stand in a 1,200-degree oven or the men's room at the "rest area" just west of Turkey Trot, Okla., until the liner fuses to your body, craft yourself a

Art by Stuart Immonen

horn out of graphite-reinforced molybdenum, shove it into the warm plastic on your forehead and voila! Instant Rhino. What? There's no way to go to the bathroom in your new togs? Try holding it for a couple of years, and see if you're not as mad as the Rhino, too. The comic-book Rhino is a burly ex-con who's talked into the trick suit by a couple of sharp-dressed dopes bent on Hulk blood or world domination, or a combination thereof. The plots are sketchy bits of flim-flam that serve no purpose other than to get the Hulk and the Rhino fighting, which they do a lot. The Hulk eventually prevails, obviously, but not without some solid tussles. And, yeah, there really isn't a fly on the Rhino suit. That pretty much answers those motivation questions.

The Sub-Mariner: Think of the Sub-Mariner as a Hulk with Spock ears. The Sub-Mariner isn't inherently evil, though some humans think he is — just like the Hulk. The Sub-Mariner distrusts humans — and with real good reason — and wow, so does the Hulk. The Sub-Mariner just wants to be left alone, and the Hulk's his willing partner in solitude. Though he and the Hulk get it on more than once, and memorably (thanks in part to the Puppet Master and his goofy radioactive clay), you come away from their battles suspecting that they're actually like Ralph and Sam, the wolf and sheepdog from the Chuck Jones Looney Tunes cartoons. They punch in, pound the heck out of each other, punch out, go home, and get together on the weekends to eat pizza and watch football. And they don't even fight over the remote.

This list could go on, but you get the idea — and you understand why so many writers of Hulk comics had him first fight ... himself. The Hulk was always sure of a good fight that way.

Tales to Astonish #79 and #87, May 1966 and January 1967

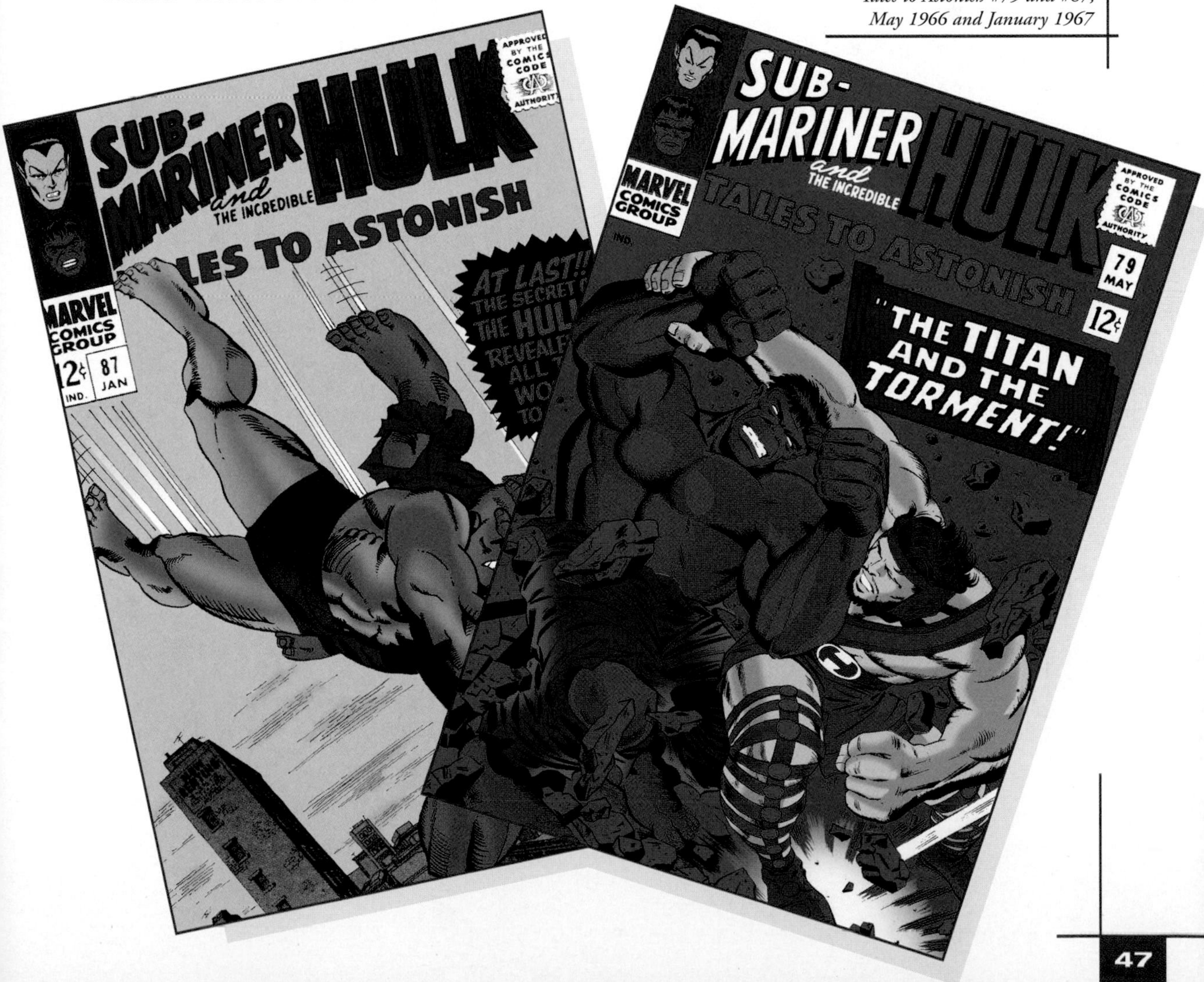
SUB-MARINER
and THE INCREDIBLE
HULK
LES TO ASTONISH
APPROVED BY THE COMICS CODE AUTHORITY
MARVEL COMICS GROUP
12¢
87 JAN
IND.
AT LAST!!
SUB-MARINER
and THE INCREDIBLE
HULK
TALES TO ASTONISH
MARVEL COMICS GROUP
APPROVED BY THE COMICS CODE AUTHORITY
IND.
79 MAY
12¢
"THE TITAN AND THE TORMENT!"

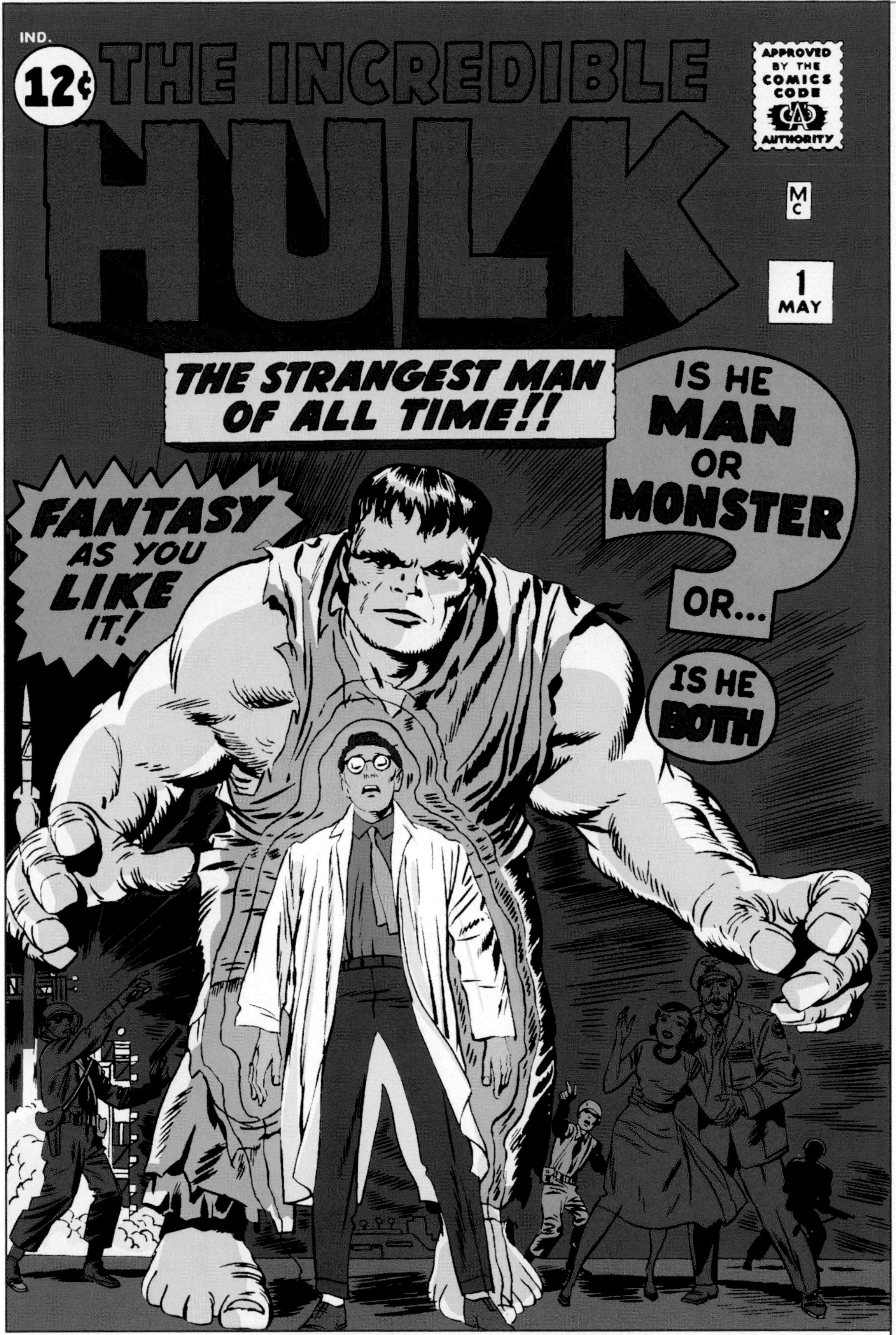
IND.
12¢
THE INCREDIBLE
HULK
APPROVED BY THE COMICS CODE AUTHORITY
MC
1
MAY
THE STRANGEST MAN OF ALL TIME!!
IS HE MAN OR MONSTER
OR...
IS HE BOTH
FANTASY AS YOU LIKE IT!

Hulk #1

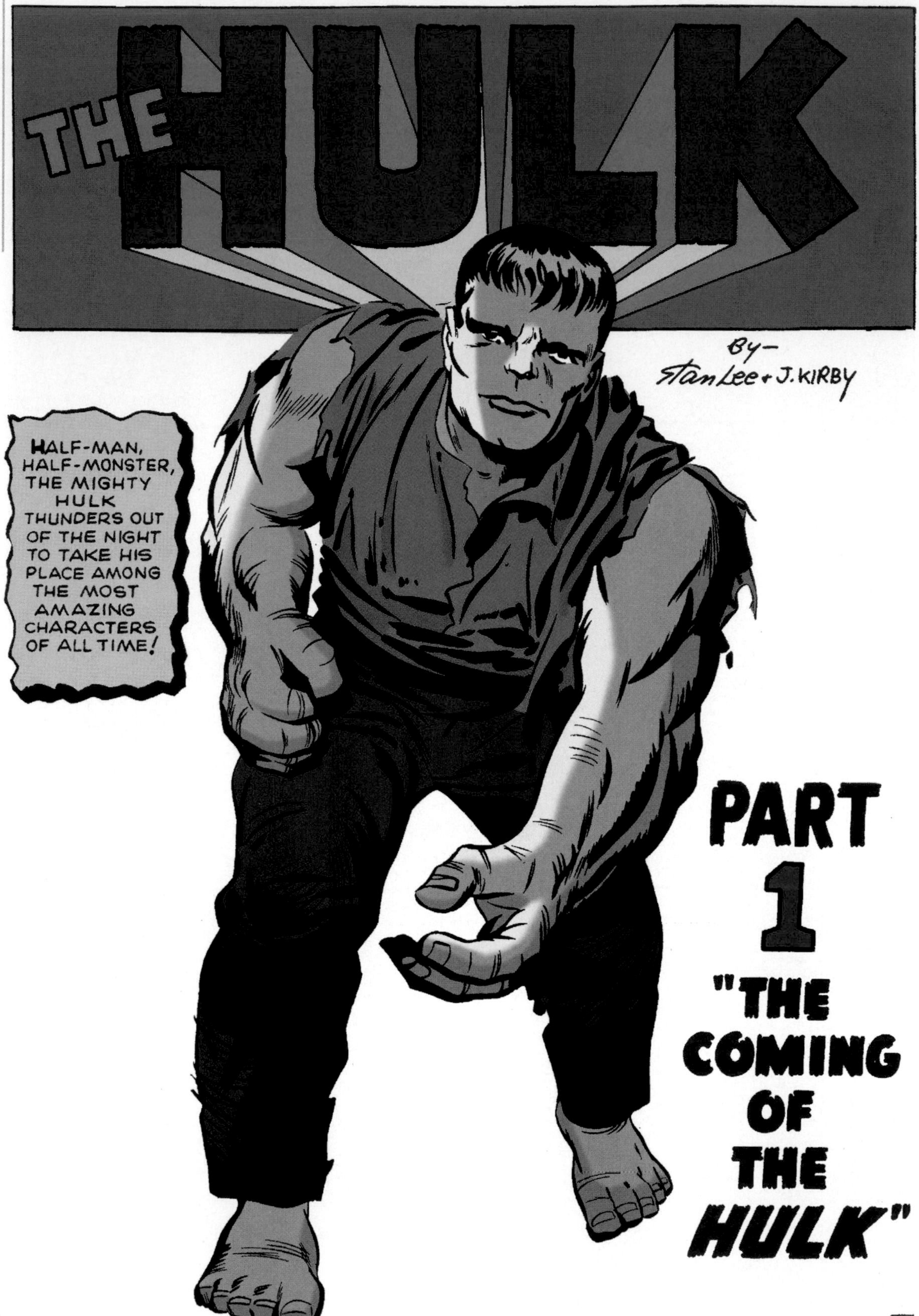
THE HULK
BY- STAN LEE + J. KIRBY
HALF-MAN, HALF-MONSTER, THE MIGHTY HULK THUNDERS OUT OF THE NIGHT TO TAKE HIS PLACE AMONG THE MOST AMAZING CHARACTERS OF ALL TIME!
PART 1
"THE COMING OF THE HULK"
V-709 1

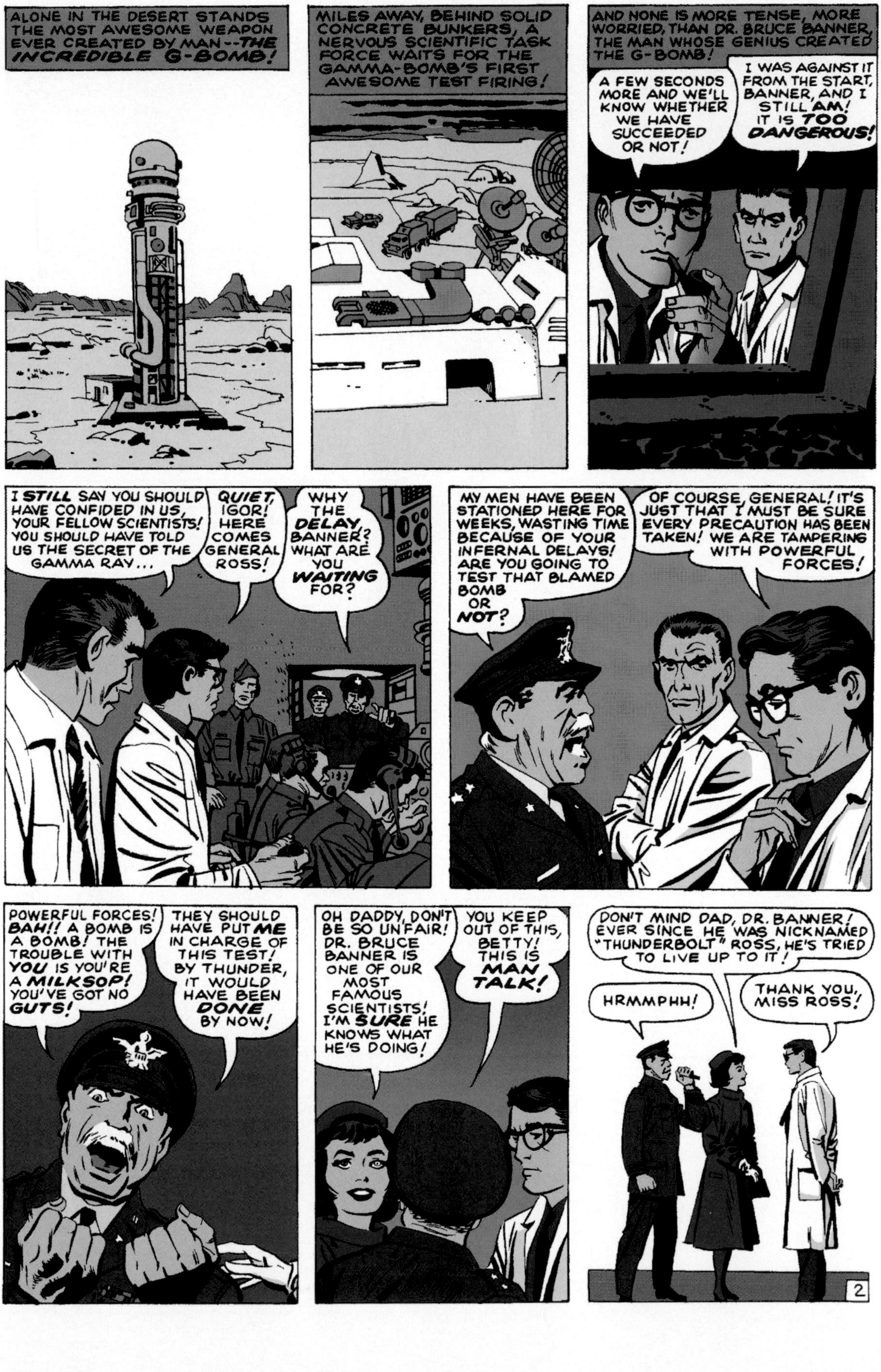
ALONE IN THE DESERT STANDS THE MOST AWESOME WEAPON EVER CREATED BY MAN--THE INCREDIBLE G-BOMB!
MILES AWAY, BEHIND SOLID CONCRETE BUNKERS, A NERVOUS SCIENTIFIC TASK FORCE WAITS FOR THE GAMMA-BOMB'S FIRST AWESOME TEST FIRING!
AND NONE IS MORE TENSE, MORE WORRIED, THAN DR. BRUCE BANNER, THE MAN WHOSE GENIUS CREATED THE G-BOMB!
A FEW SECONDS MORE AND WE'LL KNOW WHETHER WE HAVE SUCCEEDED OR NOT!
I WAS AGAINST IT FROM THE START, BANNER, AND I STILL AM! IT IS TOO DANGEROUS!
I STILL SAY YOU SHOULD HAVE CONFIDED IN US, YOUR FELLOW SCIENTISTS! YOU SHOULD HAVE TOLD US THE SECRET OF THE GAMMA RAY...
QUIET, IGOR! HERE COMES GENERAL ROSS!
WHY THE DELAY, BANNER? WHAT ARE YOU WAITING FOR?
MY MEN HAVE BEEN STATIONED HERE FOR WEEKS, WASTING TIME BECAUSE OF YOUR INFERNAL DELAYS! ARE YOU GOING TO TEST THAT BLAMED BOMB OR NOT?
OF COURSE, GENERAL! IT'S JUST THAT I MUST BE SURE EVERY PRECAUTION HAS BEEN TAKEN! WE ARE TAMPERING WITH POWERFUL FORCES!
POWERFUL FORCES! BAH!! A BOMB IS A BOMB! THE TROUBLE WITH YOU IS YOU'RE A MILKSOP! YOU'VE GOT NO GUTS!
THEY SHOULD HAVE PUT ME IN CHARGE OF THIS TEST! BY THUNDER, IT WOULD HAVE BEEN DONE BY NOW!
OH DADDY, DON'T BE SO UNFAIR! DR. BRUCE BANNER IS ONE OF OUR MOST FAMOUS SCIENTISTS! I'M SURE HE KNOWS WHAT HE'S DOING!
YOU KEEP OUT OF THIS, BETTY! THIS IS MAN TALK!
DON'T MIND DAD, DR. BANNER! EVER SINCE HE WAS NICKNAMED "THUNDERBOLT" ROSS, HE'S TRIED TO LIVE UP TO IT!
HRMMPHH!
THANK YOU, MISS ROSS!
2

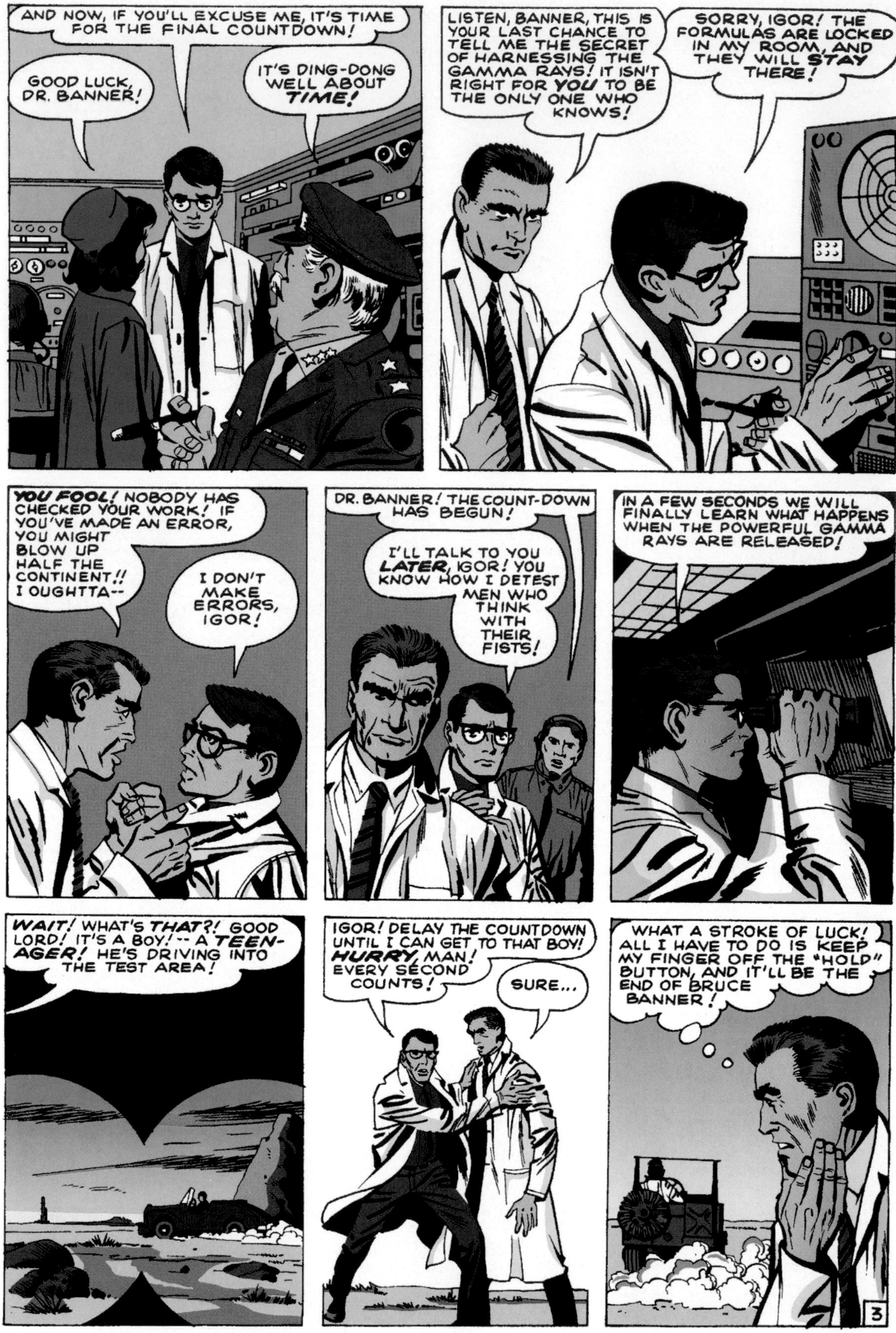
AND NOW, IF YOU'LL EXCUSE ME, IT'S TIME FOR THE FINAL COUNTDOWN!
GOOD LUCK, DR. BANNER!
IT'S DING-DONG WELL ABOUT TIME!
LISTEN, BANNER, THIS IS YOUR LAST CHANCE TO TELL ME THE SECRET OF HARNESSING THE GAMMA RAYS! IT ISN'T RIGHT FOR YOU TO BE THE ONLY ONE WHO KNOWS!
SORRY, IGOR! THE FORMULAS ARE LOCKED IN MY ROOM, AND THEY WILL STAY THERE!
YOU FOOL! NOBODY HAS CHECKED YOUR WORK! IF YOU'VE MADE AN ERROR, YOU MIGHT BLOW UP HALF THE CONTINENT!! I OUGHTTA--
I DON'T MAKE ERRORS, IGOR!
DR. BANNER! THE COUNT-DOWN HAS BEGUN!
I'LL TALK TO YOU LATER, IGOR! YOU KNOW HOW I DETEST MEN WHO THINK WITH THEIR FISTS!
IN A FEW SECONDS WE WILL FINALLY LEARN WHAT HAPPENS WHEN THE POWERFUL GAMMA RAYS ARE RELEASED!
WAIT! WHAT'S THAT?! GOOD LORD! IT'S A BOY! -- A TEEN-AGER! HE'S DRIVING INTO THE TEST AREA!
IGOR! DELAY THE COUNTDOWN UNTIL I CAN GET TO THAT BOY! HURRY, MAN! EVERY SECOND COUNTS!
SURE...
WHAT A STROKE OF LUCK! ALL I HAVE TO DO IS KEEP MY FINGER OFF THE "HOLD" BUTTON, AND IT'LL BE THE END OF BRUCE BANNER!
3

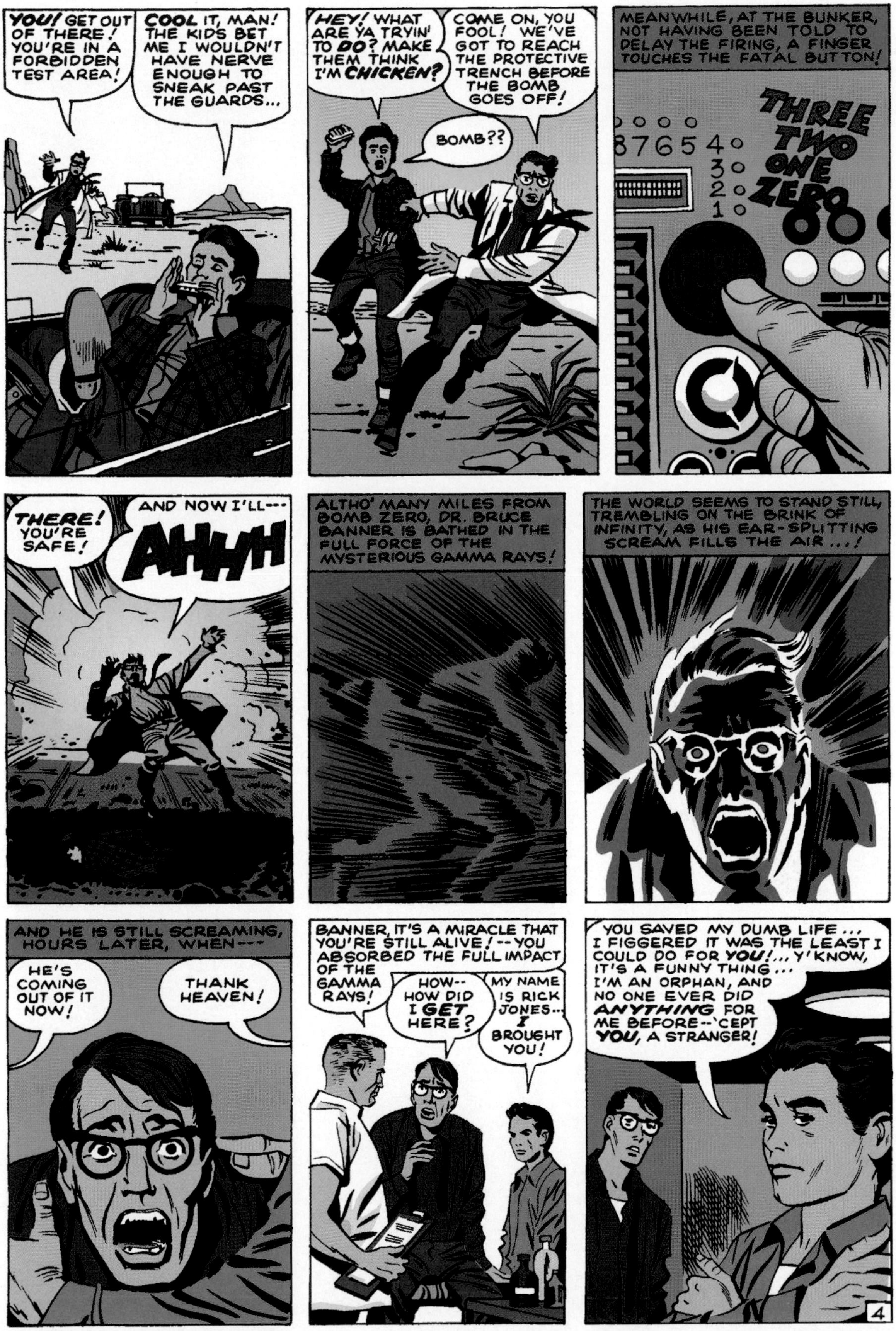
YOU! GET OUT OF THERE! YOU'RE IN A FORBIDDEN TEST AREA!
COOL IT, MAN! THE KIDS BET ME I WOULDN'T HAVE NERVE ENOUGH TO SNEAK PAST THE GUARDS...
HEY! WHAT ARE YA TRYIN' TO DO? MAKE THEM THINK I'M CHICKEN?
COME ON, YOU FOOL! WE'VE GOT TO REACH THE PROTECTIVE TRENCH BEFORE THE BOMB GOES OFF!
BOMB??
MEANWHILE, AT THE BUNKER, NOT HAVING BEEN TOLD TO DELAY THE FIRING, A FINGER TOUCHES THE FATAL BUTTON!
8 7 6 5 4 3 2 1
THREE TWO ONE ZERO
THERE! YOU'RE SAFE!
AND NOW I'LL---
AHHH
ALTHO' MANY MILES FROM BOMB ZERO, DR. BRUCE BANNER IS BATHED IN THE FULL FORCE OF THE MYSTERIOUS GAMMA RAYS!
THE WORLD SEEMS TO STAND STILL, TREMBLING ON THE BRINK OF INFINITY, AS HIS EAR-SPLITTING SCREAM FILLS THE AIR...!
AND HE IS STILL SCREAMING, HOURS LATER, WHEN---
HE'S COMING OUT OF IT NOW!
THANK HEAVEN!
BANNER, IT'S A MIRACLE THAT YOU'RE STILL ALIVE! --YOU ABSORBED THE FULL IMPACT OF THE GAMMA RAYS!
HOW-- HOW DID I GET HERE?
MY NAME IS RICK JONES... I BROUGHT YOU!
YOU SAVED MY DUMB LIFE... I FIGGERED IT WAS THE LEAST I COULD DO FOR YOU!... Y'KNOW, IT'S A FUNNY THING... I'M AN ORPHAN, AND NO ONE EVER DID ANYTHING FOR ME BEFORE--'CEPT YOU, A STRANGER!
4

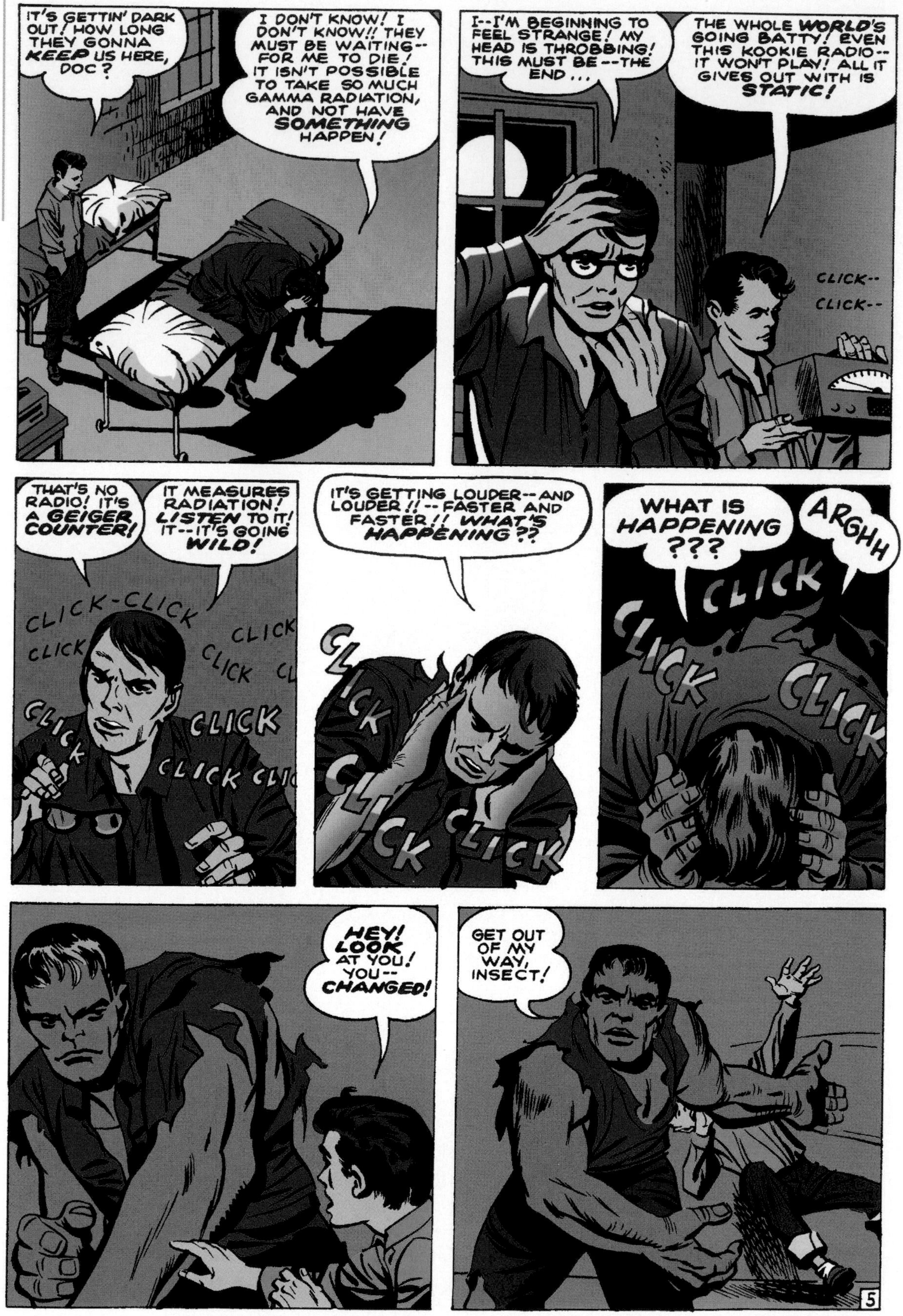
IT'S GETTIN' DARK OUT! HOW LONG THEY GONNA KEEP US HERE, DOC?
I DON'T KNOW! I DON'T KNOW!! THEY MUST BE WAITING-- FOR ME TO DIE! IT ISN'T POSSIBLE TO TAKE SO MUCH GAMMA RADIATION, AND NOT HAVE SOMETHING HAPPEN!
I--I'M BEGINNING TO FEEL STRANGE! MY HEAD IS THROBBING! THIS MUST BE --THE END...
THE WHOLE WORLD'S GOING BATTY! EVEN THIS KOOKIE RADIO-- IT WON'T PLAY! ALL IT GIVES OUT WITH IS STATIC!
CLICK-- CLICK--
THAT'S NO RADIO! IT'S A GEIGER COUNTER!
IT MEASURES RADIATION! LISTEN TO IT! IT--IT'S GOING WILD!
CLICK-CLICK CLICK CLICK CLICK CLICK CLICK CLICK
IT'S GETTING LOUDER-- AND LOUDER!! -- FASTER AND FASTER!! WHAT'S HAPPENING??
CLICK CLICK CLICK
WHAT IS HAPPENING ???
ARGHH
CLICK CLICK CLICK
HEY! LOOK AT YOU! YOU-- CHANGED!
GET OUT OF MY WAY, INSECT!
5

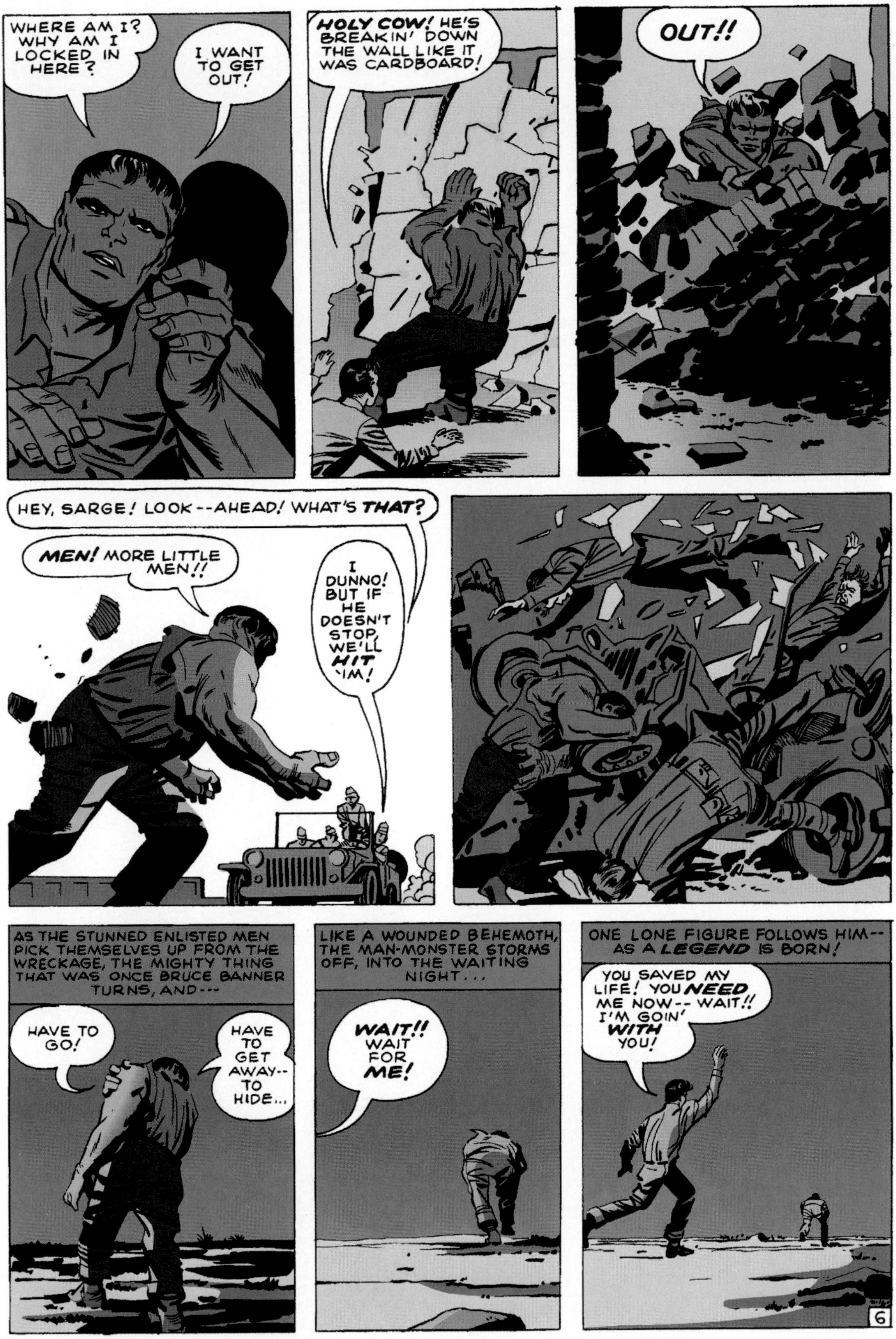
WHERE AM I? WHY AM I LOCKED IN HERE?
I WANT TO GET OUT!
HOLY COW! HE'S BREAKIN' DOWN THE WALL LIKE IT WAS CARDBOARD!
OUT!!
HEY, SARGE! LOOK--AHEAD! WHAT'S THAT?
MEN! MORE LITTLE MEN!!
I DUNNO! BUT IF HE DOESN'T STOP, WE'LL HIT 'IM!
AS THE STUNNED ENLISTED MEN PICK THEMSELVES UP FROM THE WRECKAGE, THE MIGHTY THING THAT WAS ONCE BRUCE BANNER TURNS, AND---
HAVE TO GO!
HAVE TO GET AWAY-- TO HIDE...
LIKE A WOUNDED BEHEMOTH, THE MAN-MONSTER STORMS OFF, INTO THE WAITING NIGHT...
WAIT!! WAIT FOR ME!
ONE LONE FIGURE FOLLOWS HIM-- AS A LEGEND IS BORN!
YOU SAVED MY LIFE! YOU NEED ME NOW-- WAIT!! I'M GOIN' WITH YOU!
6

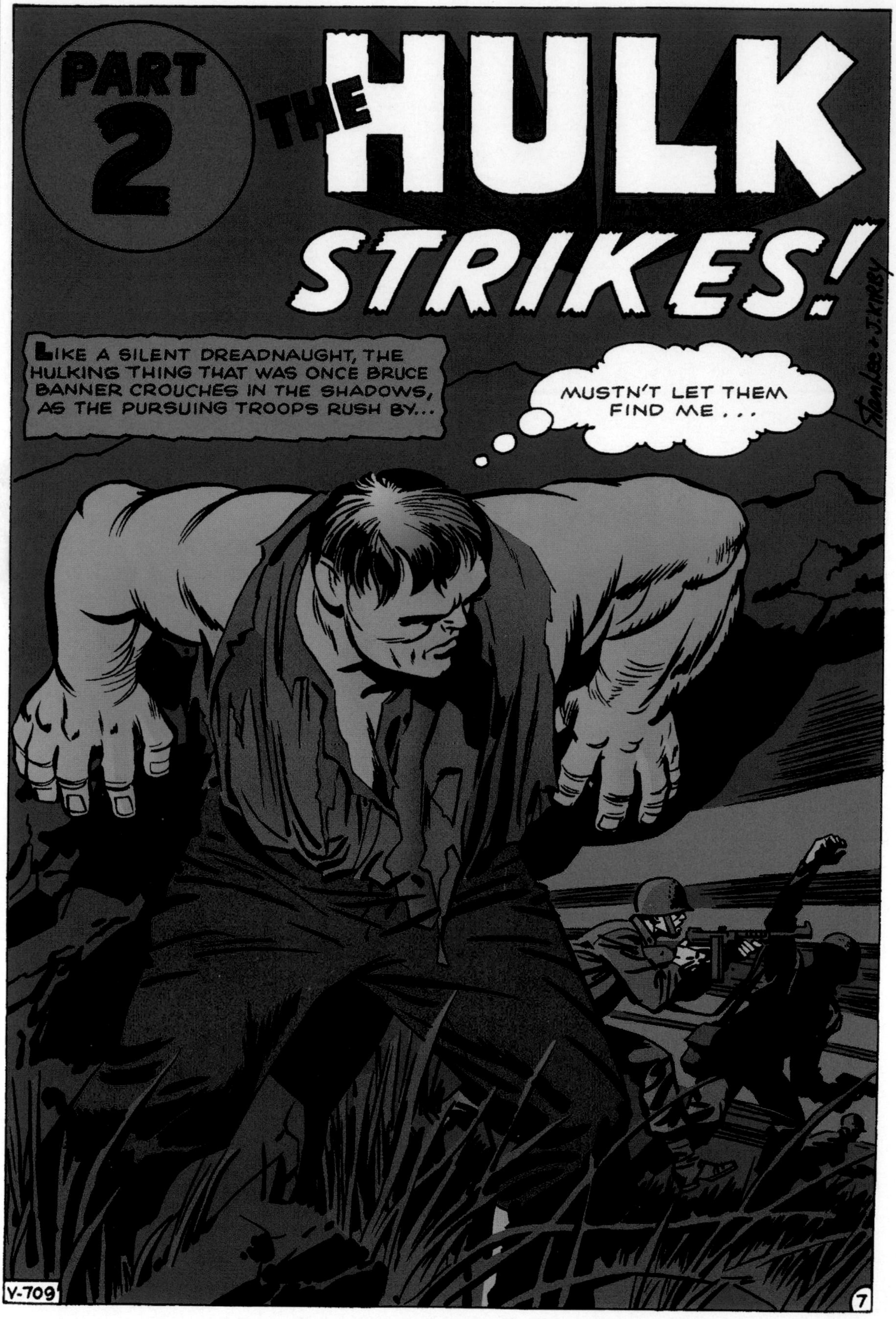
PART 2
THE HULK STRIKES!
Stan Lee + J. Kirby
LIKE A SILENT DREADNAUGHT, THE HULKING THING THAT WAS ONCE BRUCE BANNER CROUCHES IN THE SHADOWS, AS THE PURSUING TROOPS RUSH BY...
MUSTN'T LET THEM FIND ME . . .
V-709
7

FAN OUT, MEN! WE'VE GOT TO FIND THAT--THAT *HULK!!*

LOOK SHARP THERE! DON'T LET THE HULK GET HIS HANDS ON YOU!

AND THUS, A *NAME* IS GIVEN TO BRUCE BANNER'S OTHER SELF, A NAME WHICH IS DESTINED TO BECOME-- IMMORTAL!

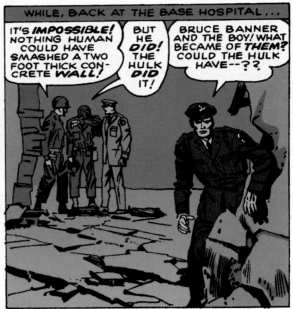

WHILE, BACK AT THE BASE HOSPITAL...

IT'S *IMPOSSIBLE!* NOTHING HUMAN COULD HAVE SMASHED A TWO FOOT THICK CONCRETE *WALL!*

BUT HE *DID!* THE HULK *DID* IT!

BRUCE BANNER AND THE BOY! WHAT BECAME OF *THEM?* COULD THE HULK HAVE--??

BUT WHO COULD EVER GUESS THE INCREDIBLE TRUTH? WHO COULD SUSPECT THAT BRUCE BANNER *IS*... THE HULK!!!

WH-WHERE IS HE *HEADED* FOR?

HAVE TO KEEP MOVING...

...HAVE TO REACH HOME! FORMULA INSIDE HOME! MUST GET FORMULA!!

DRIVEN BY SHEER INSTINCT, THE PART OF THE HULK WHICH IS STILL BRUCE BANNER HEADS FOR A SMALL COTTAGE, SMASHING ALL OBSTACLES IN HIS PATH!

MOVING WITH UNBELIEVABLE STEALTH FOR ONE SO PONDEROUS, HE STORMS CLOSER AND CLOSER TO HIS DESTINATION...

UNTIL, AT LAST, A DIM MEMORY FROM THE BRAIN OF BRUCE BANNER TELLS HIM...

THE THIRD CABIN! THAT IS WHERE I MUST GO!

8

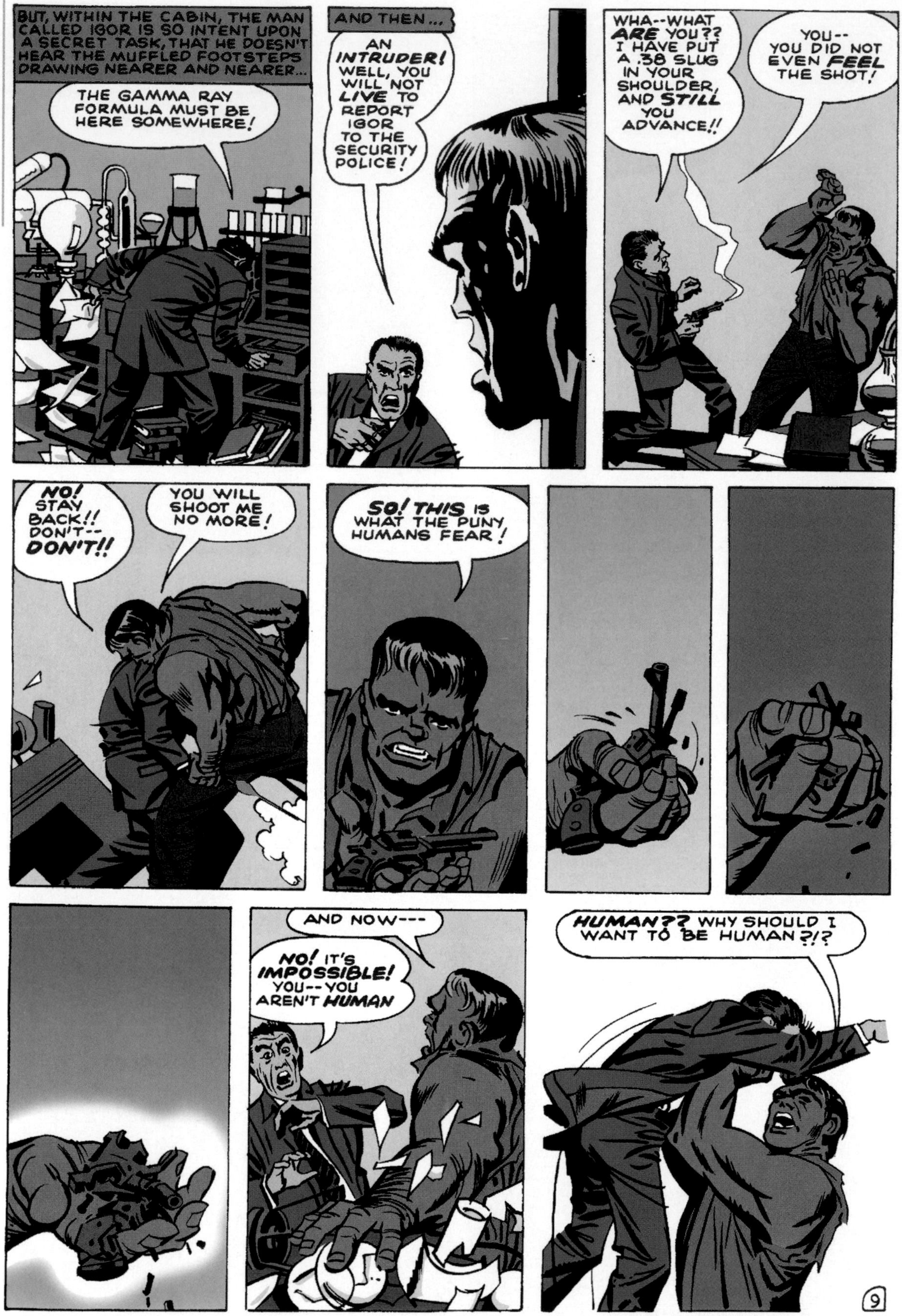
BUT, WITHIN THE CABIN, THE MAN CALLED IGOR IS SO INTENT UPON A SECRET TASK, THAT HE DOESN'T HEAR THE MUFFLED FOOTSTEPS DRAWING NEARER AND NEARER...
THE GAMMA RAY FORMULA MUST BE HERE SOMEWHERE!
AND THEN...
AN INTRUDER! WELL, YOU WILL NOT LIVE TO REPORT IGOR TO THE SECURITY POLICE!
WHA--WHAT ARE YOU?? I HAVE PUT A .38 SLUG IN YOUR SHOULDER, AND STILL YOU ADVANCE!!
YOU-- YOU DID NOT EVEN FEEL THE SHOT!
NO! STAY BACK!! DON'T-- DON'T!!
YOU WILL SHOOT ME NO MORE!
SO! THIS IS WHAT THE PUNY HUMANS FEAR!
AND NOW---
NO! IT'S IMPOSSIBLE! YOU--YOU AREN'T HUMAN
HUMAN?? WHY SHOULD I WANT TO BE HUMAN?!?
9

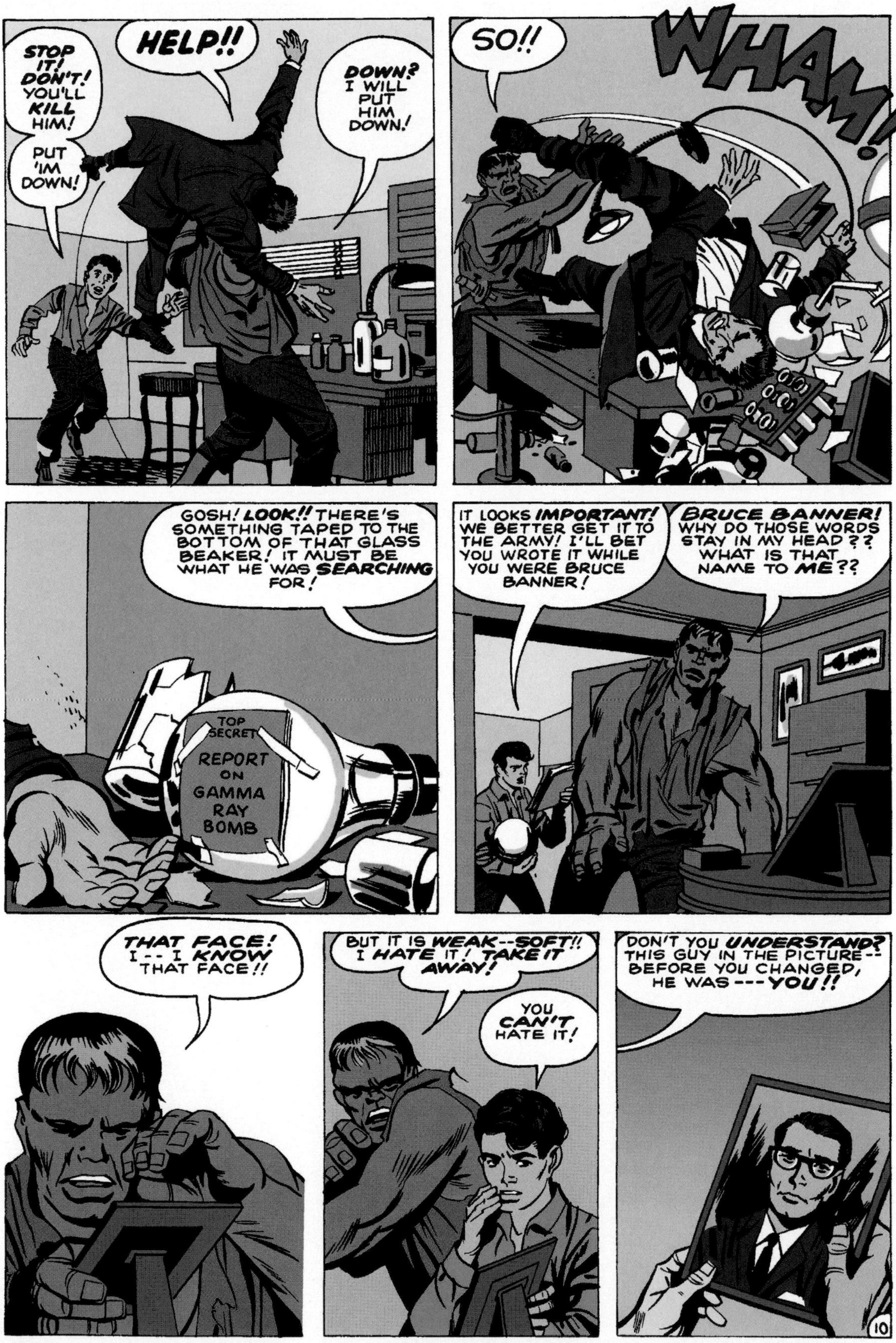
STOP IT! DON'T! YOU'LL KILL HIM!
PUT 'IM DOWN!
HELP!!
DOWN? I WILL PUT HIM DOWN!
SO!!
WHAM!
GOSH! LOOK!! THERE'S SOMETHING TAPED TO THE BOTTOM OF THAT GLASS BEAKER! IT MUST BE WHAT HE WAS SEARCHING FOR!
TOP SECRET
REPORT ON GAMMA RAY BOMB
IT LOOKS IMPORTANT! WE BETTER GET IT TO THE ARMY! I'LL BET YOU WROTE IT WHILE YOU WERE BRUCE BANNER!
BRUCE BANNER! WHY DO THOSE WORDS STAY IN MY HEAD ?? WHAT IS THAT NAME TO ME??
THAT FACE! I -- I KNOW THAT FACE!!
BUT IT IS WEAK--SOFT!! I HATE IT! TAKE IT AWAY!
YOU CAN'T HATE IT!
DON'T YOU UNDERSTAND? THIS GUY IN THE PICTURE-- BEFORE YOU CHANGED, HE WAS --- YOU!!
10

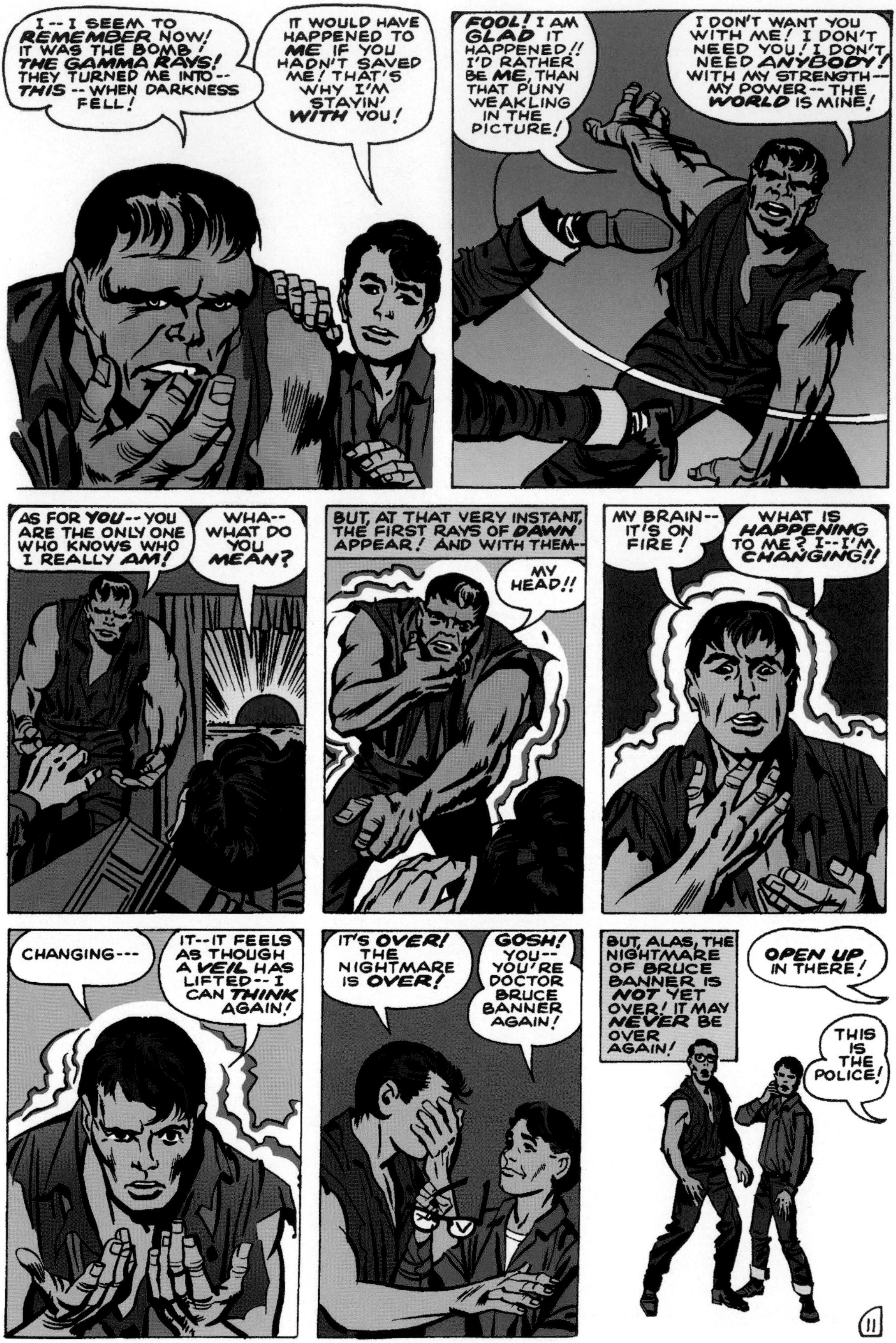
I -- I SEEM TO REMEMBER NOW! IT WAS THE BOMB! THE GAMMA RAYS! THEY TURNED ME INTO -- THIS -- WHEN DARKNESS FELL!
IT WOULD HAVE HAPPENED TO ME IF YOU HADN'T SAVED ME! THAT'S WHY I'M STAYIN' WITH YOU!
FOOL! I AM GLAD IT HAPPENED!! I'D RATHER BE ME, THAN THAT PUNY WEAKLING IN THE PICTURE!
I DON'T WANT YOU WITH ME! I DON'T NEED YOU! I DON'T NEED ANYBODY! WITH MY STRENGTH -- MY POWER -- THE WORLD IS MINE!
AS FOR YOU -- YOU ARE THE ONLY ONE WHO KNOWS WHO I REALLY AM!
WHA-- WHAT DO YOU MEAN?
BUT, AT THAT VERY INSTANT, THE FIRST RAYS OF DAWN APPEAR! AND WITH THEM--
MY HEAD!!
MY BRAIN-- IT'S ON FIRE!
WHAT IS HAPPENING TO ME? I--I'M CHANGING!!
CHANGING---
IT--IT FEELS AS THOUGH A VEIL HAS LIFTED--I CAN THINK AGAIN!
IT'S OVER! THE NIGHTMARE IS OVER!
GOSH! YOU-- YOU'RE DOCTOR BRUCE BANNER AGAIN!
BUT, ALAS, THE NIGHTMARE OF BRUCE BANNER IS NOT YET OVER! IT MAY NEVER BE OVER AGAIN!
OPEN UP IN THERE!
THIS IS THE POLICE!
11

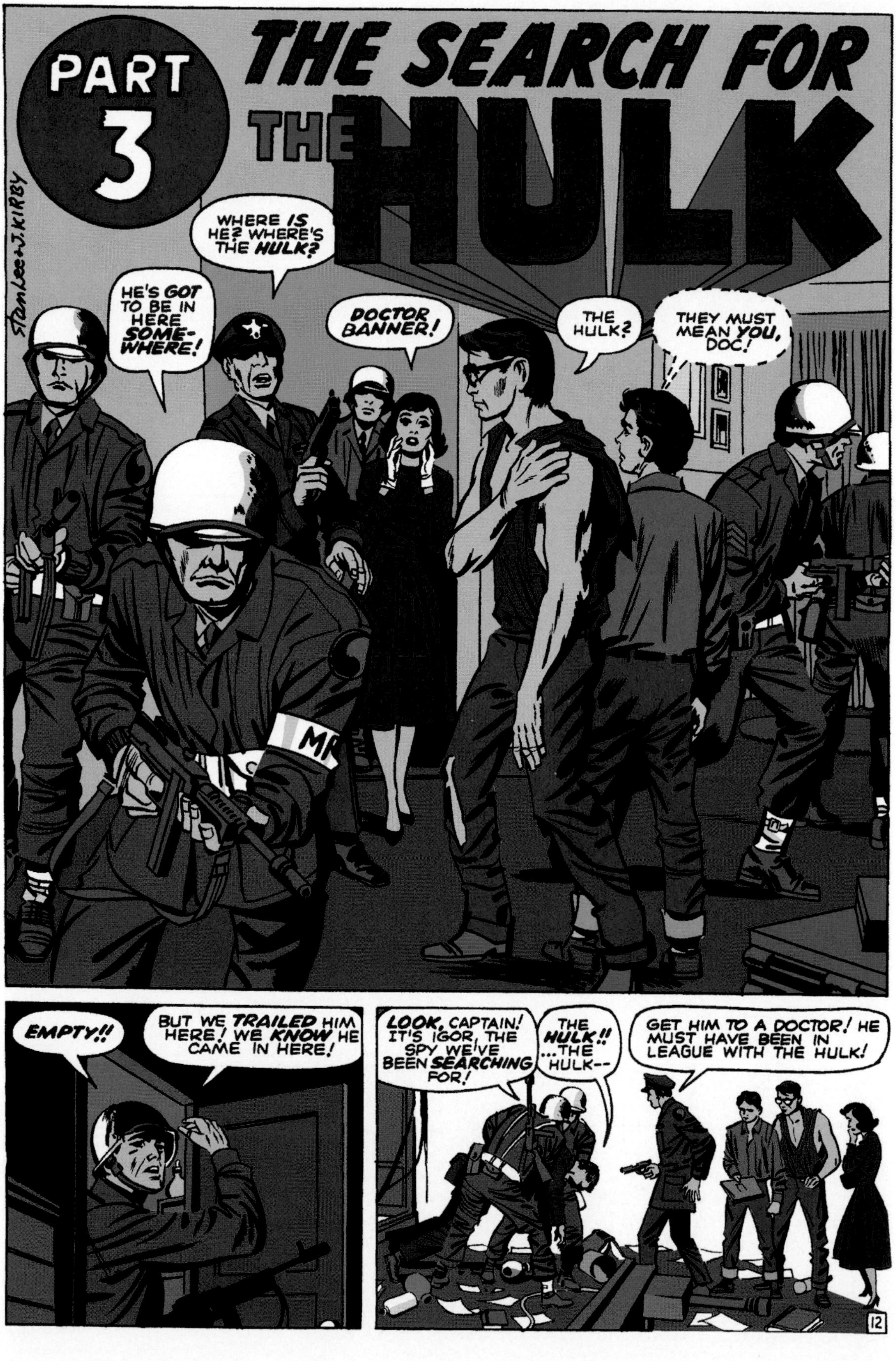
PART 3
THE SEARCH FOR THE HULK
STAN LEE + J. KIRBY
WHERE IS HE? WHERE'S THE HULK?
HE'S GOT TO BE IN HERE SOME-WHERE!
DOCTOR BANNER!
THE HULK?
THEY MUST MEAN YOU, DOC!
MP
EMPTY!!
BUT WE TRAILED HIM HERE! WE KNOW HE CAME IN HERE!
LOOK, CAPTAIN! IT'S IGOR, THE SPY WE'VE BEEN SEARCHING FOR!
THE HULK!! ...THE HULK--
GET HIM TO A DOCTOR! HE MUST HAVE BEEN IN LEAGUE WITH THE HULK!
12

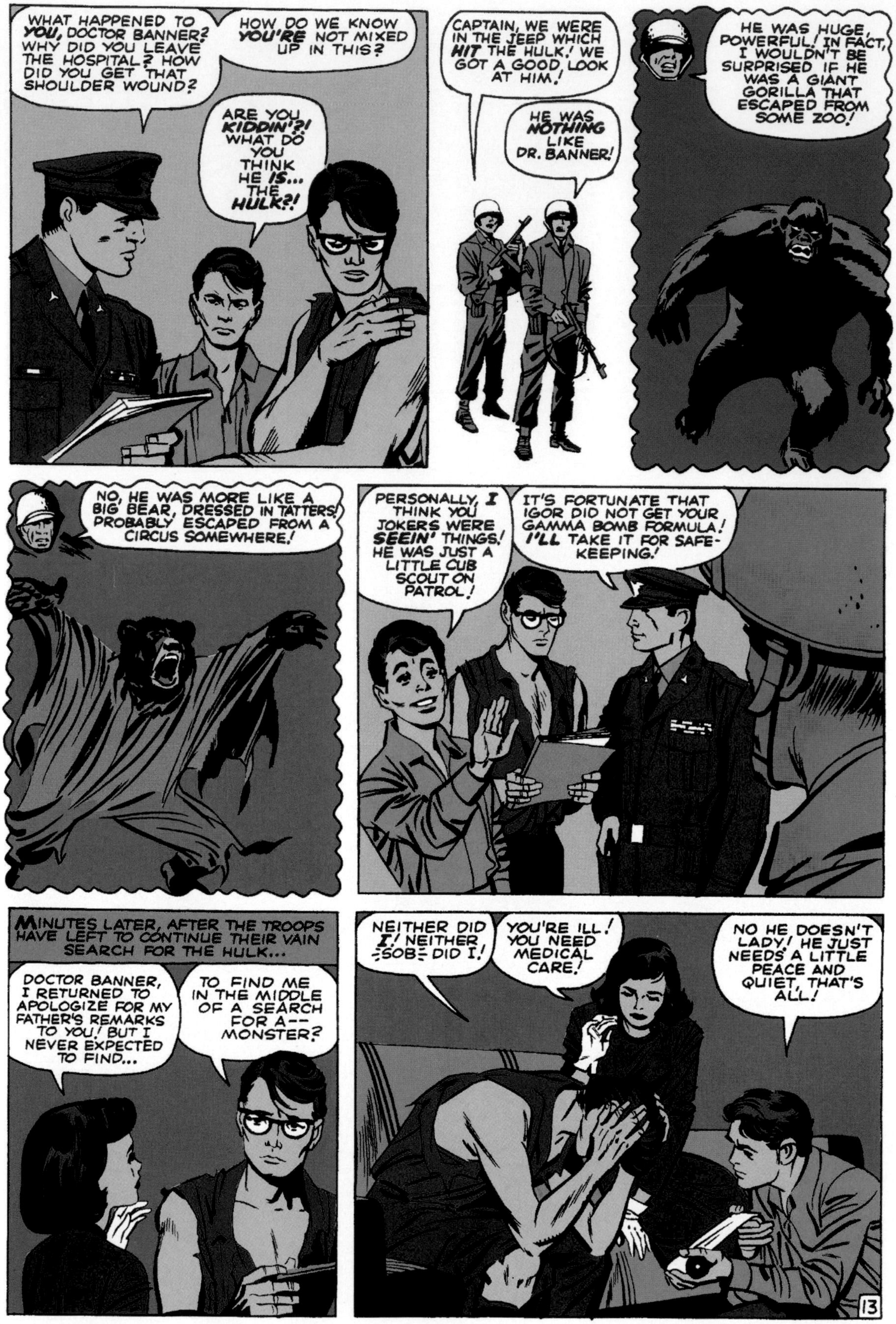

WHAT HAPPENED TO YOU, DOCTOR BANNER? WHY DID YOU LEAVE THE HOSPITAL? HOW DID YOU GET THAT SHOULDER WOUND?
HOW DO WE KNOW YOU'RE NOT MIXED UP IN THIS?
ARE YOU KIDDIN'?! WHAT DO YOU THINK HE IS... THE HULK?!
CAPTAIN, WE WERE IN THE JEEP WHICH HIT THE HULK! WE GOT A GOOD LOOK AT HIM!
HE WAS NOTHING LIKE DR. BANNER!
HE WAS HUGE, POWERFUL! IN FACT, I WOULDN'T BE SURPRISED IF HE WAS A GIANT GORILLA THAT ESCAPED FROM SOME ZOO!
NO, HE WAS MORE LIKE A BIG BEAR, DRESSED IN TATTERS! PROBABLY ESCAPED FROM A CIRCUS SOMEWHERE!
PERSONALLY, I THINK YOU JOKERS WERE SEEIN' THINGS! HE WAS JUST A LITTLE CUB SCOUT ON PATROL!
IT'S FORTUNATE THAT IGOR DID NOT GET YOUR GAMMA BOMB FORMULA! I'LL TAKE IT FOR SAFE-KEEPING!
MINUTES LATER, AFTER THE TROOPS HAVE LEFT TO CONTINUE THEIR VAIN SEARCH FOR THE HULK...
DOCTOR BANNER, I RETURNED TO APOLOGIZE FOR MY FATHER'S REMARKS TO YOU! BUT I NEVER EXPECTED TO FIND...
TO FIND ME IN THE MIDDLE OF A SEARCH FOR A-- MONSTER?
NEITHER DID I! NEITHER -SOB- DID I!
YOU'RE ILL! YOU NEED MEDICAL CARE!
NO HE DOESN'T LADY! HE JUST NEEDS A LITTLE PEACE AND QUIET, THAT'S ALL!
13

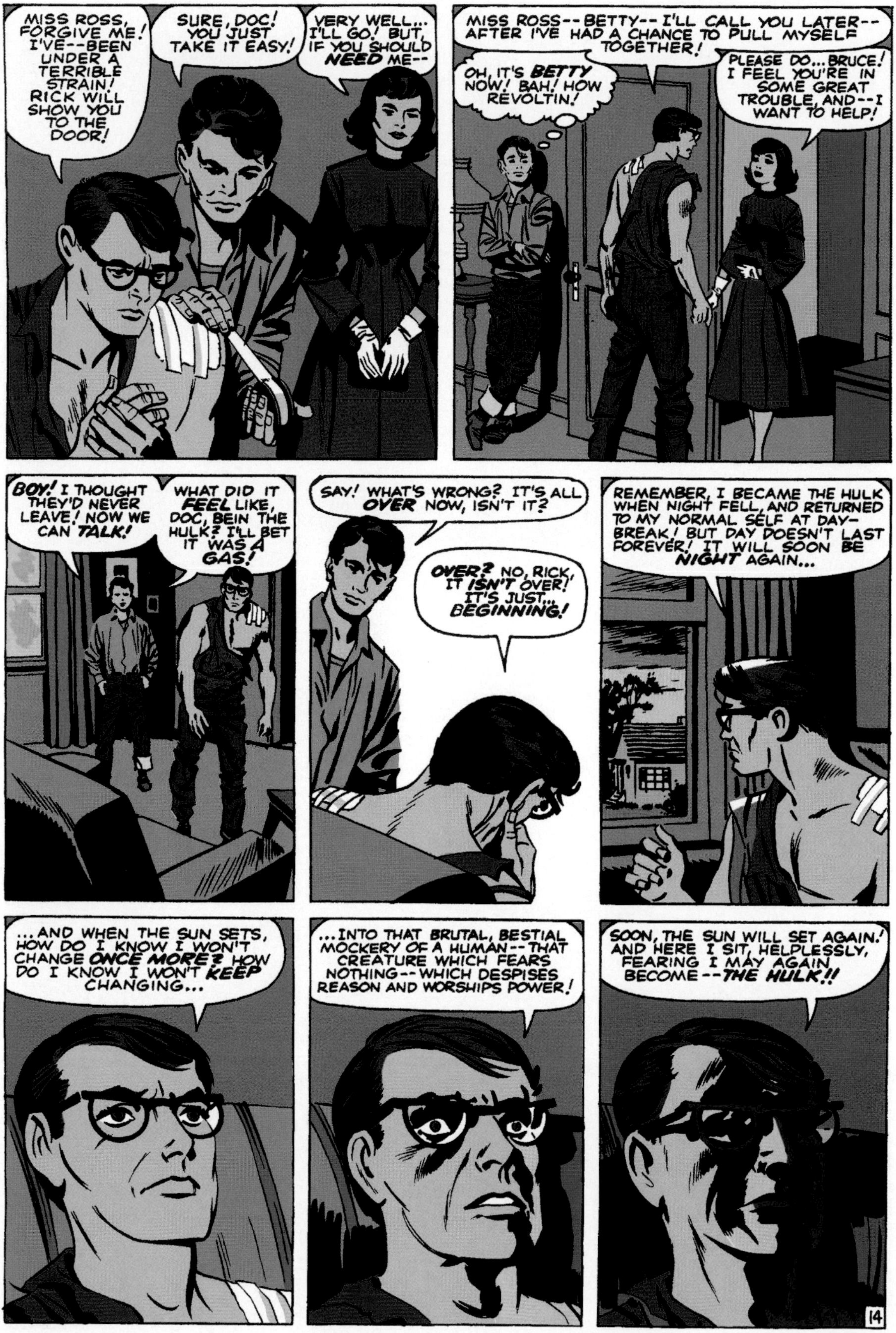
MISS ROSS, FORGIVE ME! I'VE--BEEN UNDER A TERRIBLE STRAIN! RICK WILL SHOW YOU TO THE DOOR!
SURE, DOC! YOU JUST TAKE IT EASY!
VERY WELL... I'LL GO! BUT, IF YOU SHOULD NEED ME--
MISS ROSS--BETTY--I'LL CALL YOU LATER--AFTER I'VE HAD A CHANCE TO PULL MYSELF TOGETHER!
OH, IT'S BETTY NOW! BAH! HOW REVOLTIN'!
PLEASE DO...BRUCE! I FEEL YOU'RE IN SOME GREAT TROUBLE, AND--I WANT TO HELP!
BOY! I THOUGHT THEY'D NEVER LEAVE! NOW WE CAN TALK!
WHAT DID IT FEEL LIKE, DOC, BEIN THE HULK? I'LL BET IT WAS A GAS!
SAY! WHAT'S WRONG? IT'S ALL OVER NOW, ISN'T IT?
OVER? NO, RICK, IT ISN'T OVER! IT'S JUST... BEGINNING!
REMEMBER, I BECAME THE HULK WHEN NIGHT FELL, AND RETURNED TO MY NORMAL SELF AT DAY-BREAK! BUT DAY DOESN'T LAST FOREVER! IT WILL SOON BE NIGHT AGAIN...
...AND WHEN THE SUN SETS, HOW DO I KNOW I WON'T CHANGE ONCE MORE? HOW DO I KNOW I WON'T KEEP CHANGING...
...INTO THAT BRUTAL, BESTIAL MOCKERY OF A HUMAN--THAT CREATURE WHICH FEARS NOTHING--WHICH DESPISES REASON AND WORSHIPS POWER!
SOON, THE SUN WILL SET AGAIN! AND HERE I SIT, HELPLESSLY, FEARING I MAY AGAIN BECOME--THE HULK!!
14

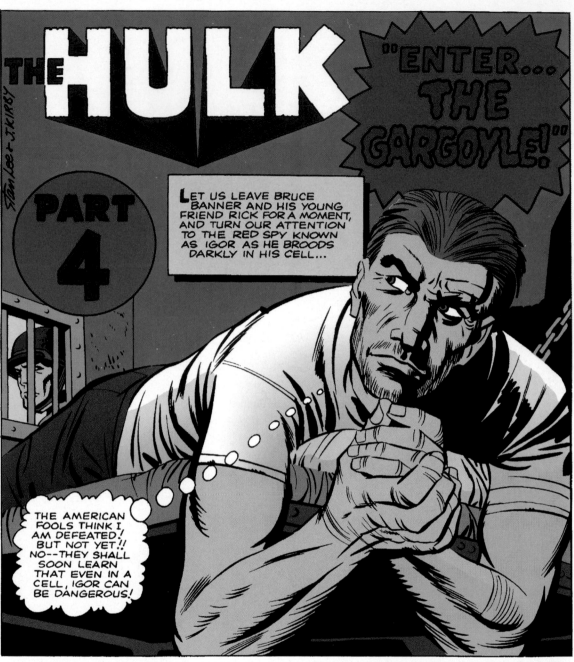

THE HULK

"ENTER... THE GARGOYLE!"

PART 4

LET US LEAVE BRUCE BANNER AND HIS YOUNG FRIEND RICK FOR A MOMENT, AND TURN OUR ATTENTION TO THE RED SPY KNOWN AS IGOR AS HE BROODS DARKLY IN HIS CELL...

THE AMERICAN FOOLS THINK I AM DEFEATED! BUT NOT YET!! NO--THEY SHALL SOON LEARN THAT EVEN IN A CELL, IGOR CAN BE DANGEROUS!

FOR THEY DO NOT SUSPECT THAT PASTED ONTO MY THUMB-NAIL IS A SUB-MINIATURE TRANSISTOR SHORT WAVE SENDING SET!

A SET WITH WHICH I SHALL NOW SEND A SECRET MESSAGE TO BEHIND THE IRON CURTAIN!

AND, THOUSANDS OF MILES AWAY...

COMRADE!! I AM RECEIVING A CODE MESSAGE FROM IGOR!

QUICK! LET ME HAVE IT!

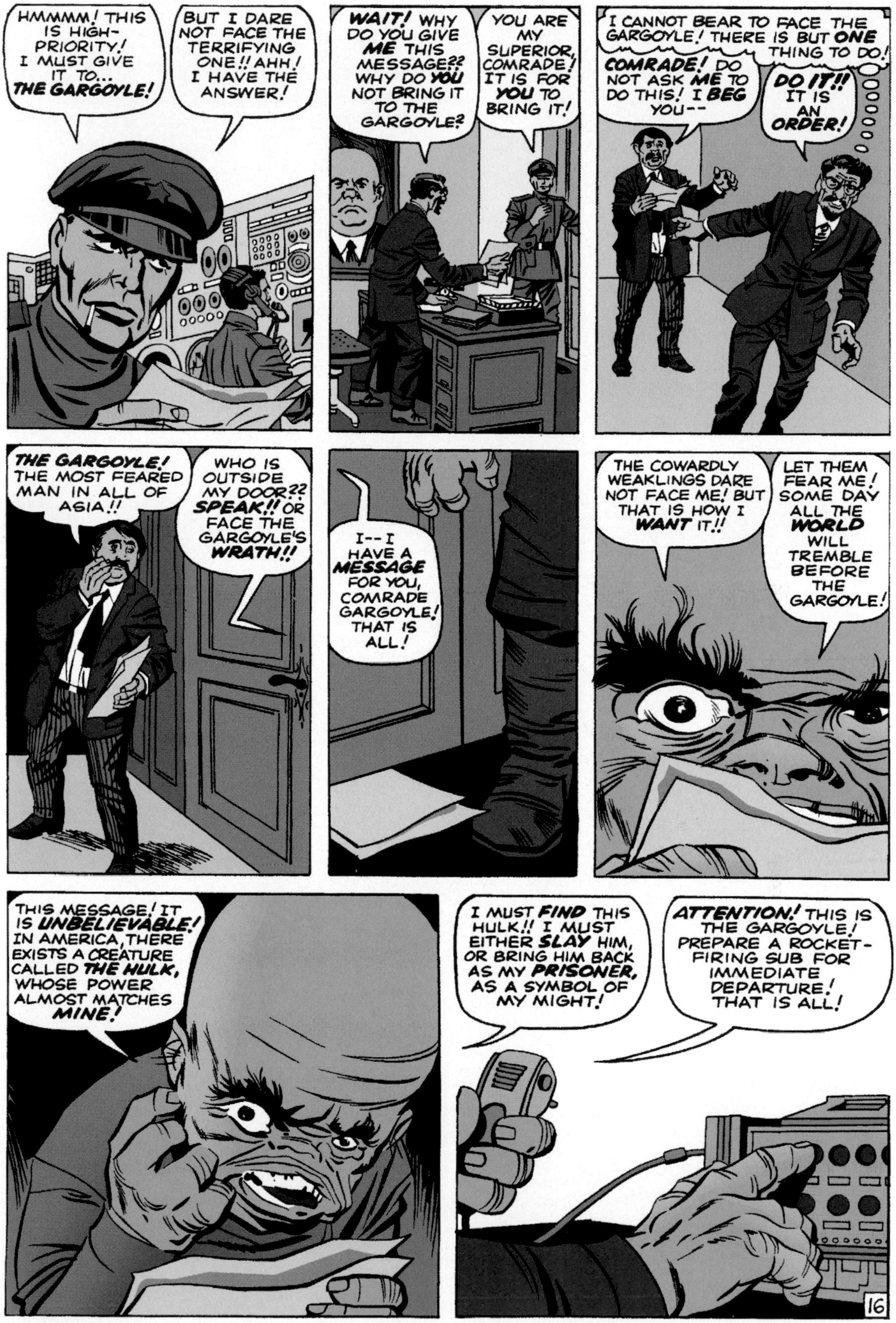
HMMMM! THIS IS HIGH-PRIORITY! I MUST GIVE IT TO... THE GARGOYLE!
BUT I DARE NOT FACE THE TERRIFYING ONE!! AHH! I HAVE THE ANSWER!
WAIT! WHY DO YOU GIVE ME THIS MESSAGE?? WHY DO YOU NOT BRING IT TO THE GARGOYLE?
YOU ARE MY SUPERIOR, COMRADE! IT IS FOR YOU TO BRING IT!
I CANNOT BEAR TO FACE THE GARGOYLE! THERE IS BUT ONE THING TO DO!
COMRADE! DO NOT ASK ME TO DO THIS! I BEG YOU--
DO IT!! IT IS AN ORDER!
THE GARGOYLE! THE MOST FEARED MAN IN ALL OF ASIA!!
WHO IS OUTSIDE MY DOOR?? SPEAK!! OR FACE THE GARGOYLE'S WRATH!!
I-- I HAVE A MESSAGE FOR YOU, COMRADE GARGOYLE! THAT IS ALL!
THE COWARDLY WEAKLINGS DARE NOT FACE ME! BUT THAT IS HOW I WANT IT!!
LET THEM FEAR ME! SOME DAY ALL THE WORLD WILL TREMBLE BEFORE THE GARGOYLE!
THIS MESSAGE! IT IS UNBELIEVABLE! IN AMERICA, THERE EXISTS A CREATURE CALLED THE HULK, WHOSE POWER ALMOST MATCHES MINE!
I MUST FIND THIS HULK!! I MUST EITHER SLAY HIM, OR BRING HIM BACK AS MY PRISONER, AS A SYMBOL OF MY MIGHT!
ATTENTION! THIS IS THE GARGOYLE! PREPARE A ROCKET-FIRING SUB FOR IMMEDIATE DEPARTURE! THAT IS ALL!
16

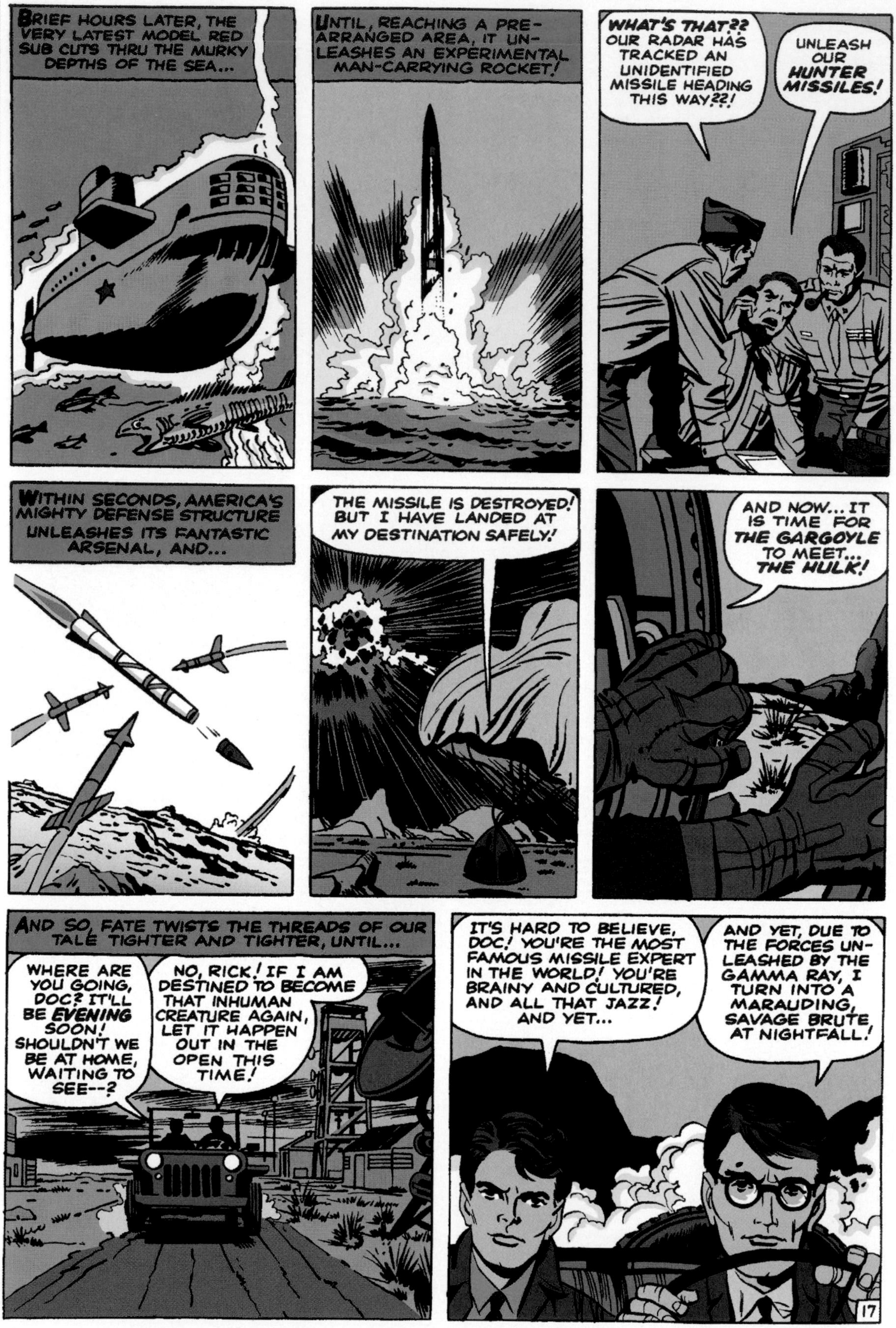
BRIEF HOURS LATER, THE VERY LATEST MODEL RED SUB CUTS THRU THE MURKY DEPTHS OF THE SEA...
UNTIL, REACHING A PRE-ARRANGED AREA, IT UNLEASHES AN EXPERIMENTAL MAN-CARRYING ROCKET!
WHAT'S THAT?? OUR RADAR HAS TRACKED AN UNIDENTIFIED MISSILE HEADING THIS WAY??!
UNLEASH OUR HUNTER MISSILES!
WITHIN SECONDS, AMERICA'S MIGHTY DEFENSE STRUCTURE UNLEASHES ITS FANTASTIC ARSENAL, AND...
THE MISSILE IS DESTROYED! BUT I HAVE LANDED AT MY DESTINATION SAFELY!
AND NOW... IT IS TIME FOR THE GARGOYLE TO MEET... THE HULK!
AND SO, FATE TWISTS THE THREADS OF OUR TALE TIGHTER AND TIGHTER, UNTIL...
WHERE ARE YOU GOING, DOC? IT'LL BE EVENING SOON! SHOULDN'T WE BE AT HOME, WAITING TO SEE--?
NO, RICK! IF I AM DESTINED TO BECOME THAT INHUMAN CREATURE AGAIN, LET IT HAPPEN OUT IN THE OPEN THIS TIME!
IT'S HARD TO BELIEVE, DOC! YOU'RE THE MOST FAMOUS MISSILE EXPERT IN THE WORLD! YOU'RE BRAINY AND CULTURED, AND ALL THAT JAZZ! AND YET...
AND YET, DUE TO THE FORCES UNLEASHED BY THE GAMMA RAY, I TURN INTO A MARAUDING, SAVAGE BRUTE AT NIGHTFALL!
17

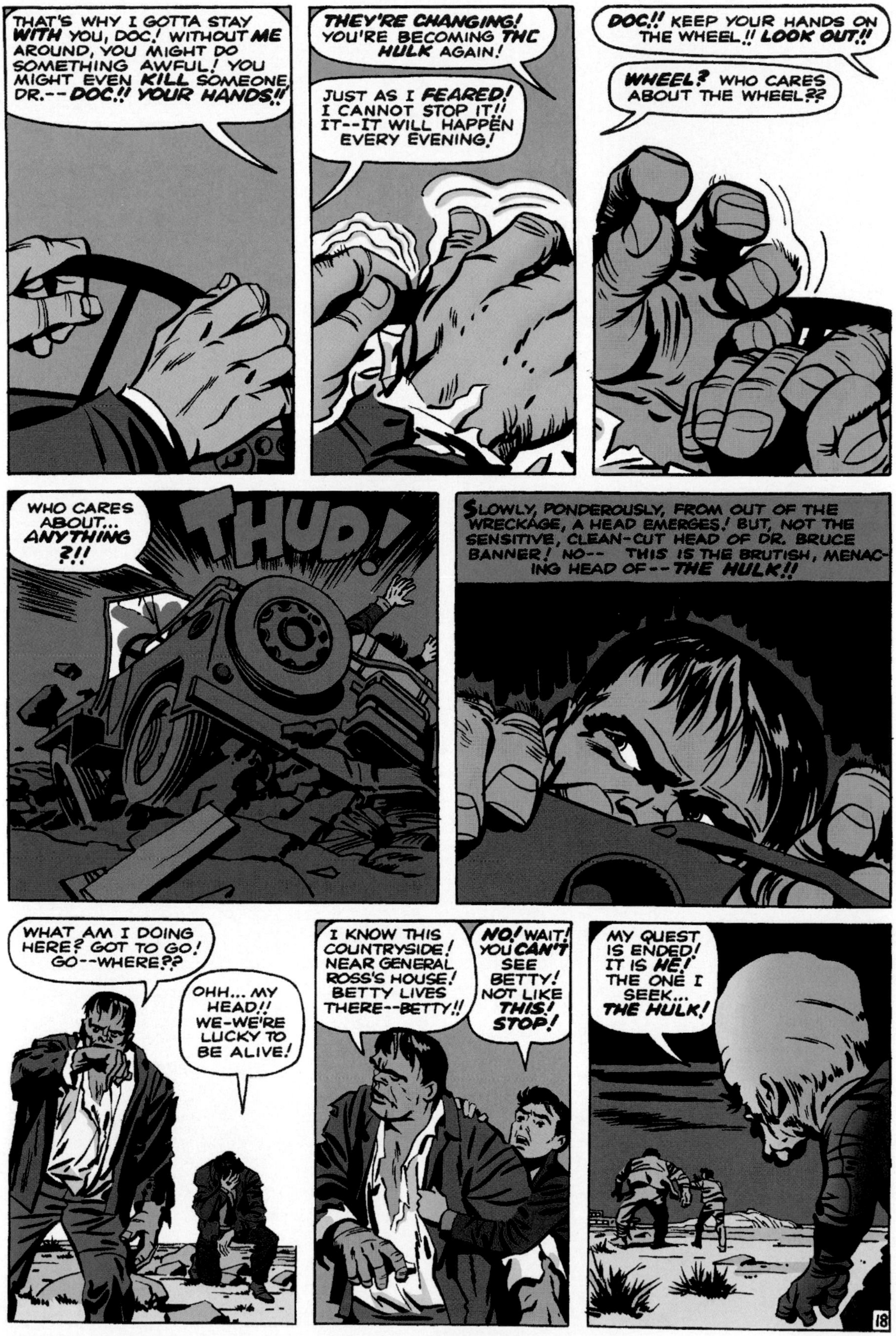
THAT'S WHY I GOTTA STAY WITH YOU, DOC! WITHOUT ME AROUND, YOU MIGHT DO SOMETHING AWFUL! YOU MIGHT EVEN KILL SOMEONE DR.--DOC!! YOUR HANDS!!
THEY'RE CHANGING! YOU'RE BECOMING THE HULK AGAIN!
JUST AS I FEARED! I CANNOT STOP IT!! IT--IT WILL HAPPEN EVERY EVENING!
DOC!! KEEP YOUR HANDS ON THE WHEEL!! LOOK OUT!!
WHEEL? WHO CARES ABOUT THE WHEEL??
WHO CARES ABOUT... ANYTHING ?!!
THUD!
SLOWLY, PONDEROUSLY, FROM OUT OF THE WRECKAGE, A HEAD EMERGES! BUT, NOT THE SENSITIVE, CLEAN-CUT HEAD OF DR. BRUCE BANNER! NO-- THIS IS THE BRUTISH, MENACING HEAD OF--THE HULK!!
WHAT AM I DOING HERE? GOT TO GO! GO--WHERE??
OHH... MY HEAD!! WE-WE'RE LUCKY TO BE ALIVE!
I KNOW THIS COUNTRYSIDE! NEAR GENERAL ROSS'S HOUSE! BETTY LIVES THERE--BETTY!!
NO! WAIT! YOU CAN'T SEE BETTY! NOT LIKE THIS! STOP!
MY QUEST IS ENDED! IT IS HE! THE ONE I SEEK... THE HULK!
18

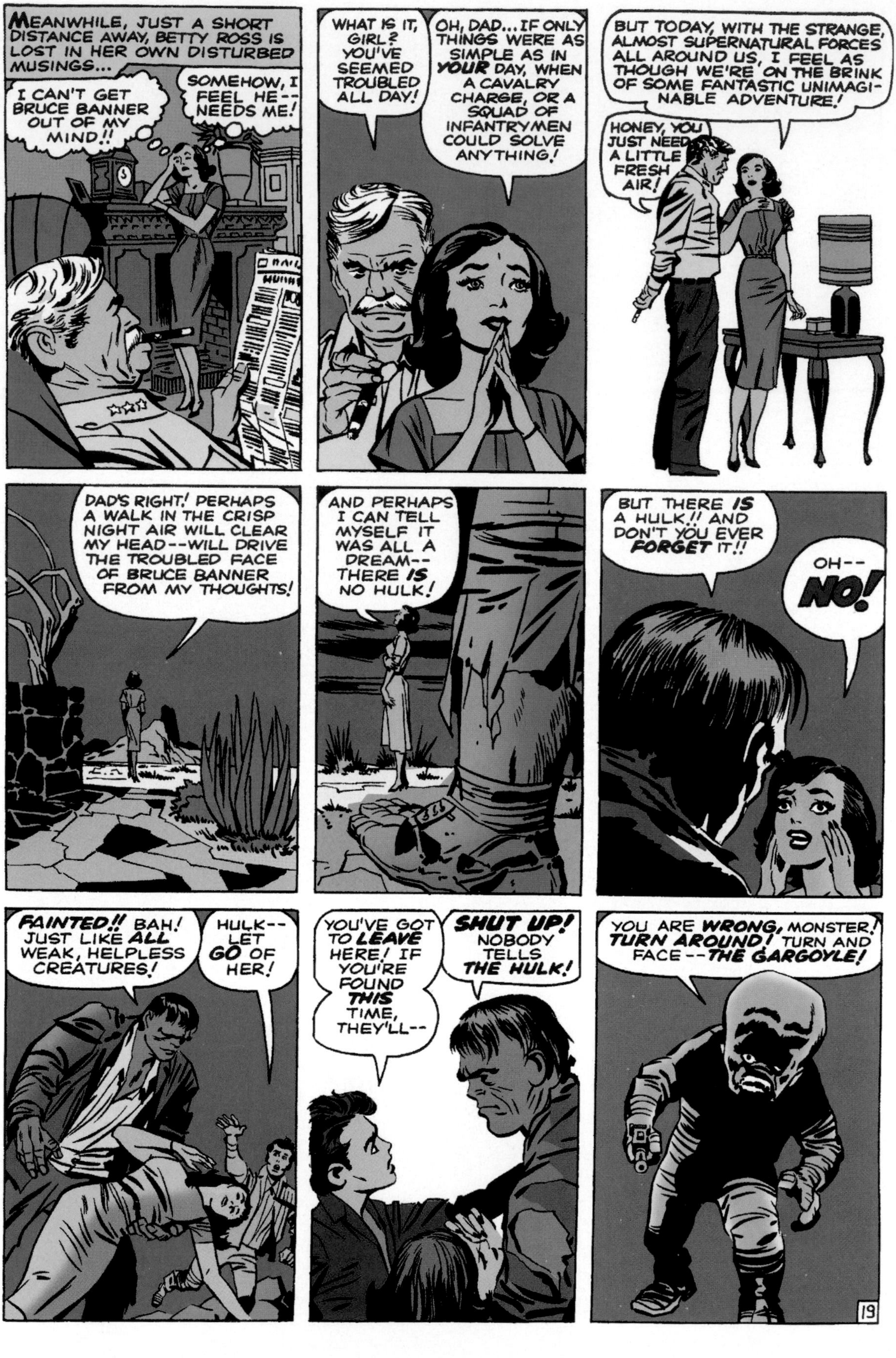

MEANWHILE, JUST A SHORT DISTANCE AWAY, BETTY ROSS IS LOST IN HER OWN DISTURBED MUSINGS...
I CAN'T GET BRUCE BANNER OUT OF MY MIND!!
SOMEHOW, I FEEL HE-- NEEDS ME!
WHAT IS IT, GIRL? YOU'VE SEEMED TROUBLED ALL DAY!
OH, DAD... IF ONLY THINGS WERE AS SIMPLE AS IN YOUR DAY, WHEN A CAVALRY CHARGE, OR A SQUAD OF INFANTRYMEN COULD SOLVE ANYTHING!
BUT TODAY, WITH THE STRANGE, ALMOST SUPERNATURAL FORCES ALL AROUND US, I FEEL AS THOUGH WE'RE ON THE BRINK OF SOME FANTASTIC UNIMAGINABLE ADVENTURE!
HONEY, YOU JUST NEED A LITTLE FRESH AIR!
DAD'S RIGHT! PERHAPS A WALK IN THE CRISP NIGHT AIR WILL CLEAR MY HEAD--WILL DRIVE THE TROUBLED FACE OF BRUCE BANNER FROM MY THOUGHTS!
AND PERHAPS I CAN TELL MYSELF IT WAS ALL A DREAM-- THERE IS NO HULK!
BUT THERE IS A HULK!! AND DON'T YOU EVER FORGET IT!!
OH-- NO!
FAINTED!! BAH! JUST LIKE ALL WEAK, HELPLESS CREATURES!
HULK-- LET GO OF HER!
YOU'VE GOT TO LEAVE HERE! IF YOU'RE FOUND THIS TIME, THEY'LL--
SHUT UP! NOBODY TELLS THE HULK!
YOU ARE WRONG, MONSTER! TURN AROUND! TURN AND FACE --THE GARGOYLE!
19

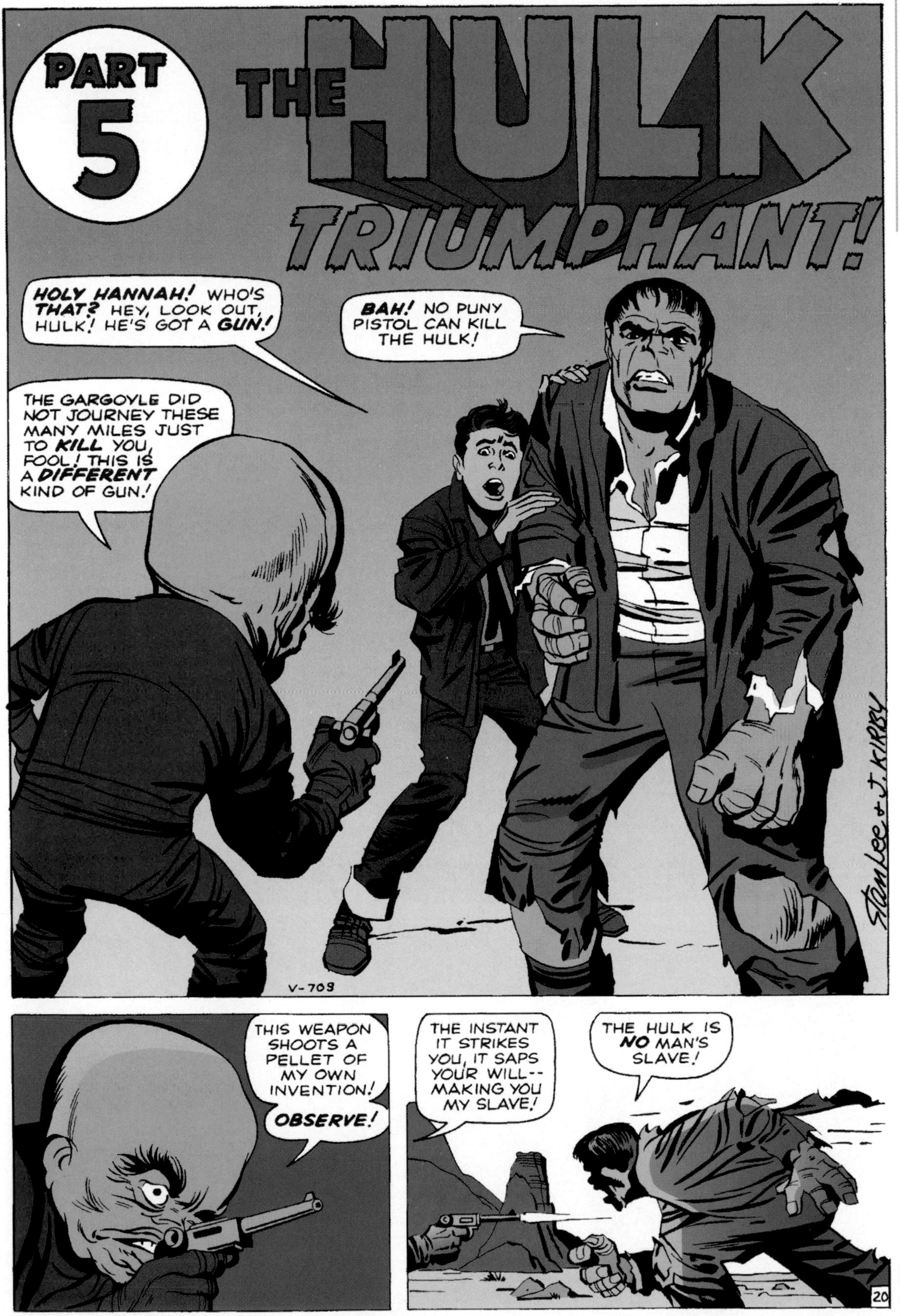
PART 5
THE HULK TRIUMPHANT!
HOLY HANNAH! WHO'S THAT? HEY, LOOK OUT, HULK! HE'S GOT A GUN!
BAH! NO PUNY PISTOL CAN KILL THE HULK!
THE GARGOYLE DID NOT JOURNEY THESE MANY MILES JUST TO KILL YOU, FOOL! THIS IS A DIFFERENT KIND OF GUN!
Stan Lee + J. Kirby
V-708
THIS WEAPON SHOOTS A PELLET OF MY OWN INVENTION! OBSERVE!
THE INSTANT IT STRIKES YOU, IT SAPS YOUR WILL-- MAKING YOU MY SLAVE!
THE HULK IS NO MAN'S SLAVE!
20

HAH! THE GARGOYLE IS NEVER WRONG!

AND THOUGH **YOU** SEEM TOO UNIMPORTANT TO WASTE ANOTHER PELLET ON, I BELIEVE IN TAKING NO CHANCES!

IT IS **DONE!** BOTH OF YOU... RISE, AND FOLLOW ME!

RISE...

FORTUNATELY, IN THE EXCITEMENT OF THE MOMENT, THE GARGOYLE DOES NOT NOTICE THE UNCONSCIOUS GIRL LYING IN THE SHADOWS BEHIND HIS TWO HELPLESS PRISONERS!

HOW EASY IT IS FOR THE GARGOYLE TO BE VICTORIOUS!

AND MOMENTS LATER...

BETTY! BETTY!

DAD... IT-- IT WAS HORRIBLE!

IT WAS **THE HULK!** HE CAME FROM OUT OF THE DARKNESS! HE--HE WAS **TERRIFYING!**

THERE, THERE, MY DEAR! YOU'RE SAFE NOW!

BUT WHERE DID HE **GO?** WHAT DID HE **WANT?** OR--OR DID I **IMAGINE** THE WHOLE THING?

I'LL **FIND** HIM, BETTY! I **SWEAR** TO YOU, MY CHILD, I'LL FIND HIM AND DESTROY HIM!

AND YET, IN SPITE OF EVERYTHING, THERE WAS SOMETHING... SOMETHING **SAD** ABOUT HIM!! ALMOST AS THOUGH HE WAS SEEKING... HELP!

I'LL FIND HIM! IF IT TAKES AN **ETERNITY,** I'LL FIND THAT MONSTER!

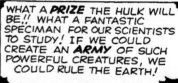

AND, IN A SPEEDING TRUCK, DRIVEN BY A DRIVER WHOSE WILL HAS ALSO BEEN SAPPED, THE GARGOYLE AND HIS PRISONERS SPEED TOWARD THE COAST... RACING TO REACH THEIR DESTINATION BEFORE THE DAWN!

FASTER! FASTER!

WHAT A **PRIZE** THE HULK WILL BE!! WHAT A FANTASTIC SPECIMAN FOR OUR SCIENTISTS TO STUDY! IF WE COULD CREATE AN **ARMY** OF SUCH POWERFUL CREATURES, WE COULD RULE THE EARTH!

21

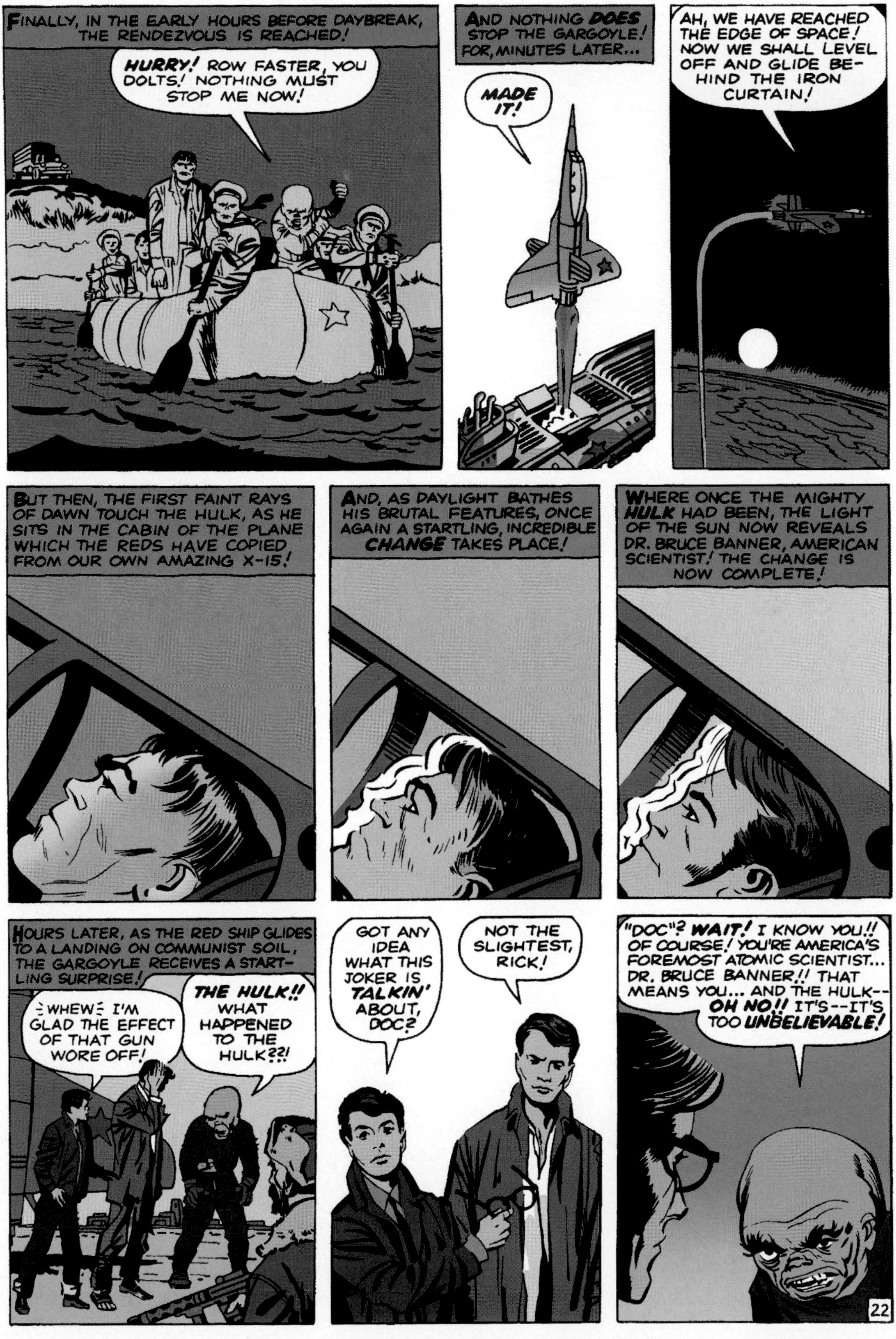
FINALLY, IN THE EARLY HOURS BEFORE DAYBREAK, THE RENDEZVOUS IS REACHED!
HURRY! ROW FASTER, YOU DOLTS! NOTHING MUST STOP ME NOW!
AND NOTHING DOES STOP THE GARGOYLE! FOR, MINUTES LATER...
MADE IT!
AH, WE HAVE REACHED THE EDGE OF SPACE! NOW WE SHALL LEVEL OFF AND GLIDE BEHIND THE IRON CURTAIN!
BUT THEN, THE FIRST FAINT RAYS OF DAWN TOUCH THE HULK, AS HE SITS IN THE CABIN OF THE PLANE WHICH THE REDS HAVE COPIED FROM OUR OWN AMAZING X-15!
AND, AS DAYLIGHT BATHES HIS BRUTAL FEATURES, ONCE AGAIN A STARTLING, INCREDIBLE CHANGE TAKES PLACE!
WHERE ONCE THE MIGHTY HULK HAD BEEN, THE LIGHT OF THE SUN NOW REVEALS DR. BRUCE BANNER, AMERICAN SCIENTIST! THE CHANGE IS NOW COMPLETE!
HOURS LATER, AS THE RED SHIP GLIDES TO A LANDING ON COMMUNIST SOIL, THE GARGOYLE RECEIVES A STARTLING SURPRISE!
WHEW! I'M GLAD THE EFFECT OF THAT GUN WORE OFF!
THE HULK!! WHAT HAPPENED TO THE HULK??!
GOT ANY IDEA WHAT THIS JOKER IS TALKIN' ABOUT, DOC?
NOT THE SLIGHTEST, RICK!
"DOC"? WAIT! I KNOW YOU!! OF COURSE! YOU'RE AMERICA'S FOREMOST ATOMIC SCIENTIST... DR. BRUCE BANNER!! THAT MEANS YOU... AND THE HULK-- OH NO!! IT'S--IT'S TOO UNBELIEVABLE!
22

UNDER CLOSE GUARD, THE GARGOYLE RUSHES HIS PRISONERS TO HIS SECRET STRONGHOLD, AND THEN...

YOUR SECRET IS A SECRET NO LONGER, BANNER! I KNOW THAT YOU AND THE HULK ARE THE SAME!!

DOC! WHAT DO WE DO NOW?

EASY, RICK! IT'S HIS PLAY SO FAR!

BUT WHY? WHY WOULD YOU WANT TO BE A MONSTER? YOU MUST BE INSANE! IT--IT'S THE MOST HORRIBLE THING IN THE WORLD TO BE A FREAK-- A GARGOYLE! LIKE ME!

DOC! HE'S CRYING!

I'D GIVE ANYTHING TO BE NORMAL! ANYTHING!

SO WOULD I--BUT I AM AS HELPLESS AS YOU!

WAIT! LISTEN TO ME! I CANNOT STOP MYSELF FROM TURNING INTO THE HULK-- BUT YOUR CASE IS DIFFERENT!

I'VE SEEN CASES LIKE YOURS! I KNOW HOW TO CURE YOU...BY RADIATION! BUT ALTHOUGH YOUR FEATURES WOULD BECOME NORMAL, YOUR BRAIN WOULD SUFFER! YOU WOULD NO LONGER BE A BRILLIANT SCIENTIST!

DOC! YOU AIN'T GONNA HELP THAT CREEP, ARE YOU??!

QUIET, RICK!

NO MATTER WHAT HAPPENS TO ME... EVEN IF I DIE... SO LONG AS I COULD DIE AS-- A MAN!

THEN, AT A COMMAND FROM THE GARGOYLE, ALL IS MADE READY...

NOW!

AND, WHERE A GARGOYLE HAD BEEN LYING...

DOC! IT'S WORKING!

...A MAN ARISES!

YOU DID IT!

YOU DID IT!

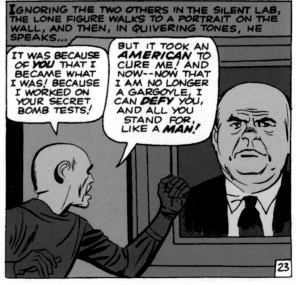

IGNORING THE TWO OTHERS IN THE SILENT LAB, THE LONE FIGURE WALKS TO A PORTRAIT ON THE WALL, AND THEN, IN QUIVERING TONES, HE SPEAKS...

IT WAS BECAUSE OF YOU THAT I BECAME WHAT I WAS! BECAUSE I WORKED ON YOUR SECRET BOMB TESTS!

BUT IT TOOK AN AMERICAN TO CURE ME! AND NOW--NOW THAT I AM NO LONGER A GARGOYLE, I CAN DEFY YOU, AND ALL YOU STAND FOR, LIKE A MAN!

23

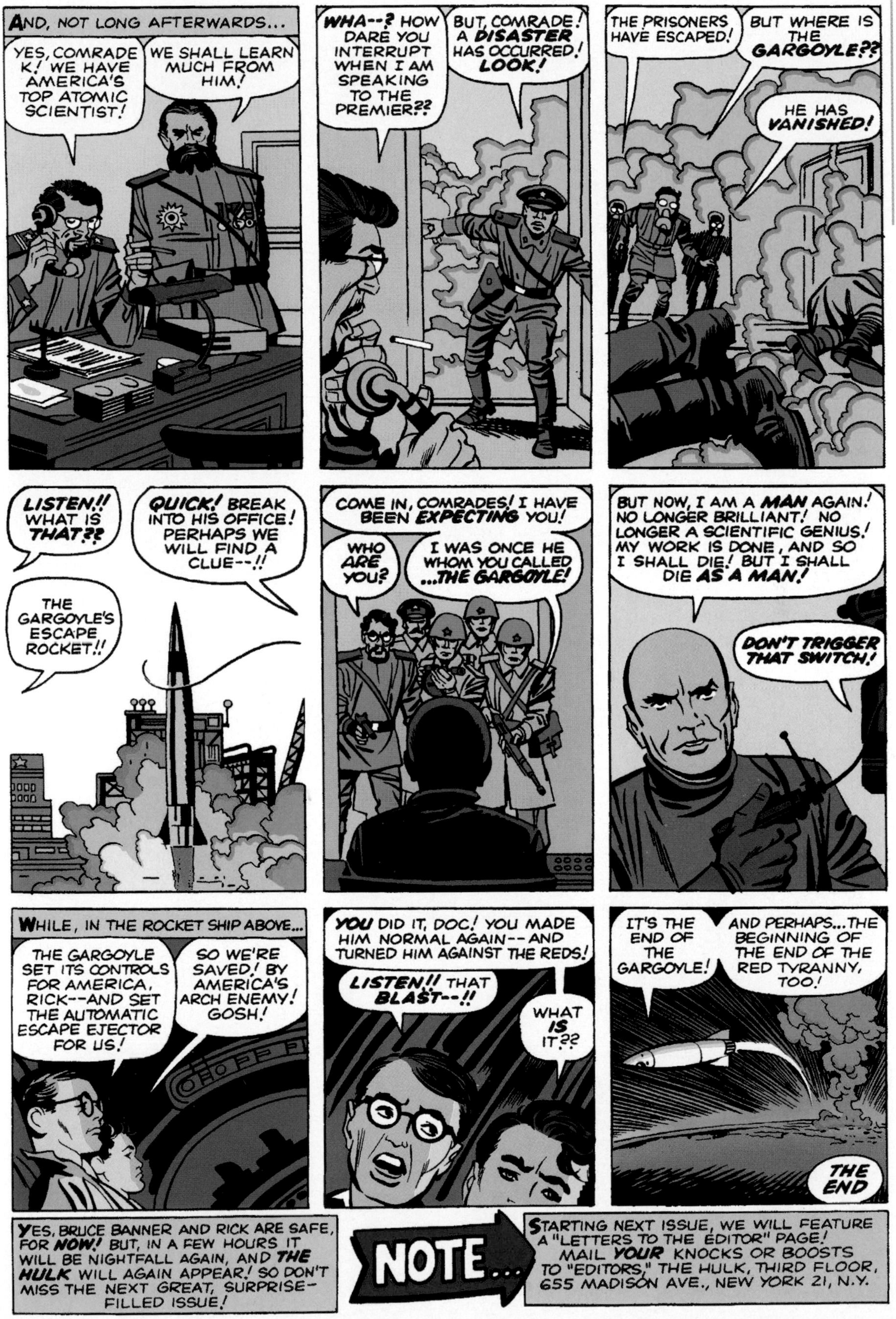
AND, NOT LONG AFTERWARDS...
YES, COMRADE K! WE HAVE AMERICA'S TOP ATOMIC SCIENTIST!
WE SHALL LEARN MUCH FROM HIM!
WHA--? HOW DARE YOU INTERRUPT WHEN I AM SPEAKING TO THE PREMIER??
BUT, COMRADE! A DISASTER HAS OCCURRED! LOOK!
THE PRISONERS HAVE ESCAPED!
BUT WHERE IS THE GARGOYLE??
HE HAS VANISHED!
LISTEN!! WHAT IS THAT??
QUICK! BREAK INTO HIS OFFICE! PERHAPS WE WILL FIND A CLUE--!!
THE GARGOYLE'S ESCAPE ROCKET!!
COME IN, COMRADES! I HAVE BEEN EXPECTING YOU!
WHO ARE YOU?
I WAS ONCE HE WHOM YOU CALLED ...THE GARGOYLE!
BUT NOW, I AM A MAN AGAIN! NO LONGER BRILLIANT! NO LONGER A SCIENTIFIC GENIUS! MY WORK IS DONE, AND SO I SHALL DIE! BUT I SHALL DIE AS A MAN!
DON'T TRIGGER THAT SWITCH!
WHILE, IN THE ROCKET SHIP ABOVE...
THE GARGOYLE SET ITS CONTROLS FOR AMERICA, RICK--AND SET THE AUTOMATIC ESCAPE EJECTOR FOR US!
SO WE'RE SAVED! BY AMERICA'S ARCH ENEMY! GOSH!
YOU DID IT, DOC! YOU MADE HIM NORMAL AGAIN--AND TURNED HIM AGAINST THE REDS!
LISTEN!! THAT BLAST--!!
WHAT IS IT??
IT'S THE END OF THE GARGOYLE!
AND PERHAPS...THE BEGINNING OF THE END OF THE RED TYRANNY, TOO!
THE END
YES, BRUCE BANNER AND RICK ARE SAFE, FOR NOW! BUT, IN A FEW HOURS IT WILL BE NIGHTFALL AGAIN, AND THE HULK WILL AGAIN APPEAR! SO DON'T MISS THE NEXT GREAT, SURPRISE-FILLED ISSUE!
NOTE...
STARTING NEXT ISSUE, WE WILL FEATURE A "LETTERS TO THE EDITOR" PAGE! MAIL YOUR KNOCKS OR BOOSTS TO "EDITORS," THE HULK, THIRD FLOOR, 655 MADISON AVE., NEW YORK 21, N.Y.

Chapter Three

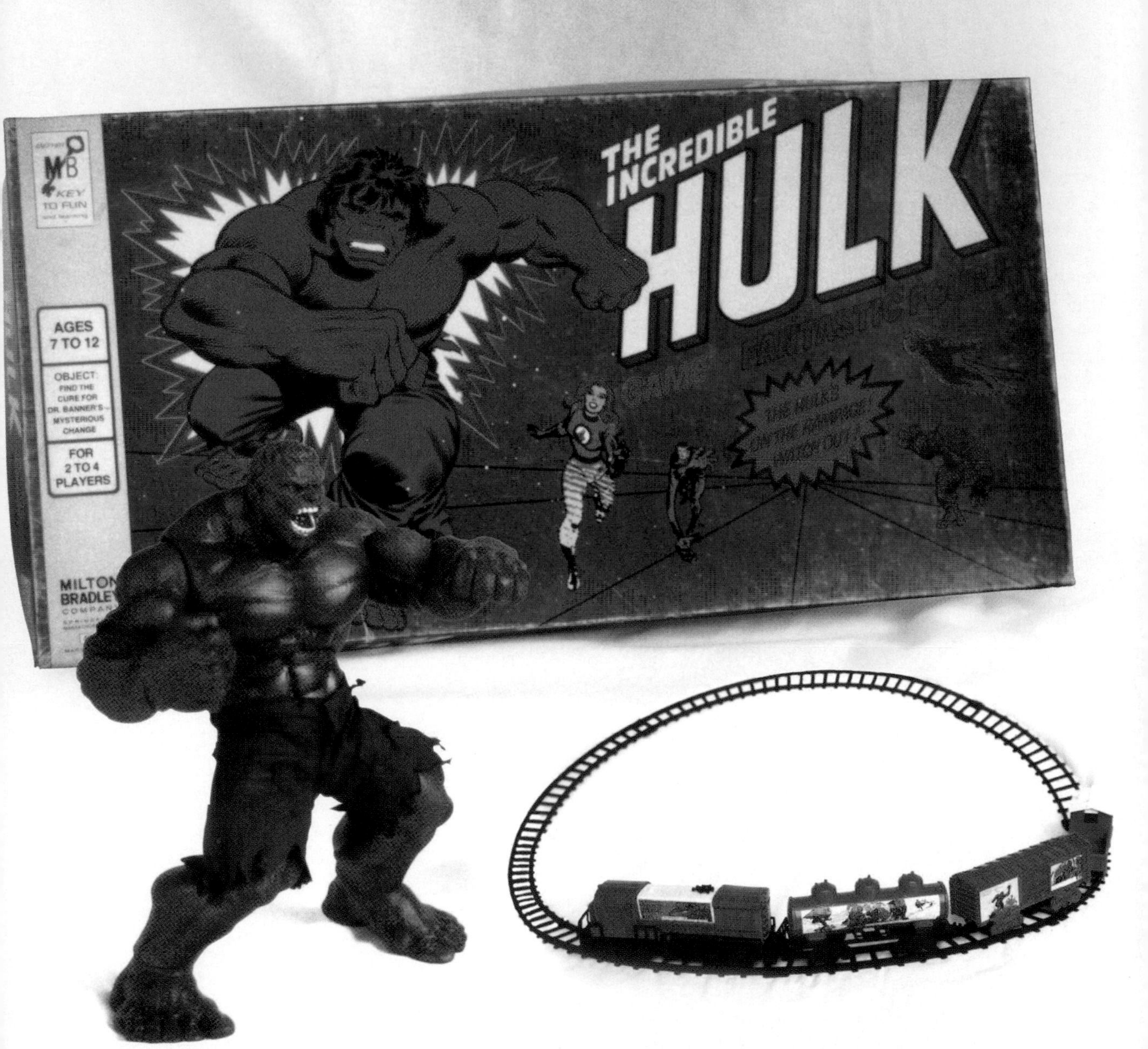
MB
KEY TO FUN
AGES 7 TO 12
OBJECT: FIND THE CURE FOR DR. BANNER'S MYSTERIOUS CHANGE
FOR 2 TO 4 PLAYERS
MILTON BRADLEY COMPANY
THE INCREDIBLE HULK

HULK, AS IN BULK

From Flying Fists to Fun Putty, and back again

Thank God for eBay.

Without eBay, the wired two-thirds of the world would have no way of knowing there's such a thing as an Incredible Hulk toothbrush, or a Hulk bicycle license plate or trick-or-treat pail or especially an Incredible Hulk shower-head cover with matching shampoo. Best of all, any of these treasures could be yours. All it takes is the high bid.

Wait. You want more? You got more: The holographic Incredible Hulk yo-yo. The Incredible Hulk Hero Head game. Incredible Hulk puffy art. The Incredible Hulk sponge-boat bath toy. Incredible Hulk candy cigarettes (which aren't called "candy cigarettes" but instead the more politically reasonable "candy sticks," though anyone over the age of seven knows better). The Incredible Hulk hang glider. The Incredible Hulk thermos, to keep hot things hot and cold things cold. Incredible Hulk bubble gum. (Described as follows in a recent eBay auction: "1978 Incredible Hulk bubble gum MIP." "MIP," by the way, stands for "mint in pack," and you can believe that's how this gum is going to stay. It hasn't been opened for 25 years. Why tempt fate now? After all, this isn't the sort of delicacy that improves with age.)

Had enough yet? Didn't think so: The Incredible Hulk Flying Fist. The Incredible Hulk trash can. The Incredible Hulk kazoo. An Incredible Hulk Hallmark ornament. (When you care enough to send the very best, and want to say, "I think your Christmas needs more repressed anger and all-out rage.") The Incredible Hulk slot car. The Incredible Hulk train. The Incredible Hulk Hummer. The Incredible Hulk VW van. The Incredible Hulk Monster Jam truck. The Incredible Hulk Kia Sephia. (Just kidding!) Incredible Hulk Fun Putty. An Incredible Hulk head bank. (How many times have you seen the Hulk and wished you had a head like that full of nickels? Well, you just got your wish. And that ain't his brain rattling you hear when you shake it back and forth, boy.) An Incredible Hulk soap dish. The Incredible Hulk transistor radio, so you can see if the Hulk really and truly is picking up a station that doesn't come in on anyone else's radio.

Can't forget the contradictions in terms, either: the talking Incredible Hulk figure, which represents the most useless application of talking-doll technology this side of George W. Bush, and an Incredible Hulk record album. (You think James Brown jumps off the vinyl? Wait till you hear Lou Ferrigno do "In-A-Gadda-Da-Vida." Actually, the Hulk record consists of issue #171 being read aloud, for those who find reading a comic too mentally taxing.)

Okay, you've

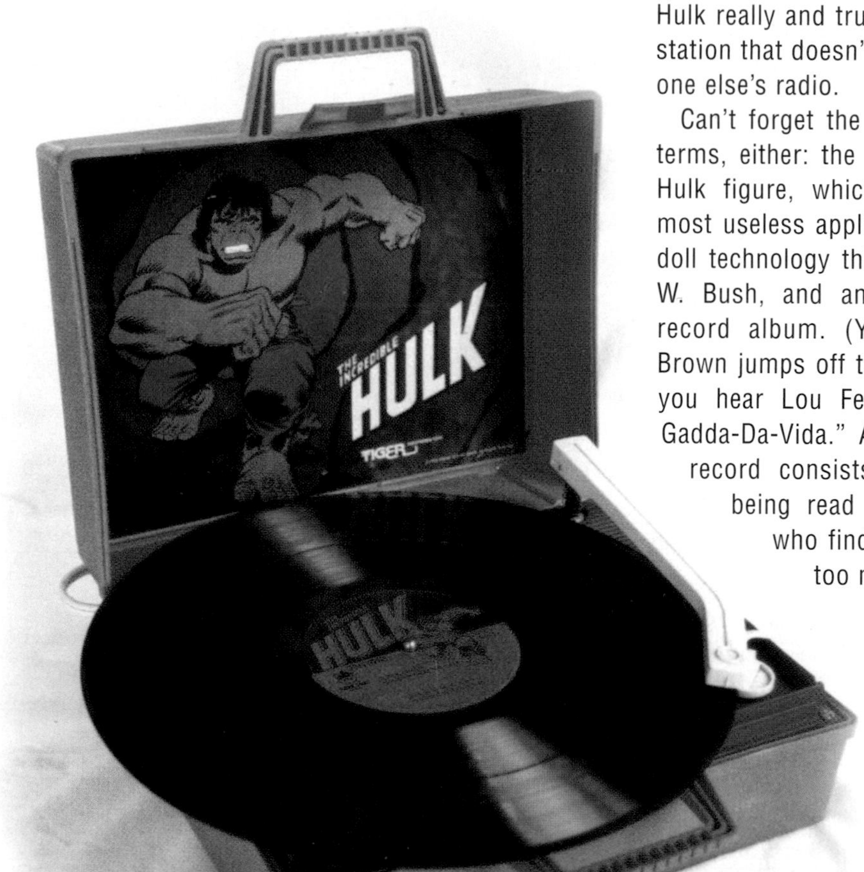
THE INCREDIBLE
HULK
TIGER

Hulk comics for those who find reading a Hulk comic too mentally taxing: Tiger's Hulk record player and record of Incredible Hulk #171.

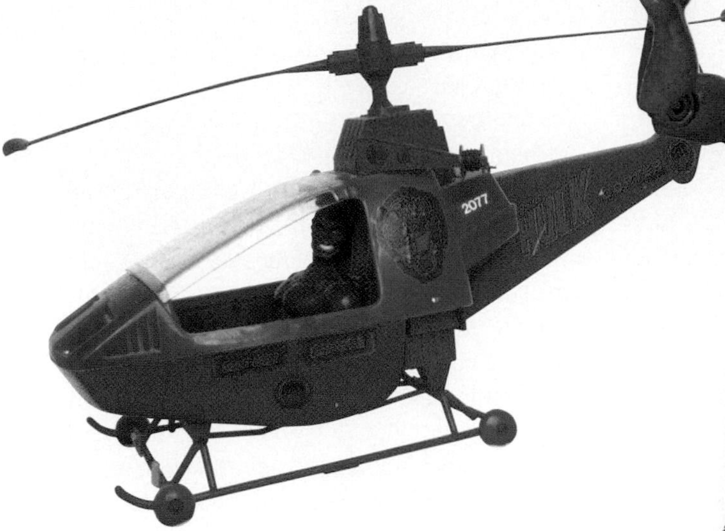
2077

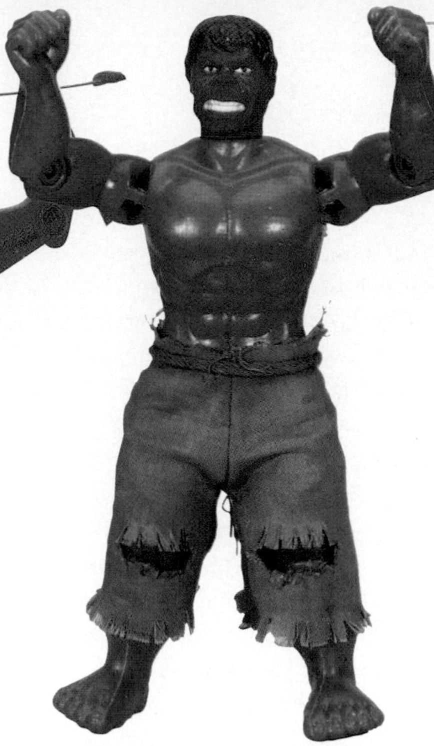

The Hulk Mego: The prototypical action figure with the pants that rip in exactly the same place. The Empire Toys Hulk copter: Like the Hulk needs a second career as a traffic reporter.

suffered enough. By now, it should be apparent that not only is the Hulk the world's most unstoppable green human bean, he's also an unstoppable licensing machine.

So why stop at shower heads and hang gliders? Why not use the Incredible Hulk wherever strength is of the essence? Incredible Hulk drain cleaner. Incredible Hulk alpha-hydroxy lotion. ("For clean, green, younger-looking skin in days.") Incredible Hulk garlic. Incredible Hulk super glue. Incredible Hulk zit-be-gone. Incredible Hulk Everclear. The marketing mind goes a-boggle at the possibilities.

The Incredible Hulk has been featured on an awful lot of toys in his 40-year lifetime. And why not? "Hulk smash" has natural appeal to the younger, less-restrained set. It only makes sense that if your little Hulk is going to smash anyway, he ought to have genuine Hulk-branded stuff to smash with.

Okay, that doesn't explain Incredible Hulk shampoo. ("I'm gonna get really, really, really mad and lather, rinse and repeat.") But it definitely explains the Incredible Hulk Rage Cage, the Incredible Hulk Crash/Smash Play Set with Doc Samson and the Incredible Hulk Hummer, which is about as good as it gets for the quintessential monster SUV now that it's been reduced to a Rodeo Drive cruiser.

It also explains Incredible Hulk action figures. It makes sense that some of the first modern superhero action figures depicted the Hulk. Those figures were called Megos, and they're still fanatically cherished by a cadre of collectors. Not the same cadre that considers He-Man and the Masters of the Universe to be the pinnacle of western civilization, but close.

Megos weren't the first action figures, though sorting out which figures were is like trying to figure out who first got their peanut butter in someone else's chocolate, or vice versa. If you stretch the definition enough, little Hittites were doing power dives with the terra-cotta equivalents of Super Saiyan Goku figures long before Christianity, or Saturday-morning TV, for that matter. Besides, action figures are in the use, not the definition. To the Hulk, Michaelangelo's David could be an action figure, though those so-called posable arms are a total crock.

Yeah, yeah, yeah, but the normal world pegs the start of the action-figure era as the late '50s with the introduction of that super-powered (at least super-endowed) heroine, Barbie. The dark secret in a Manga Spawn's past is that most of its key attributes — articulated joints, semi-realistic costumes, caricatured body features and petrochemical-based construction — evolved from Barbie, and if not Barbie, her pal Skipper. Bamboo shoots under the fingernails won't get Kenner to admit the real inspiration for the Boba Fett Fortress Play Set With Light-Up Laser Immolation Action is the Barbie Boulevard Beauty Salon With Light-Up Hair-Dryer Action, but it's a fact, Jack: Toys get their inspiration from other toys, and if you're gonna steal, steal from the toys that work.

Barbies and G.I. Joes pretty much dominated the action-figure scene until Mego crashed the party in 1972. Mego was essentially an importer and distributor of Hong Kong-made figures. The Hong Kong company that exported to Mego, Lion Rock Trading, also exported ladies' underwear and leisure suits to the United Kingdom, which explains the wacky threads on the Starsky and Hutch Megos but does absolutely nothing to explain why David Banner's pants never split open when he becomes the Hulk (which is the closest thing male comics superheroes have to, "What holds that thing up, anyway? Scotch tape? It sure ain't gravity.").

Mego also farmed out the plastic molding of its figures, which saved money but resulted in figures with hands often described as "oven mitts." These aren't hot-dog fingers; these are pork-chop hands. If real people had hands like these, finger-puppet sales would plummet. Wedding rings would be worn on

The DIY Hulk Head: Any resemblance to Deion Sanders is coincidental.

the feet. Manicurists would be begging for change on San Francisco street corners. The Isotoner folks would have to open a drive-through liquor store.

In fact, the reason Mego went bankrupt in 1982 was because it built its own plastic factory to make better-quality figures. Let that be a lesson.

Mego's first superhero figures hit U.S. shelves in 1972 as part of the Official World's Greatest Super Heroes series. The eight-inch figures were clothed in leisure-suit leftovers and were fully posable, though that term didn't have the same meaning then it does now. Same with "realistic" and "lifelike," which cause an eyebrow to raise when the subject is action figures. How can a molded-plastic rendering of a fictional character with a torso that has a full 360-degree range of motion and arm hinges that wouldn't look out-of-place on a Daewoo be true-to-life? There's one for Kirkegaard.

The first Mego figures showed DC characters, but Mego wised up fast and added Marvel superheroes. The Hulk was one of the first eight-inch Marvel Megos, and he comes off pretty well, if a bit short compared to a normal-height superhero like Spider-Man, who also got an eight-inch figure.

The Hulk ought to come off well. If ever a character was created with the proportions of an action figure, it's the Hulk. That's why Hulk action figures have always sold better than Clearasil a week before the prom.

Not content with superheroes, Mego expanded its figure line into super-villains. By definition, that should leave the Hulk further out in the cold than the Little Match Girl, but Mego figured the Hulk would soon tire of pounding the polyfill out of the Shore Patrol G.I. Joe and thoughtfully added a Leader figure to the villain line. This lets you experience the pulse-pounding action of the Leader thinking his foes into submission — but should you somehow not find that stimulating enough, you can get two full servings of pretend fries by running the Leader's plastic head through a Play-Doh McDonald's Happy Meal Maker.

If outsmarting the Leader didn't leave the Mego Hulk plumb tuckered out, he could always hop on the "Supervator: Super Action Flyby." Then, in a scene that couldn't have been more true to Stan Lee's comic vision if it had involved Teletubbies, he could lurch and stagger down a string to snatch up the "Nasty Secret Plans," which a Hulk needs like he needs anabolic steroids.

To the Hulk, a vehicle can be lumped in the same category as anabolic steroids, but Mego would simply not take "no" for an answer. Whether he wanted them or not, the Hulk got more inexplicable vehicles than there are on a no-credit-no-problem used-car lot, starting with the three-wheeled Mego Hulk Explorer.

The Hulk Explorer is a rebadged Hyperion vehicle from Mego's Micronauts line — a swoopy, Gundam-y thing that's scary in the same way *Sailor Moon* is scary and gives the Hulk just what he needs most: missile-shooting capability. Right. Give the world's biggest, strongest, least rational, most enraged human being a missile, and put it on a flying tricycle named after the tire-blowing scourge of the nation's freeways. Look the hell out, Freddie Prinze Jr.

The Hulk also got a Mego van, an Econoline-looking affair he used after work to take kids to dance class. (Come on: The Hulk can get across Manhattan in, what, two jumps, can cross the deserts of the great Southwest in five, and he needs an eight-miles-to-the-gallon, 0-to-60-in-half-an-hour *van*? Is it really that important for him to be able to lay a four-by-eight sheet of plywood flat in the back and carry eight adults in comfort?)

The Hulk, being one of the more popular superheroes of the late '70s, showed up in many Mego lines, including the jumbo-size line, the magnetic line (a European release that came with Authentic Amputation Action! — you could pull off and reattach magnetically affixed arms and legs), the die-cast line and the smaller-than-life 3-¾" Comic Action Heroes. These figures had all the detail of Malt-O-Meal, but the playsets are cool. The Hulk never got a hideout/playset of his own, but he was right at home in the Exploding Tower, which came with the imminently useful "Comic Action Activator" (i.e., the air pump that made the walls fall down).

For all their cheddarness, or maybe because of it, vintage Megos aren't cheap. You might spend $50 for the privilege of snuggling with your very own soft-plastic eight-inch figure with genuine cloth pants that always have the rips in the same places.

Fortunately — or not, depending on your feelings toward barely molded lumps of green plastic — Megos aren't the only Hulklings from the '70s and '80s. There's a

THE INCREDIBLE HULK
CANDY STICKS
Free Tattoo Inside!
BOP BAG
THE INCREDIBLE HULK
36 inch* (90 cm) Inflatable
BOP BAG
Ages 3-10
MADE IN CHINA

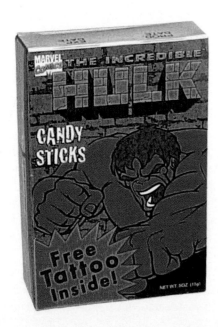

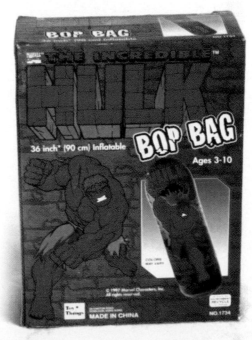

The Hulk Bop Bag proves once again that even if you knock down the Hulk, he doesn't stay down for long. The Hulk Candy Sticks keep the Hulk toothbrush busy.

bendy Hulk, a hard-plastic Hulk, a soft-plastic Hulk, a log-throwing Hulk, and of slightly later vintage, a Santa Hulk. (Yeah, with him coming down your chimney, you can bet there's going to arise such a clatter you'll have to spring to the window to see what's the matter. If the window's still there.) Even before these Hulks, Marx made a small Hulk figure in the '60s to complement its World War II soldiers, cowboys and Indians, and Civil War fighters, which it does perfectly. Think Gettysburg would have been different if the Hulk had led Pickett's Charge? There's one way to find out.

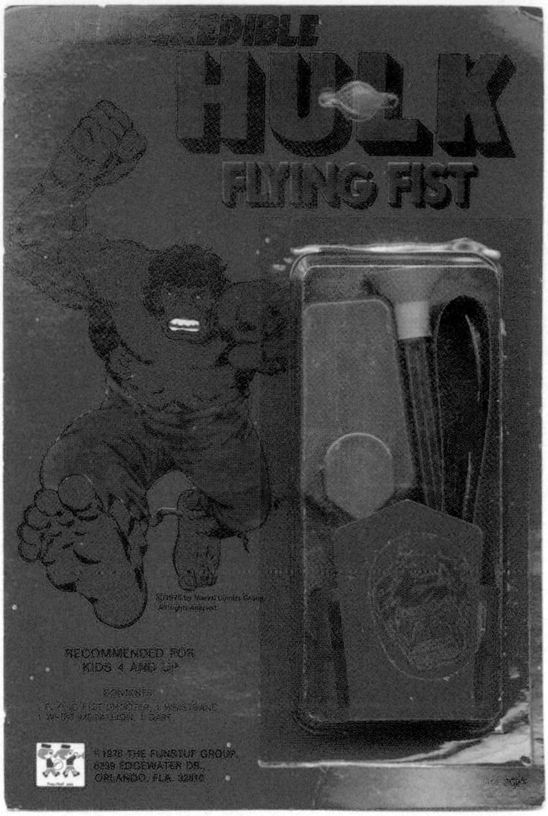
HULK
FLYING FIST

Note: It's the Hulk that's incredible, not the Flying Fist. Use the Flying Fist in a real fight, and you're liable to get a flying trip to the hospital.

Subsequent Hulk action figures are more — here's that word again — realistic, though none ever really improved on the playability of the original Megos. The Hulk's a little different in that regard: He doesn't need hands to hold an atomic-powered Easy-Bake Oven or a Hulkarang. He just needs to be able to head-butt a wall of Lincoln Logs and give a big sister an action-figure noogie. Any old Hulk figure suffices just fine. Still, if you must have a Hulk figure that looks not realistic, not lifelike, but merely awesome, it's hard to go wrong with the Hulk from ToyBiz's Avengers boxed set and the Dale Keown-era Smart Hulk. To him is awarded the ultimate Hulk complement: He sure doesn't look smart.

To return to the Hulkmobile thing again, the ex-Banner sure has a lot of internal-combustion contraptions at his disposal for someone who's 10 feet tall and can't even fit into the front seat of a Hummer without cranking the seat adjuster back to the tailgate. The reality-defying Mego van has already been mentioned, but don't forget the Hulk slot car (yeah, that's another brainstorm — put the Hulk in a 500-horsepower race car, and tell him *not* to throw the other cars into the grandstand) and MPC's snap-together Hulk Hauler — a late '70s Chevy truck with some nifty sidepipes and even better graphics.

Most miscellaneous Hulk stuff dates from that late '70s era, when superheroes were cooler than virgin polyester and the Hulk was at his apex. That popularity prompted brainstorms like the Hulk kazoo, the Hulk flashing-color spinner, the Hulk finger puppet, Hulk putty and the Hulk hang glider. While it's easy to make fun of these geegaws, the fact is they're the stuff of kids' play, and simple toys always seem cheap and cheesy to grownups. It's what you put into them that makes them fun. Truth be told, there's a heck of a lot more fun in a parachuting Hulk toy than there is in a $200 cold-cast-resin Hulk statue. And neither would be out of place on an executive desk, squatting between the Mont Blanc and the cut-crystal candy dish.

Sometimes, it seems like there's a never-ending supply of fun, cool and inexplicable Hulk toys. Take the Hulk/Fantastic Four board game. It's curious the same way the Osbournes are curious, only with less hair tinting. The game has the Fantastic Four chasing the Hulk around the board, and the first player to complete his picture of Bruce

Banner wins. How delightful. The game could only be more anti-Hulk if Rainbow Ponies were doing the chasing. A real Hulk game would start with the first player shaking the dice, rolling a one, plowing to the finish line, forcibly inserting the dice into a cavity of utter darkness and screaming "Hulk SMASH!!!!!!!" Authentic, but not exactly hours of fun.

Come to think of it, Incredible Hulk trading cards are a contradiction in terms, too. The Hulk would not be one to sit around cracking packs and trading doubles of the Martian Manhunter with the kid down the street. Still, during the halcyon days of trading cards in the early '90s, the Hulk was right in there pitchin' with the Emmitt Smiths and Mark McGwires of the card world.

The Hulk on trading cards goes back to 1966, when superhero comics and non-sport trading cards were in their relative infancy. That year's set of Marvel Super Heroes cards devoted 11 cards to the Hulk, attaching punch lines to existing art that are funny the same way roofing nails are funny. (Example: the "But I wanted an A-bomb for Christmas" card.)

The comedic brilliance of these cards is mirrored in the Marvel Comics sets of 1978-79. The only thing funnier than these cards is Carrot Top on C-Span. For instance: A kid hitting a baseball says, "Our team loves to play dirty. Watch this dirty slide into second base." In the next panel, he's shown crashing into the Hulk while a player from another team says, "He didn't know we have the Hulk playing second for us." Get it? He didn't know the Hulk was playing ... haw, haw, haw — see, he didn't know the Hulk ... hee, hee. Isn't that just the funniest thing you ever heard?

Right up there with that priceless fusion of art and literature is the Marvel Hulk glider from the 1966 Marvel Flyers, which features a Hulk head and torso printed on a Styrofoam glider with hulk arms printed on the wings. It gets stuck in trees more often than any gamma-irradiated human ever did, though it's also a lot quieter.

Hulk cards started appearing in earnest in 1990, when SkyBox issued its first Marvel Universe cards. Then, the prevailing wisdom was that you couldn't sell cards that didn't show baseball players, but SkyBox's retort to the prevailing wisdom was short and to the point: Oh, yeah? Sez who? Actually, its *other* retort to the prevailing wisdom wasn't much longer: Okay, if you can't sell cards that don't show baseball players, we'll make comics superheroes look like baseball players. That's

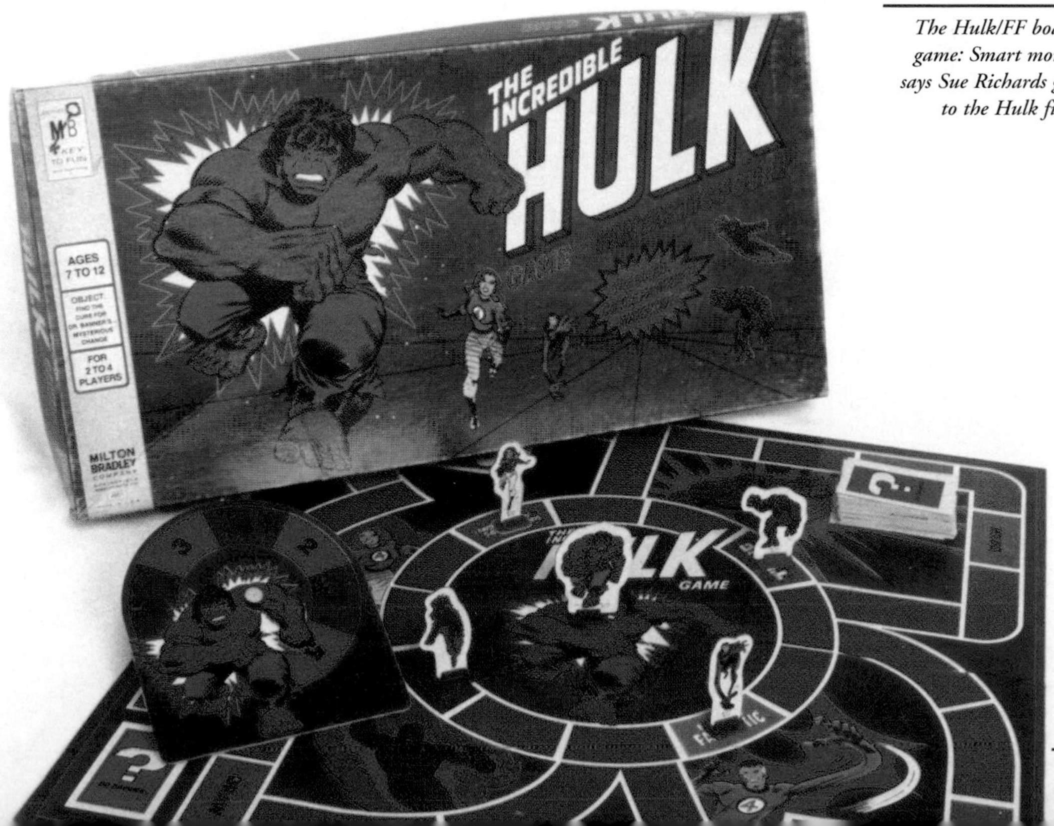
THE INCREDIBLE HULK
AGES 7 TO 12
FOR 2 TO 4 PLAYERS
MILTON BRADLEY COMPANY
GAME

The Hulk/FF board game: Smart money says Sue Richards gets to the Hulk first.

essentially what the Marvel Universe cards do, and they do it great.

Marvel Universe cards brought quality and style to non-sport cards with entertaining backs and fronts that featured original art, not stuff borrowed from whatever issue the art director happened to have on his desk. They continued and expanded for the better part of a decade, and were joined by great sets like Marvel Masterpieces, which showcased the original art of some fantastic artists — including Joe Jusko, Dave Dorman, Bill Sienkiewicz and the Hildebrandt brothers. Yeah, they're just trading cards, and yeah, they got mixed up along the way with Internet stocks to the detriment of both — but when you take a step back, you can appreciate some of the Marvel cards for what they are: great art in a cheap pack.

Along with the memorable Marvel cards came the less-than-memorable cards. Most of them have already been forgotten, but no such luck with the Marvel vs. WildStorm set, which pits the legendary characters of the Marvel Universe against the derivative, blasé characters from the WildStorm universe. Here's the say-no-more on this set: The set's two Hulk cards pitted the Green Monster against WildStorm foes Slag and Grunge. Now that the dust has settled, any guesses as to who came out on top of those tussles?

Also on the forgettable pile is Marvel QFX, which used the costly, breathtaking, barrier-breaking technique called "cut and paste" to place the art of current Marvel editor-in-chief Joe Quesada into real-life scenes of New York City. Want to see Mr. Fantastic pull himself up through an authentic New York City sewer grate? You got your wish, cowboy. Marvel QFX rang down the curtain on the greatest comics-on-cards era in history. The era was headed in that direction anyway; QFX just got it there quicker.

Stranded somewhere on the desert highway between forgettable and memorable are the Marvel Overpower cards from the early '90s. Overpower was a collectible card game that was Marvel's answer to Magic: The Gathering, the game that spawned the collectible-card-game craze. Unlike Magic's universe of wizards, monsters, freaks and DMV employees, the Overpower characters were based on characters whose identities, powers, strengths, weaknesses, origins and dispositions were well-known to anyone who could look at the pictures and turn the pages. Also unlike Magic, Overpower found itself painted into a corner by the fact that its characters were so well-known and powerful. How many strongest beings in the universe can you have, anyway? Stan Lee gave his superheroes human touches, but not nearly enough to create the broad spectrum of heroes, villains, actions and bit players a successful CCG needs.

Overpower's other problem was that tactically it was only slightly more advanced than Go Fish. The game got better and more complex with expansions, but even then hundreds of characters were left out that could have made Overpower into a serious competitor for Magic. The game

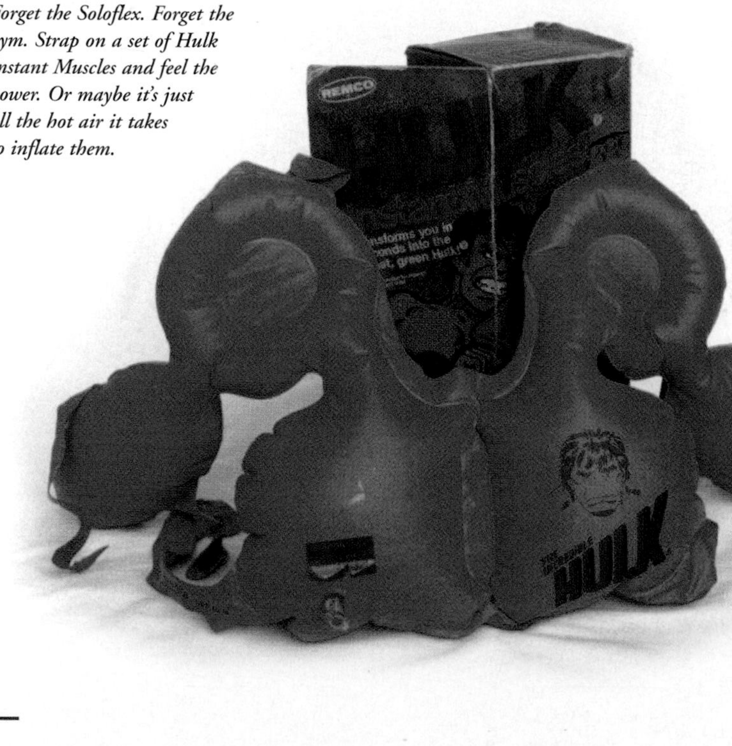
REMCO
HULK

Forget the Soloflex. Forget the gym. Strap on a set of Hulk Instant Muscles and feel the power. Or maybe it's just all the hot air it takes to inflate them.

Hulk in a box: Big green video games

Crossing from comics to video games and video games to comics isn't as easy as it looks. Super Mario Bros. comics haven't displaced the X-Men, and Spider-Man for PS2 hasn't bumped Grand Theft Auto. That's okay. Multimedia properties don't have to dominate every medium; they just have to be there when the money's counted, like the IRS. Besides, spreading the wealth is democratic. Sharing is nice.

When it comes to video games, the Hulk has shared more nicely than Pollyanna, which is a little odd — first because the words "Hulk" and "Pollyanna" are used in the same sentence, and second because the Hulk seems custom-made for the small, small screen. Hulking Out and Hulk Smash are nothing if not great video-game moves without the video game.

The first Hulk video game of note was the Incredible Hulk: Pantheon Saga Playstation game, created by Eidos (the company that foisted Tomb Raider on a panting world) and released in 1997. The game put the player in the Hulk's size-30 shoes and had him fight grade-Z villains like the Pantheon, Trauma, Piecemeal, U-Foes and Maestro.

The game didn't look the best and didn't have the best Hulk material to work with, but it's tolerable fun and quite cheap these days.

Debuting later this spring is quite a different mess of clams. Vivendi/Universal's Hulk: The Movie game is coming to the three big platforms — GameCube, PS2 and Xbox — in summer 2003 and promises to bring the multi-layered power and mental instability of the movie to gamers. It might not have the artistic wallop of Ang Lee's picture, but the wallop it brings to a different medium will be real enough.

*All in all, the **Hulk** has mostly kept his distance from the video boxes — but that may be changing.*

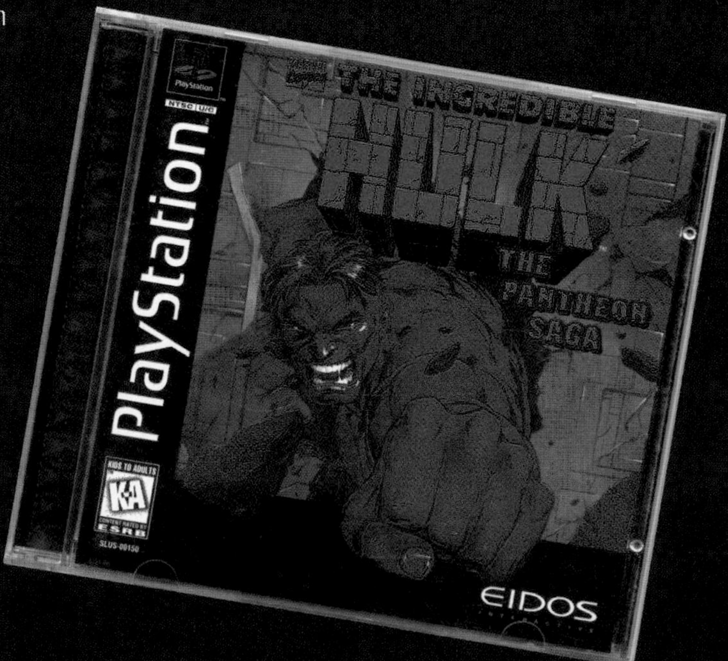
PlayStation
THE INCREDIBLE
HULK
THE PANTHEON SAGA
KIDS TO ADULTS
K-A
ESRB
EIDOS

faded away without fanfare in the late '90s, and while there are people who still collect the cards and play the game, there are also people who collect and listen to eight-tracks.

From a Hulk fan's standpoint, there are more than a dozen Hulk-related Overpower cards to collect — but surprisingly, none of them are killers in the context of the game. The Hulk is more vulnerable than Captain America, for instance, even though they're both well-nigh indestructible human beings. The difference is that there are times when the Hulk isn't the Hulk, but Captain America is always Captain America. Hulk's somewhere-between-good-and-evil persona also doesn't play well in the CCG context.

In what would have been a sweet ironic twist, Wizards of the Coast, the company that rode Magic: The Gathering to untold wealth and won the American license to distribute Pokemon cards, announced in 1999 that it had landed the Marvel CCG license and would be making Marvel CCGs that would have all the complexity of Magic (or, at the very least, Skip-Bo). WotC made the announcement flush with Pokemon's staggering success, a success that was as massive as it was short-lived. Within 18 months, WotC was a Hasbro subsidiary, Pokemon began hemorrhaging Oddishes and Snubbils faster than an Internet startup, and the Marvel-CCG project had ground to a halt, with nothing much more

than an abortive X-Men CCG to show for it.

That's okay, though, because by 1999 a new gaming force was hitting the scene — the collectible-miniature game. CMGs combine the fast-paced action of CCGs with the tactical manipulations of board and role-playing games, and if you believe the previous statement, you're probably a 16-year-old

who plays the bass drum in pep band and has seen the *Lord of the Rings* movies 17 times each, even though they totally blew the casting of the magic lichen.

The original CMG was a Magic-y sort of thing called Mage Knight, a great game to be sure. It was quickly followed by HeroClix, which fuses Marvel's classic characters to the hottest game platform going.

HeroClix beats previous Marvel CCGs eight ways to Sunday because the game's figures and board add previously unknown levels of complexity and strategy and ... oh, forget it. If collectible card games float your boat, and you get a little tired of chess, chess, chess morning and night, HeroClix is your kinda diversion.

Just like the Overpower Hulk, the HeroClix Hulk is not king of the hill. He's strong and indestructible, but not indestructible enough. Should the

The Hulk's role in collectible-card games (like Overpower, below) and collectible-miniature games (like HeroClix, above) has always been as the semi-heroic heavy. Interestingly, the Hulk is not the strongest creature or the toughest fighter in Overpower or HeroClix.

Hulk ever tangle with Captain America, the Hulk goes down 80 percent of the time. Ah, but it's that 20 percent that keeps the players playing.

Four things make HeroClix a monster game: It's fun, fast-paced and very playable, as games of this sort go, and the figures are fantastic. They're small and bottom-heavy, since dials on the base vary a figure's powers and weaknesses, but they're also quite detailed and far more than blobs of plastic on a lump of plastic. The Hulk features a dynamic pose and a startling amount of anatomical correctness; it's collectible even if you have no interest in the game, which makes the HeroClix marketers prone to dancing in the aisles, in addition to being quite rich.

Take a HeroClix figure off its base, and you have a mini-sculpture. Make the off-base figure a little larger and you have a statuette, which is also one of the more popular collectibles du jour. Bowen Designs made most of the Hulk statuettes and mini-busts until early 2003, and its Hulk and Gray Hulk statuettes from earlier this year are powerful, richly detailed and neatly crafted. The license for Hulk statuaries has since passed to Dynamic Forces, and its first effort, a sort of takeoff on Rodin's "The Thinker" with the Gray Hulk as the title character, is killer. Put this in between the Mont Blanc and the Frango mints on your desks and see if the other VPs don't treat you with a whole new brand of respect.

The statuettes and mini-busts are extremely nice, but unlike Megos, they're collectibles designed to be collectibles, and priced like collectibles from the getgo. This is like spending $40 million *trying* to make a movie as cheesy as *Plan 9 From Outer Space*; go ahead, but you're better off buying a case of hard lemonade and a camcorder, letting the chips fall where they may and spending the remaining $39.9 million on a really nice recliner.

Time, not marketers, will determine tomorrow's great Hulk collectibles. eBay, or whatever the future version of eBay looks like, will have a hand in it, too. HeroClix Hulks probably will be high on the list. Incredible Hulk shampoo probably won't be. But for those special times when you need Hulk-soft hair, it's nice to know the answer is as close as your computer.

Now, when does that auction close?

Maybe you can't have the Hulk's physique, but between the Hulk Instant Muscles and the electronic Hulk Hands, you're more than halfway there. Get some ripped jeans and a Beatles wig, and you're in business.

INCLUDES 4 "AAA" BATTERIES
Ages 6 & Up
Item No. 70516
TRY ME!
TAP HANDS FOR SOUNDS
SEE BACK OF PACKAGE FOR CAUTIONS
ELECTRONIC
HULK HANDS
WITH SMASH 'N BASH SOUND EFFECTS!
SMASH!

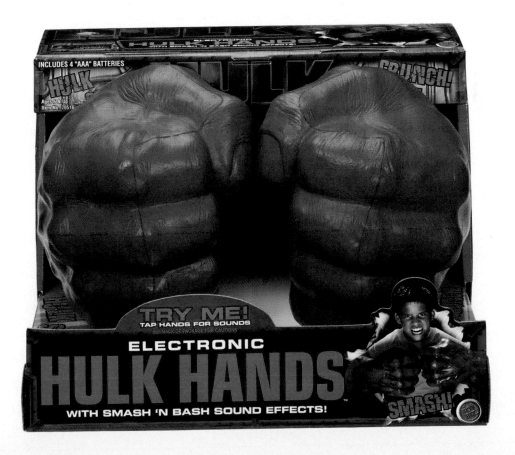

Crouching toys, hidden figures:
The story behind the Hulk movie toys

One of the best things about blockbuster movies isn't the movie itself but all the stuff it generates. The world is still coming to grips with *Battlefield Earth* action figures, not to mention the Fearless Leader Halloween costumes left over from *The Adventures of Rocky and Bullwinkle*.

Licensing is one of the names of one of the games that go along with a blockbuster movie. Licensing gives the moviemakers a cushion in case the movie-going public doesn't equate the LL Cool J remake of *Rollerball* with boffo box-office. It also can work for licensors when they jump onto the back of a *Lord of the Rings* or *Spider-Man* and ride it all the way to the bank.

Licensors are more conservative these days, which makes sense all around unless you really dig the idea of *Divine Secrets of the Ya-Ya Sisterhood* boxers. As a result, the licensing push for a movie like *Hulk* — which five years ago would have included trading cards, stickers, paint-with-water books, 3-D puzzles, HO trains, dragon kites, drum sets, bean plush and craft kits — now only focuses on the bare essentials.

With the Hulk, that naturally means action figures. ToyBiz has seven eight-inch action

figures that really are action figures in the sense that they all do something other than pose. The Rapid Punch Hulk features a "Wall Smashing Action" move; take him out on the job site or donate him to your local SWAT team. Throwing Hulk has "Boulder Throwing Action," making him just the thing you need when the Gauls attack and you're all out of boiling oil. The Absorbing Man has a "Transforming Texture" move; he comes in handy when you've just taken the last paper towel off the roll. Rage 'n' Roar Hulk has "Punching Action and Electronic Sound" — sort of the best of both worlds. The Hulk Dog merely has sound, which is a good thing when you consider what most dogs do. Superposeable Hulk has a wall-mountable base, and no one knows why. The Punching Hulk punches. Big surprise there.

Toy Biz also has a 13-inch superbendy Hulk with roaring action and the one thing every businessman needs for the big sales meeting: The Hulk mask with Voice Changer, which lets you look like the Hulk and sound like the CEO.

Ang Lee's movie isn't meant to be a licensing smash. It's meant to be a meticulously crafted, impressionistic take on a classic character. If you think the movie deserves more neat products, write the toy companies. Better yet, see the movie a couple of dozen times and buy the DVD when it comes out. The trend in licensed products with any movie this side of *Harry Potter* is for many of the coolest products to come out after the movie's released and before it heads to video. At that time, toy companies know what sort of audience they're dealing with, what products will work best and how they ought to sell — good questions all.

If you're hoping for a *Hulk*-movie-based chess set, you may be disappointed. But everything else is on the table.

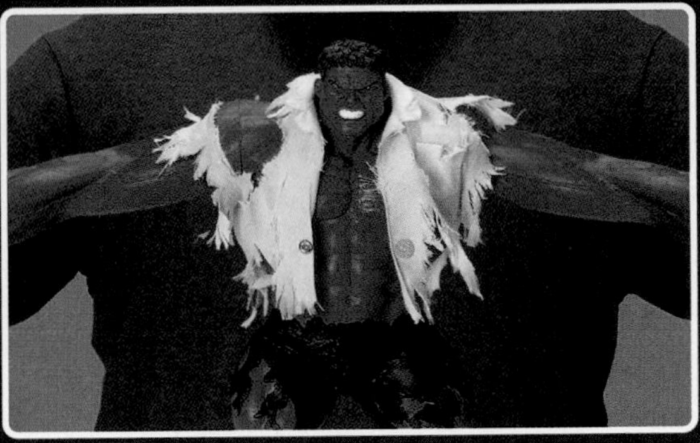

Electric Stretch 'n' Roar Hulk

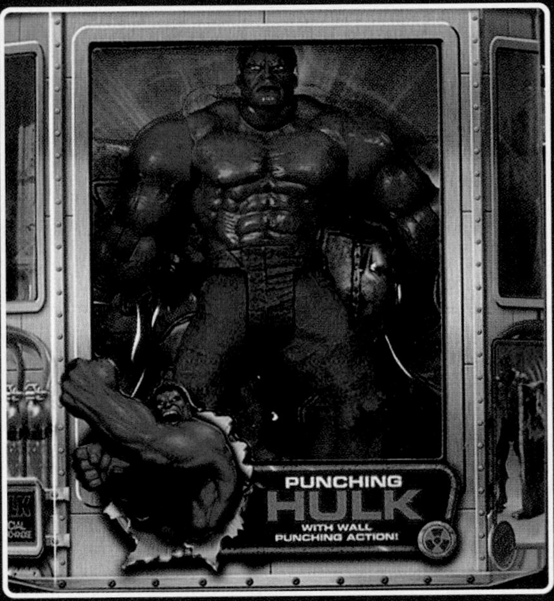
PUNCHING
HULK
WITH WALL
PUNCHING ACTION!

Punching Hulk

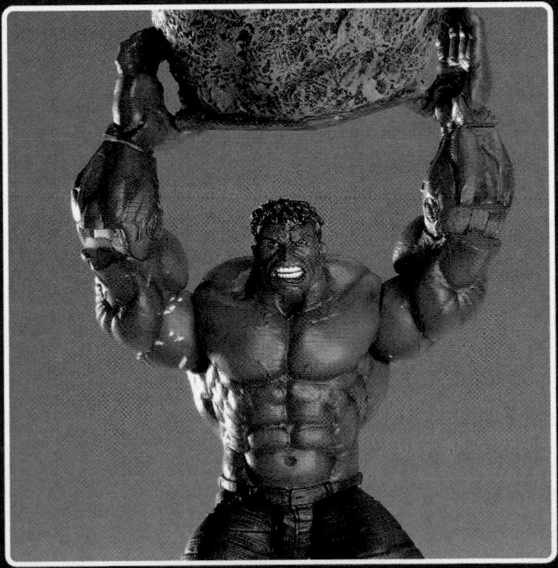

Throwing Hulk

Chapter Four

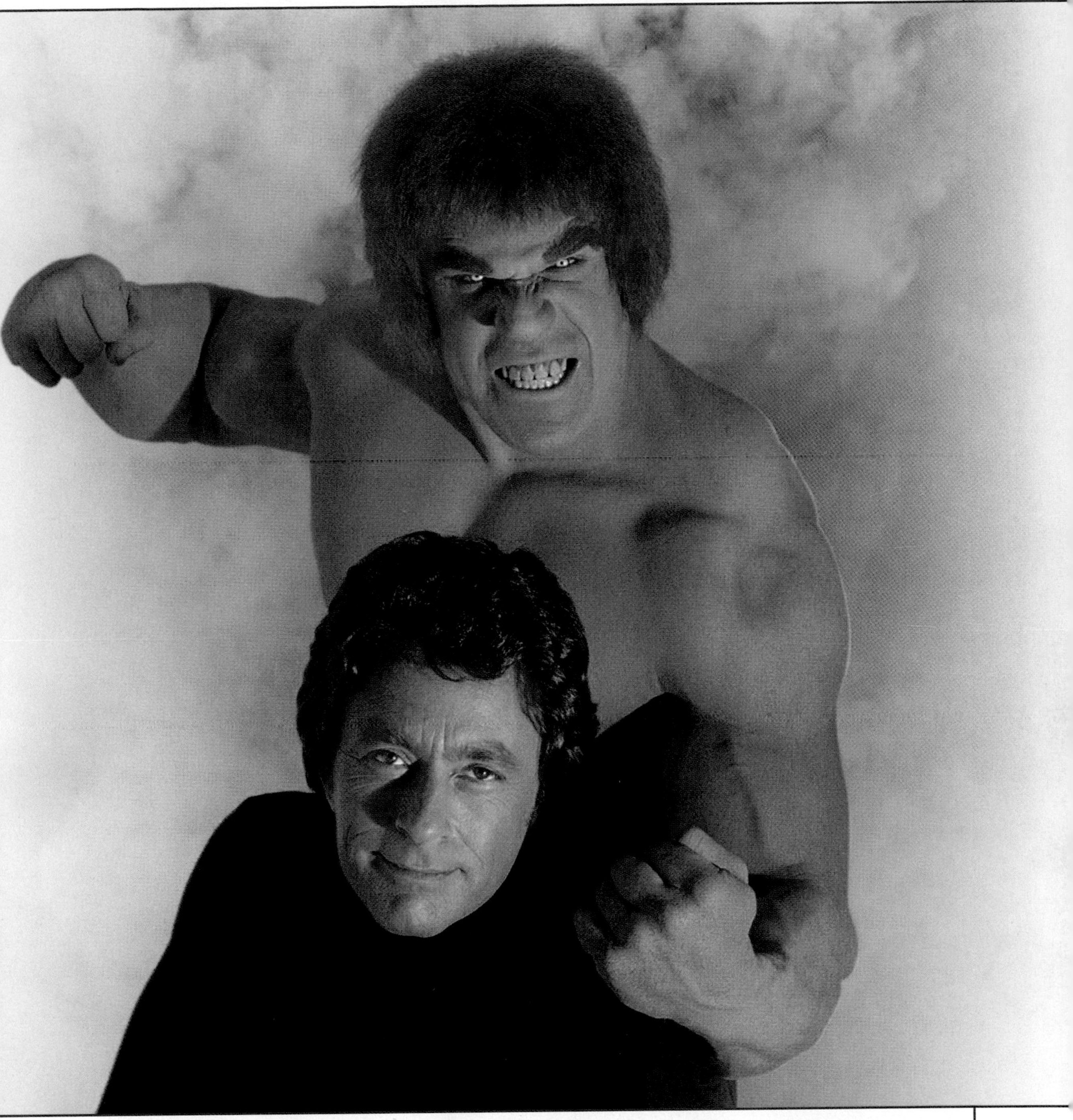

BIG HULK, SMALL SCREEN

The Hulk on TV

Eddie's father was the star. Lurch was the narrator. A former Teen Mr. Universe was the guy in the yak's-hair wig. Mariette Hartley was the dead woman with the Emmy. Arnold Schwarzenegger was the muscle-bound guy on the sidelines. '70s television doesn't get any more quintessentially '70s — or any better — than *The Incredible Hulk.*

Scratch a casual Hulk fan and chances are you'll find someone who watched the Hulk TV series and thought it was really cool. That's not to say there aren't casual fans of the comic or hardcore fans of the TV series. (Geez, are there ever, especially the latter.) But it took money and motivation to buy a comic book, which was the way most people got to read *Incredible Hulk.* You probably didn't get a haircut every month — especially in the '70s — and bumming a copy from a friend was also not a long-term solution. On the other hand, how much money or motivation did it take to turn on a TV set? Even a teenager could manage that.

One of the big reasons the Hulk TV series was cool was because it wasn't the comic book and didn't try to be. The similarities between the comic book and TV series are the bare underpinnings of the character and plotline, and nothing more: An atomic scientist gets a dose of gamma radiation. When he gets mad, he turns into the Incredible Hulk. As the Hulk, he's hunted by mostly evil people who want to turn his strength to their wicked ends. That's it. The vehicles built on that chassis are as different — and as desirable — as a Bimmer and a Hummer. It's just that sometimes, you need to go fast — and sometimes, you gotta have the ground clearance.

Maybe you don't really understand how different the TV show is from the comic book. For instance, in the TV show, Bruce Banner is David Bruce Banner, most often called "David." In the movie, David Banner is the father of the current Robert Bruce Banner, most often called "Bruce." Does that mean David Bruce Banner is the father, the son or the father *and* the son? Uh, yes. And no. Bruce Banner is the guy who turns into the Hulk. In the comics and the movie, he's Robert Bruce Banner; in the TV show, he's David Bruce Banner. Got that? Sure you do.

As for why Robert Bruce is Bruce and David Bruce is David, your guess is as good as anyone's. Supposedly, the show's producer, Kenneth Johnson (who later produced *V*, among other sci-fi treats) didn't like alliterating names. (Good thing he never hung around Stan Lee in the '60s.) Also, Bruce was not the manliest name to be sporting in the '70s, though the Bruces of the philosophy department of the University of Woolamaloo would consider you a pooftah for saying

How do you skirt the issue of whether the Hulk's pants rip in the same place every time? Dress him in shorts. Lou Ferrigno strikes the classic pose.

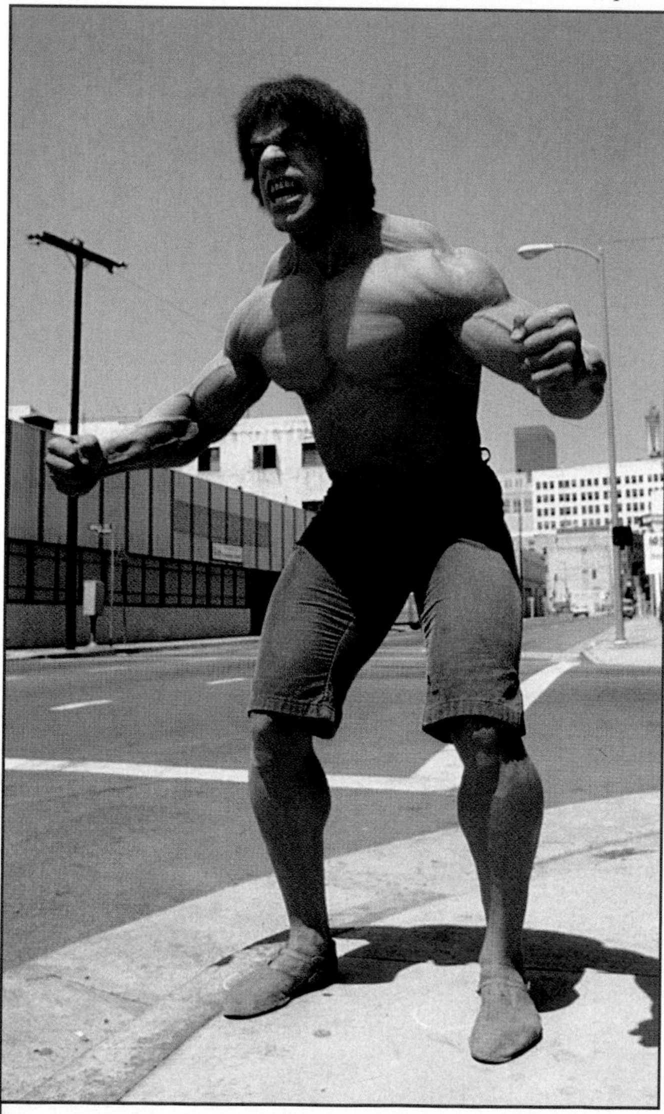

CBS Photo Archive

so, and it never did Bruce Jenner any harm.

Okay, so David Bruce Banner's wife dies in a car fire in part because he lacks the strength to save her. The tragedy compels him to investigate the way people's strength seems to increase in times of extreme physical or emotional stress. He determines that gamma radiation is the key and gives himself a shot of the good green stuff. No selfless rush to rescue Rick Jones here: The genesis of this Hulk is all about science, givin' it up for ol' Poly Tech, just like the legendary Doc Hyde.

You know what happens next; the scene is a classic of '70s television. Even if you weren't around to see it, you've seen it. David Banner's car gets a flat tire in a rainstorm. When he tries to change it and hurts his hand, he flies into a rage. The rage accelerates. Bill Bixby's face contorts; his skin tone changes; his body swells. Noises become chaotic, otherworldly. Hair sprouts with the time-lapse speed of a Chia Pet commercial. In less than a minute, Bixby changes from his normal self into a bare-chested green monster who flips the flat-tired car like it was a toy (which it was, but that's another story).

Congratulations: You've just witnessed the first-ever live-action TV Hulk-out — and the start of a TV phenomenon.

Believe it. Long before anyone smelled what the Rock was cookin', the Rock smelled what the Hulk was cookin'. And it wasn't Niblets corn in a Boil-In Bag.

But because this is the Hulk, there has to be a dark spot in this sunny portrait of primal rage, and it appears the next day. When Banner tries to un-gamma himself, a fire destroys the lab. His colleague dies, and an investigative reporter from the *National Register* (thinly veiled pointed reference there,

Bill Bixby infused David Banner with warmth and humanity, and added class to what could have been second-rate kitsch.

CBS Photo Archive

huh?) named Jack McGee sees the Hulk fleeing the scene, and puts two and two together. Sensing the scoop of the century, he vows to track down the monster. David Banner hits the road, always one small step ahead of McGee, vainly searching for the cure that never comes.

Nice setup — but where's Betty? Where's Thunderbolt Ross? Where are the Mole Men, for criminy's sake? The answer is: They're not there — and there was never a thought they might be there. For all their merits as comic-book characters, Ross, Betty, and the premium assortment of nuts and chews in the Hulk's villains sampler would look stupid(er) in a medium that struggled vainly with the logistics of getting the monkey to smile on cue in *B.J. and the Bear.* Knowing that, producer Johnson, with Stan Lee's blessing, overhauled the Hulk so it would work on prime-time live-action '70s TV.

The first thing the Hulk did was shrink. While the original comic-book Hulk was 10 feet tall and weighed 1,000 pounds, the Hulk had his stomach stapled for TV. He withered away to a mere seven feet and 330, though most of that was makeup and trick camerawork necessitated by a shortage of seven-foot-tall, 330-pound, car-flipping thespians.

The TV Hulk remained earth's strongest human, but he couldn't manage the real heavy lifting of the comic Hulk without a truss. The comic Hulk could press more than 100 tons, but the TV Hulk had to be content flipping Gran Torinos and beating up abusive dads. The TV Hulk could also be hurt by bullets, but better aim true: He was such a quick healer that if you plugged him before a commercial break, he was usually good to go after the Armour Hot Dog jingle. Falls from great heights were capable of causing some

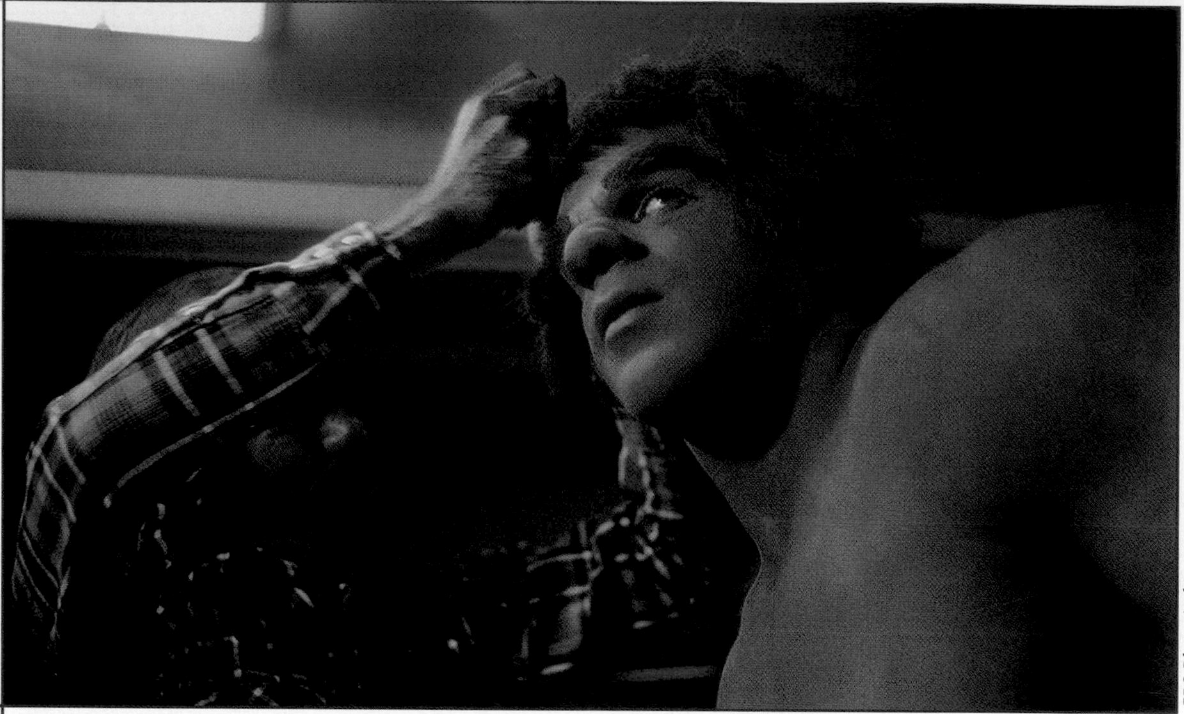

CBS Photo Archive

John Fogerty sang about Green River, Lou Ferrigno lived it. His makeup ran when he sweated, forcing him to spend the time between takes spread-eagled in his air-conditioned trailer.

discomfort, but even those ... well, Houston, we have a problem with the falls from great heights.

We'll get to that in a minute. First, let's meet the cast.

There aren't many. The Hulk series kept things simple: just a man, a monster and the investigative reporter who loved him.

The man was the best-known actor of the three. Bill Bixby had tasted small-screen success with *My Favorite Martian* and *The Courtship of Eddie's Father* in the '60s. He also had pretensions of being a serious stage and movie actor, but what TV star doesn't? Heck, even Flipper turned into a prima donna after a while.

Journeyman actor Jack Colvin played Jack McGee. Years of bit parts and walk-ons had prepared Colvin (who was and is a respected acting teacher) for the role of his life: a dusty, slightly down-at-heel, shirt-collar-outside-of-the-sport-coat reporter obsessed with finding a green-painted, yak-hair-wearing bodybuilder. Colvin nailed it. It wasn't a springboard to a record deal or a Pepsi commercial, but it put food on the table. It still does.

Bixby was the name above the title, but the real star of *The Incredible Hulk*, as it should be, was the Hulk ... and the guy who played him. Lou Ferrigno was a bodybuilder with an equally pumped-up resume: 1970 Teen Mr. America, 1973 Mr. America, and 1973 and 1974 Mr. Universe; a co-starring role with Arnold Schwarzenegger in the landmark body-building documentary *Pumping Iron*; the obligatory brief football career, with the Toronto Argonauts of the Canadian Football League; and measurements to die for: 22 ½-inch biceps and a 59-inch chest. Ferrigno has a hearing impairment, which affects his speaking voice, but that was no issue for the TV Hulk. The only sounds he made were roars and growls, and those were dubbed — originally by Ted Cassidy (Lurch from *The Addams Family),* and then, after Cassidy's death, from a taped assortment of animal noises and other sounds.

Because he's six feet tall and had never acted (documentaries don't count), Ferrigno wasn't the first choice to play the Hulk. Richard Kiel was. About the only nearly seven-foot-tall actor in Hollywood, Kiel was "Jaws" in the James Bond film *Live and Let Die* and actually shot some scenes for the first Hulk movie, one of which made it to the final cut. (If you really want to know, it's the overhead shot at the lake where the Hulk pushes a tree into the water to help rescue a little girl. The Hulk in that shot is Richard Kiel.)

Kiel was big enough, but he wasn't Hulk enough. Sensing that fact, Kenneth Johnson

Everything you ever wanted to know about the Hulk, but were afraid to ask

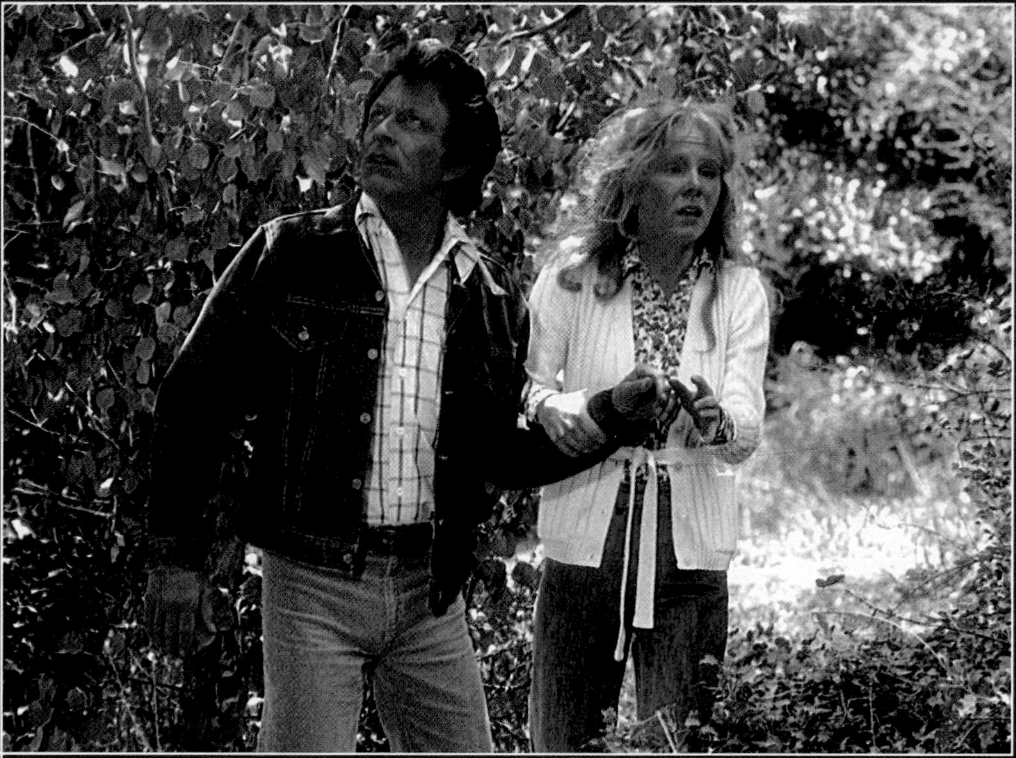

CBS Photo Archive

A pre-Proto-Hulk David Banner leads Laurie Prange through the southern California jungles in the classic "Prometheus" two-parter.

There have always been people who keep track of things that shouldn't really be kept track of. The difference now is that thanks to the Internet, these people can share their discoveries with the world. Gosh, thanks, Internet! Still, without the Internet, these bits of Hulk TV-series effluvia — gathered by Mark Rathwell, Marina Bailey, David Jones, Bryan Kennedy and their friends (all of whom all were willing to give their names, amazingly) — would remain the property of a select few. Instead, they now belong to the world. Take good care of them.

If you find trivialities like these have the same appealing greasy aftertaste as microwave pork rinds, you can find lots more at http://tmar.za.net/hulkfaq.htm. We won't wait up for you.

When the Hulk wasn't chasing around Southern California backlots, he was running down New York alleys. One alley in particular had special appeal to the Hulk. He ran down it in four episodes: "Final Round," "Captive Night," "Metamorphosis" and "Kindred Spirits." Did he ever get an odd sense of déjà vu? If he did he never let on.

To protect his true identity, David Banner used aliases — lots of aliases. He used aliases like a three-year-old uses Kleenex. Among them: Bailey, Ballant, Balon, Banion, Bannister, Barker, Barnes, Baron, Barr, Barrett, Barton, Baxter, Becker, Beckwith, Beddiger, Bedford, Beeman, Beldon, Bellemy, Beller, Belson, Beemon, Benchely, Benedict, Bennet, Bennings, Benson, Benton, Bernard, Bernett, Betson, Bettman, Betton, Bishop, Blackwell, Blaine, Blair, Blake, Blakeman, Bosky, Bowman, Bradburn, Bradshaw, Bramer, Breck, Brennan, Brent, Breyman, Brown, Burnett, Burns and Butler. No Bavid Danner or Aviday Annerbay? They must have been saving those for season six.

Continued on page 95

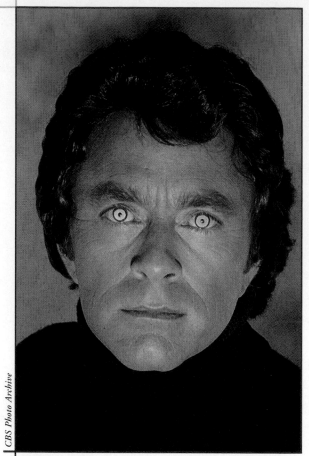

Don't shoot till you see the whites of his eyes: Thanks to the wonders of colored contact lenses, David Banner makes it clear that a change is in the air.

tabbed his second choice, giving Ferrigno the nod over Schwarzenegger, another fellow non-actor, because Ferrigno was taller. (Had Schwarzenegger been a little taller and Ferrigno a little shorter, would Lou have gone on to mutter, "I'll be baaaack," and marry Maria Shriver? Don't ask.)

Ferrigno's heavy features and awesome frame turned out to be the perfect raw material for the Hulk. All the producers had to do was add a yak's-hair wig and green body paint (which came off on *everything,* from the walls the Hulk crashed through to the bears he wrestled), and keep Ferrigno from sweating and — shades of Earl Scheib! — ruining the paint job. In fact, between takes Ferrigno had to lay spread-eagled on the floor of his air-conditioned trailer to keep his makeup from running.

Ferrigno would sometimes wear a sticker on his arm reading, "Caution: Being green may be hazardous to your health." But there were perks, too: At the height of his popularity, Ferrigno received 2,000 pieces of fan mail a week.

Bixby endured similar hardships with less fan mail. As part of the Hulk-out process, he had to wear white contact lenses that required anesthetic to put in, and caused his eyes to blur and burn for hours afterwards. The pain went away, though, and during the show's run and for years thereafter, Bixby remained one of the Hulk's greatest fans, starring gladly in all the sequels and even directing one of the better episodes. (Not to be outdone, Jack Colvin directed two fine episodes, as well.)

"At first, everyone was saying, 'You're doing what?'" Bixby told the Chicago Tribune in 1979. "'After *Steambath, Rich Man, Poor Man, [The Courtship of] Eddie's Father,* you're going to do that?' I said, 'Just watch the show.' You hear the title *The Incredible Hulk* and it brings out the intellectual snobbery in the viewing audience. We have overcome not only our title, but the negativism.

"When we started, everyone said, 'pooh, pooh,'" he added. "Here it is, six months later and everyone is saying 'We've got to have a show like the Hulk.'"

Bixby credited the writers — "It's very difficult; it takes tremendous writing" — and then added something curious: "We have to go back and ... make it as real as we can," he said. "The more we stay with reality, the better the Hulk will be."

It's not often you hear one of the key figures in a sci-fi hit say the series needs to stay firmly rooted in reality. But the closer you look at the Hulk TV show, the more it looks like *The Rockford Files* with James Garner changing into the strongest human on earth when the bad guys kidnap Rocky.

Yeah, it's a long ways from Tyrannus and the Space Parasite, but (and this'll be the last time this point is made — promise) the TV series worked because it was a little bit dusty and definitely down to earth, and not campy like *Wonder Woman.* If Lyle Waggoner had dared bare a bicuspid on *The Incredible Hulk,* Lou Ferrigno would have shoved him in a grease trap.

The Hulk series ran for four and a half seasons, from 1979 to 1982. A made-for-TV movie kicked it off and three more TV movies aired after the show was axed. A fourth TV

Continued from page 93

The folks at the Hulk FAQ site have also tracked some of the feats of strength performed by the TV Hulk. While any one of them would elicit a "Puny human!" from the comic Hulk, they sure beat heck out of anything Hulk Hogan did in *Santa with Muscles*. They include:

Smashing through brick walls
Overturning cars
Snapping chains
Kicking over a mobile home
Spinning a ferris wheel
Holding down a helicopter
Overturning a tank
Smashing through doors
Throwing people across a room
Lifting up a (filled) jury box
Overturning a fork-lift
Breaking out of a freezer
Uprooting large trees

Creating a gale-force wind with
    his voice
Stopping a bus with his hands
Breaking a boulder in half
Breaking out of a safe
Punching through several
    feet of concrete
Lifting an elevator
Resisting a car crusher
Bending steel bars
Tipping a crane
Breaking a football helmet
Wrestling a bull to the ground

And finally, here's their list of things that caused David to turn into the Hulk (and can't we relate to any of these, particularly electrocution and being caught in a printing press?):

Getting beaten up
Electrocution
Intense frustration
Having a car collapse on him
Being hit by a car
Being attacked by animals
    (snakes, dogs,
        scorpions, bears)
Nightmares
Being shot
Sinking in quicksand
Drowning
Being poisoned
Involvement in a car accident
Struggling to break free
    of restraints
Being buried alive
Traffic jams
Extreme heat
Hypnosis
Fires
Being trampled
Personal injuries
Being caught in a
    printing press

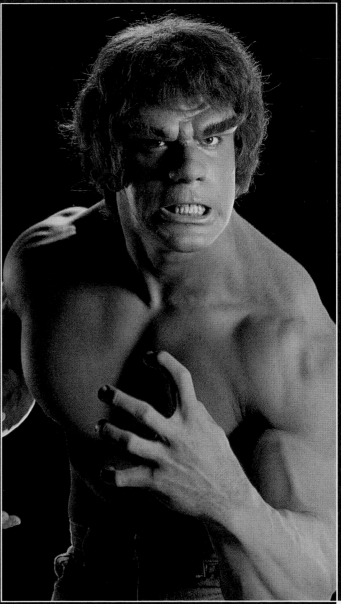

CBS Photo Archive

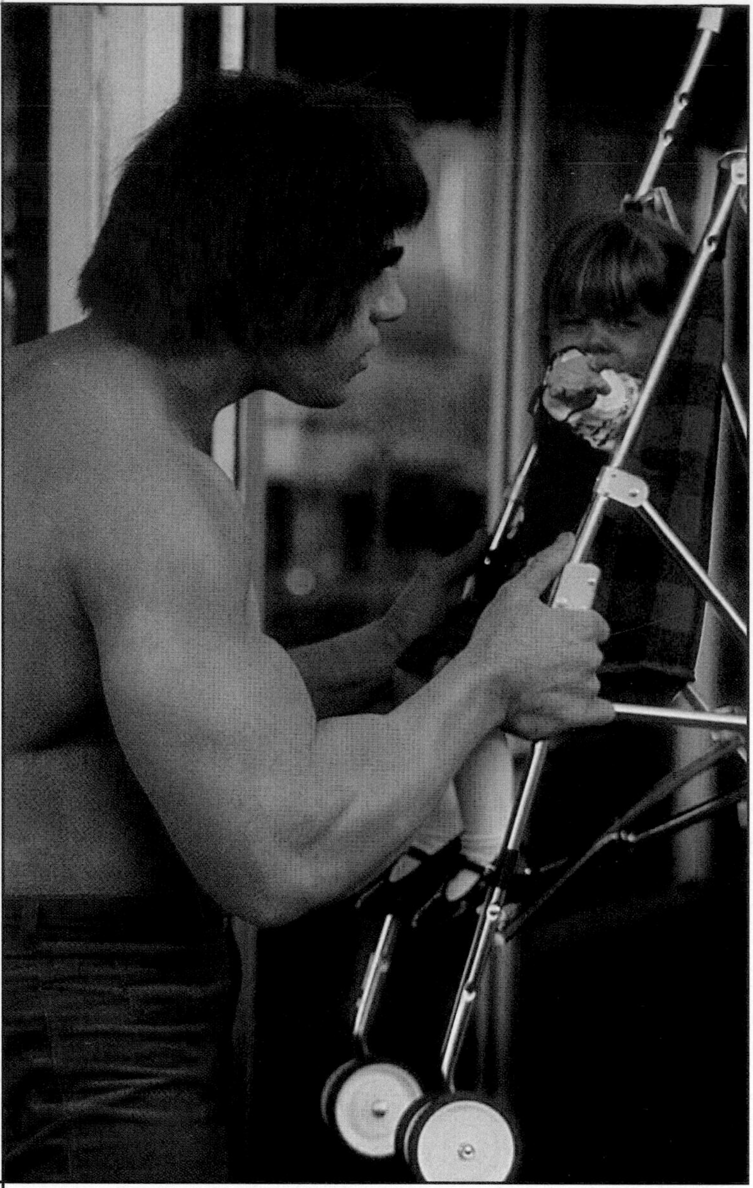

CBS Photo Archive

Who says guys never ask for directions? The Hulk learns the way to the nearest Tank 'n' Tummy in the 1979 episode "Like a Brother."

short. They run out of plots or the actors bolt or the viewers move on to *Knight Rider*, scary a thought as that seems today. Compounding the situation for the Hulk series was its expense: Episodes cost upwards of $660,000 to make — a real chunk of money in those days, considering you could crank out a whole season of *Three's Company* for $857.50, plus a new *Potty Time Joke Book* for the writers. As soon as Universal (which made the episodes) and CBS (which paid for them) sensed the Hulk had outlived its usefulness, they dispatched Miami Steve Van Zandt to pay the series a little call. Which he did in the fall of 1981, though episodes ran through May 1982.

But like a Monty Python corpse, the Hulk wasn't dead yet. Demand from fans and the networks' insatiable desire for programming (the same desire that brought us *America's Funniest Outtakes from America's Funniest Home Videos* and Regis Philbin) meant the Hulk could come back. The Hulk *had to* come back. And the Hulk came back in three increasingly more mediocre made-for-TV movies: *The Incredible Hulk Returns, The Trial of the Incredible Hulk* and *The Death of the Incredible Hulk.*

movie was stopped only by Bill Bixby's death.

The TV series made the whole world go Hulk-mad for a time. It was the No. 1 show on Friday nights for its first couple seasons and a perennial power in the top-10 lists. The two-hour pilot episode was released in Europe and was the top-grossing movie on the continent for two months. The two-part episode where David Banner marries a terminally ill psychiatrist played by Mariette Hartley (otherwise known as the Polaroid camera lady) also got the feature-film treatment overseas; as *The Bride of the Incredible Hulk*, it packed the popcorn houses from Portugal to Poland.

If shows like *The Incredible Hulk* have a shortcoming, it's that their life spans are

Taken by themselves, the movies weren't bad, and actually had some things to offer comics fans. The Hulk teams up with the Mighty Thor in the first flick and is defended by Matt Murdock, a.k.a. Daredevil, in the second. But the Hulk and Thor in tandem couldn't keep a helicopter from taking off, an outcome that must have had Stan Lee wondering why he bothered to add "Mighty" and "Incredible" to their names. Furthermore (and here's where the falls-from-great-heights thing comes into play), the Hulk dies in *The Death of the Incredible Hulk* after falling from a plane. In the TV series, he fell from a similar plane flying at a similar height, and he got up and walked away. Boy oh boy, and you wonder why fans just snap.

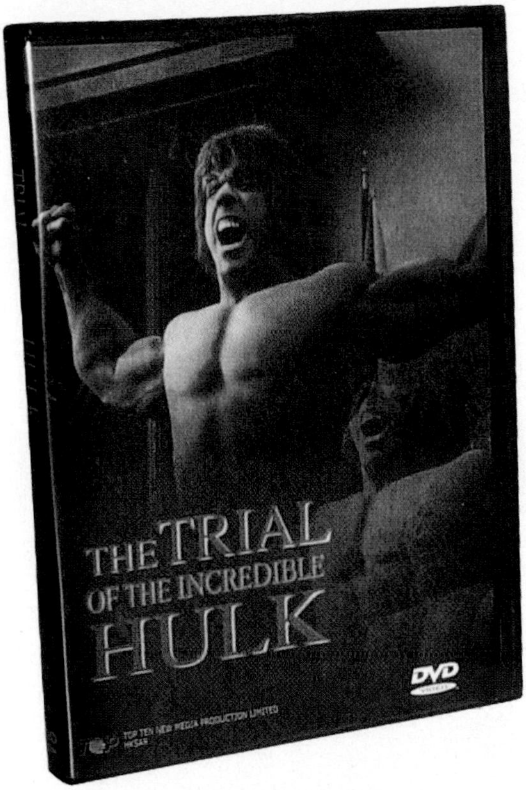
THE TRIAL
OF THE INCREDIBLE
HULK
DVD

Trial of the Incredible Hulk DVD

Fans hoping the movies would build on the plot lines, themes and character development of the TV series came away sorely disappointed. But they kept the Hulk on the small screen and kept the momentum moving toward a big-screen movie that would render all the small-screen movies as forgettable as they ultimately were.

The Hulk TV series is a perfectly contained entity, like Spaghetti O's. Nothing that came after it, except for the made-for-TV movies that are really just extensions of the series, use it as a jumping-off point. No comics are based on it, no animated series, no theatrical movies. It's a shrewd modification of a comics archetype and an extremely well-realized reflection of its place and time — and if you want to know what those statements mean, put the Sci-Fi Channel on the flat-screen and buy some episodes on video for the home theater.

If you do, be warned: You may never view Bruce Banner the same way again. You may even start calling him "David." Just don't start comparing the comic Hulk to Lou Ferrigno. The yak's-hair wig throws you for a loop every time.

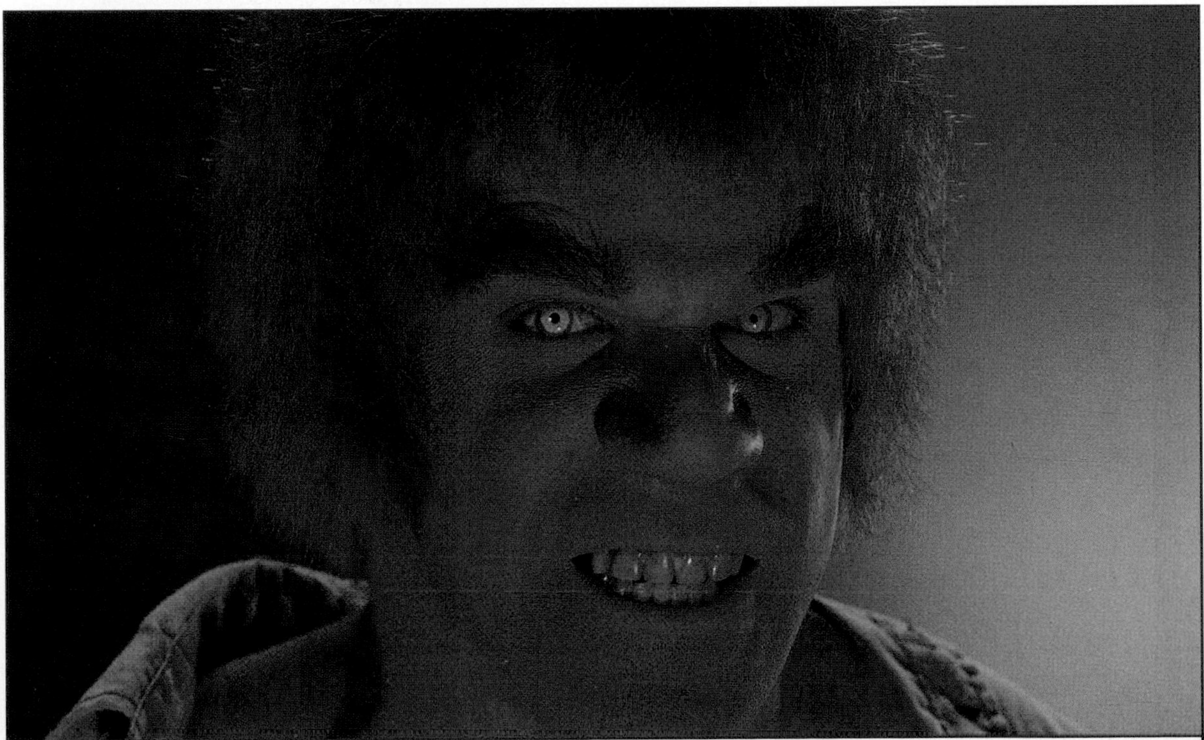

CBS Photo Archive

The Hulk's Greatest Hits: Five million film buffs can't be wrong

The main thing a top-10 list proves is that there's no accounting for taste. Everyone has their favorite Hulk episode, and if that episode isn't on a top-10 list, even if it's a top-10 list that has nothing to do with the Hulk, stand the heck back. You'll see for yourself that hell really has no fury like a Hulk fan scorned.

Understood, but there's space to fill and duty calls, so leave us to press on. If you're looking for 10 episodes that give you a good idea of what *The Incredible Hulk* is, was and could be, start with these:

The Incredible Hulk *(pilot episode/made-for-TV movie)*: Is it cheating to list the pilot as a must-see episode? Well, it's a whole lot easier to understand the rest of the episodes if you've seen the pilot, the plot summation that kicks off every episode notwithstanding. And the pilot is exceptionally well-done. Five million European film buffs can't be wrong, even if they do like Jerry Lewis way too much. First aired Nov. 7, 1977.

"Married" (a.k.a. The Bride of the Incredible Hulk): The Hulk gets hitched, only it's not the Hulk that gets hitched but Banner, and one of the reasons he gets married is because he knows that his bride (played by Polaroid camera pitchlady Mariette Hartley, in a performance that won her the first Emmy ever awarded to a sci-fi series for reasons other than technical — which tells volumes about the Emmy people's opinions of the acting abilities of William Shatner, Leonard Nimoy, et. al.) is about to head off to that Great Psychiatric Clinic in the Sky. Haul out the Kleenex, and prepare to say "awwwwwww" more than once. Two-hour episode, first aired Sept. 22, 1978.

"Homecoming": David Banner reunites with his brother and sister, and they all have a quasi-happy — and occasionally green — Colorado Thanks-giving. No family feuds but an obligatory showdown with a shady land developer. This is Colorado, after all. Diana Muldaur shines as David's sister. Aired Nov. 30, 1979.

"Proof Positive": You know this plot: About three years into the run of a successful series, there's an episode that uses flashbacks to give the writers and actors time

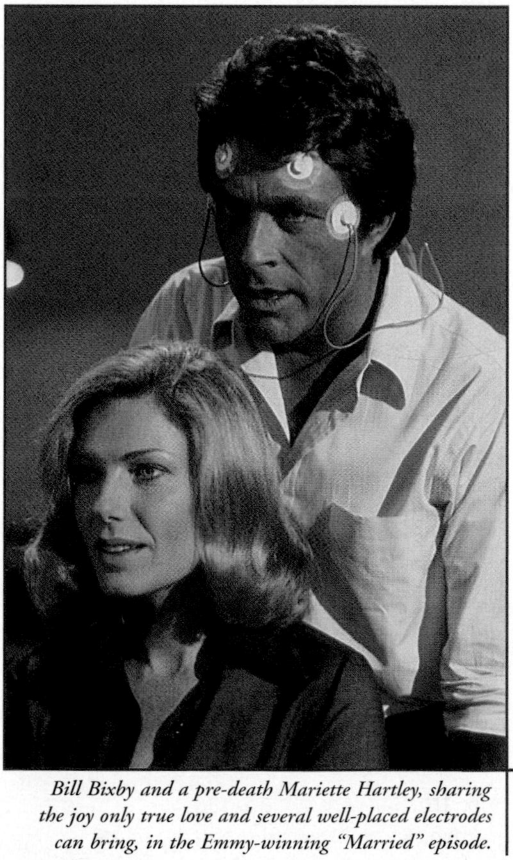

CBS Photo Archive

Bill Bixby and a pre-death Mariette Hartley, sharing the joy only true love and several well-placed electrodes can bring, in the Emmy-winning "Married" episode.

for that second jumbo latte. This one is better than most, not because Bill Bixby never appears, but because it has a plot. Not much of a plot — the daughter of the *National Register*'s publisher takes over the paper temporarily and asks Jack McGee to justify his existence, more or less — but enough. Aired Jan. 11, 1980.

"Prometheus": If you remember your mythology, Prometheus was the god who defended man before Zeus and for his troubles was chained to Mount Caucasus while a vulture pecked at his liver throughout eternity. While that would have made an interesting Hulk episode (Woody Woodpecker himself couldn't crack the Hulk's epidermis, and what chain could have held the Hulk to what rock?), *this* tale played better on the tube. The Hulk gets stuck halfway in his transformation, and the Army captures the Proto-Hulk. A strong supporting cast, including the eternally watchable Monte Markham, help make this a classic piece of '70s sci-fi. Aired Nov. 7 and Nov. 14, 1980.

"Bring Me the Head of the Hulk": Isn't that supposed to be "Bring Me the Head of Alfredo Garcia"? Ah, well; all's fair in episode titles. Bill Bixby makes his directorial debut in this nifty episode, which places Jack McGee in the unusual position of having to defend the Hulk from attack by a hired gun from a rival tabloid. Not

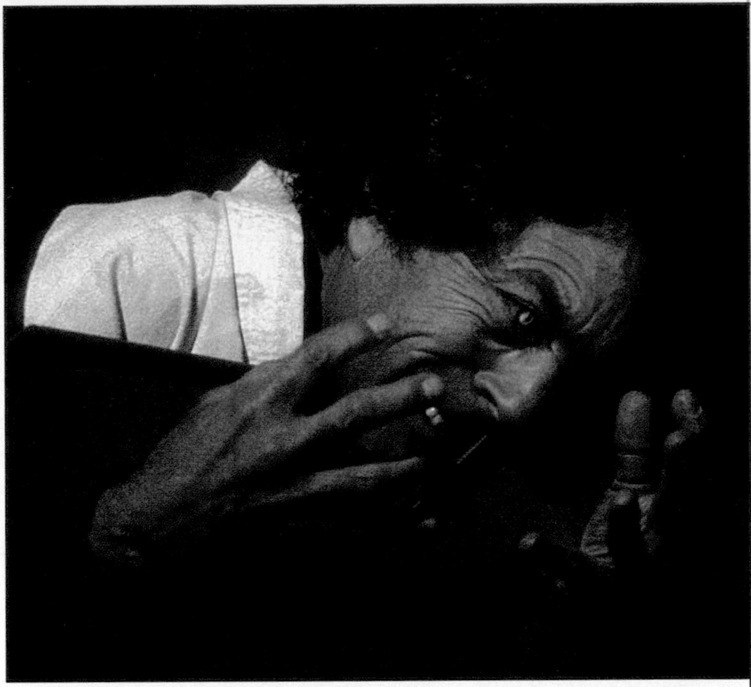

CBS Photo Archive

Now that's acting: Bill Bixby made his transformation into the Hulk totally believable (by late-'70s TV standards) without relying on a bevy of special effects (top), and the Hulk totes Dr. Jane Cabot (Jane Merrow) in Bill Bixby's directorial debut, "Bring Me the Head of the Hulk" (bottom).

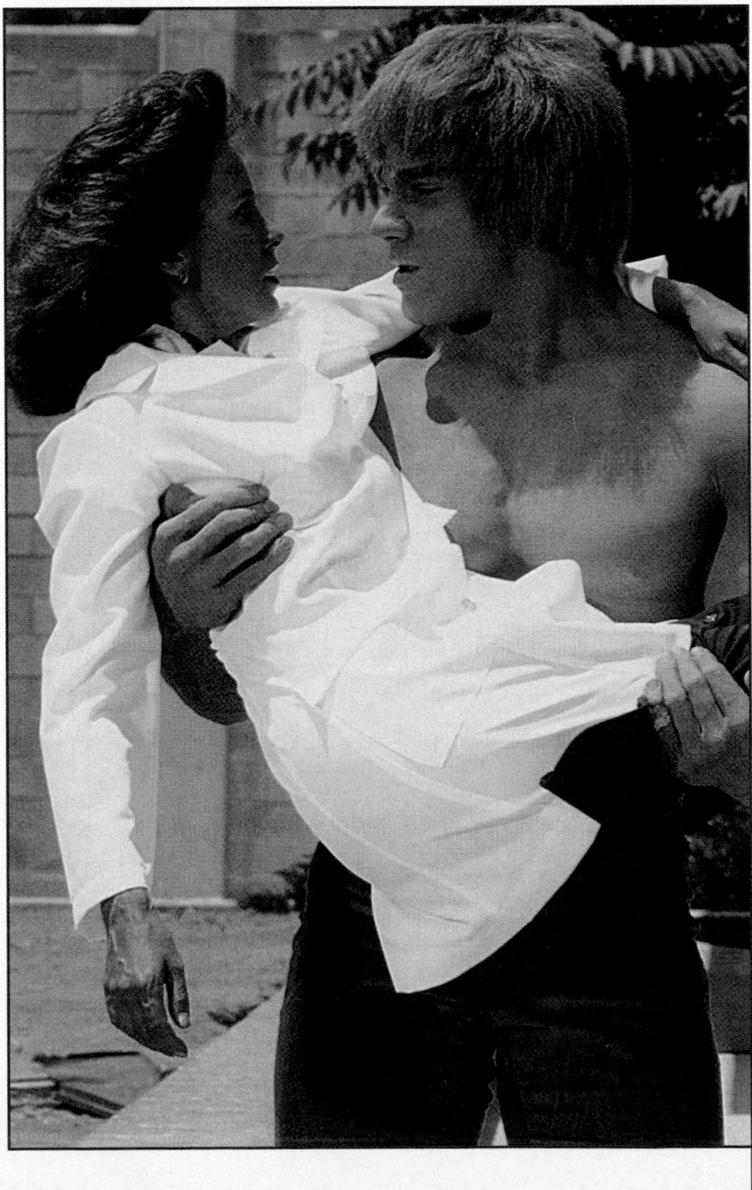

CBS Photo Archive

the *Weekly World News,* certainly. It's too busy fleshing out its latest scoop: Nostradamus actually listed "an ABBA revival" as a sign that the world would end soon. Aired Jan. 9, 1981.

"Good-bye, Eddie Cain": The Hulk meets '40s film noir in this Raymond Chandleresque episode. The first episode directed by Jack Colvin rates sorta high on the suspended-disbelief scale, but who said anything about any of this stuff having to be believable? You want believability, watch C-Span. Then again, don't. Aired. Jan. 23, 1981.

"East Winds": Jack Colvin directs this tale of intrigue — and bathtubs — in Chinatown, and does a darn fine job of it. Not a typical Hulk episode, but man does not live by Hulk alone. Not this man, anyhow. Aired Feb. 20, 1981.

"The First": If it seems like all the two-hour and two-part Hulk episodes were good, that's because they were. No frustrating season-ending cliffhangers here: David Banner discovers that a Dr. Clive cured another Hulk, but when he finds Clive's notes and tries to cure himself, the ex-Hulk interferes and becomes a Hulk again — an evil Hulk! Dirk Durock, the TV Swamp Thing, makes a scary Evil Hulk, and homages abound to great Universal monsters and their movies. The Hulk-vs.-Hulk showdown is the series' best fight. Aired March 6 and March 13, 1981.

"The Harder They Fall": David Banner learns what it means to be physically challenged when he's hit by a car and paralyzed from the waist down. Not a lot of Hulkarific action but some great acting by Bill Bixby. All in all, as sensitive as a bomb-sniffing dog at Washington National. Aired March 27, 1981. (The episode's name was borrowed from one of the all-time-great boxing movies, if anyone cares.)

"Interview with the Hulk": Michael Conrad, of *Hill Street Blues* fame, plays a reporter on the skids who uncovers the scoop of a lifetime: David Banner is alive and well and playing Jack on *Three's Company.* (Sort of.) The reporter blackmails David to get the truth about the Hulk, but learns something about himself in the process. And believe it or not, it's not that he's the king weasel of all time. Aired April 3, 1981.

Headin' off to that oft-photographed alley again, the Hulk cranks it up in "Terror in Times Square."

CBS Photo Archive

The forgettable Hulk

By law, every 10-best list has to be balanced by a 10-worst list. It's not nice to call attention to some nasty odors emanating from the direction of your TV screen, but on the other hand, you can never have enough cheap laughs, especially in a book this expensive. So here goes.

"Never Give a Trucker an Even Break": The highlight, if you can call it that, of this Hulk-meets-the-CB-crowd episode is footage borrowed from Steven Spielberg's epochal TV movie *Duel*. It also stole its title from the W.C. Fields flick *Never Give a Sucker an Even Break*. If you're gonna steal, steal from the best. But like momma said, you shouldn't have to steal at all. Aired April 28, 1978.

"Earthquakes Happen": Now *there's* an original title. No wonder they have to steal from dead, drunken comedians. David tries to borrow a cup of gamma radiation from a nuclear power plant, but then a massive earthquake hits, spilling the gamma radiation all over the floor. If you laughed all the way through *The Poseidon Adventure*, you'll love this; otherwise, you'll yearn for Lloyd Bridges to burst through the door and proclaim, "I picked the wrong week to stop sniffing glue!" Aired May 19, 1978.

"Babalao": The obligatory trip to Louisiana's steamy swamps produces the obligatory encounter with voodoo and possession and strange curses in the moonlight. Scooby-Doo did this one, and better, and it's not often you can say that. Aired Dec. 14, 1979.

"Fast Lane": David rents a car filled with stolen money and is pursued through the desert by gangsters. It takes the better part of 45 minutes for the Hulk to do what you knew he was going to do all along: Stop the gangsters' car, yank them out and beat them up. Not a truly bad episode, but it's not a good sign when you know what's going to happen 15 minutes before it happens. Aired Jan. 16, 1981.

"Long Run Home": Three of the worst episodes in Hulk history aired back-to-back-to-back. This is the Hulk-meets-the-motorcycle-gang one. Think the motorcycle gang is tough but the Hulk is tougher? You've been reading ahead. Aired Feb. 1, 1980.

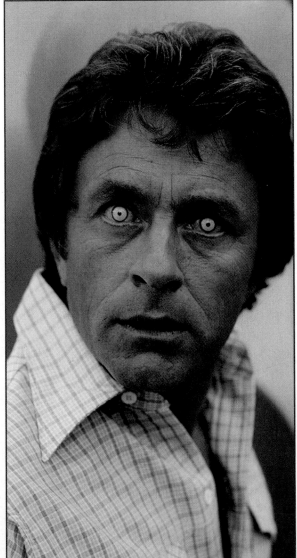

That voodoo you do so well has Bill Bixby seeing green in "Babalao."

CBS Photo Archive

CBS Photo Archive

When the Hulk is bad, as he is in "Fast Lane," the obvious happens obviously: Lou Ferrigno grabs the mobsters (top) and launches them (bottom).

CBS Photo Archive

"Falling Angels": Having just savaged *The Wild Bunch*, the Hulk writers now take their dull knives and chisels to *Oliver Twist*, with the anticipated ugly result. The Hulk finds himself in the middle of a pickpocket ring where all the dips are orphans. No one sings "Consider Yourself," thankfully. Only professional intervention kept the writers from next taking on *Pride and Prejudice.* Aired Feb. 8, 1980.

"The Lottery": David wins the lottery; that's the good news. The bad news is there's no way he can collect his winnings without revealing his identity. When he asks a friend to collect on David's behalf, the friend uses the money to launch a scam. Just in the nick of time, David changes into the Hulk and straightens out the books before the IRS guy does his audit. Something like that, anyway. Aired Feb. 15, 1980.

"Half Nelson": The following statement only has impact when you say it in the tones of the donkey from *Shrek* after he realizes the dragon guarding the castle is female. "Why, of course you're a *girl* dragon," he says, dragging out every syllable. Why, of course the Hulk takes on midget wrestling is this episode. Haven't seen *Shrek*? Do yourself a favor: See it before you see "Half Nelson." And if you never get around to "Half Nelson," that's okay, too. Aired April 17, 1981.

"Patterns": The Hulk crashes the runway of a fashion show trying to help a clothing manufacturer who's under the gun from loan sharks. A frustrating episode, if for no other reason than the crucial Hulk clothing question is never asked: How come the shirt always rips but the pants never do? Aired May 22, 1981.

"Slaves": An escaped African-American convict forces David to work as a slave in a gold mine. Since the Hulk's writers never shied away from borrowing movie plots, why not just borrow *The Defiant Ones* instead? Why not send Lou Ferrigno and, say, Sherman Helmsley careening madly through Southern California backlots, one step ahead of the bloodhounds? Or why not just forget about the whole thing? Aired May 5, 1982.

Hulk animated

The live-action Hulk series is by far the most popular Hulk TV show, but it's not the only one. The Hulk first hit the tube in 1966 as part of the syndicated *Marvel Superheroes* series. The storylines mixed traditional comics plots with *Perils of Pauline* endings, and the cheapo animation made Hanna-Barbera look good. The Hulk shared air time with the Sub-Mariner, Captain America and Iron Man, which was probably just as well. A series as bad as this shouldn't have to be endured alone.

A cartoon Hulk returned to the small screen in 1982 in a Saturday-morning pairing with the Amazing Spider-Man. The Hulk got top billing — and why not? His live-action show did better than Spidey's — and his episodes featured all the familiar comic-book plot twists and characters: Thunderbolt Ross, Betty, Bruce Banner (but no Glenn Talbot, thankfully) and the usual assortment of thrift-store villains.

The show was a quality piece of work by '80s animation standards, but the Hulk portion of it didn't last. Too much Lou Ferrigno too fresh on viewers' minds, evidently. NBC was never much of a Saturday-morning network, anyway.

As the demand for animated television in the mid '90s accelerated like an Italian two-seater, there was no keeping a cartoon Hulk off the small screen. In September 1996, *The Incredible Hulk* half-hour animated series debuted on upstart network UPN (the descendant of Universal, the studio that produced the Hulk live-action series).

As animated series go, the UPN Hulk wouldn't make anyone forget *Rocky and Bullwinkle* — but by weekend-morning animation standards, it was fine. The Hulk rampaged just the way he's supposed to, the gray Hulk and She-Hulk made cameos, and the voiceover cast couldn't be beat: Neal McDonough as Dr. Bruce Banner, Luke Perry as Banner's sidekick Rick Jones, Genie Francis as Betty Ross, Matt Frewer as the Leader, Mark Hamill as Gargoyle, Shadoe Stevens as Doc Samson, Kevin Schon as Major Talbot, John Vernon as Thunderbolt Ross, Thom Barry as Gabriel Jones, Cree Summer as She-Hulk/Jennifer Walters and, best of all, Lou Ferrigno as the Hulk.

The Hulk had a good run on UPN, but things change quick on smaller networks. By the second season, the series was renamed *The Incredible Hulk and She-Hulk*; by September 1999, it was gone.

Gone but not forgotten. With a blockbuster movie under its belt, you'd have to think the chances are good that the Hulk will be back. And with all the cutting-edge animation going on these days ... well, the thought of the Hulk done a la *Samurai Jack* is enough to make your brain water. More or less.

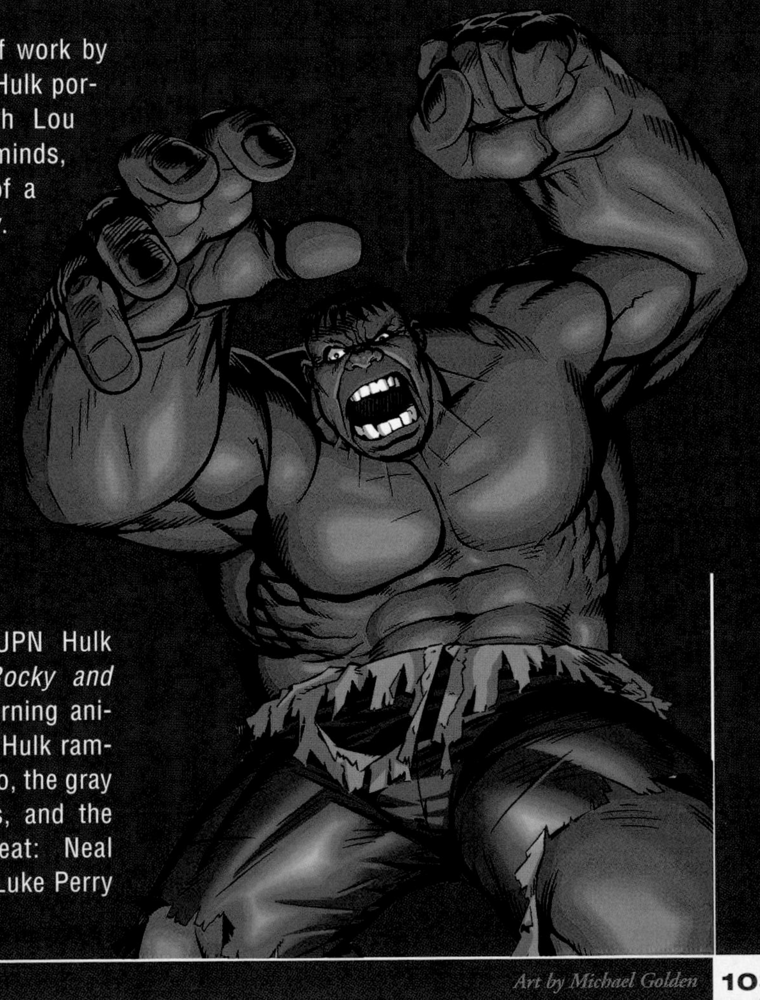

Art by Michael Golden

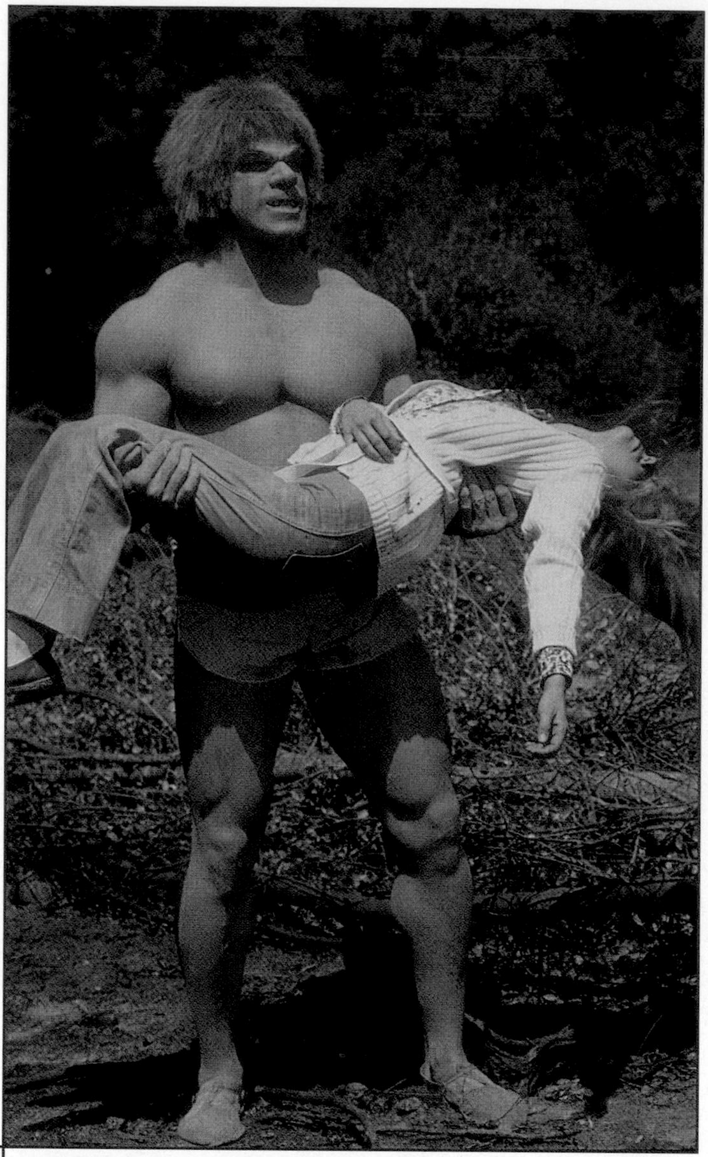

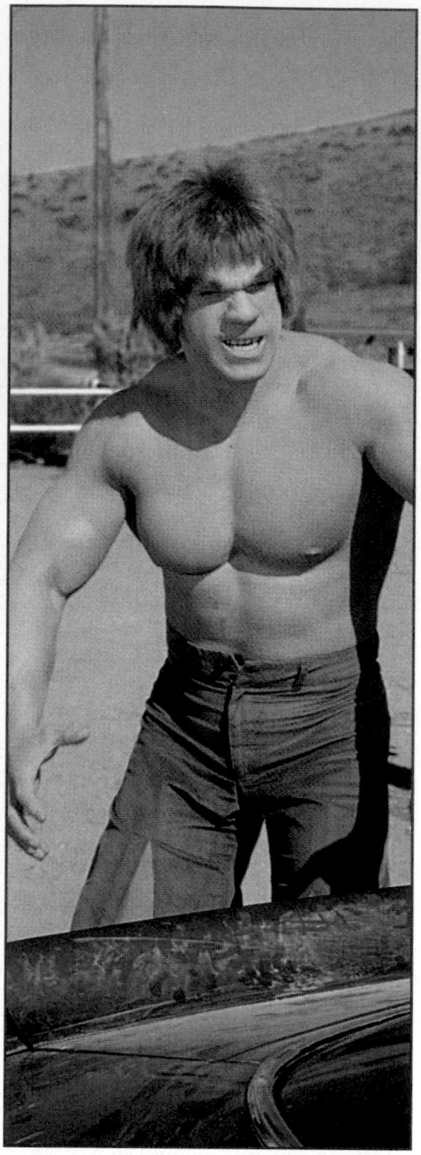

The many faces of the Hulk turn out to be one face, whether he's carrying an unconscious beauty Frankenstein-style (top), taking on the mob (top right) or hangin' with his homies (bottom).

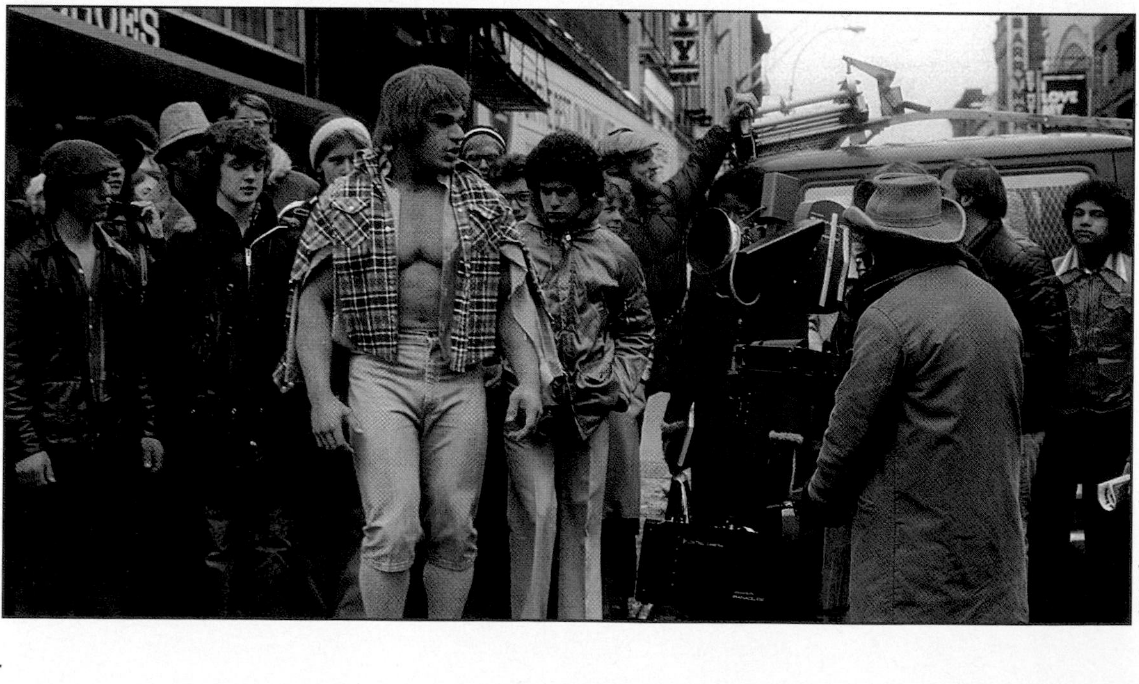

CBS Photo Archive

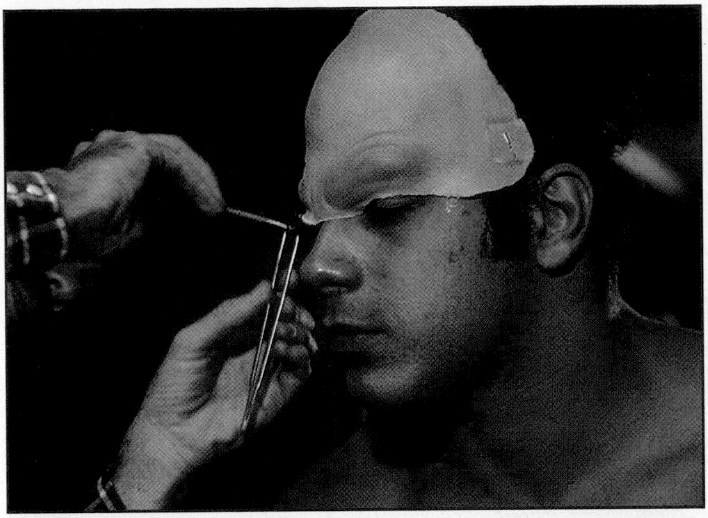

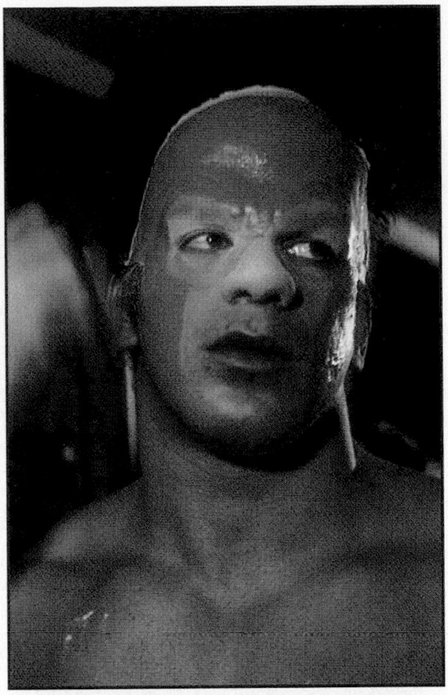

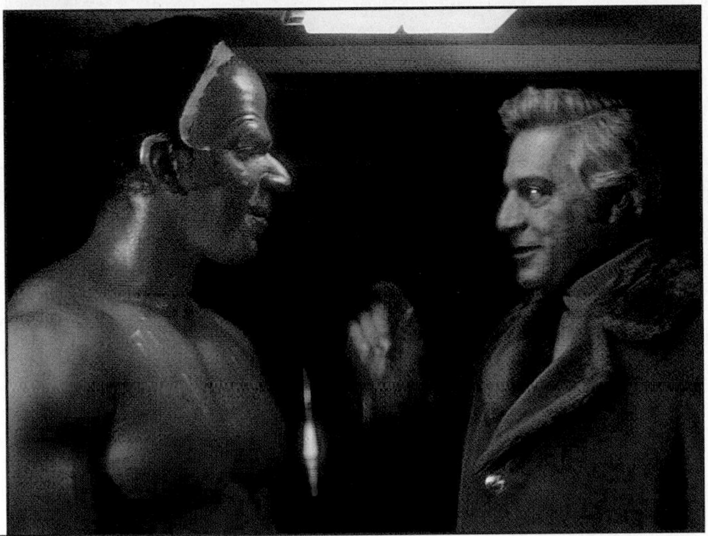

The transformation of Lou Ferrigno into the Hulk was by no means rapid, taking several hours on a good day and involving all manner of glues, masks and putties. That's Lou with his dad, above.

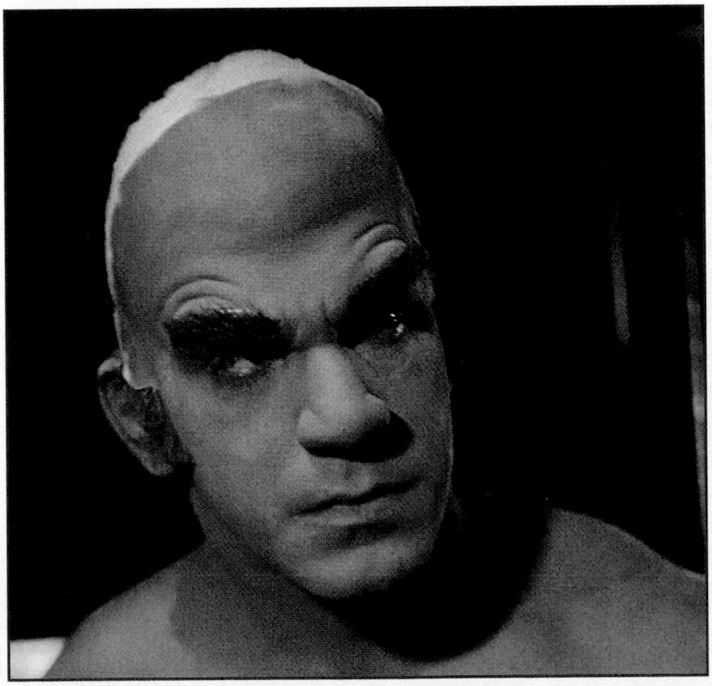

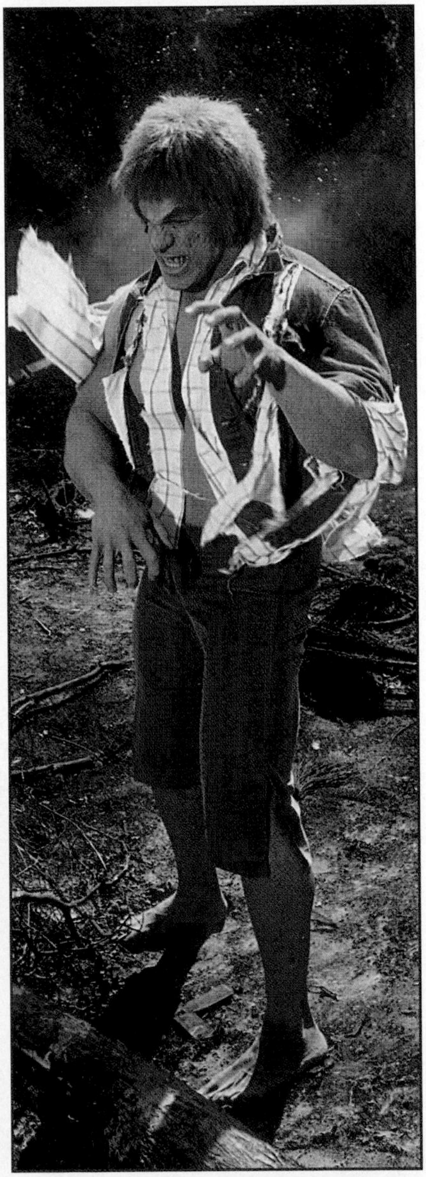

CBS Photo Archive

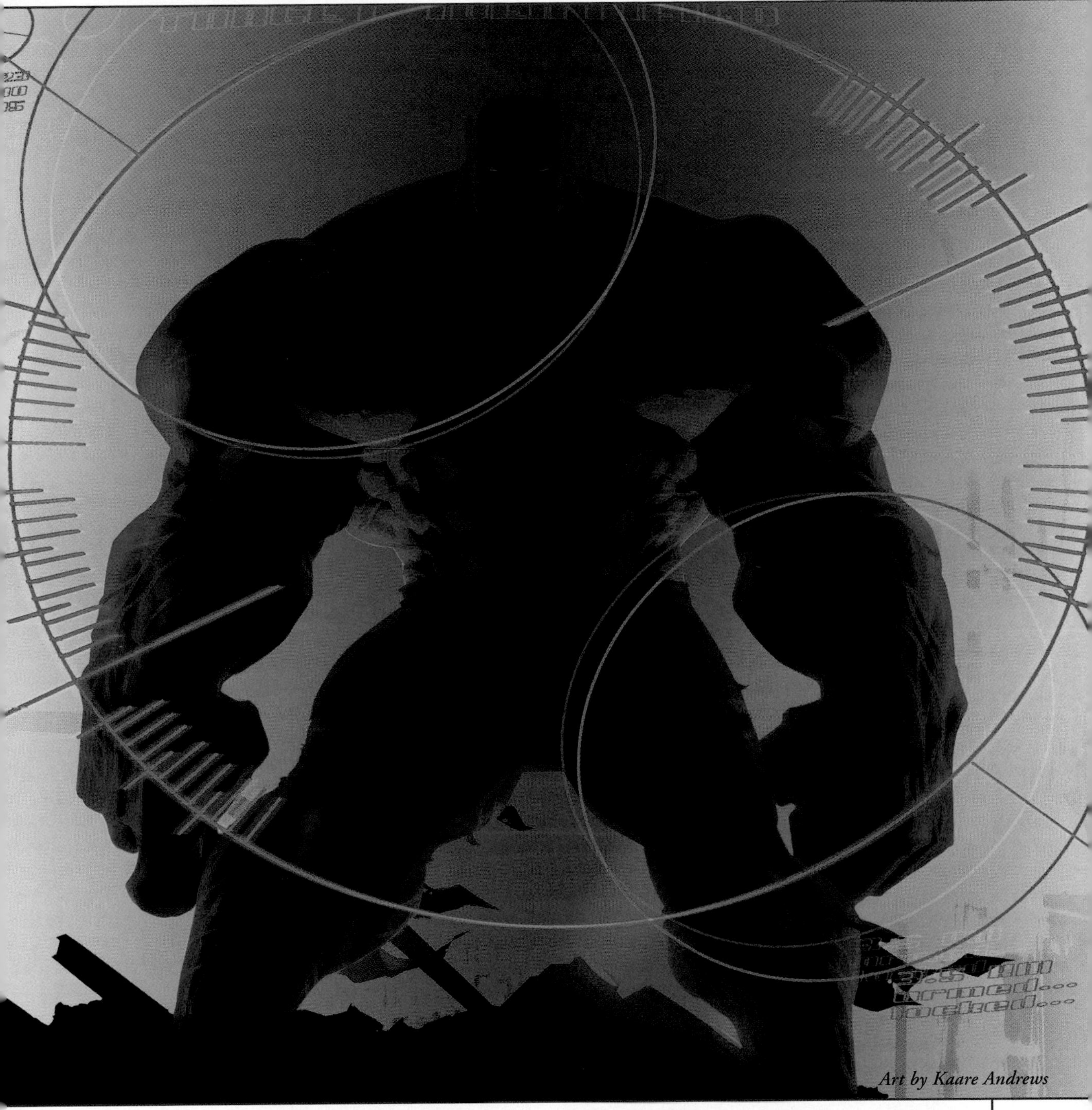

Art by Kaare Andrews

THE HULK REBORN

This ain't your Daddy's Hulk

"Why It's Cool: Writer Bruce Jones has resurrected a classic staple of adventure fiction — the secret evil organization bent on world domination — and we're behind him 100 percent! Gone are the goofy costumes of A.I.M. and the Secret Empire, instead replaced by shadowy types in Gucci suits who hatch elaborate schemes and get electrocuted where they sit when they fail. As Bruce Banner found out in Incredible Hulk #44, *he's dealing with a whole new enemy that he can't just punch out as the Green Goliath."*

The previous paragraph wasn't created specifically for this book. It's too well-written for that. It's from *Wizard*, the leading newsstand magazine covering comics and the people who make them. *Wizard* is as restrained as a howler monkey on crystal meth, and it's written by people who really care that SuperMutantPowerBoy used to wear his rocket-launching prosthetic sinus over *here* and now it's over *there*. But it covers all the comics from *Little Bunny Foo Foo* to *Anatomically Impossible Amazons*, and it actually dislikes many of them.

Liking Hulk comics was not something *Wizard* often did several years ago. The title was in a malaise, which is a polite way of saying it read like the Federal Tax Code. It had lost its focus, which is the only thing that ever made the Incredible Hulk special. If it wasn't Bruce Banner channeling on how he could stop being the Hulk, it was Thunderbolt Ross' obsession with capturing the Hulk, the Leader's single-(big-)minded desire to eradicate the Hulk, or the Hulk just being the Hulk, less dimensional than a wireless-camera pop-up ad and as shaded as a West Texas pitch-'n'-putt.

Most comics are freewheeling, like Ben Affleck pre-J. Lo: They travel the world — and other worlds — interact with humans and non-humans and everything between, and make it seem totally logical. The fact that there are no boundaries, no restraints, no restrictions give these comics their appeal. It

They look like comic creations with only the slightest smidgen of realism, but they look right. This is unreality, after all.

ain't real, and it positively wallows in its unreal-ness. It's why Stan Lee put "fantasy" in the titles of his first superhero comics. Don't try this at home, kids. Not that you ever could.

The Hulk, on the other hand, welcomes outside influences with the same warm-hearted open-mindedness as old-order Amish. What you see here, what you read here, what you say here, stays here. Reading the Hulk should feel like a lockdown at the CIA. It should be stuffy as heck in between the covers. That way when Banner finally goes off, it's the comics equivalent of pearl diving and coming up for air at the last instant. The pressure is finally released; you can breathe again. But before you know it, you're back underwater, back in the pressure, back where you can't breathe, chasing another pearl.

Like your favorite buggy-riding religion, the Hulk thrives on simplicity, which is typically the antithesis of comics plotting. Less-is-more as a comics concept usually goes over like Snoop Dogg at a tent revival. It's usually about pumping up the volume, giving previously buffed superheroes muscles that look like prize zucchini after a summer of Miracle-Gro. Fortunately, the new leaders of Marvel Comics, President Bill Jemas and Editor-in-Chief Joe Quesada, were willing to give less-is-more a shot with the Hulk.

Freethinking Marvel editor Axel Alonso was put in charge of the back-to-basics Hulk. "I was told to make Hulk accessible to new readers, and make it sell better," he says. "Sales figures show we've accomplished the latter, which implies we've done the former." His first project: 2001's *Banner*.

Describing *Banner* in the context of the Hulk is akin to drilling a hole in water. Alonso's take on things is pretty simple, and provides a start: "Bill Jemas wanted to see more monster in the Hulk" — and these days around Marvel what Bill Jemas wants, Bill Jemas gets.

It's just a start, though. Jemas got his super-size monster plus some tremendous writing in the deal. Replacing universal conspiracies and villains that looked like flatworms were the old key adversaries, Thunderbolt Ross and Doc Samson, working their way through a wonderfully claustrophobic plot with a suitably paranoid backstory. The series' title was the tip-off: It's about Banner. Even when it's about the Hulk, it's about Banner — because if you scratch the Hulk deep enough, you'll always find Banner underneath.

The art is another matter entirely. Richard Corben's pencils are unlike anything that ever appeared between the pages of a big green book. Not only that, they go against the fine-lined quasi-manga look of a lot of modern superhero comics. They're stumpy and blocky, and very three-dimensional. They're equal parts *Chicken Run*, Herb Trimpe and *Mad* magazine. And the thing is, they work great. The Hulk and his supporting cast never looked like this in almost 40 years of Hulking; they look like comic creations with only the slightest smidgen of realism, but they look right. This is unreality, after all. There are no gamma-irradiated physicists running around the real world, no green-haired physicians with biceps that seat four comfortably and no half-crazy generals

willing to blow up the whole desert Southwest to accomplish one simple goal. None that we know of, anyway. So who the heck said they were supposed to look *real?*

One more great thing about *Banner:* The part where Doc Samson challenges the Hulk to give him his best shot is better than the best Led Zepplin riff. It blows away a decade of convoluted plots and multiple personalities with one huge shot to the chops. It's definitely one of the 10 best sucker punches in comics history.

Banner laid the groundwork for a revitalization of the *Incredible Hulk* series that kicked off later in 2001. As the *Wizard* review at the top of the chapter says, the new books go back to basics, to the archetypal plots of adventure fiction, to the stuff that made the Hulk such an appealing

Richard Corben's distended artwork on Banner *displayed a cool sort of unreal realism.*

The most personal interpretations of the Hulk occur on covers of Incredible Hulk. *Here, Kaare Andrews does the appropriately disturbing honors on issue #46.*

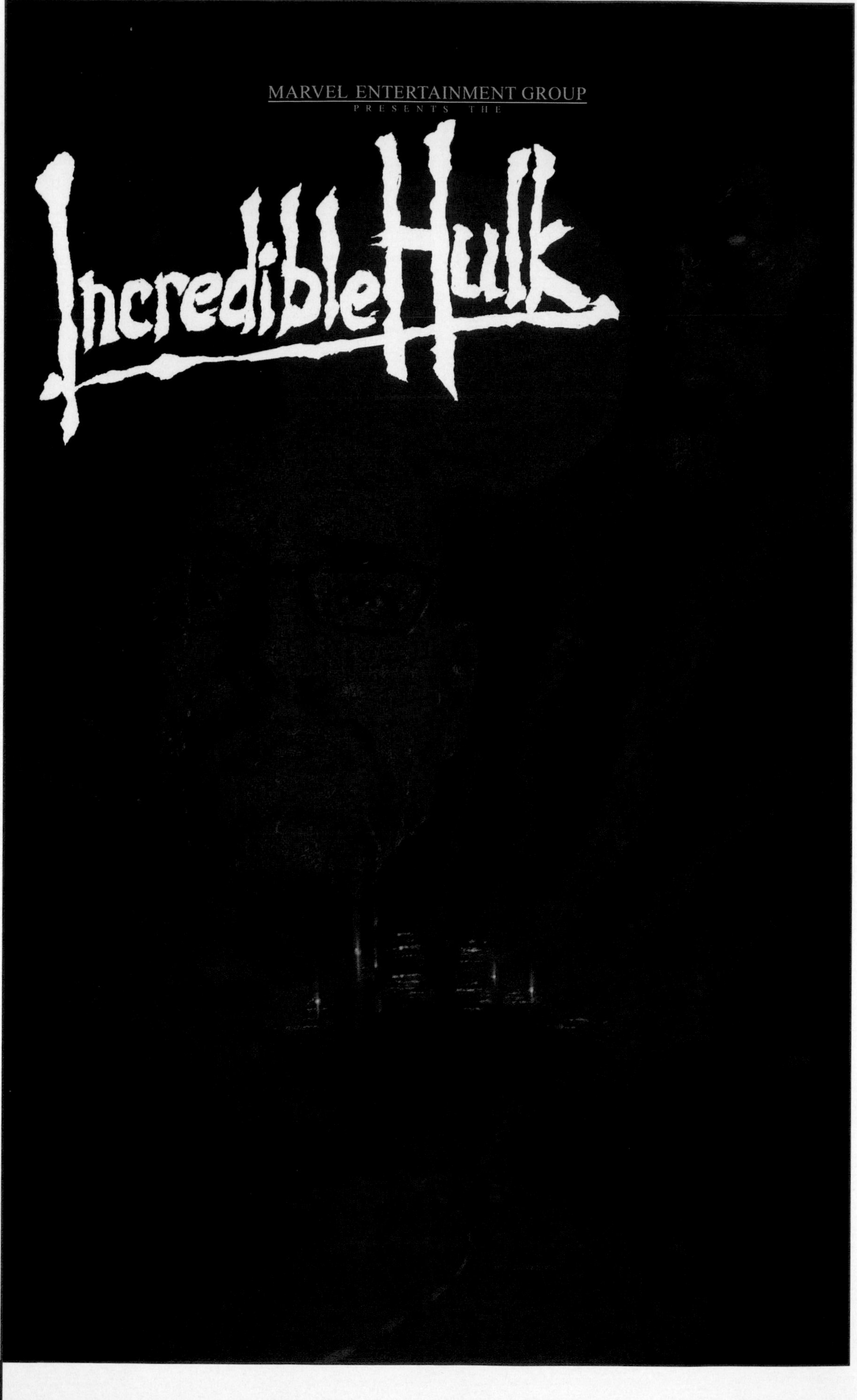
MARVEL ENTERTAINMENT GROUP
PRESENTS THE
Incredible Hulk

hero/anti-hero to start with.

That's where Alonso's coming from, anyway. "For me, the Hulk is Banner's id — times twenty," he says. "I grew up reading the Herb Trimpe Hulk, the 'Bah, puny humans!' Hulk who was always fighting some new monster every issue."

That may be where Alonso's Hulk is coming from, but that's not where he is. The difference between the Trimpe Hulk and Alonso's Hulk is the difference between the old Datsun 280Z and the new Z car, the difference between Robert Johnson and Stevie Ray Vaughan. The books are streamlined like an Olympic bobsled and take you on the same kind of ride: a takeoff sprint, gradual turns at the top, building speed down the straightaway, then the chicane, the big hairpin turn at the bottom and a screeching, skidding finish. Stick an arm out of the sled on the way down, and it's liable to be ripped off. Miss the turn, and you wind up in the hay bales with one hell of a headache. Breathing during the ride is optional but not required.

*Andrews takes the **styles** of 20th-century advertising and popular art — Norman Rockwell, N.C. Wyeth, Hadden Sundblom — and gives them wicked little **voodoo-doll** twists.*

"I was given *Incredible Hulk* with the mandate to make it more accessible," Alonso continues. "For me, that meant getting back to basics, and that meant asking some basic questions. Who is the Hulk? What type of story does this character exist to tell? Certain themes emerged — anger management principal among them. As we all know, when you or I lose our cool, we might break a plate or two; when Bruce Banner loses his cool, he can destroy a city. This has been Banner's lot for 40 years. But this inspired a new question: Is it always a burden? I mean, the bad thing about being Bruce Banner is that you turn into a thousand-pound monster who can level anything in his sight, but it's also true that the good thing about being Bruce Banner is that YOU TURN INTO A THOUSAND-POUND MONSTER WHO CAN LEVEL ANYTHING IN HIS SIGHT. There's a genie inside

you that you can uncork at any moment. And haven't there been moments in your life when you wished you could turn into the Hulk? Isn't there some primal thrill to be found in knowing you've got a thousand-pound Ace up your sleeve?"

The new look of *Incredible Hulk* starts with Kaare Andrews' covers. They're not of this comics world. They're pop art, Roy Liechtenstein in reverse. Liechtenstein made a career of turning comics images into hundred-thousand-dollar works of art; Andrews takes the styles of 20th-century advertising and popular art — Norman Rockwell, N.C. Wyeth, Hadden Sundblom — and gives them wicked little voodoo-doll twists. The result ain't your daddy's Hulk covers, but only in appearance. The inspiration is the same as it ever was.

The insides prove a lesson first taught long ago — taught to Hollywood to great effect by Alfred Hitchcock, and recently rediscovered by claustrophobic, paranoid series like *CSI* and *Alias*: You don't need a lot of plot. You just need a little, provided you do the right things with it.

In the case of the Hulk, the plot is the same old simple thing it's been bringing to the dance since the early '60s: Bad people want to get the Hulk. Bruce Banner wants to stop being the Hulk. Banner is chased. Hulk is chased. Hulk fights back. Hulk smash. Q: If you can't trust your friends, who can you trust? A: Not a damn soul. Not a lot of messing with secret identities here. It's strap it on boys and let's go.

With a plot like this, style points count for an awful lot. It's the difference between Hitchcock's *Rear Window* and the Monty Python version of *Rear Window*, which consists of five seconds of footage of — you guessed it — a rear window. ("Well, let's see now … there's the rear window. He sees the murder. The murderer's come into the room

Shades of the Dragon Lady: The new Hulk stories <u>owe as</u> much to film noir and classic comics like Will Eisner's Spirit *and Milt Caniff's* Terry and the Pirates *as they do to Lee and Kirby. Art by Stuart Immonen*

to kill him, but he's outwitted him and he's all right. The end. I mean, Alfred Hitchcock, who's supposed to be so bloody wonderful, padded that out to one and a half hours.")

Front-flip-nailing figure skaters have nothing on the new Hulk when it comes to style points. The new Bruce Banner is a Zen sort of guy, passive and impassive, in the world but not of the world. The thing he most resembles is a police sketch of a serial killer. He drifts past images of a small boy the Hulk supposedly killed and tries to reconcile him with *him*. Meanwhile, all around him, forces of good and evil are at work — spinning their webs, laying out plans and never ceasing to keep Banner in their crosshairs. You get a real sense that Bruce Banner is more uncomfortable than the back seat of a Yugo, but you're not allowed to dwell on it. Things happen just too damn fast.

You hear about books being real page-turners, quick reads, stories you just can't put down. The new Hulk is all that and more. It's like the front cover comes with skin-activated Super Glue. The minute it hits your hands, it stays there until the last page is

turned. You find yourself racing to the finish like funny cars at the Winternationals. You even read the ad on the back cover. That's how good this book is. And that's mainly Bruce Jones' writing.

"I'd been a fan of Bruce Jones' work from his days at Warren Publications," Alonso says. "He'd dropped out of comics for more than a decade when I first contacted him. I was an editor at Vertigo at the time, and he wrote a number of wonderful short stories for me for my anthologies. When I came to Marvel, and I was assigned Hulk, he immediately came to mind. I gave him a call, and we were on the same page from day one."

Oh, yeah. The Hulk. There's been lots of talk about what Bruce Banner looks like in the new Hulk books, but not much said about what the Hulk looks like. Here's what the Hulk looks like: He looks like he's way too big for this book or any book this side of the Domesday Book.

It looks like he's a size 10 trying to fit into a size three. He looks like steroids on steroids. He looks *real* big. And mean. Probably is mean, too. But in the new Hulk, much of the violence is implied, not shown. The splash pages overflow with violent acts, but for the most part, it's not the Hulk committing the acts. Sometimes — and here's a switch — it's Bruce Banner.

The effect is brilliant. The upshot is that the Hulk smashes like an earthquake, like a tornado. One second it's there and the next it's not. How can you show that sort of instantaneous destruction? The only reasonable answer: You can't.

Chalk that one up to the artists — and Alonso's sure hand guiding the artists.

"As for artists, I was lucky enough to launch with John Romita Jr. and Tom Palmer, both of whom knocked the ball out of the park," he says. "After that, my game plan has been to have a new artist per arc, with Lee Weeks and Stuart Immonen following J.R., and also turning in fantastic work. Next up, Mike Deodato Jr., whose first issue premiered in February. All these artists are different, but what links their work is the fact that they are amazing storytellers."

The supporting cast is pretty memorable

by Hulk standards, too. Villains recite Coleridge — "The Rime of the Ancient Mariner," specifically. Boy hitmen and girl hitmen cohabitate, albeit uneasily. The good guys are sometimes the good guys — but sometimes, they're the bad guys. And vice versa. Shoot-'em-ups that would make the Cosa Nostra proud take place in roadside diners. And in the middle of it all is Bruce Banner, who sometimes goes off and transforms into the Hulk.

If it seems like knives being flung at you from every direction, wait until you read the comic. It's like *North by Northwest* recorded at 33⅓ and played at 78.

The beauty of the new Hulk is that it's totally open-ended. Picture this police-sketch serial killer walking down a country road. A car careens around a corner and nearly hits him. A sniper draws a bead on him but is struck dead by a blow dart just before he pulls the trigger. A boobytrap nails a would-be assassin instead of its intended victim. Mayhem and murder swirl around this impassive walking figure like spun sugar in a cotton-candy machine, but he keeps walking. If he ever stops walking, look the hell out. But he can keep walking forever. At the end of the day, though, he's a lone character walking down a road. It doesn't get any simpler.

Putting it into simpler terms, Alonso explains, "The vision has expanded. Bruce Jones is attempting to explore the line between the man and the monster. What parts of the man can be found in the beast — and vice versa? Early on, we had a conversation where we talked about Bruce Banner's predicament. If the Hulk is a completely different entity than Banner, then that implies moral separation for him, does it not — a get-out-of-jail-free card? However, if the Hulk is NOT an entirely separate entity than Banner, then this raises a host of questions, not the least of which is how account-

able he is for the monster's actions … and to what degree can he hope to exert control over its actions? The plot thickens."

Although inspired by the same source material, the comic book and movie are simply not cut from the same cloth. The movie takes the characters and plotline from the first Hulk comics and filters them through the perspective of a moviemaking genius. The movie is an artist's rendition of a classic hero/anti-hero. It's full of images and effects that only work in a movie. On the other hand, the new Hulk comics are an artist's (and writer's) rendition of a classic hero/anti-hero, full of images and effects that only work in a

Mayhem and murder
swirl around this impassive walking figure like spun sugar in a cotton-candy machine, but he keeps walking. And if he ever stops walking, **look the hell** out.

Art by Stuart Immonen

comic book. Different artists are doing the rendering, and their end products are vastly different. It's okay to like the movie and the comics even though they bear scant resemblance to each other. And people will definitely come to the comic via the movie.

"The movie should bring heightened visibility to the comic for a month or two, but there's no evidence that movies have a long-term impact on the sales of the periodical comics," Alonso says. "There's a window of time during which people look for the char-

It's hard to *imagine* any film fan with taste not liking the cinematic *style* and *pacing* of the new Hulk comics. And it's equally hard to imagine any old-line Hulk fan not being similarly *impressed*.

acter — but after that, things settle back to normal. Spider-Man sales were up well before the movie was released last year. The same is true for Hulk."

Even though the book and movie are a good Pacific Ocean apart in tone and style, it's hard to imagine any film fan with taste not liking the cinematic style and pacing of the new Hulk comics. And it's equally hard to imagine any old-line Hulk fan not being similarly impressed. The Hulk's new creators are Hulk fans, after all.

"It's easier to keep a book going if you have reverence for the character you are editing, which I do with Hulk," Alonso says. "I think that the Hulk is a unique character with lots of pop appeal. We try to tap into this in the comics and on the covers. Hell, the first words uttered in Bruce Jones' first issue were by a street thug to Bruce Banner: 'Those are some ill pants.' That was a shout-out to the old-school fans, for whom purple pants will always be in fashion."

The Ultimates is a different matter entirely. Purple pants are not in fashion in *The Ultimates*. There's no *Ultimates* movie to yank people back into the comics. There doesn't need to be. The comic is part of a Marvel line that's meant to drag a lot of the Marvel pantheon kicking and screaming into the 21st century. Think of them as the comics equivalent of the remake of *Ocean's Eleven*. Some people are really going to groove on George Clooney and Brad Pitt playing like Frank Sinatra and Dean Martin (though not really), and some people wouldn't trade the original Rat Pack for all the counterfeit Julia Roberts DVDs in China. It's all taste — though seeing the Brooklyn Bridge blown to smithereens in the Ultimates/Ultimate X-Men crossover is worth the ticket to that dance.

Think of *The Ultimates* and *Incredible Hulk* as talented teammates in an uneasy partnership. Each one wants to be the star and each one pushes the other higher, faster, farther, bigger. The creative freedom expressed in one is expressed slightly differently in the other. The result is not only good comics but also good comics getting better all the time. Who's against that?

Art by Stuart Immonen

A big green guy on the move: Valuing trends for Hulk comics

"If you want good friends they're gonna cost you," the late great Townes Van Zandt sang (okay, sort of sang-talked), and that's especially true when the friends are issues of *Incredible Hulk.* Hulk comics in general command higher prices now than they ever have — and as long as the comic stays hot and the movie commands attention, that situation's not about to abate. Still, as there are with any collectible, there are peaks and valleys with Hulk comics, and it might be helpful to know where they are if you choose to navigate this particular collectibles minefield.

The Incredible Hulk debuted during comics' Silver Age, which means it's going to take a lot of silver to get a copy of an early Hulk comic over your transom. (Just be thankful the Hulk didn't debut during comics' Golden Age.) A Mint, unrestored copy of *Hulk #1*, the comic that ushered the Green … er, Gray Goliath into the legion of Stan Lee-created superheroes, will set you back in the neighborhood of $15,000 — reasonable for double-wides, pricey for comic books.

If the comic is graded (see below for that whole sordid story) the price can approach that of a six-passenger family sedan, nicely equipped. On the other hand, if the copy is restored — given the comic-book equivalent of botox, with split seams repaired, rips fixed, colors brightened, pages bleached and creases smoothed — you might be able to come away with *Hulk #1* for $5,000 … or less! At that price, why not buy two?

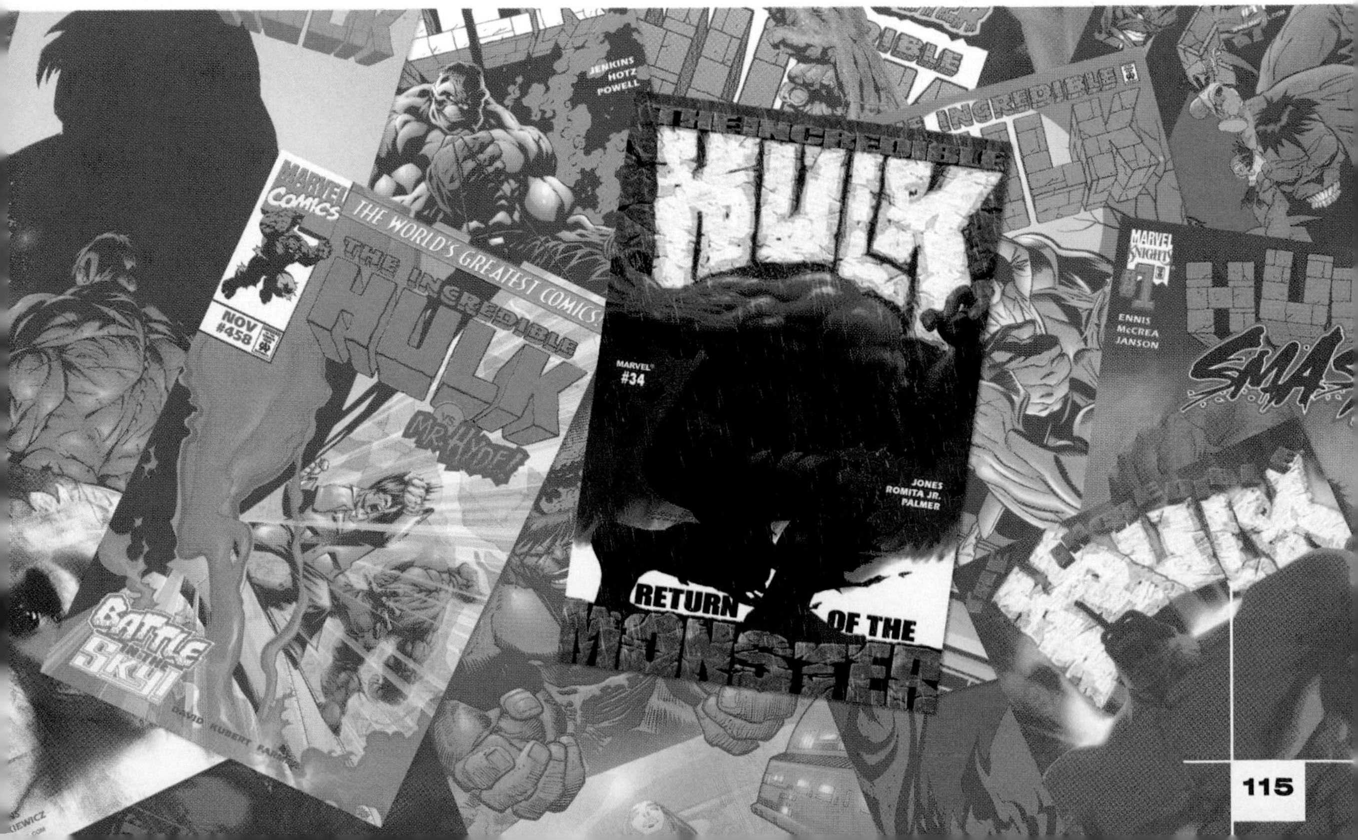
JENKINS
HOTZ
POWELL
MARVEL COMICS
THE WORLD'S GREATEST COMICS!
THE INCREDIBLE HULK
NOV #458
VS MR. HYDE!
THE INCREDIBLE HULK
MARVEL #34
JONES
ROMITA JR.
PALMER
RETURN OF THE MONSTER
MARVEL KNIGHTS
ENNIS
McCREA
JANSON
BATTLE IN THE SKY

On the other hand, the Hulk's first issues are a whole lot cheaper than the issues featuring the first appearances of some other Marvel Silver Age icons. The first issue of *Amazing Spider-Man* books for a cool $33,000. *Fantastic Four #1* will set you back at least $25,000. That makes 15 grand for the Hulk or eight large for *Uncanny X-Men #1* look like a steal of a deal.

And compared to those prices, the price-guide values for garden-variety issues of *Tales to Astonish* are nothing: $75 to $125 can get you one of these — and what they lack in historical significance compared to *Hulk #1*, they more than make up for in virtues like coherence. That is, if you consider coherence a virtue.

The Hulk debuted during comics' Silver Age, which means it's going to take a lot of silver to get a copy of an early Hulk comic over your transom.

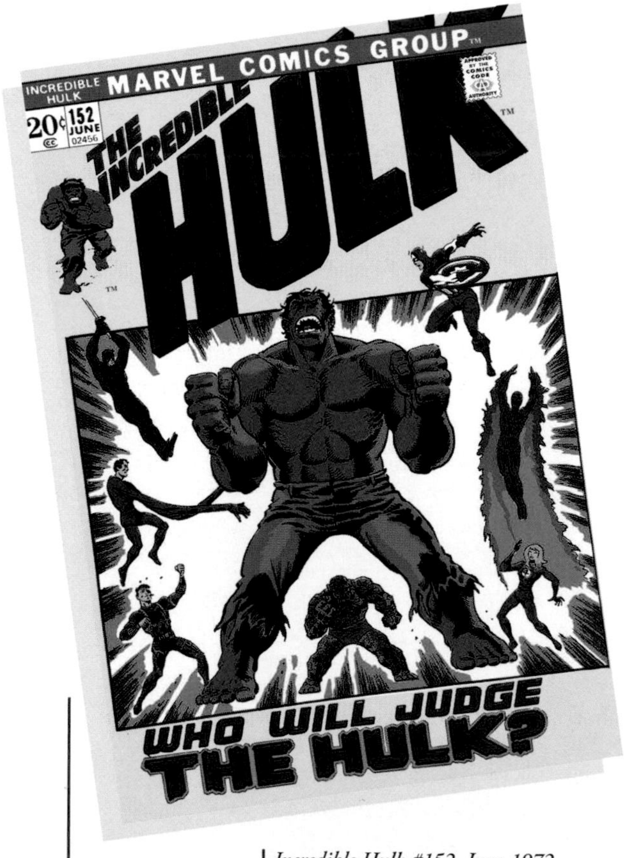
INCREDIBLE HULK
MARVEL COMICS GROUP
20¢ 152 JUNE 02456
THE INCREDIBLE HULK
WHO WILL JUDGE THE HULK?

Incredible Hulk #152, June 1972

When the Hulk got his book back in 1968, he really hit his stride, though you wouldn't know that by reading a comic-book price guide. (The problem is not with your set. The values for comic books are set by complex factors like perceived scarcity, condition rarity, collector demand, eBay listings, winning lottery numbers and whatever sum you get by repeatedly hitting a calculator with your fist.) With the exception of the Hulk's relaunch as a standalone title, most issues from the late '60s and early '70s can be snapped up for $2 to $50, depending on the issue and its condition. The big exception: *Hulk #181A*, the special variation of the Hulk-vs.-Wolverine issue, which brings 20 times the usual rate because it has a fight scene between the Hulk and some mutant Canadian guy.

Among the hottest comics on the current-comic market are *Incredible Hulk #34-42,* from the re-relaunched Bruce Jones *Incredible Hulk* series. Individual books range from around $2 to $20, with *Incredible Hulk #34* leading the way.

Occasionally, huge collections of Hulk comics show up on eBay. For collectors or Hulk fans who don't have many Hulk comics, these collections are fantastic deals on a per-comic basis. On the other hand, if a collection duplicates many of the comics a collector already has, they ought to pass on the collection — unless the comics in the collection are in much better shape than the comics the collector has in his collection. Then it becomes a question of how important it is to have a collection of higher-grade comics as opposed to just a collection of comics. (Answer: If you're thinking there's even the remotest chance you may want to sell a comic at some distant point, buy the best grade you can afford. Otherwise, buy cheap, read it until it falls apart, toss it, and buy another one.)

People are fond of saying that the valuation of comics is an inexact science. They're close. It's not a science. And it's not even inexact.

The real green monsters:
The most valuable Hulk comics

A list of the 10 most valuable Hulk comics is just a space-wasting effort to prove the author knows how to read a price guide, a mindless ploy to titillate readers with comic books they don't stand the chance of a Vespa rider in a Harley bar of ever reading, a paean to the market-inflating numerically graded comics that have taken over more thoroughly than the compact disc. And here it is.

Okay, but this list is different. Many of the 10 most valuable Hulk comics *are actually affordable.* Imagine that. If you're willing to bite the bullet and settle for a comic that looks and feels just like the comic books you grew up with, you can get almost all the comics on this list for less than $1,000 total. That's not chump change for most chumps — but compared to the moola it would cost to snag other 10-most-valuable lists, Hulk readers are getting off easy.

A couple of caveats amidst the cheeriness: You won't be able to buy graded comics at these prices. You'll have to settle for comics that are in their raw state, with pages you can turn and covers you can smell, instead of commoditized comics sealed in plastic more impervious than a Huggies Overnite. Also, the concept of buying the best grade you can afford is temporarily altered to read, "buy the best issue for the money." If you can get a Good copy of *Hulk #2* for $350 and a pristine *Incredible Hulk #187* for the same price, take the lower-grade *Hulk #2.* It's a superior comic, albeit in an inferior grade.

One final warning: Don't believe everything you read in the price guides. (Oh sure. Just when you're able to read a price guide, here comes some goon telling you not to read them.) Price guides take a snapshot of a place in time that's as obsolete as last month's computer. Also, the real worth of a collectible isn't in what a price guide says. It's in what someone is willing to pay. That's why eBay isn't just the world's ultimate marketplace; it's the world's ultimate price guide, too.

Forget the Abomination. *That's* scary.

Hulk #1: $10,000 to $15,000. That's in tip-top-above-the-tip-top-*plus* grade, what the comic-grading services would consider a 9.5-and-above grade, and what are the chances of one of those walking into the local comics emporium? Seriously, who's going to buy the very first issue of a comic and then not touch it for the next 40 years? It happens sometimes — rarely — and that's what this price is: a sometimes — rarely — price. Most of the nicer issues actually changing hands in the marketplace grade out in the 5.0 to 7.0 range and bring $2,000 to $3,000 each, which is still a big price. It's one-tenth of an entry-level BMW, if that's any help.

Hulk #2: $3,500. You figured #2 would be worthless because all the big money was headed after #1? Guess again. Furthermore, a rule around the magazine business is that anyone can sell the debut issue of a magazine; selling the *second* issue is the hard part. Makes sense; you do see fewer copies of #2 — and fewer still of issues #3-6 — which is one of the reasons why the Hulk devolved from a standalone book into half of *Tales to Astonish.* The price for a top-grade non-graded copy is a conceit, since there are no top-grade non-graded copies. Prices drop quickly from those Near Mint heights. You can find a very readable Good to Fine copy of

Hulk #2 for a couple hundred bucks, which is as bargain-priced as semi-scarce Silver Age comics get.

Hulk #3-6: $1,000 to $1,500. The most expensive, professionally graded examples start at $1,000 and reach up toward the sun, only to have their wax wings melt and be sent plummeting back to earth. Readable copies — the unplastic-wrapped ones that actually allow you to turn the pages — go for a couple hundred dollars. Based on contemporary circulation and condition rarity, that's a great price. Just remember: These comics are quaint, jingoistic time capsules, like those healthed movies featuring Mr. Spirochete. If you want something with a plot line that doesn't read like a Quinn Martin production, go for the modern stuff.

Incredible Hulk #181: $1,000 to $1,250. Amazingly, a CGC 9.2 (i.e., Near Mint) graded copy of this book sold for $1,400, which is a whole lotta money for a book that isn't that old and isn't going to be read because it's closed up in an acrylic mausoleum. Still, it's a key book in comics continuity, it pits the two greatest fighters in the Marvel Universe, and the price guide says it ought to sell for $1,000 — so $1,400 is still in the ballpark. The suspicion is that the days of this being a $2,000 comic aren't far off — and might actually be here, should a CGC 9.7 hit the boards.

Incredible Hulk #102: $500. This is the first issue of the relaunched Hulk, and you get what you'd expect for what in essence is a second *Hulk #1:* a price bubble. The bubble isn't that big, but it's there. Lesser-grade copies barely bubble at all.

Tales to Astonish #60 and #61: $250 to $300. The Hulk debuts in Marvel's showcase anthology book. These are darn good comics that are not very expensive. Here you can actually afford to buy the best, and nice-looking collector specials go for less than $100. They aren't true bargains — it's just plain wrong to call something that originally sold for a dime and now sells for $100 a bargain — but they're more than reasonable in the big picture … whatever that picture happens to look like at the moment.

Art by Leinil Francis Yu

Top 10 Hulk battles

These aren't in any order because choosing a favorite Hulk battle is a matter of preference, like Mr. Green vs. Red Fusion vs. Pepsi Blue. With a blindfold on, they all taste like cough syrup and look like a Rorschach blot.

Hardly an issue of the Hulk goes by without Marvel's own Mr. Green doing some memorable rearranging of carbon atoms and elemental iron. Still, just as in *Trading Spaces*, some of the rearrangements work better than others. Those would include:

Hulk vs. Wolverine I, ***Incredible Hulk #181:*** When probably the two greatest fighters in the whole fight-happy Marvel Universe strap it on for the first time, you would expect skyrockets and roman candles. You pretty much get what you expect. Not the most elegantly choreographed fight scenes — but what they lack in execution they more than make up for in blood and fury.

Hulk vs. Wolverine II, ***Incredible Hulk #340:*** The first one went over so well you knew a second one was coming. There isn't much staging for this tussle, not even the Christmas-tree lights used to start drag races. They just wade into each other with fists and claws flying. Great stuff.

MARVEL COMICS GROUP
25¢
181
NOV
THE INCREDIBLE
HULK
AND NOW... THE WOLVERINE!
Incredible Hulk #181, November 1974

Hulk vs. Rhino, ***Incredible Hulk #104:*** The Rhino is clothed in an indestructible hide. The Hulk is indestructible. The Rhino has the unflinching attitude of someone who did 15 hard in Sing Sing. The Hulk seethes primal rage. Who has the advantage? You're right, but the outcome's a lot closer — and much more exciting — than you might think. The first of the great Hulk battles.

Hulk vs. Doc Samson, ***Banner #3:*** There is just nothing in the whole literally bloody Hulk lexicon that can compare with Doc Samson daring the Hulk to hit him with his best shot. Samson dares, the Hulk hits, and the result is about what you'd expect — squared. The punch that turns the Doc's face into a lunar landscape minus the Sea of Tranquility is the single best shot in the Hulk books. Unless you're Doc Samson, of course.

Hulk vs. Hulk statue, **some time after *Incredible Hulk #319:*** Just before John Byrne's run as the Hulk's mastermind ended at six issues, the Superman writer-to-be disclosed his plans for one of the next issues. The Hulk — a truly mindless engine of destruction in Byrne's incarnation — would encounter a statue of himself crafted from the tougher-than-dirt element adamantium (the same stuff that made Wolverine and his claws well-nigh indestructible) and imbued with a life force. It would be the Incredible Hulk vs. the Indestructible Hulk. Talk about your battle for the ages.

Hulk vs. the Ultimates, ***The Ultimates #5:*** You don't usually remember a fight scene for the dialogue, but some of the lines the Hulk cracks off in the course of this head-knocking with Captain America and the gang are funny enough to give Shaquille O'Neal a bladder-control problem. The action's pretty active, too; the scenes of Captain America getting tossed around by an unlucky-in-love Hulk — and vice versa — have all the bite of habanero-jalapeño Altoids.

Continued on page 121

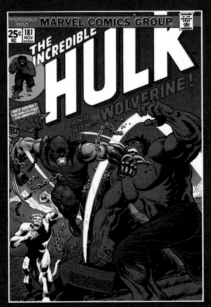

I'm not bad, I'm just drawn that way

The ever-changing Hulk

Times change, people change, and no one looks like they did 40 years ago — not even Bart Simpson. God put pictures on driver's licenses to remind us of that fact. But when it comes to changing looks drastically overnight, Robert DeNiro has nothing on the Incredible Hulk.

Of course, there are reasons for this other than just an artist's desire to assert his view of how the Hulk should look. The Hulk has been through a lot on the plot-and-character side during the last 40 years, and many of those story-borne changes have required the Hulk to alter his appearance. In a very small nutshell, the Hulk's creators have never been in complete agreement on how smart the Hulk should be. Every time his IQ changes a couple of points, his looks change, too.

Thank goodness this just happens to the Hulk. Imagine if everyone's appearance was IQ-related. Would George W. Bush be distinguishable from an armadillo? Only when he lays on his back.

Another dilemma the Hulk has that other super-creations don't is that his costume is his birthday suit. When it changes, he has to change. Spider-Man and Daredevil have it soft; all it takes is a trip to Ballet Bob's Leotardland for them to change colors. The Hulk needs 12 pages of continuity and/or a new creative team.

Even a simple streamlining takes work. Tony Stark changes his Iron Man getup more often than Christina Aguilera changes hair colors. Big deal: It's just sheet metal. For the Hulk to go from semi-prehistoric to quasi-Rambo, it takes 24 pages of continuity *and* a new creative team *and* yet another twist on the origin story *and* an IQ adjustment — to the Hulk, not necessarily to his readers.

These obstacles haven't stopped the Hulk from making with the makeovers. Hulk historians in turn have cataloged all these variations and given them names: the Savage Hulk, the Bannerless Hulk, Savage Banner, the Gravage Hulk, the Gutenberg Hulk, the Professor and Mary Ann. They're available for the viewing, along with pages and pages of 100-percent-accurate (right down to the last

The early Hulk definitely owed a debt to Universal's Frankenstein. Art by Jack Kirby

Continued from page 119

Captain America's well-nigh indestructible. So is the Hulk. This fight could go on a while. Art by Bryan Hitch

Hulk vs. Absorbing Man, *Hulk* **movie:** Does anyone stage fights with more style than Ang Lee? Errol Flynn and Douglas Fairbanks may have swashed more and buckled down — but when it comes to setting the mood, taking the angles and assuming the positions, Lee is the unsurpassed master. The Hulk's climactic battle substitutes Stravinsky, Sterno and death metal for the rice wine and poetry of the duels in *Crouching Tiger, Hidden Dragon,* but the result is every bit as breathtaking. Movies are a bottom-line art; it's hard for them to be good if they don't look good. The movie builds and builds to this single fight, so it has to look good. And does it ever.

Hulk vs. Abomination, *Incredible Hulk*

There are no friends like old lovers, or words to that effect: The Hulk and the Abomination (shown here in modern garb) go back a ways. Art by Mike Deodato Jr.

#54: The preview in *Wizard* showing the new-and-improved Abomination is all the justification you need. It doesn't matter that the only part of the Abomination that's shown is his eye. That's one evil eye, and it has the calming effect of Muhammad Ali staring down Joe Frazier before the Thrilla in Manila. You just know this one's gonna hurt.

Hulk vs. Sub-Mariner, *Tales to Astonish* **#100:** The cover says it all: a duel to the near-death high above the Sun and Fun Capital of the World, Miami Beach. The inside pages are just as swell, too. Forget the setup for the fight — an ultimately lame plot about the Puppet Master making a Hulk figure out of radioactive clay, and using it to control the Hulk and send him headlong into an initially peaceable Sub-Mariner. Focus instead on the dynamic fight pages, courtesy of the underrated Marie Severin. The story ends with a typical-for-the-time anticlimax, but face it: the Hulk and the Sub-Mariner held down either end of *Tales to Astonish.* You think one would really kill off the other?

Hulk vs. Thing, *Incredible Hulk #122:* Any lover of the Fantastic Four will find this issue irresistible, though the outcome is absolutely no surprise. If it had ended logically, the Fantastic Four would have been the Fantastic Three from that point forward, because the Hulk had already taken down villains more powerful than the Thing. It would take all the Marvel Bullpen's powers of manipulation to keep the Thing's balls in the air. Bottom line: Ain't it great to read, "It's clobberin' time" within a Hulk comic?

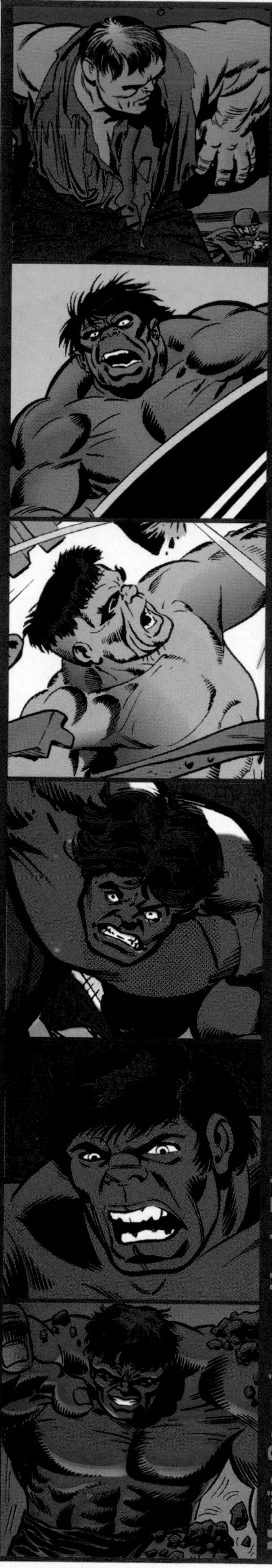

Jack Kirby · John Buscema · Steve Ditko · Gil Kane · Herb Trimpe · Marie Severin

footnoted appearance of the Bi-Beast) Hulk facts and fun, at the outstanding Hulk fan site Leader's Lair (leaderslair.crosswinds.net/gammapeople/incarnations/incarnations.html). If you regard this book as the first step toward all-out Hulk love, Leader's Lair supplies steps two through ten.

Jack Kirby's Hulk, whether gray or green, was straight do-not-pass-GO-do-not-collect-$200 out of the Frankenstein movies. It's not the shape of his body so much as the look around the eyes that says, "You'd really like me if I don't tear you to pieces first." Kirby's Hulk is actually good-looking the same way Howie Long or Dolph Lundgren is good-looking. The only difference is the Hulk's never pitched TV antennas for Radio Shack. Lucky Hulk.

Kirby's Hulk, like most of his Marvel superheroes, perfectly complemented Stan Lee's stories. The First Comic-Book Soap Opera needed a protagonist that looked like a soap-opera hero, and the Hulk's heavy brow and dreamy eyes were straight out of *The Edge of Night.*

From Kirby, the Hulk passed to Marvel house artists like Gil Kane and Steve Ditko, whose Hulks were more massive and muscular than Kirby's, with faces that wouldn't have looked out of place on NFL football cards. Compared to some recent Hulks, these Hulks looked about as threatening as Charlie Brown, but don't be fooled. The power's there. Dump K2 on one, and he'd pop out the crest grunting, "Puny human! Second-largest mountain in Himalayas no match for Hulk!" What was huge in comics then was simply different from what's huge now. Perspective wasn't overblown. Ten feet tall meant 10 feet tall. And simple desk calculators cost $500.

Herb Trimpe's take on the Hulk is only a couple years removed from Kirby's, but almost everything about the character is different — from his posture to his facial features to his hairstyle. Trimpe was more influenced by *National Geographic* than Universal monster movies. His Hulk is straight out of the Cro-Magnon era as opposed to the black-and-white era. Not only did Bruce Banner get bigger and stronger when he changed into the Hulk, but he took two big steps back down the evolutionary ladder — which dovetails perfectly with the whole primitive-superego-Freudian-manifestation thing that was a big part of the late-'60s Hulk.

Trimpe's Hulk served as *the* Hulk until the mid-'70s, when the Green Goliath assumed the "classic Hulk" look. The creature was more massive, proportioned more like a modern comic-book superhero, but the face was less prehistoric. That look worked for a decade, with only slight variations in details like the length of his hair as the character passed from artist to artist, writer to writer and Freudian motivation to Freudian motivation.

This is the Hulk of the Hulk Flying Fist and the Hulk Bop Bag, though thankfully not the constipated-caveman Hulk of the Hulk Power Putty.

Top 10 Hulk comics

Top-10-comics-of-all-time lists are jive. They're ego-stroking exercises for the intermittently informed people who compile them, feeble shouts of, "Look at me! My opinions are bigger than yours!" directed at a world that could care less, infantile expressions of opinions formed no more distinctly than instant oatmeal. They're idiotic and pathetic, and make the people who compile them look idiotic and pathetic, too. So here's mine.

Actually, this isn't a 10-best-Hulk-comics list. That *would* be a useless ego-stroking exercise. This is a you-can't-go-wrong-with-these-10-or-so-issues list. Want 10 or so great issues of the Hulk you'll read again and again and never dream of locking away behind tamper-evident plastic? Here you go. And the best thing about these comics is that every one except the origin issue can be picked up used for a reasonable price, proving once more that great art not only doesn't have to cost an arm and a leg, it doesn't even have to cost a toenail job.

Hulk #1: No matter how many times the origin story has been redone, there's nothing like the first time. The story shows its age, but so does every other 40-year-old comic book. You want contemporary storytelling, buy a contemporary comic. Other issues would fill in the ample backstory to the origin, but this one just chugs along like Rick Jones' roadster, speeding to a by-now inevitable conclusion.

Tales to Astonish #90: The Abomination shows up for the first time, and seeing how he's still around giving the Hulk all he can handle, and seeing as how he made Betty Banner the Hulk's ex for good, it might not be a bad idea to check out his surprisingly humble origins.

Incredible Hulk #147: As mentioned repeatedly, as fine a Hulk issue as there is. As fine a comic as there is. As fine a fusion of art and literature as there is. And it can spin straw into gold, too! Somewhere, Rod Serling is smiling.

Incredible Hulk #314-319: John Byrne's run on the Hulk was unlike anything before or since. If you like what he did with Superman, you'll love what he does with the Hulk. If you've never heard of John Byrne, this'll get you introduced. If you've never heard of Superman, there's

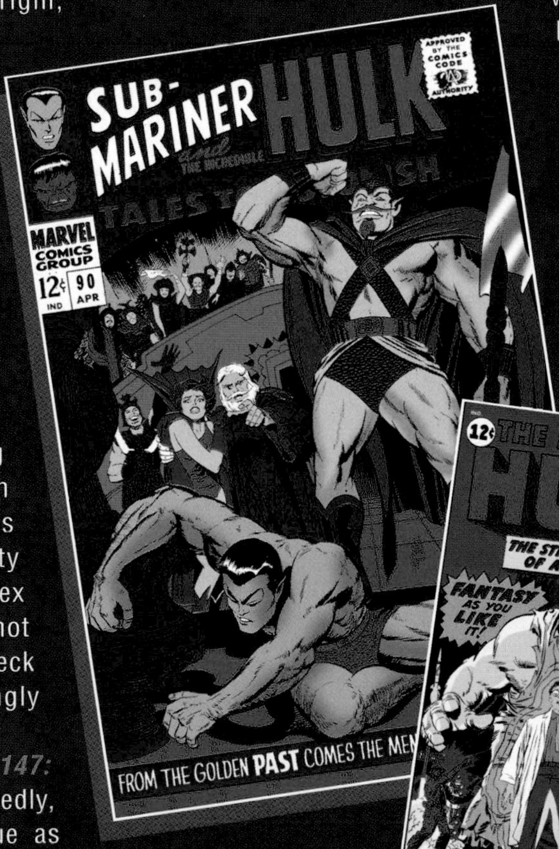
APPROVED BY THE COMICS CODE AUTHORITY
SUB-MARINER
HULK
and THE INCREDIBLE
MARVEL COMICS GROUP
12¢
90 APR
IND
FROM THE GOLDEN PAST COMES THE ME

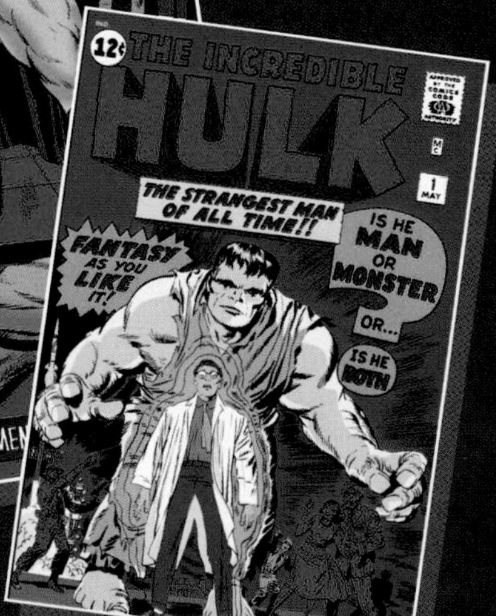
12¢ THE INCREDIBLE
HULK
1 MAY
THE STRANGEST MAN OF ALL TIME!!
FANTASY AS YOU LIKE IT!
IS HE MAN OR MONSTER
OR...
IS HE BOTH

Continued on page 125

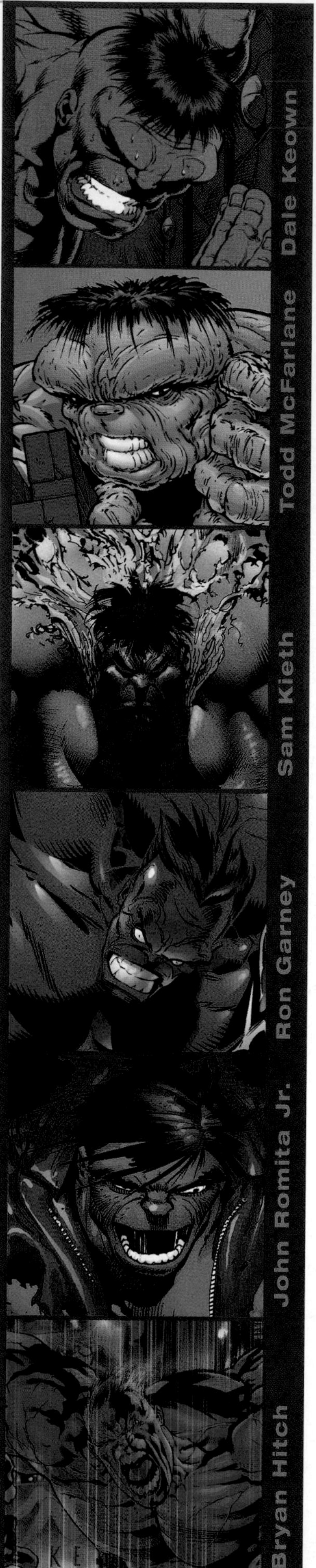
Dale Keown
Todd McFarlane
Sam Kieth
Ron Garney
John Romita Jr.
Bryan Hitch

From the mid-'80s through decade's end, the Hulk's appearance evolved subtlely. Not only did he trade his faded green epidermis for a shiny new gray skin, but he also got corners. Like a new Cadillac less the incongruous Led Zeppelin soundtrack, the Hulk became more angular and stylized as he sprang from the pencils of energetic young artists like *Spawn* creator and Mark McGwire home-run-ball owner Todd McFarlane.

Corners on the Hulk were just the start. Winds of change were sweeping through comics, but no one realized it at first. They just thought someone left the door open at the House of Ideas.

In the end, change was mostly good. Getting there was occasionally hell.

Now is not the time to get into everything the Hulk endured in the late '80s and early '90s. Suffice it to say he went through the whole *Lord of the Rings* trilogy, a couple of *Star Wars* movies, the *Godfather* saga, *Lost Weekend* and *A Beautiful Mind*, with snatches of *Monsters Inc.* thrown in. On the other hand, the various Hulks spun out of the plot machinations of the early '90s looked great, and very much unlike the Hulks of the past. From the Gray Hulk/Joe Fixit to the Professor, from the Future Hulk to Shrapnel (Shrapnel?!?), the Hulks of the early '90s were huge, stylized, small-headed and angular, very much in keeping with the savage-big-guy style of new-wave superheroes like Dale Keown's The Pitt. The old Marvel war-horse Hulk was gone; equally gone was the classic Hulk. This was the new new Hulk. How new? He often slung bandoliers over his shoulders and took after his enemies with a really big machine gun, like Rambo with a punk cut. That's how new.

From those Hulks, it's a sharp left turn down a gravel road to Richard Corben's stumpier, more cartoonish Hulk, which looks nothing like anything in the Hulk pantheon before or since. And from there, it's another quick right to the Hulks of the new *Incredible Hulk* comics and *The Ultimates*. The upcoming Loeb-and-Sale *Hulk: Gray* promises yet another Hulk look, different from the McFarlane and Kirby gray Hulks while retaining those Hulks' power and style.

All these modern Hulks balance the hugeness of the early '90s comics with the humanness of the '70s and '80s versions. They fit their books; they look right. Do they represent the quintessential Hulk? It depends — or, as Bill Clinton said, "What exactly do you mean by 'the'?"

The Hulk's artists have given readers their money's worth through the years without giving them the same Big Green Guy all the time. That's tough to do, because it's not just reworking the sheet metal. It's messing with the skin. Considering that the Hulk has had his skin messed with at least as much as Michael Jackson, he still looks good. For a Hulk.

Continued from page 123

really nothing to suggest, short of asking Marvel President & COO Bill Jemas for a job.

Incredible Hulk #367-368: Sam Kieth *(The Maxx)* and Dale Keown *(Pitt)* went on to draw big guys for Image, the creator-owned comics company that hauled comics kicking and screaming into the modern era. In these two issues they show their chops on the biggest big guy of all. Peter David's stories stick to the white line, avoid the ditches and give plenty of room for the Hulk to do what he does best.

Banner #1-4: There are four issues in the miniseries; they read incredibly well and breathtakingly quickly. The only thing they leave to doubt is which is better: Richard Corben's art or Brian Azzarello's writing.

***Incredible Hulk #34,* etc.:** Biased assessment? Maybe. Caught up in the heat of the moment? Possibly. Certainly the latest incarnation of the Hulk builds on much of what has gone before, and there couldn't be the new one without the old one. By the same token, there couldn't be a Corvette without a Model T — yet when someone comes looking for a car that performs as good as it looks they don't linger over Lizzie. All comic books are products of their time and place. They're as ephemeral as printed literature gets. But if any comics are built to last, and able to transcend styles and eras, it'd be the new Hulk books.

***The Ultimates #1,* etc.:** Unlike *Incredible Hulk*, *The Ultimates* swill in their time slot. Like the Hulk books, *The Ultimates* do what they do with such incredible skill and style they can't be put down. Few comics are as out-and-out fun — and remember, that's why people started reading comics in the first place.

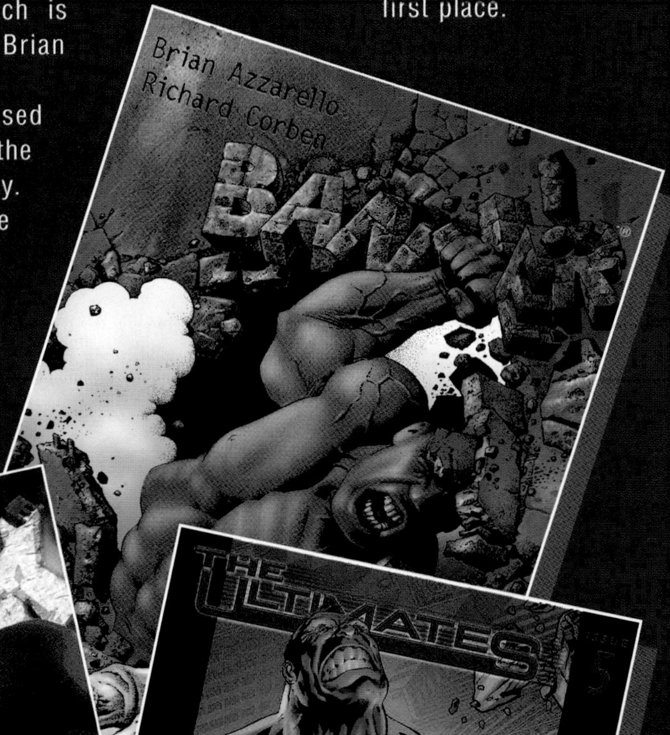
Brian Azzarello
Richard Corben
BANNER

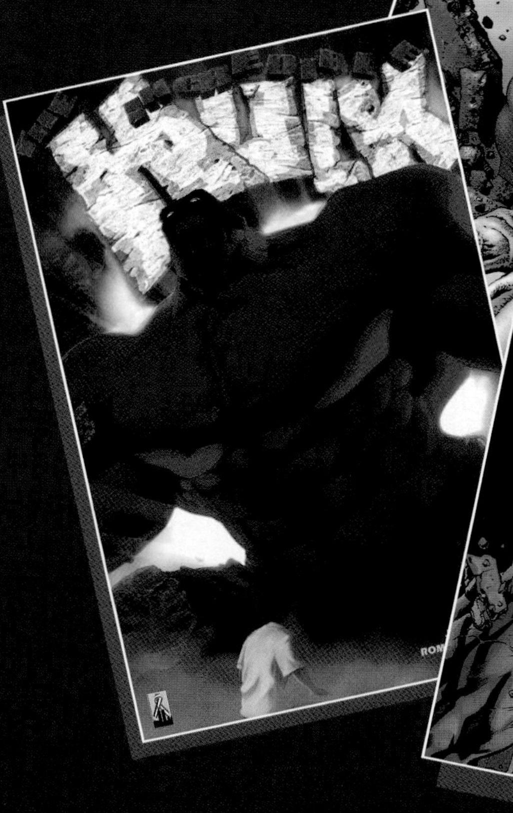
THE INCREDIBLE HULK

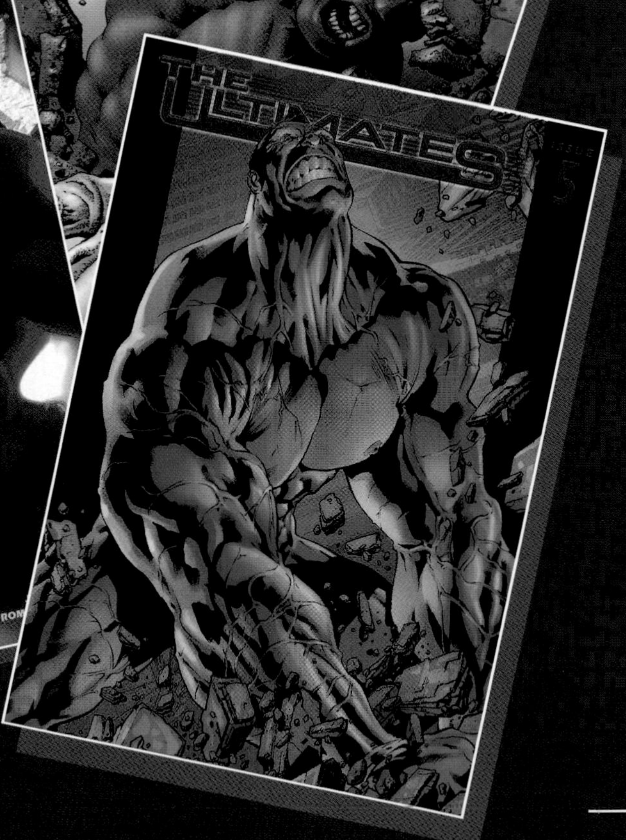
THE ULTIMATES

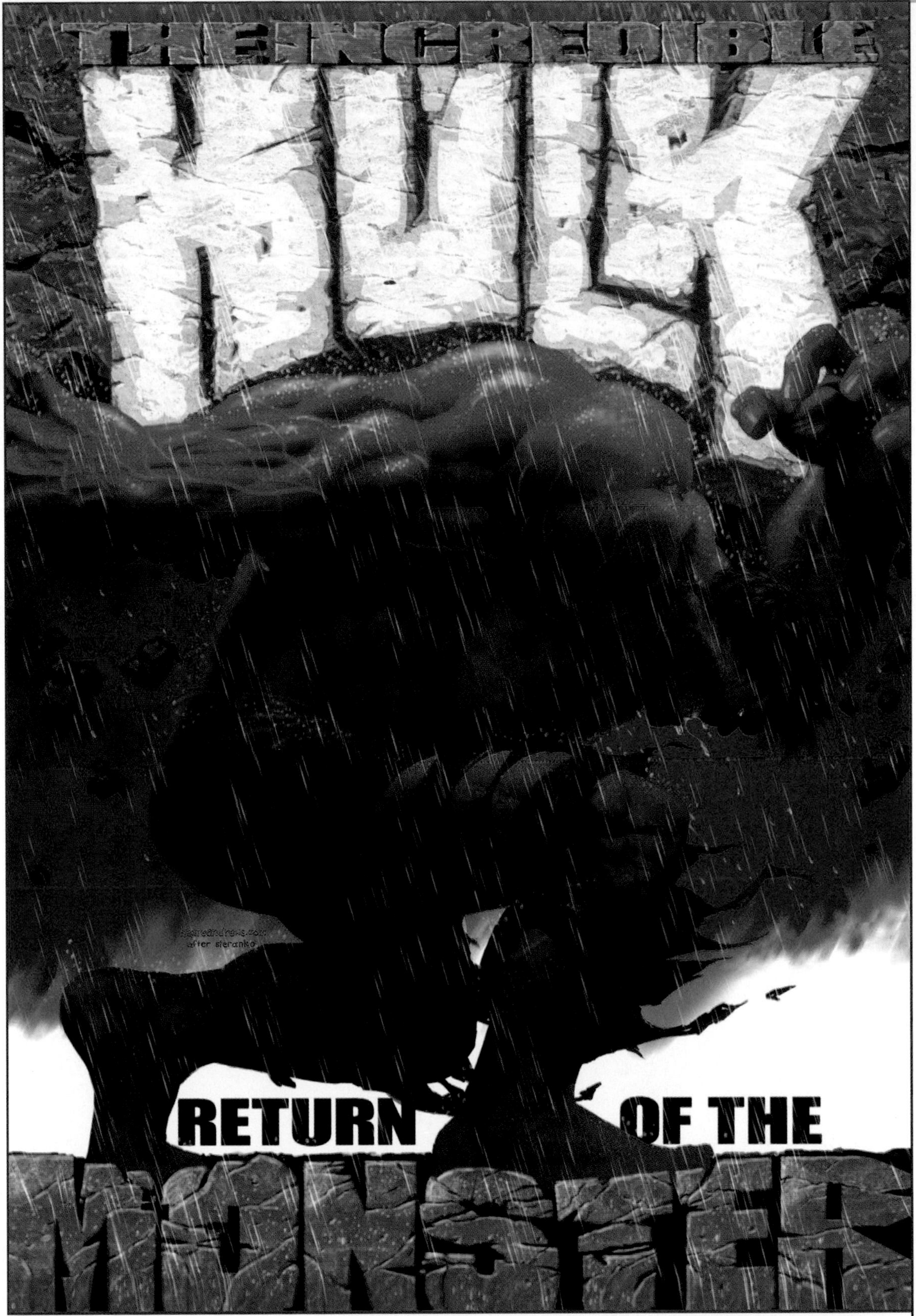
THE INCREDIBLE
HULK
RETURN OF THE
MONSTER

Incredible Hulk #34

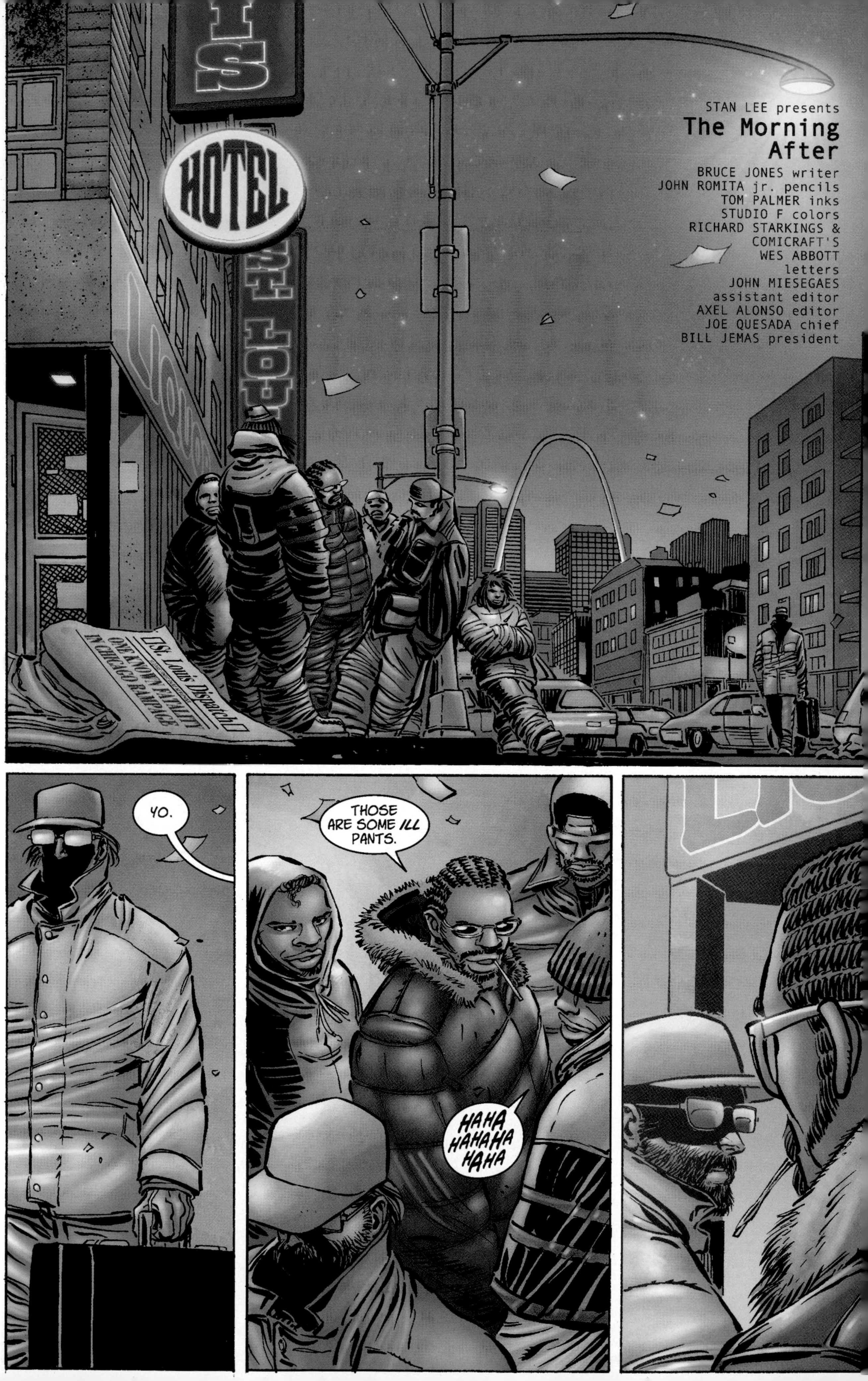
STAN LEE presents
The Morning After
BRUCE JONES writer
JOHN ROMITA jr. pencils
TOM PALMER inks
STUDIO F colors
RICHARD STARKINGS & COMICRAFT'S WES ABBOTT letters
JOHN MIESEGAES assistant editor
AXEL ALONSO editor
JOE QUESADA chief
BILL JEMAS president
HOTEL
St. Louis Dispatch
ONE KNOWN FATALITY IN CHICAGO RAMPAGE
YO.
THOSE ARE SOME ILL PANTS.
HAHA HAHAHA HAHA

-- REPORTS SO FAR CONFIRM ONE OFFICIAL DEATH -- THAT OF NINE-YEAR-OLD RICKY MYERS. MIRACULOUSLY, NO ONE ELSE WAS HURT IN THIS BRUTAL, DELIBERATE ATTACK ON DOWNTOWN CHICAGO BY THE --

TWENTY BUCKS A NIGHT. NO TV. BATH DOWN THE HALL.

ONE NIGHT.

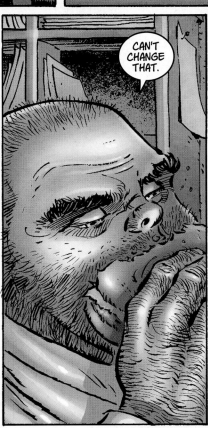

CAN'T CHANGE THAT.

TWO NIGHTS.

-- NOW HAVE SOME TAPE FROM CNN SHOWING THE CHILD'S PARENTS, MR. AND MRS. TRAVIS MYERS, AT MT. PROSPECT HOSPITAL WHERE THEIR SON RICKY WAS PRONOUNCED DEA--

KLK

-- PRESENT WHEREABOUTS OF THE CREATURE ARE NOT KNOWN. IT IS SUSPECTED THAT THE MONSTER IS ONE *BRUCE BANNER*, THE NUCLEAR PHYSICIST WHO --

-- CAN'T BLAME BANNER. IT'S NOT LIKE HE CAN CONTROL IT. IT'S LIKE A *JEKYLL N'* --

-- MUST BE DONE. A LITTLE KID'S DEAD. I DON'T CARE IF HE'S *RESPON*--

HAIR COLOR

Exercises in Mind-Control Yoga

TAMING INNER

-- MILITARY CAN'T HOLD HIM AND HE CAN'T CONTROL HIMSELF THEN THERE'S ONLY ONE THING TO DO AS FAR AS --

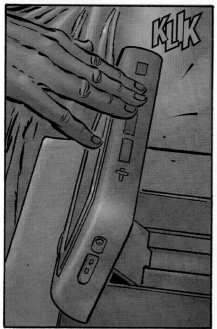

KLK

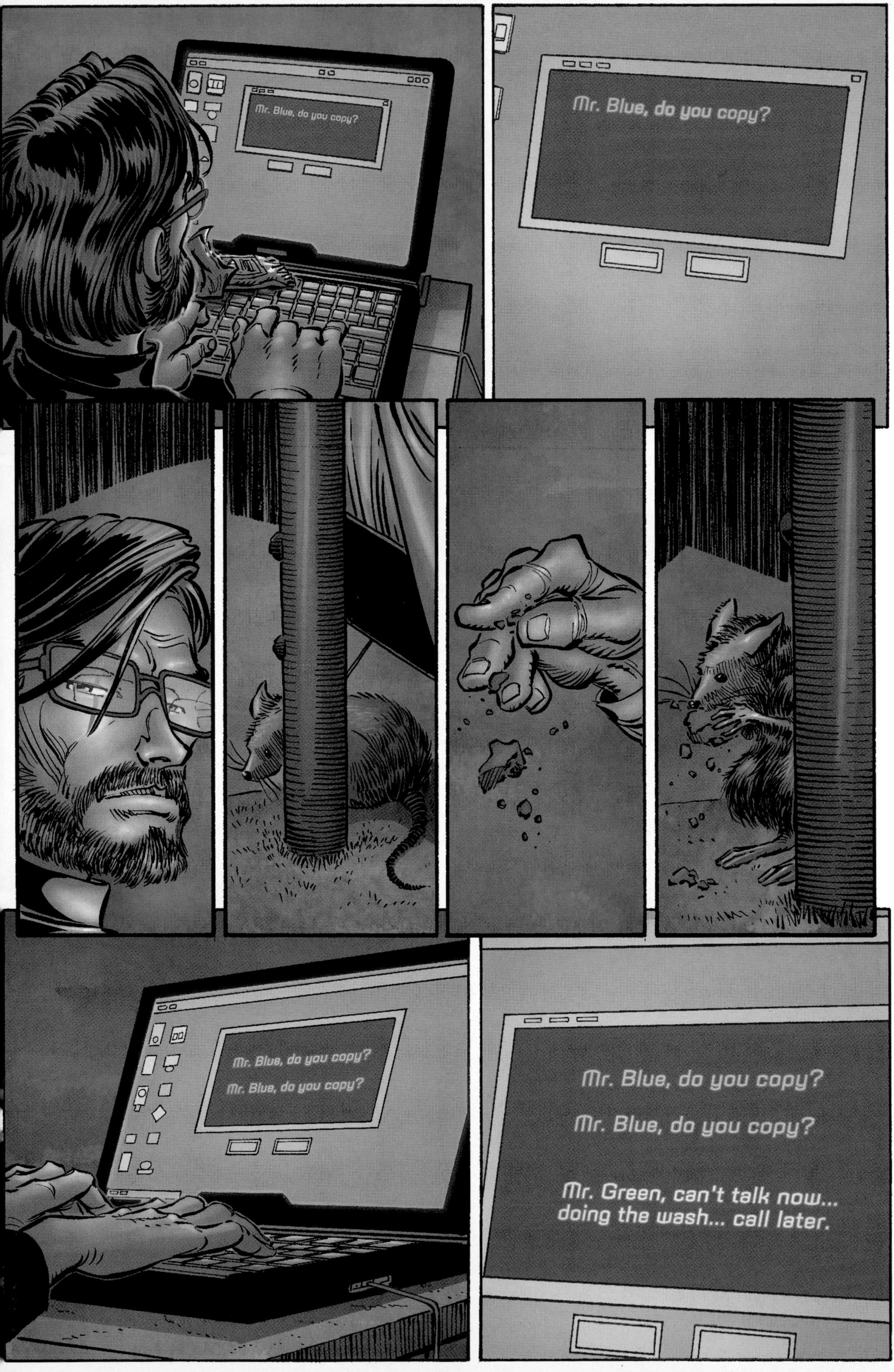
Mr. Blue, do you copy?
Mr. Blue, do you copy?
Mr. Blue, do you copy?
Mr. Blue, do you copy?
Mr. Blue, do you copy?
Mr. Blue, do you copy?
Mr. Green, can't talk now... doing the wash... call later.

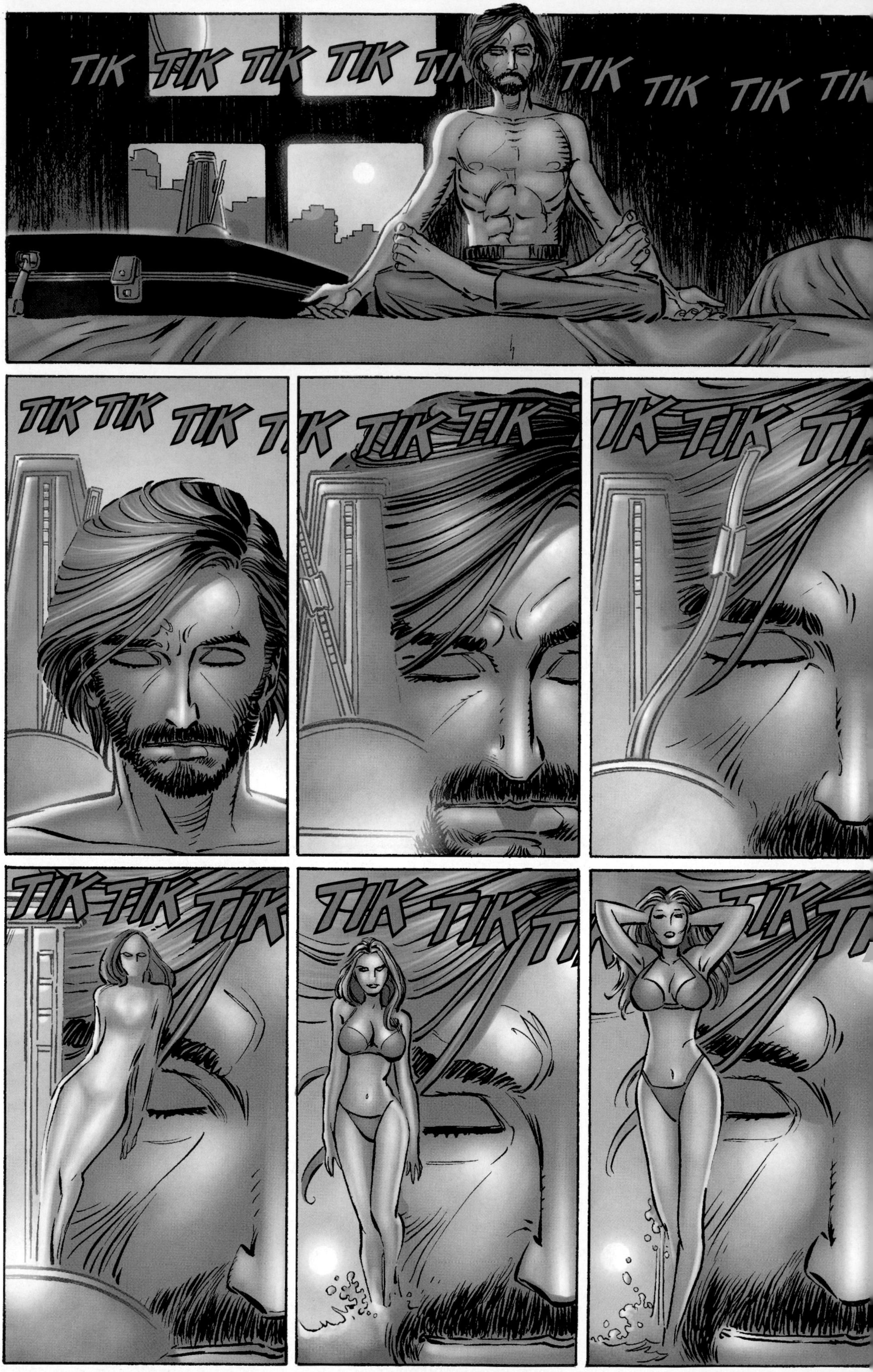
TIK TIK TIK TIK
TIK TIK TIK
TIK TIK TIK
TIK TIK
TIK TIK
TIK TIK TIK
TIK TIK
TIK

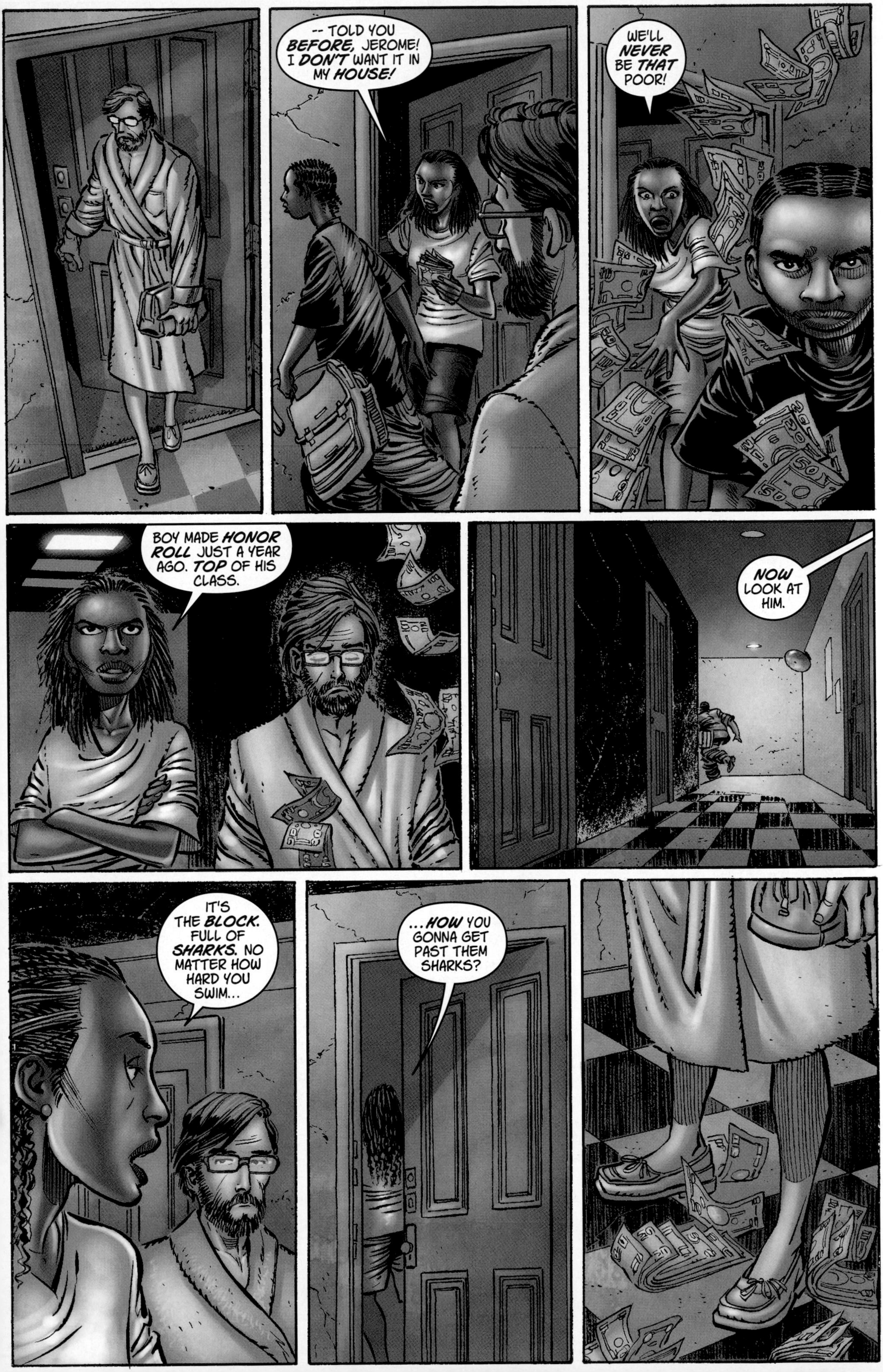
-- TOLD YOU BEFORE, JEROME! I DON'T WANT IT IN MY HOUSE!
WE'LL NEVER BE THAT POOR!
BOY MADE HONOR ROLL JUST A YEAR AGO. TOP OF HIS CLASS.
NOW LOOK AT HIM.
IT'S THE BLOCK. FULL OF SHARKS. NO MATTER HOW HARD YOU SWIM...
...HOW YOU GONNA GET PAST THEM SHARKS?

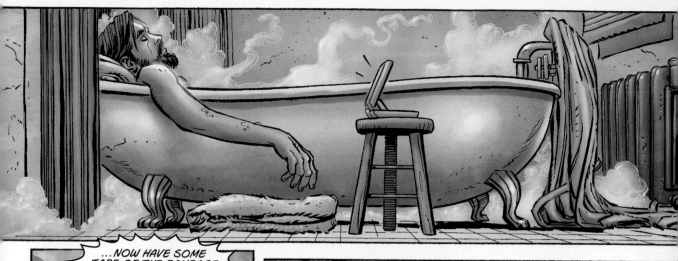

...NOW HAVE SOME TAPE OF THE RAMPAGE IN CHICAGO SHOT BY AN AMATEUR PHOTOGRAPHER, SHOWING THE CREATURE IN ACTION...

IF YOU SEE **THIS MAN,** DO **NOT** APPROACH. NOTIFY THE POLICE IMMEDIATELY BY DIALING THE 911 EMERGENCY NUMBER. THE SUSPECT IS NOW BELIEVED TO BE WEARING A **BEARD.**

REPEAT: DO NOT APPROACH!

EXPIRES 08-17-01

ROBERT BRUCE BANNER
1205 MEOHFSVLKVFNZVDF
SANTA FPOJFDKRISA OEN

SEX: M   HAIR: BRN   E
HT: 5-09   WT: 140   D

Robert B.

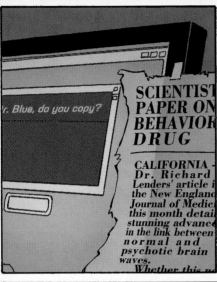

SCIENTIST
PAPER ON
BEHAVIOR
DRUG

CALIFORNIA —
Dr. Richard
Lenders' article i
the New England
Journal of Medic
this month detail
stunning advance
in the link between
normal and
psychotic brain
waves.
Whether this

r. Blue, do you copy?

Mr. Blue, do you copy?

Mr. Green, Aunt June sick...
forced to leave present
location... will contact you
later... avoid unnecessary
exposure.

Mr. Blue, will wait
to hear from you...
Best to your aunt.

RREEEEEOOOOOOOWWWW

RREEEEEOOOOOWWWW

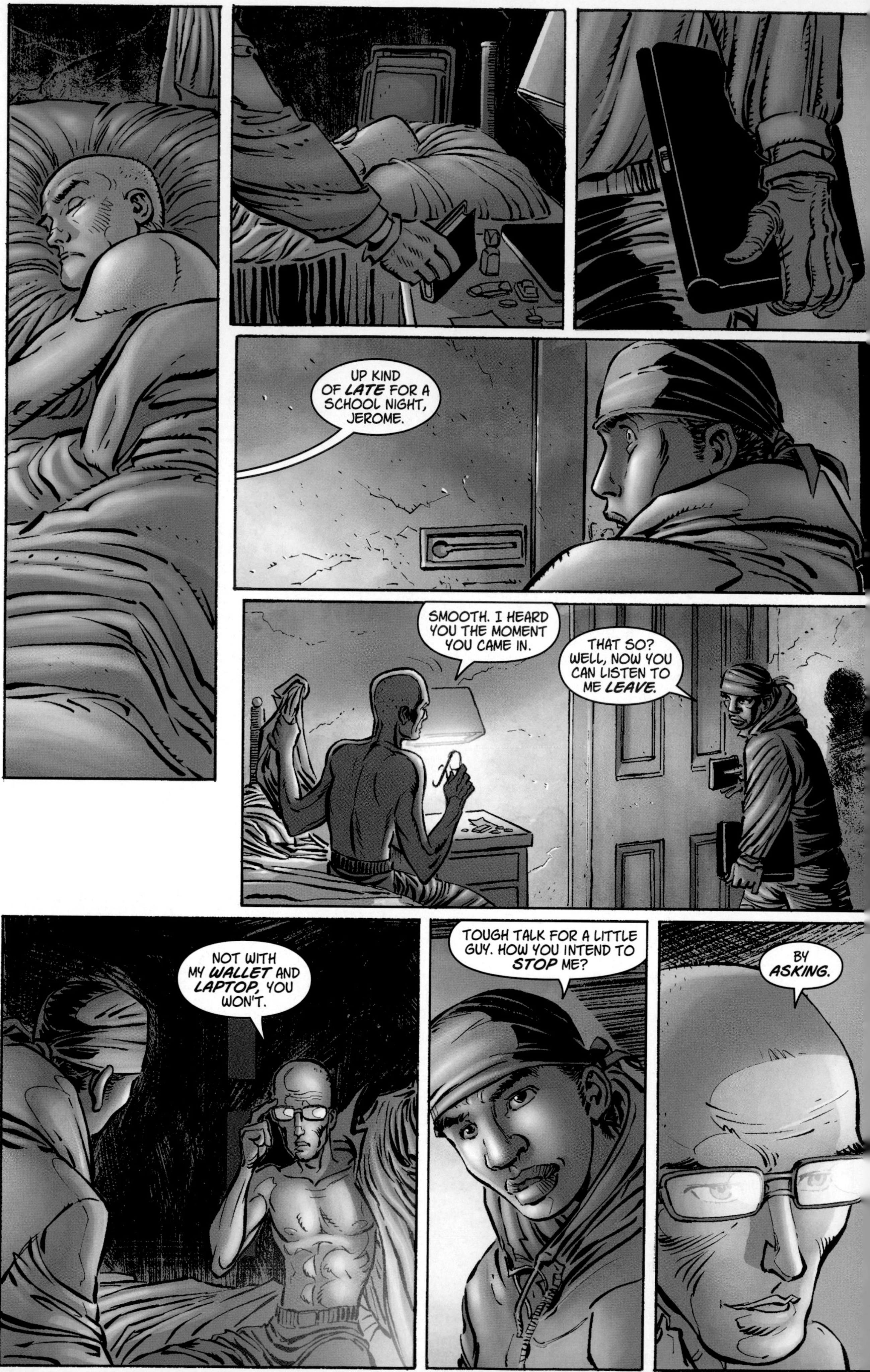
UP KIND OF LATE FOR A SCHOOL NIGHT, JEROME.
SMOOTH. I HEARD YOU THE MOMENT YOU CAME IN.
THAT SO? WELL, NOW YOU CAN LISTEN TO ME LEAVE.
NOT WITH MY WALLET AND LAPTOP, YOU WON'T.
TOUGH TALK FOR A LITTLE GUY. HOW YOU INTEND TO STOP ME?
BY ASKING.

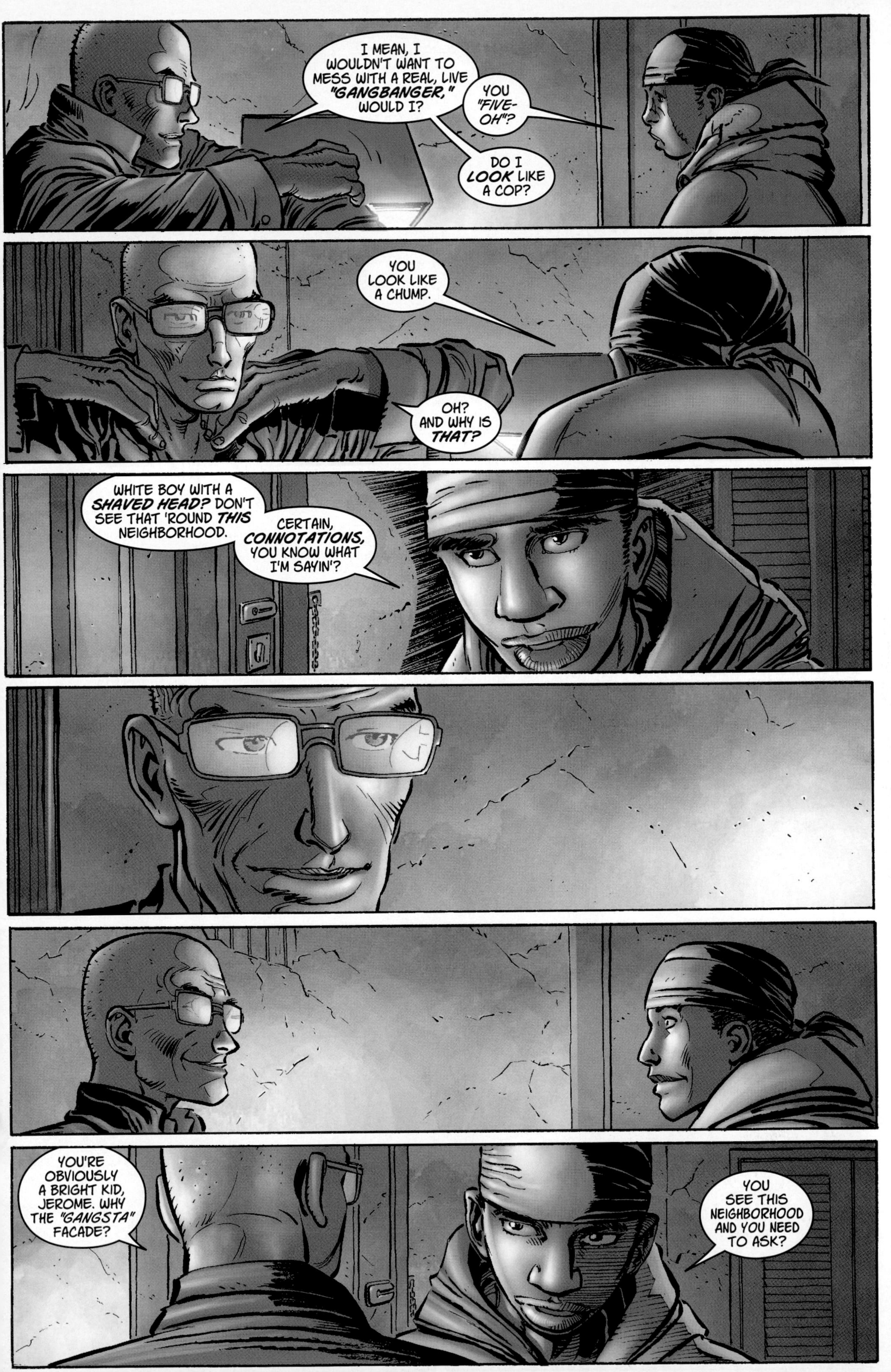

I MEAN, I WOULDN'T WANT TO MESS WITH A REAL, LIVE "GANGBANGER," WOULD I?
YOU "FIVE-OH"?
DO I LOOK LIKE A COP?
YOU LOOK LIKE A CHUMP.
OH? AND WHY IS THAT?
WHITE BOY WITH A SHAVED HEAD? DON'T SEE THAT 'ROUND THIS NEIGHBORHOOD.
CERTAIN, CONNOTATIONS, YOU KNOW WHAT I'M SAYIN'?
YOU'RE OBVIOUSLY A BRIGHT KID, JEROME. WHY THE "GANGSTA" FACADE?
YOU SEE THIS NEIGHBORHOOD AND YOU NEED TO ASK?

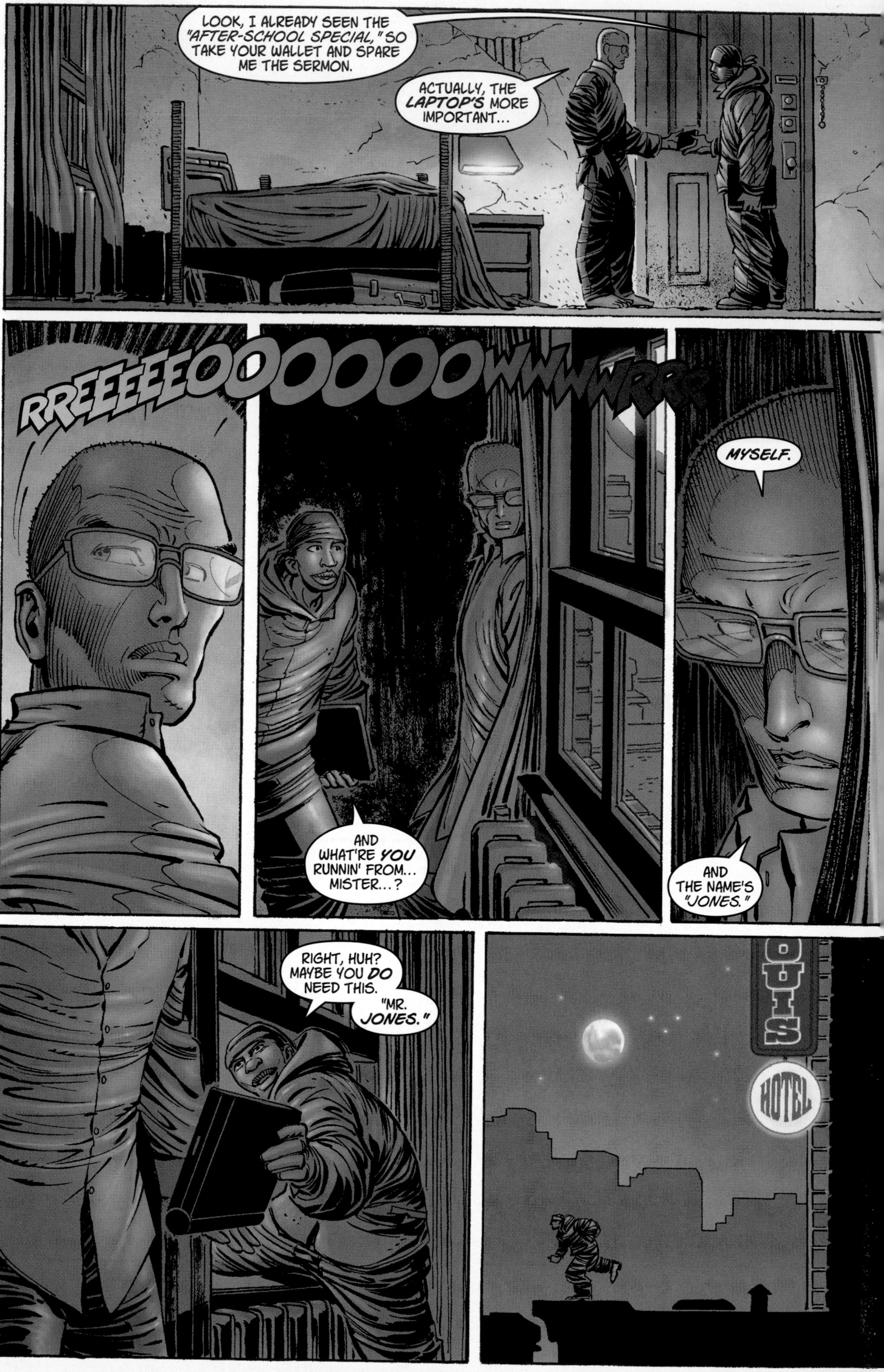

LOOK, I ALREADY SEEN THE "AFTER-SCHOOL SPECIAL," SO TAKE YOUR WALLET AND SPARE ME THE SERMON.
ACTUALLY, THE LAPTOP'S MORE IMPORTANT...
RREEEEEEOOOOOOOWWWWRRR
AND WHAT'RE YOU RUNNIN' FROM... MISTER...?
MYSELF.
AND THE NAME'S "JONES."
RIGHT, HUH? MAYBE YOU DO NEED THIS. "MR. JONES."
HOTEL

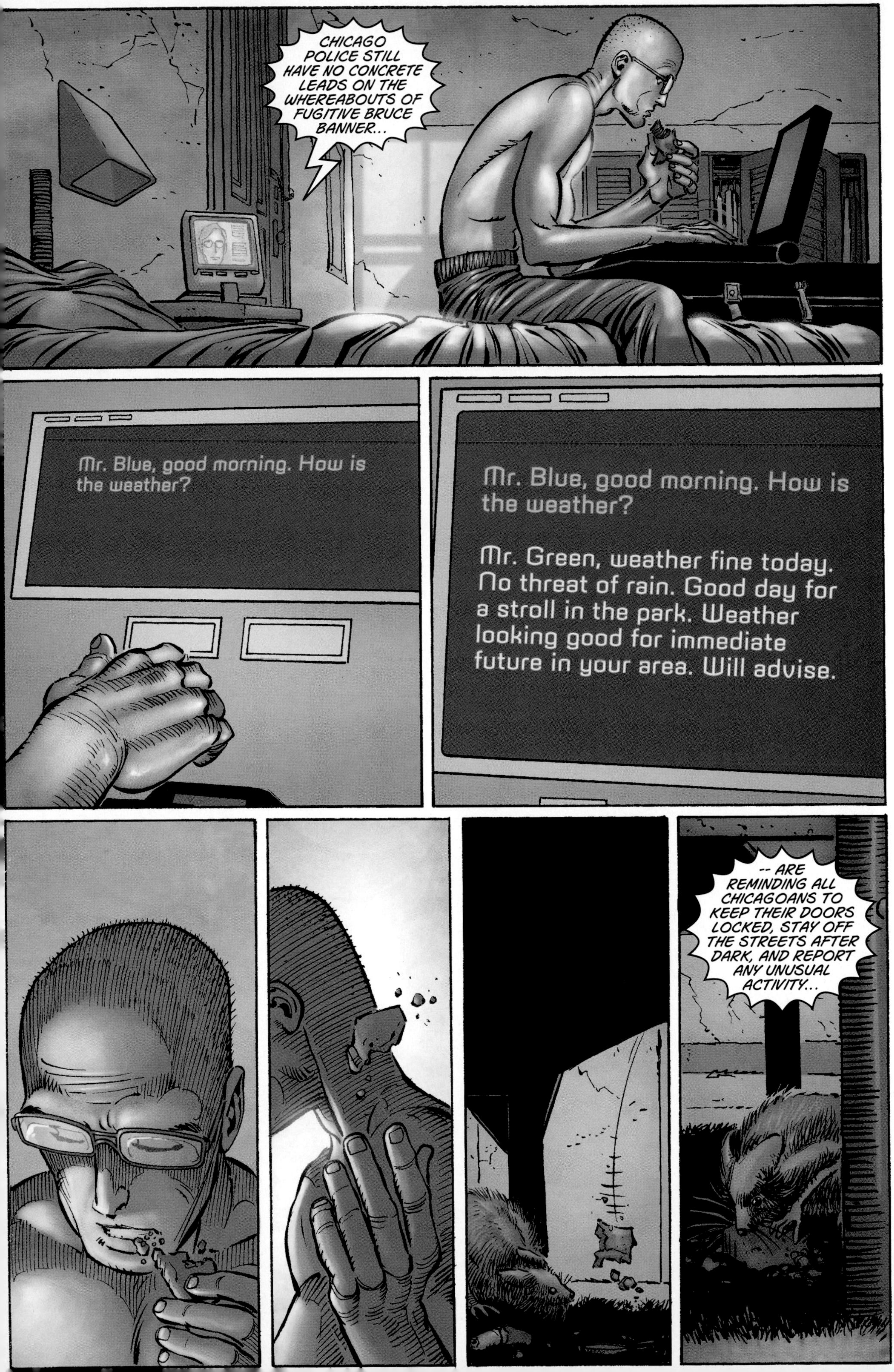
CHICAGO POLICE STILL HAVE NO CONCRETE LEADS ON THE WHEREABOUTS OF FUGITIVE BRUCE BANNER...
Mr. Blue, good morning. How is the weather?
Mr. Blue, good morning. How is the weather?
Mr. Green, weather fine today. No threat of rain. Good day for a stroll in the park. Weather looking good for immediate future in your area. Will advise.
-- ARE REMINDING ALL CHICAGOANS TO KEEP THEIR DOORS LOCKED, STAY OFF THE STREETS AFTER DARK, AND REPORT ANY UNUSUAL ACTIVITY...

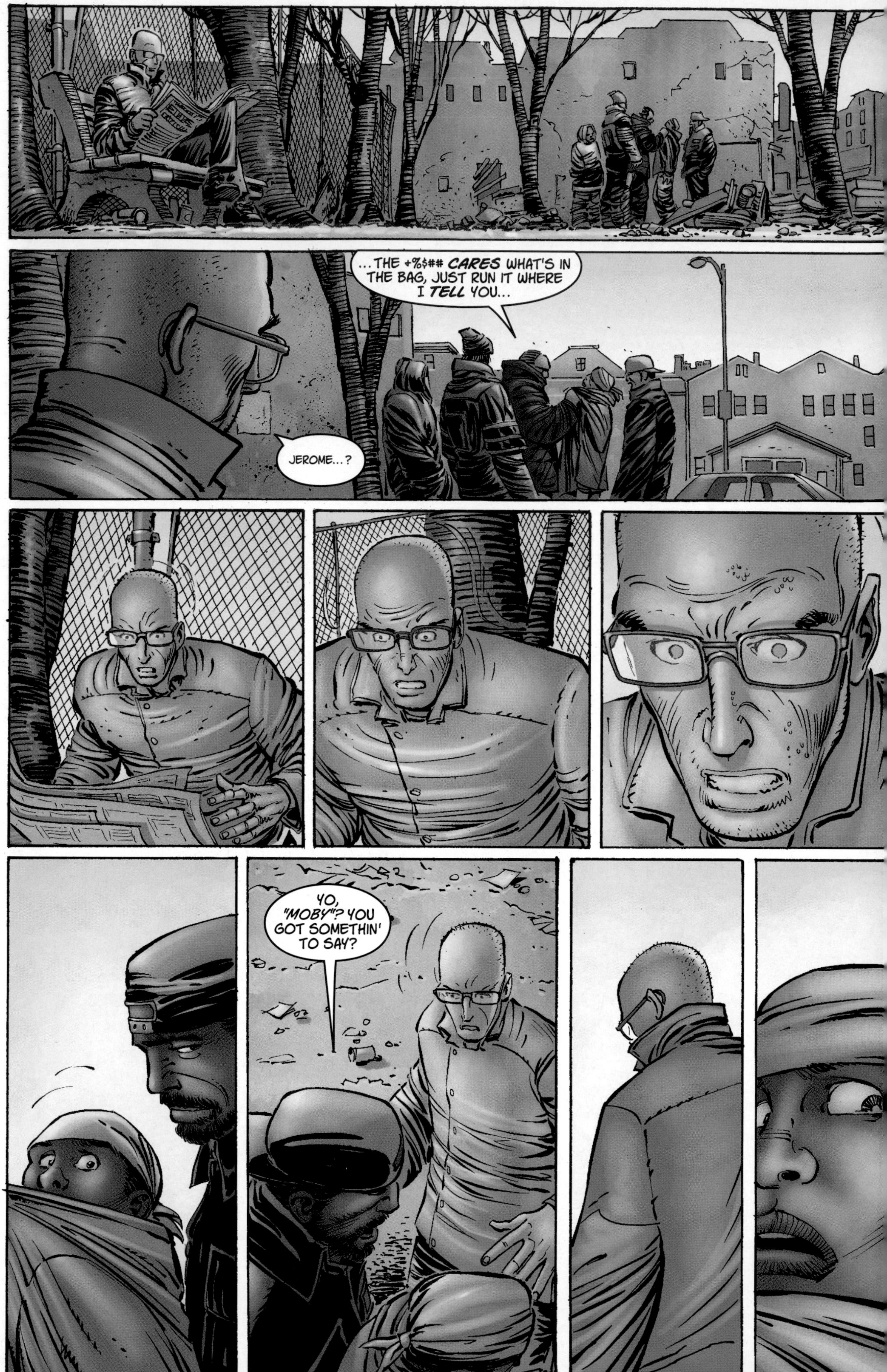
...THE +%$## CARES WHAT'S IN THE BAG, JUST RUN IT WHERE I TELL YOU...
JEROME...?
YO, "MOBY"? YOU GOT SOMETHIN' TO SAY?

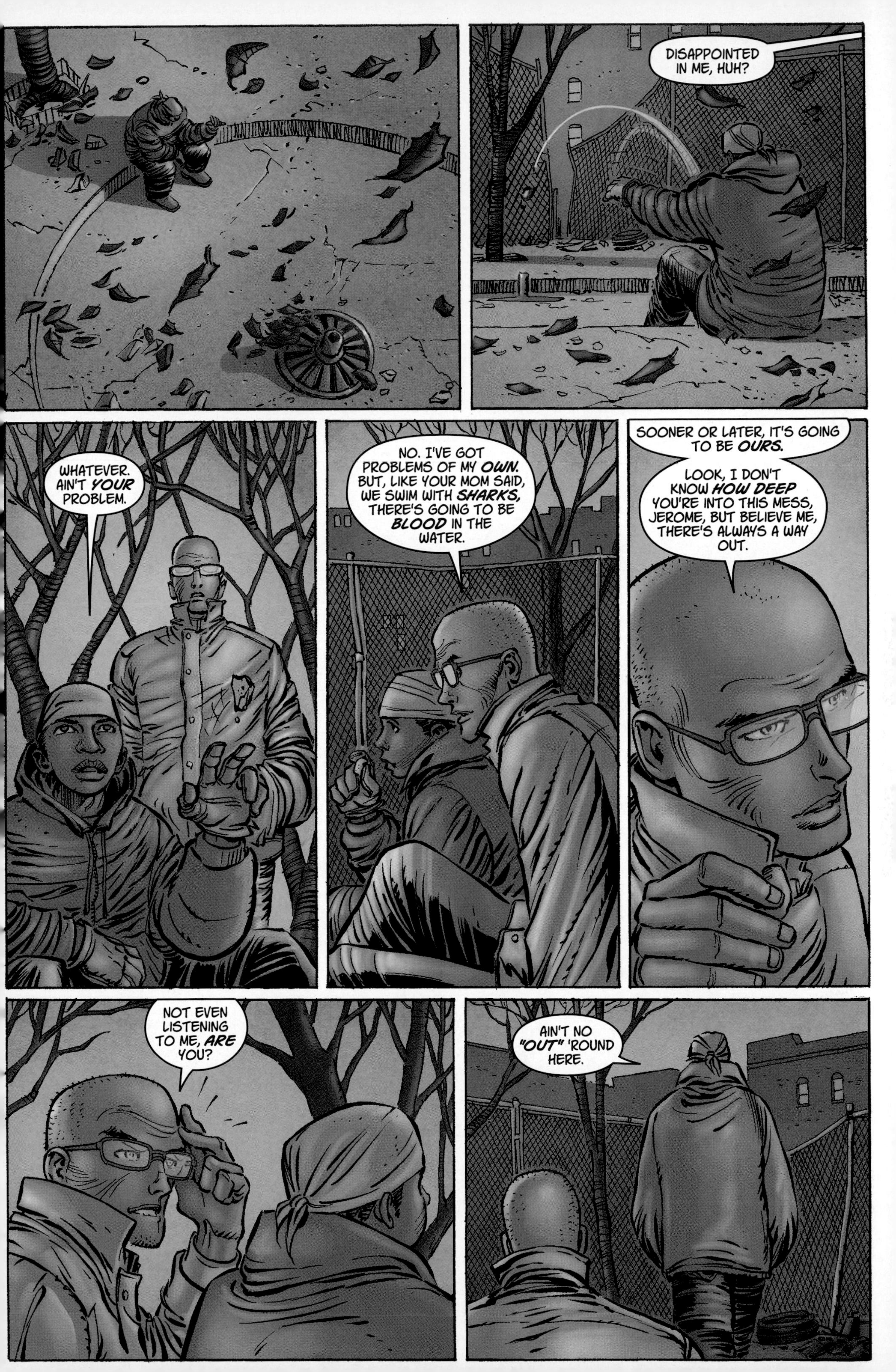
DISAPPOINTED IN ME, HUH?
WHATEVER. AIN'T YOUR PROBLEM.
NO. I'VE GOT PROBLEMS OF MY OWN. BUT, LIKE YOUR MOM SAID, WE SWIM WITH SHARKS, THERE'S GOING TO BE BLOOD IN THE WATER.
SOONER OR LATER, IT'S GOING TO BE OURS.
LOOK, I DON'T KNOW HOW DEEP YOU'RE INTO THIS MESS, JEROME, BUT BELIEVE ME, THERE'S ALWAYS A WAY OUT.
NOT EVEN LISTENING TO ME, ARE YOU?
AIN'T NO "OUT" 'ROUND HERE.

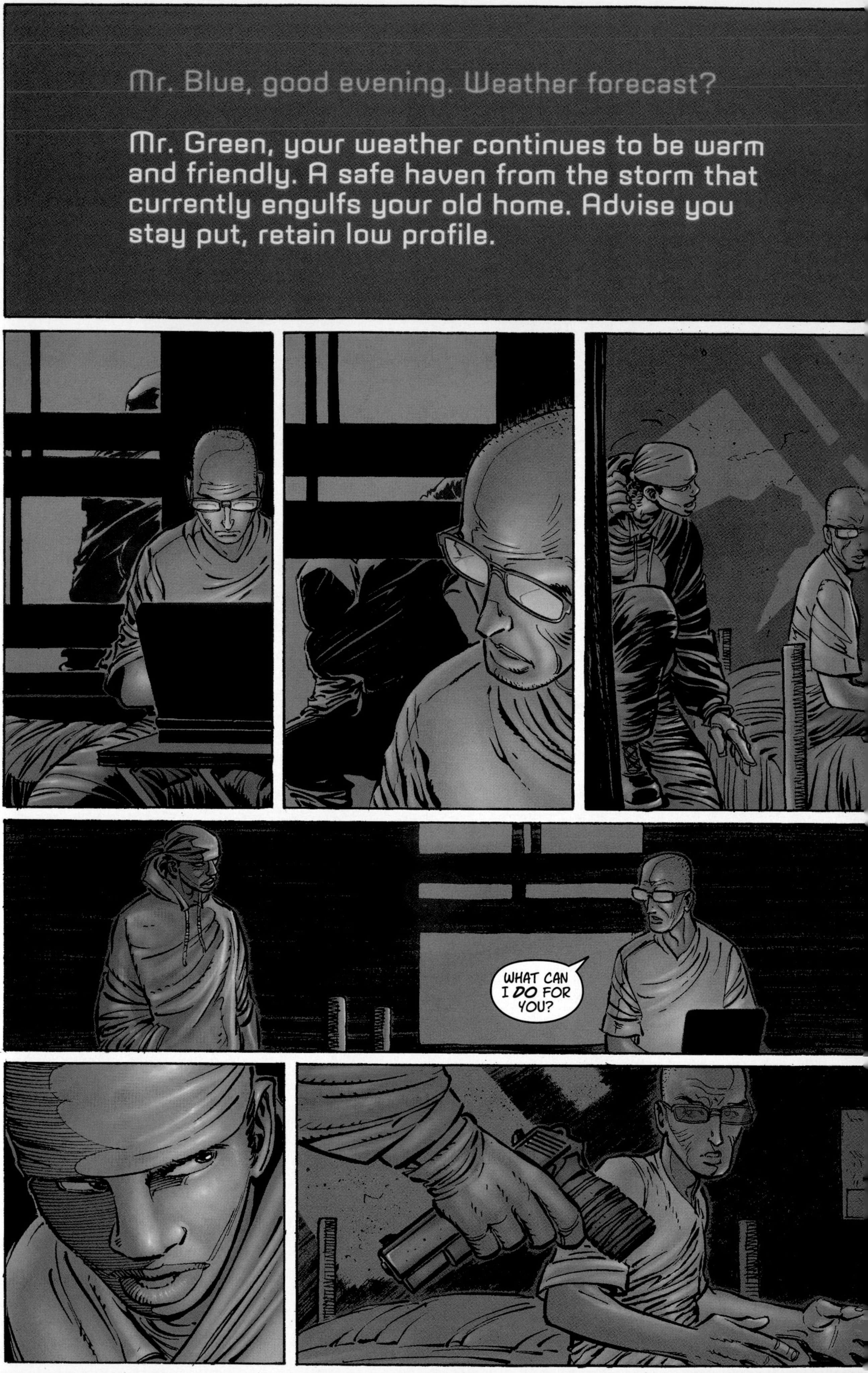
Mr. Blue, good evening. Weather forecast?
Mr. Green, your weather continues to be warm and friendly. A safe haven from the storm that currently engulfs your old home. Advise you stay put, retain low profile.
WHAT CAN I DO FOR YOU?

"JUICE." POWER. THAT'S WHAT LIFE'S ALL ABOUT, ISN'T IT-- WHO HOLDS IT?

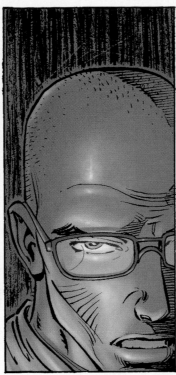

WELL, THAT CREW ON THE CORNER GOT PLENTY OF JUICE. I KNEW THAT WHEN I HOOKED UP WITH 'EM, BUT I WAS TOO STUPID TO...

I WAS TOO STUPID.

WHATEVER. I'M IN. DEEP. TOO LATE TO SWEAT ABOUT IT.

IS IT NOW?

WHAT?! YOU THINK I CAN JUST WALK AWAY FROM THE GAME? PICK UP AN' LEAVE?

YOU TELL ME.

YOU NEED ME TO SPELL IT OUT FOR YOU? "MR. JONES," YOU BEST GO BACK WHERE YOU CAME FROM.

I CAN'T.

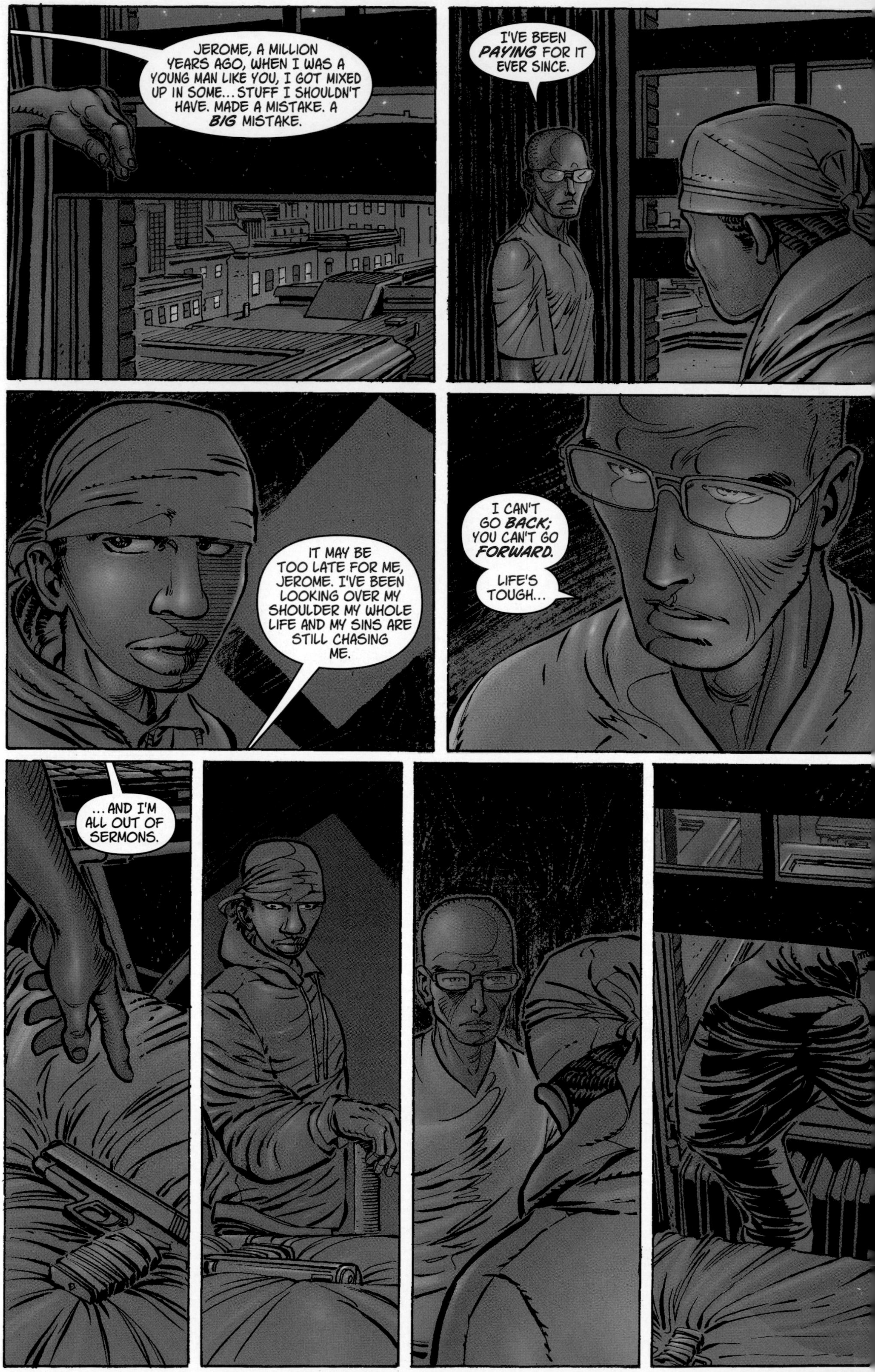
JEROME, A MILLION YEARS AGO, WHEN I WAS A YOUNG MAN LIKE YOU, I GOT MIXED UP IN SOME... STUFF I SHOULDN'T HAVE. MADE A MISTAKE. A BIG MISTAKE.
I'VE BEEN PAYING FOR IT EVER SINCE.
IT MAY BE TOO LATE FOR ME, JEROME. I'VE BEEN LOOKING OVER MY SHOULDER MY WHOLE LIFE AND MY SINS ARE STILL CHASING ME.
I CAN'T GO BACK; YOU CAN'T GO FORWARD.
LIFE'S TOUGH...
...AND I'M ALL OUT OF SERMONS.

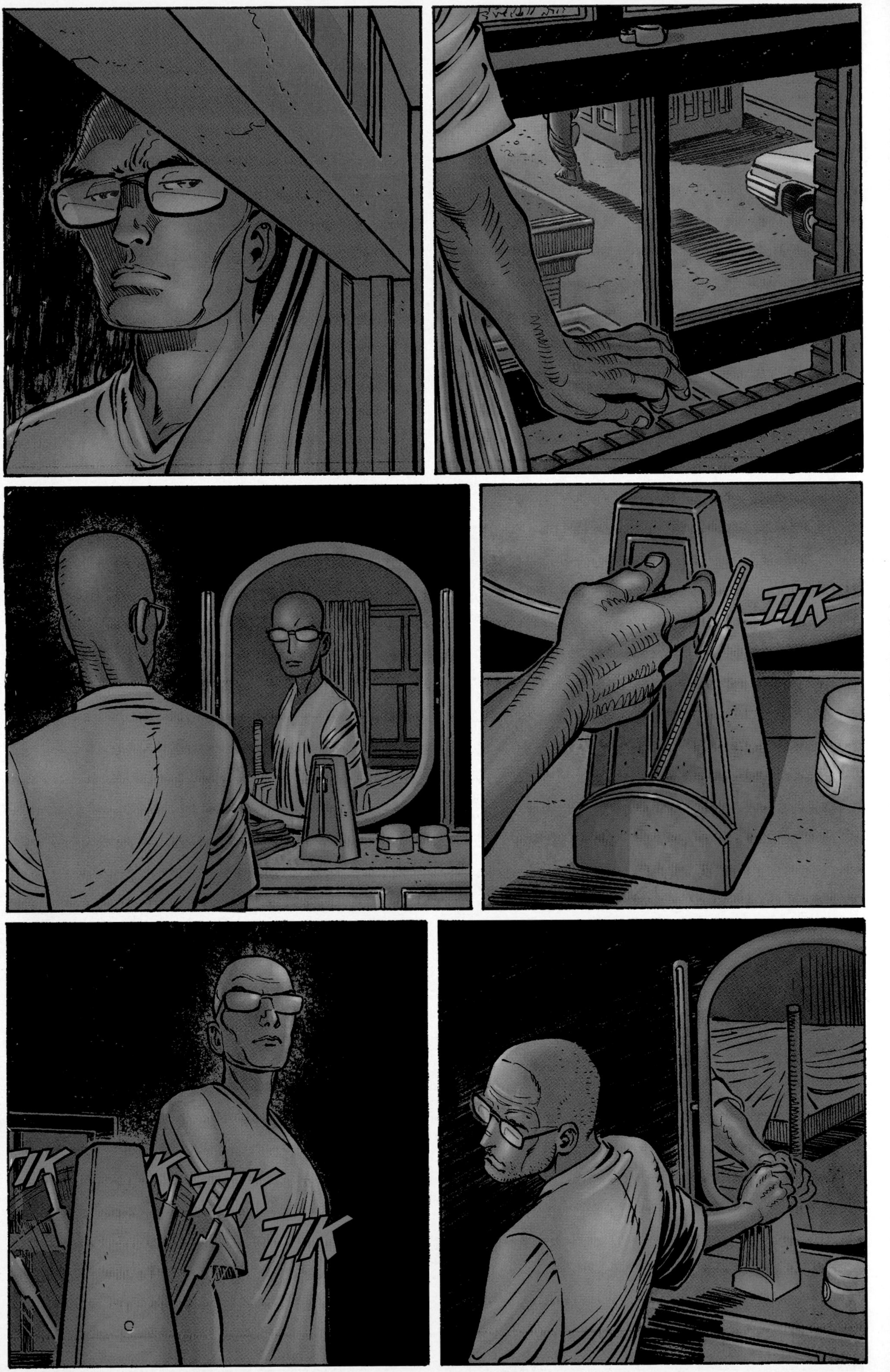

TIK
TIK
TIK
TIK

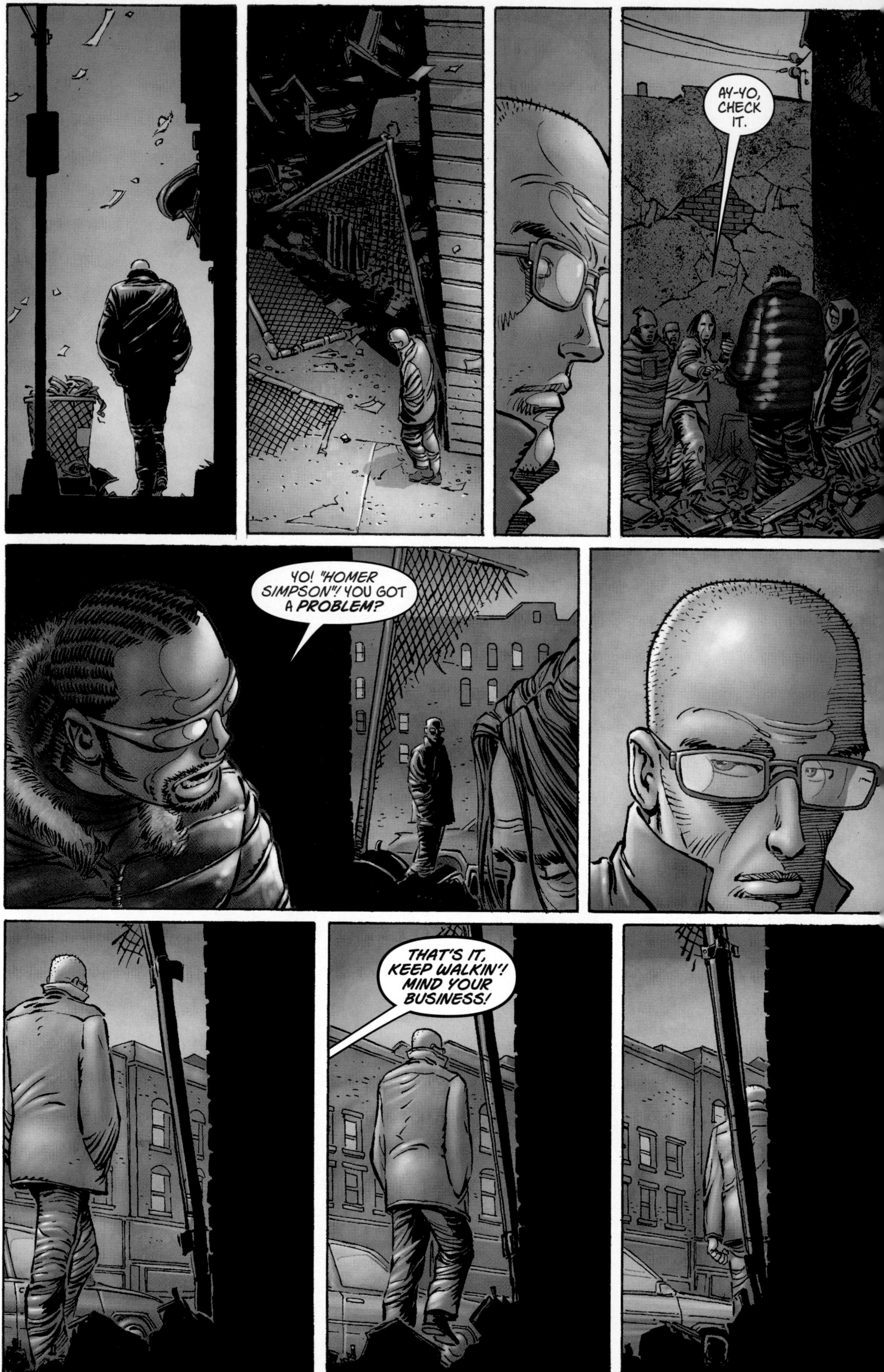
AY-YO, CHECK IT.
YO! "HOMER SIMPSON"! YOU GOT A PROBLEM?
THAT'S IT, KEEP WALKIN'! MIND YOUR BUSINESS!

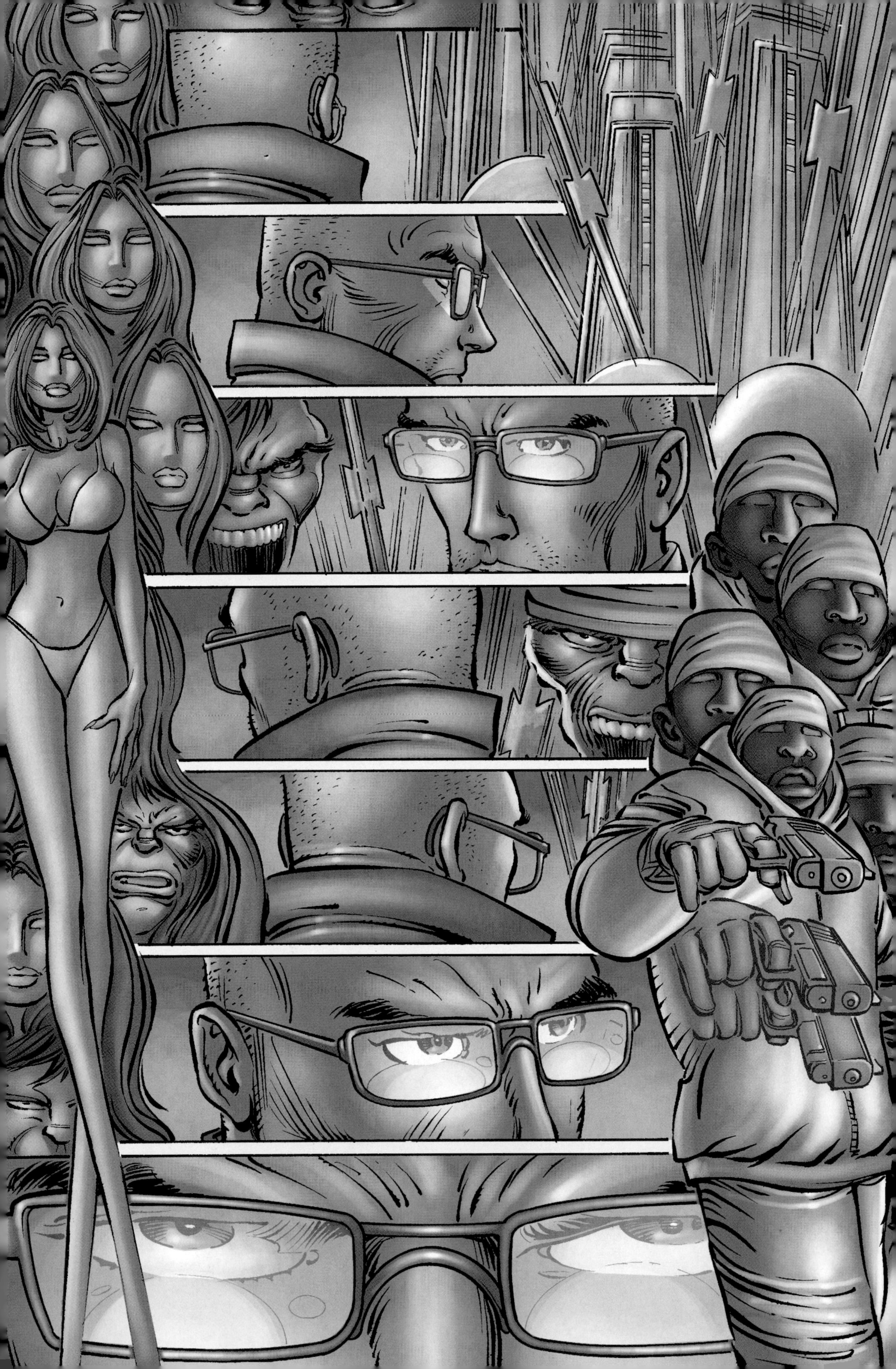

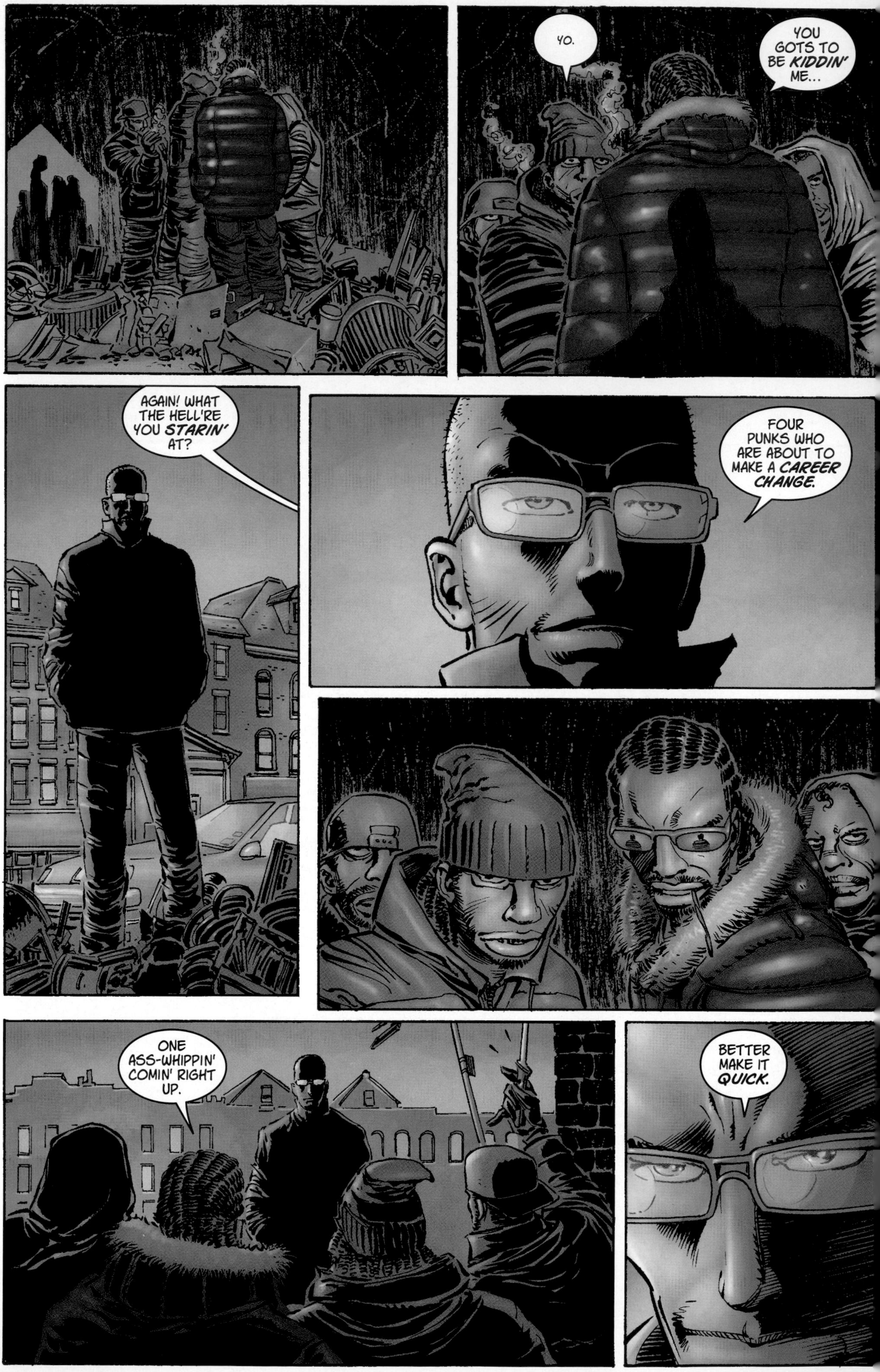
YO.
YOU GOTS TO BE KIDDIN' ME...
AGAIN! WHAT THE HELL'RE YOU STARIN' AT?
FOUR PUNKS WHO ARE ABOUT TO MAKE A CAREER CHANGE.
ONE ASS-WHIPPIN' COMIN' RIGHT UP.
BETTER MAKE IT QUICK.

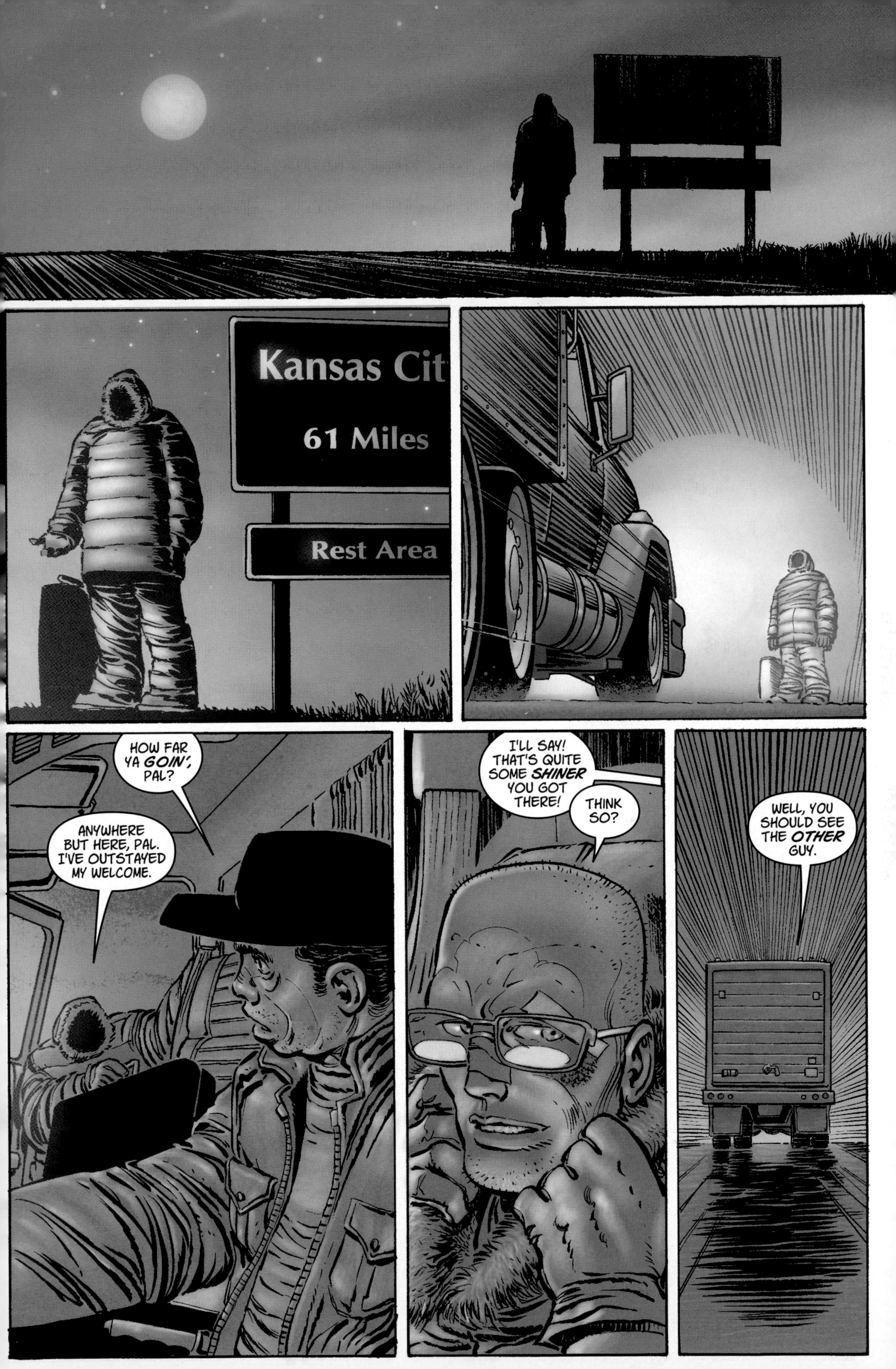
Kansas City
61 Miles
Rest Area
HOW FAR YA GOIN', PAL?
ANYWHERE BUT HERE, PAL. I'VE OUTSTAYED MY WELCOME.
I'LL SAY! THAT'S QUITE SOME SHINER YOU GOT THERE!
THINK SO?
WELL, YOU SHOULD SEE THE OTHER GUY.

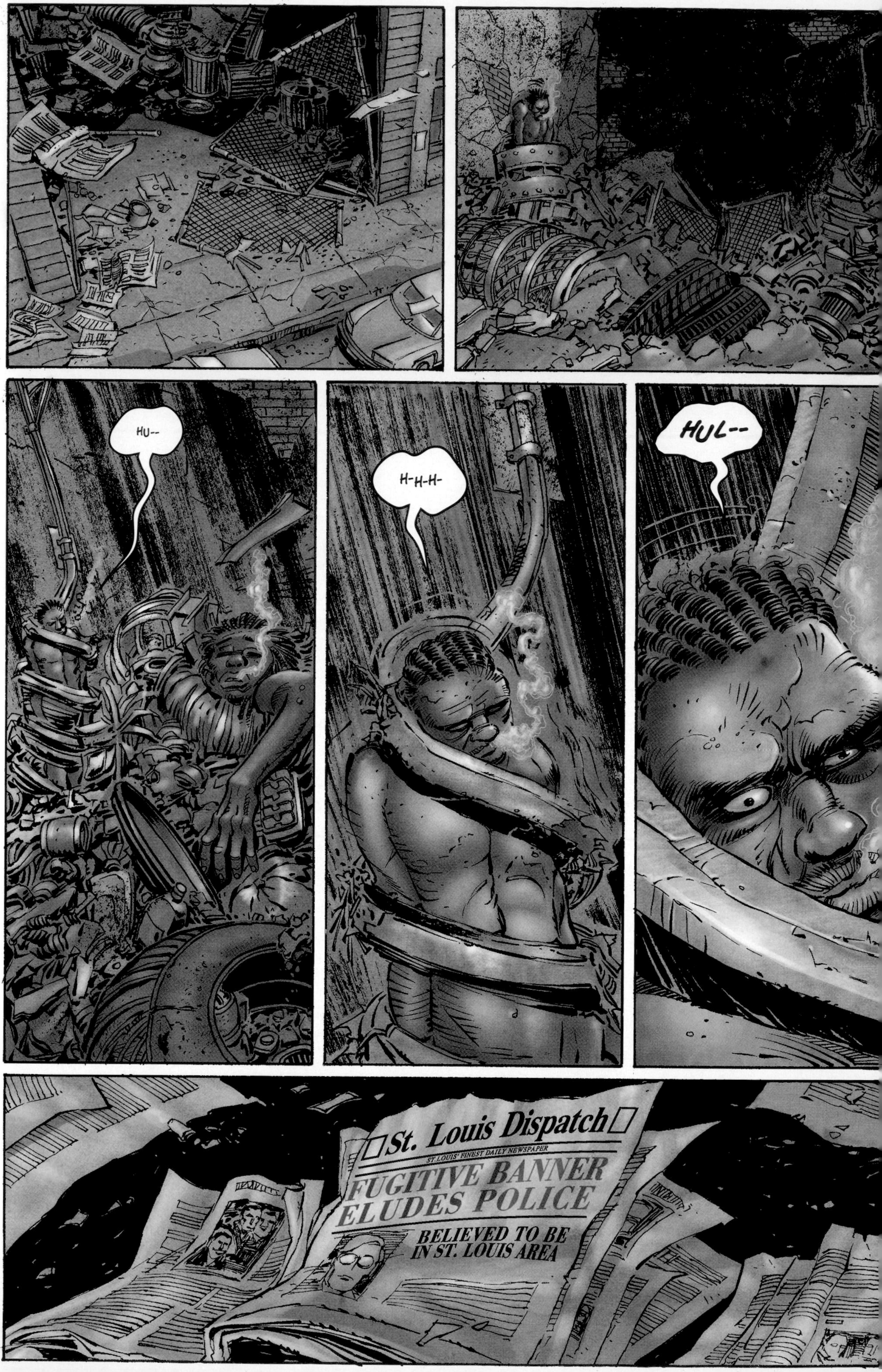
HU--
H-H-H-
HUL--
St. Louis Dispatch
ST. LOUIS' FINEST DAILY NEWSPAPER
FUGITIVE BANNER ELUDES POLICE
BELIEVED TO BE IN ST. LOUIS AREA

Continued in the *Incredible Hulk Vol. 1: Return of the Monster* Trade Paperback

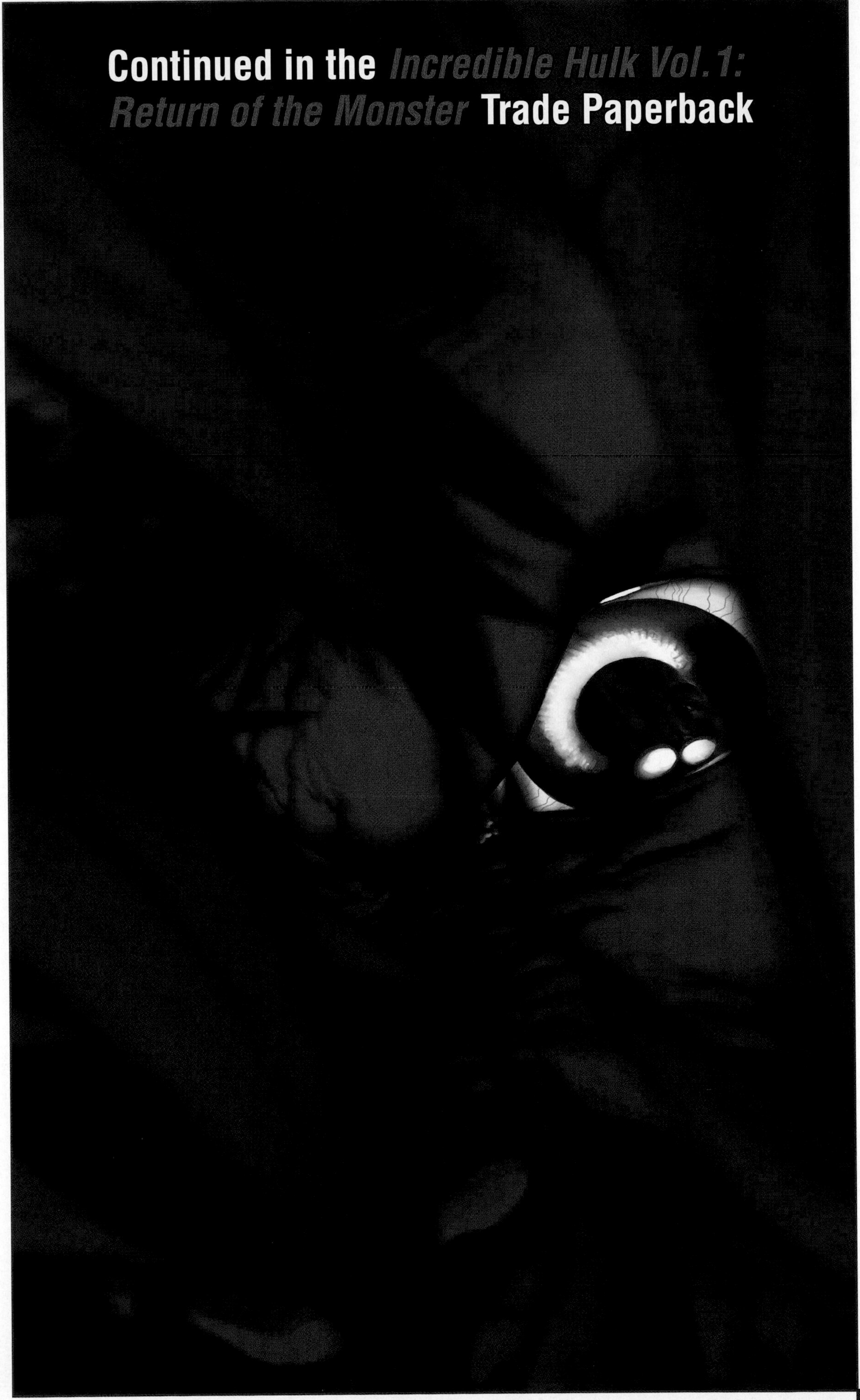

Art by Kaare Andrews

Chapter Six

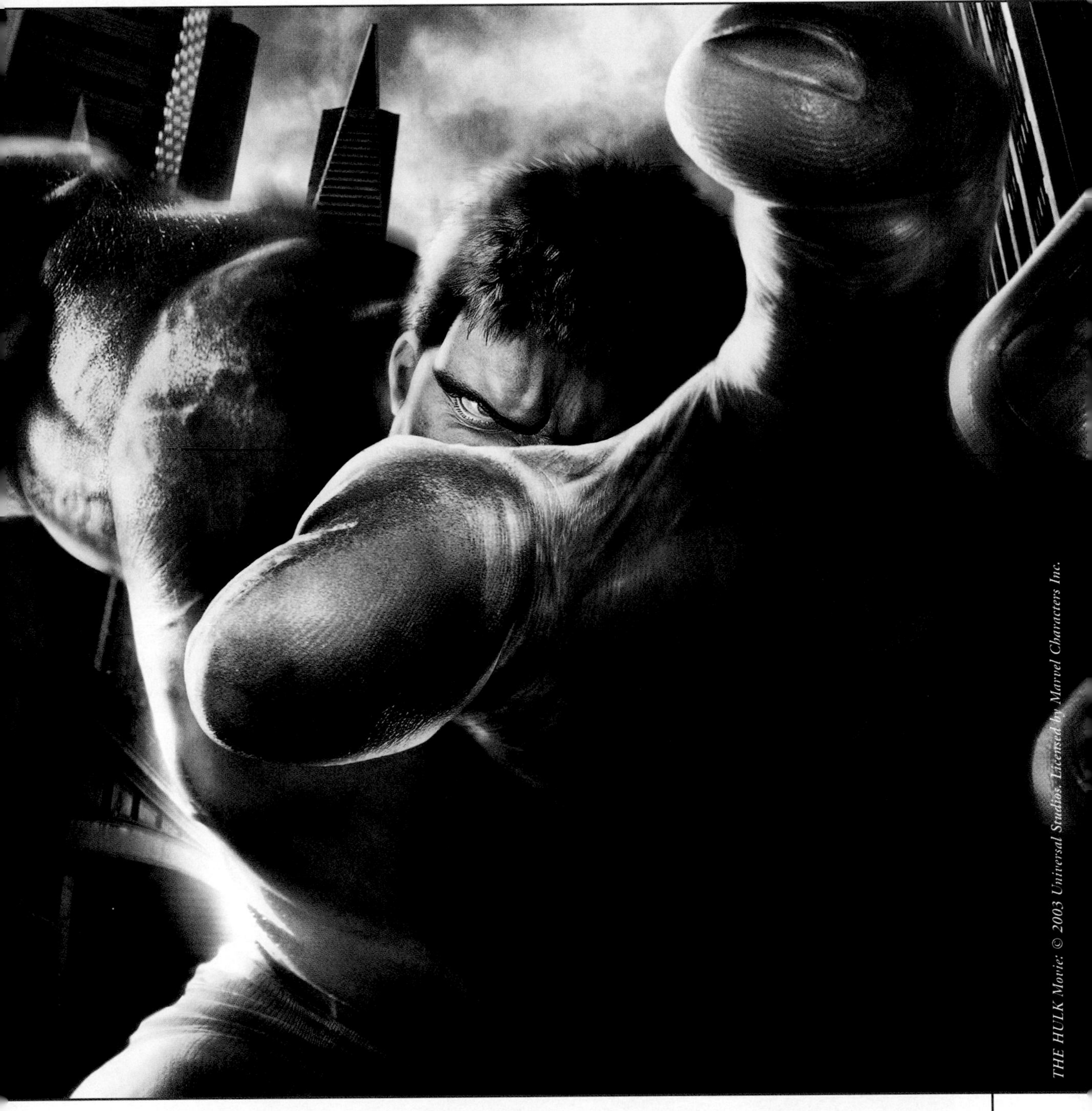

BIG HULK, BIG SCREEN

The Hulk at the movies

The scene is as film noir as you can get in a movie that isn't filmed in grayscale and isn't based on a Raymond Chandler novel. Bruce Banner peers through a Venetian blind while his voice says, "I don't know who I am … I don't know what I'm becoming. There's only one thing I know for sure: You wouldn't like me when I'm angry." The cuts show a tensed hand, a scientist in a darkened room peering through a microscope, abnormal blood cells and finally a close-up of Banner's bloodshot eyeball. The blood vessels multiply. The white of the eye turns green. As the tribal drumming intensifies, the obligatory nod to the director appears, followed by Nick Nolte's beat-up visage saying, "My son is unique. Because he is unique, the world will not tolerate his existence." And then all hell really breaks loose. To the strains of a dimed guitar the scenes come

fast and furious: soldiers running helter-skelter; tanks rolling; the Hulk bursting from a water tank; houses exploding; helicopters spinning across desert; and best of all, the Hulk grabbing a tank by the barrel and flinging it discus-style over the hills and far away. The barrage of images ends when the movie logo and summer release date crash onto the screen.

After that full-frontal assault, a return to the Super Bowl — especially this particular Super Bowl — was like slipping "Sheep May Safely Graze" into the CD player after a day at the blast furnace. The season of waiting and watching for the *Hulk* movie began with a nuclear-sized bang.

This might not be the optimum time to ask this question, but what's your idea of the perfect *Hulk* movie? Bruce Banner trying to change a tire in the rain *again?* Thunderbolt Ross looking like the Wizard

Like the current Incredible Hulk *comic, Ang Lee's movie proves the suggestion of violence is often more compelling than violence itself.*

of Oz with scrambled eggs on his shoulders? The Hulk in the ultimate showdown with the Space Parasite, played for all he's worth by Keanu Reeves? A 30-minute Hulk-out followed shortly by a 60-minute Hulk-out?

Sorry. Maybe in the sequel.

The consensus of the moviemakers at Marvel Entertainment is that the perfect Hulk movie is a disturbing, dynamic, powerful piece that does a Bruce Banner job of balancing the psychological and the physical. The perfect Hulk movie places a disparate yet talented cast under the direction of Hollywood's most distinctively

THE HULK Movie: © 2003 Universal Studios. Licensed by Marvel Characters Inc.

*The smart script keeps the leash on the **screen-smashing, speaker-blowing** action until the **tension** has built to a point where that **action** is the only reasonable release.*

can circulate worldwide in less time than it takes to toast a Pop-Tart.

One bit of blog was true: The budget for *Hulk* was huge. Of course, these days, $100 million doesn't buy as much movie as it used to — but even so, the thrills in this movie aren't cheap. Hulk fans wishing the movie had been semi-cheezoidal and totally tongue-in-cheek take note: *Hulk* reaches for the sky, not for another bag of Funyuns. It comes from better stock: *The Outer Limits. Godzilla vs. Mothra. Public Enemy. The Fugitive. Crouching Tiger, Hidden Dragon. Citizen Kane.*

Hulk takes cues

skilled all-around filmmakers. The perfect Hulk movie delivers one heck of a Hulk. And because the Marvel moviemakers sign the checks, their consensus packs a Hulk-size wallop.

Sure, we get it *now* — but back when there was more hush-hushing going on with this movie than a three-year-old boy encounters at 8 a.m. mass, the consensus was barricaded behind a closed set at Universal and a lot of locked lips at Marvel HQ. In the upcoming-movie biz, no news is definitely bad news — so the bloggers blogged, and the rumors flew. The film's budget was out of control, the cast was at each other's throats, and the plot turned on a gamma-infused poodle. It's always nice when your fans care enough about you to insert Poodle-Hulks into your movies, but moviemakers have good reasons for keeping their movies under wraps — especially these days, when outtakes

from all these great works of visual pop culture, but it goes its own way as stubbornly as the Big Green Guy. It uses the comic book for its characters, but it makes the comic's extremely two-dimensional characters extremely three-dimensional. The reasons why it's able to nail this combination shot are the reasons why behind all great movies: The quality of the actors playing heretofore cardboard cutouts Thunderbolt Ross, Glenn Talbot, Betty Ross and David Banner; the skill and vision of director Ang Lee (whose last big-screen action epic, *Crouching Tiger, Hidden Dragon*, did nothing less than create a brand-new genre of action-art-foreign-language film); and a smart script that keeps the leash on the screen-smashing, speaker-blowing action until the tension has built to a point where that action is the only reasonable release.

People who don't make movies don't

Hulk's starkly lit sets conjure up echoes of the labs of Dr.Frankenstein — and not by accident.

realize how hard it is to make a movie. That's natural; people who don't make moussaka don't realize what it takes to make moussaka. The difference between moussaka and movies, outside the taste, is the amount of logistical coordination moviemaking demands. (This is true for all movies except, of course, for *My Big Fat Greek Wedding*, where there is absolutely no difference between the moussaka and the movie.)

Hulk was filmed on four stages on the Universal Pictures backlot. One stage houses the containment chamber, the water-filled tank where Bruce Banner first transforms into the Hulk. Another houses Banner's laboratory and was partially decorated by Ang Lee's wife, who just happens to be a biochemist. An outdoor set encompasses Banner's boyhood-home nightmarescape. And the fourth stage is suburbia redux, with replicas of four colorful country-style houses singled out by Lee on drives around Berkeley and recreated down to the last morsel of fascia by the set designers.

A lot of what went on in these stages was a secret kept by Lee, his cameramen and actors. Much filming time was spent on closed sets getting the people scenes right, creating and conveying the proper shades of emotion through details as subtle as the way Eric Bana eats a chicken wing. In some scenes, Lee experimented with camera positions and lighting just to see what they would look like.

If you get the feeling Ang Lee brought the same sort of mad-scientist intensity to his filmmaking that Bruce Banner brought to his research, go to the head of the class.

It's a quality actors find attractive.

"Ang brought such a lyricism to movies like *The Ice Storm* and *Crouching Tiger*," said Jennifer Connelly, who plays Betty Ross. "I just wanted to be around him."

"Ang is making a movie that's totally different from anything you've ever seen," explained Josh Lucas, a.k.a. Major Glenn Talbot. "We have an extraordinary challenge because we have a director who's not going to let one moment go by that doesn't seem like you're actually watching a beast."

"You had to work extremely hard in every facet," added Eric Bana, the Australian actor-comic who plays Bruce Banner. "Ang's a perfectionist, and he has a very determined vision. We all worked hard — not just hours; everyone works long hours — but in intensity. The level of intensity was extreme. He made me dig deep and go places that I found pretty uncomfortable. But I'm weirdly attracted to that, so that was fine by me."

If you're wondering why *Hulk* needed a director with Ang Lee's artistic sensibility and impressive resume (which also includes *Sense and Sensibility*), you just ran over your answer. Go back, pick it up and listen for a heartbeat. Lots of directors can make movies that run the emotional gamut from a car exploding to a helicopter exploding, with a soundtrack featuring Limp Bizkit available wherever rap-metal is sold. The Hulk is superficially about action — but without motivation, he's barely a green King Kong. His actions need to flow from his emotions, so you want a director who made something refined like *Sense and Sensibility* to take the movie smoothly from justification to explanation to action.

"It's been great working on *Hulk*," Lee told the comics magazine *Wizard*. "Universal has given me an opportunity to be creative with the filming. They've made me feel like I'm back on the set of *Crouching Tiger, Hidden Dragon*."

Now, about that action. The *other* reason why you want Ang Lee directing is because when you're done with the explanations and want to start smashing things, you want the director of *Crouching Tiger,* *Hidden Dragon* choreographing the smashing. In fact, you want the director of *Crouching Tiger, Hidden Dragon* choreographing the smashing even when less than half the smashings he's choreographing are live. A huge portion of the action on the screen comes from the mind-blowing special effects and the people behind them.

Mind-blowing special effects are everywhere in films. Even Tom Hanks-Meg Ryan movies have mind-blowing special effects. In fact, so many minds have theoretically been blown by movie special effects you half-expect to find bits of gray matter scattered in with the spilled popcorn when you plunk down in your stadium seat for the 9:00 show.

In this case, the hype is no hype. The special effects (courtesy of Industrial Light and Magic, the Microsoft of special effects) do blow minds — and other body parts. They're also spectacular. Words don't do justice. Lots of moviemakers saunter in with their big-budget action films claiming, "Anything we can imagine, we can put on the screen," and do nothing more than establish how pitiful their imaginations are. Not this time. The imaginations are incredible, and so are the effects.

Many members of the crew working on *Hulk* wore baseball hats with Chinese characters on the side that roughly translate as

Hulk earnestly duplicates the scruffy desert landscape that was an integral part of Kirby and Lee's original vision of the Hulk.

"kick ass." The special effects could well be what the hats are referring to.

Numbered first among those effects must be the Hulk himself.

The reason for that, of course, is that the big-screen Hulk really is a Freudian manifestation of the superego. In other words, he's just pretend. "Pretend" in Hollywood lingo is spelled "CGI," and it stands for "computer-generated image," or something close. CGI is the rage in action and animation moviemaking because if you can imagine it and make a mouse go back and forth, you can put it on the screen. *Toy Story* and its offspring are CGI movies; so are films like *Jimmy*

The big-screen Hulk really is a Freudian **manifestation** of the **superego**. In other words, he's just pretend.

Neutron and *Shrek*. *Final Fantasy* was supposed to be the grand vizier of all these, the CGI film that changed sci-fi moviemaking forever and sent video games flying to the big screen like the monkeys in *Wizard of Oz*, but someone forgot to tell the scriptwriters.

The trickiest thing you can do with CGI is combine it seamlessly with live-action footage. When it's done in small amounts and with a modicum of taste and logic, like in the *Harry Potter* and *Star Wars* movies, it can be stunning; when it's made the star of the show, such as in the less-than-classic live-action remakes of the classic Saturday-morning cartoons *Scooby-Doo* and *Rocky and Bullwinkle*, the result has been more scary than entertaining. A new young generation equates terror not with Bela Lugosi sipping O-positive but images of a sausage-shaped 3-D computer graphic scarfing Scooby Snacks and a robotic moose trading hip banter with Robert DeNiro.

If 3-D images of traditional 2-D characters really are extra-scary, then making the Hulk a CGI image was a good idea.

No Bullitt here, Karl Malden need not apply: The Hulk takes to the streets of San Francisco.

Besides, the filmmakers didn't have much choice if they didn't want to abandon reality altogether for the goofball reality of the *Godzilla* movies, where no one could live in the cities he destroys and no one could drive the cars he crushes. Ray Harryhausen was great, but not here, thanks.

"It's true to the classic Hulk, but with the advantages you have today," Marvel Studios head Avi Arad said of the CGI Hulk. "It's much more human than animal. When you see the face, there's human emotion."

Okay, but no one's expecting the Hulk to exhibit any more facial expressions than prime Katherine Hepburn (when Dorothy Parker wrote, "she runs the gamut of emotions from A to B"). His mission, should he decide to accept it, is to manipulate a few objects — some living, some not and some a little of both. *That's* the proper use of a CGI character.

All right, already. The CGI Hulk looks very, very good. Good enough to occasionally make you forget he's CGI, that's how good. The best CGI character ever? That's

The CGI Hulk is up to the standards of everything else in the movie. In other words, he looks very good.

hard to say. The new boss becomes the old boss in about as much time as it takes a computer to become obsolete. This is for sure, though: You believe Eric Bana evolves into a computer graphic. You believe that when the Hulk plays track-and-field with an M-1 Abrams it's not accomplished with a couple of keystrokes. Best ever? Who knows? But up to the standards of everything else in the movie? Oh, yeah.

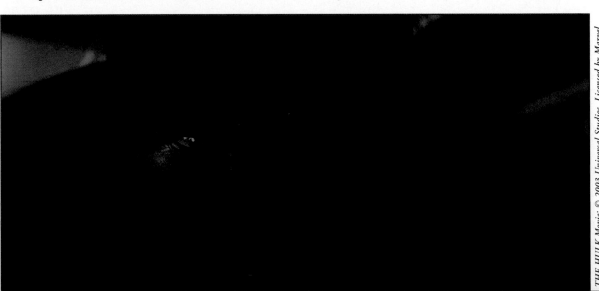

That eye needs no introduction.

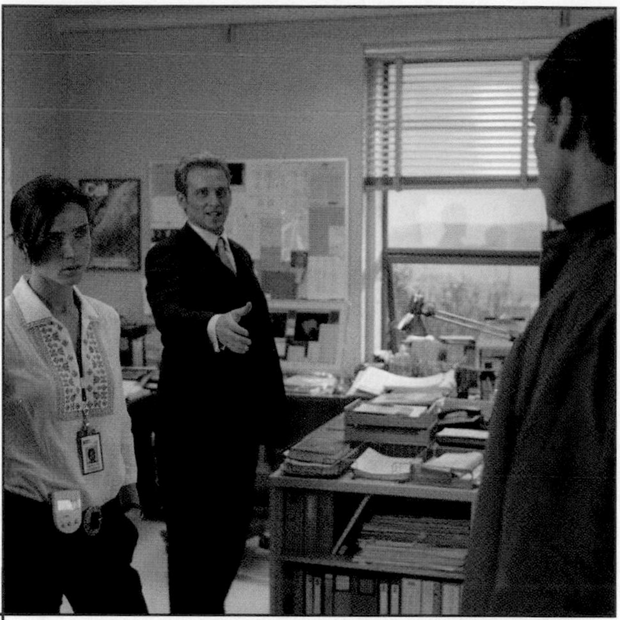

Glenn Talbot tries to impress himself on a less-than-impressed Bruce Banner.

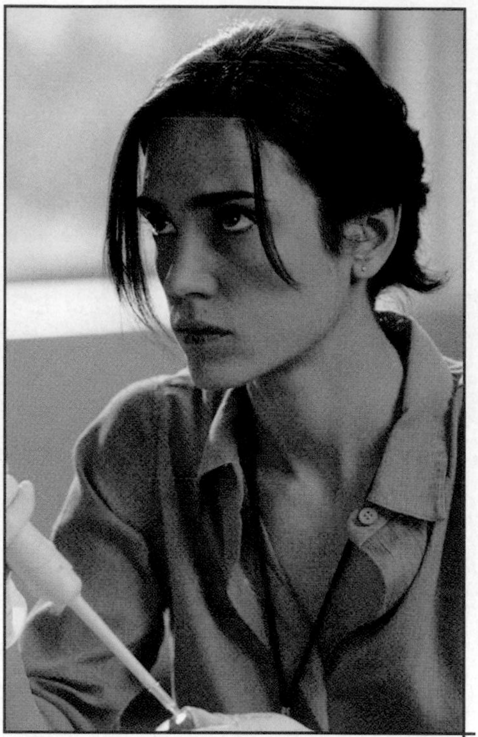

Betty Ross (That's no home-perm kit she's messing with.)

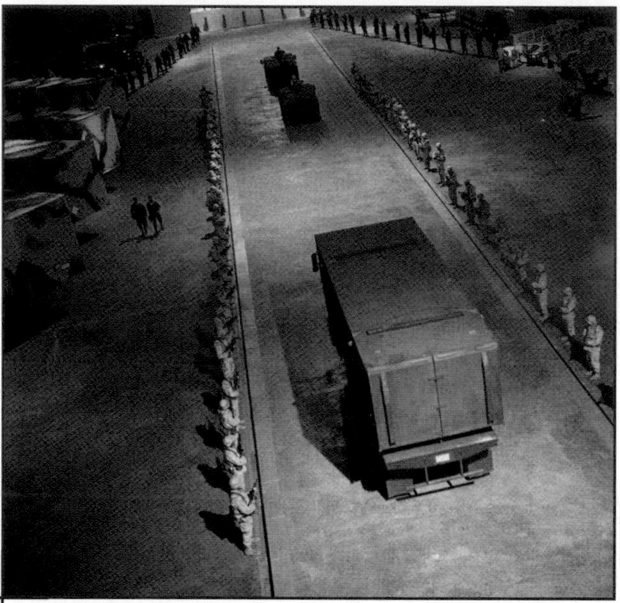

The military mobilizes.

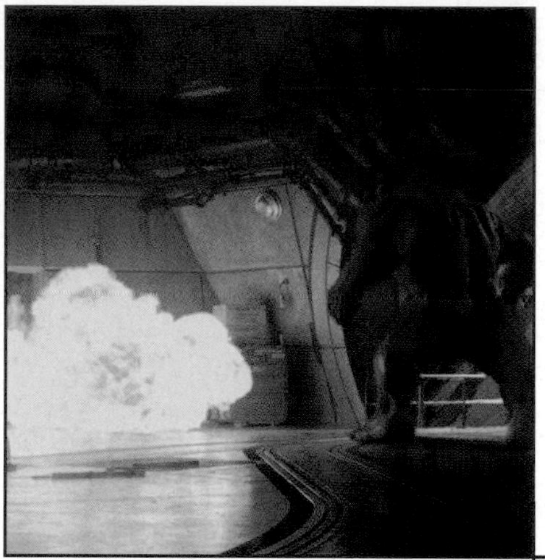

The Hulk on the loose where he shouldn't be.

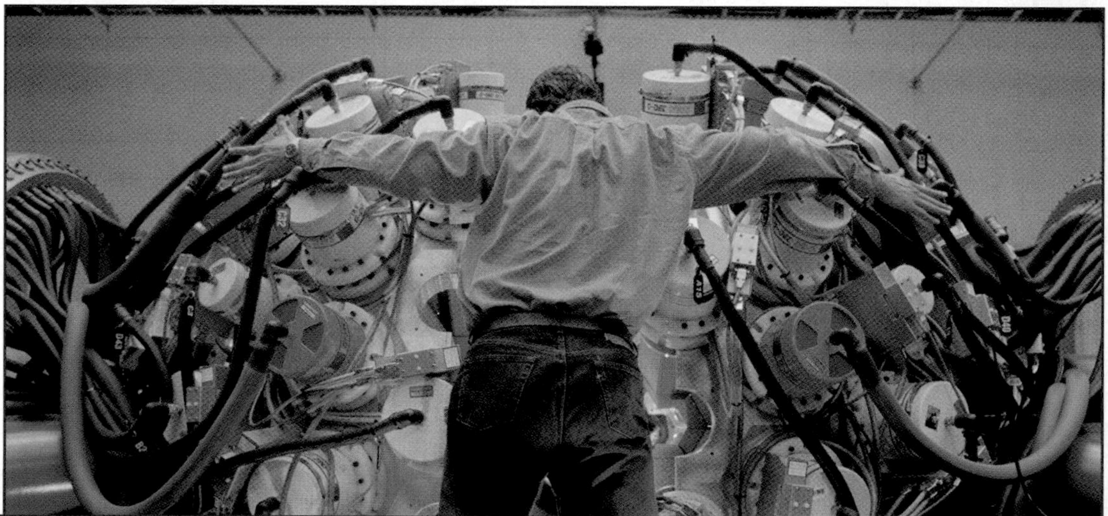

Bruce Banner bear-hugs one of his greatest creations, the transformation chamber.

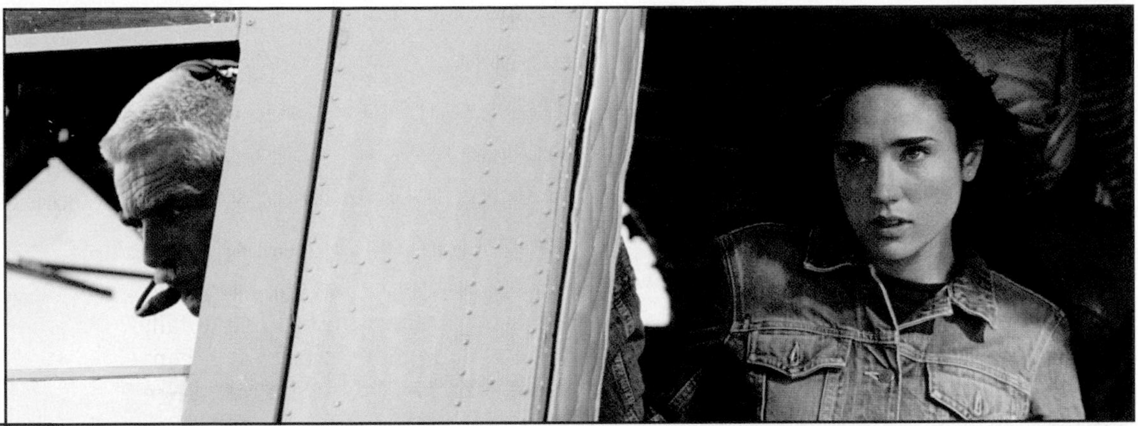

Sam Elliot and Jennifer Connelly bring a welcome heft to their roles.

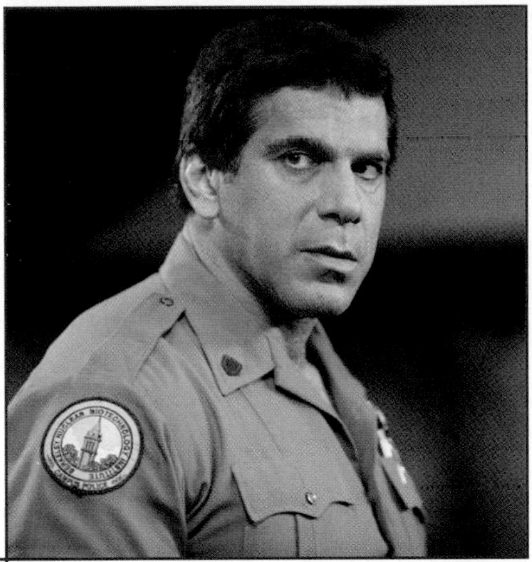

Shades of the past, Lou Ferrigno cameos as a security guard.

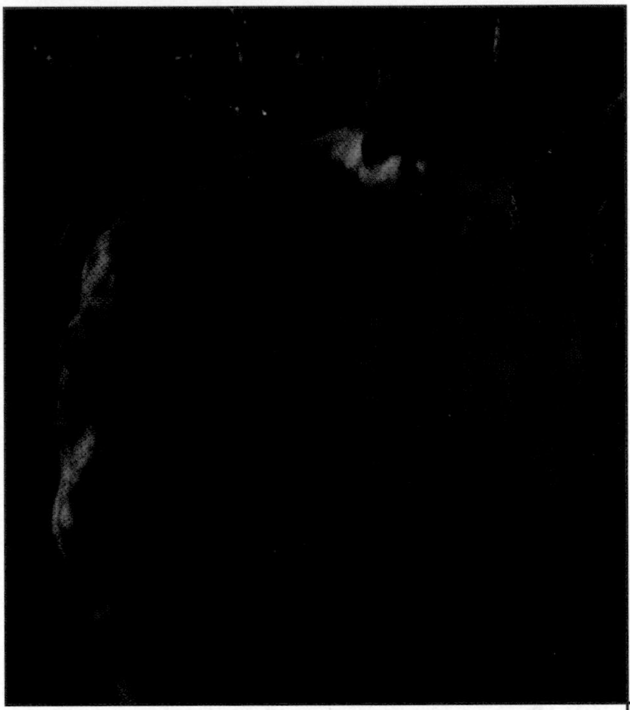

You believe Eric Bana transforms into the Hulk. That's the important thing.

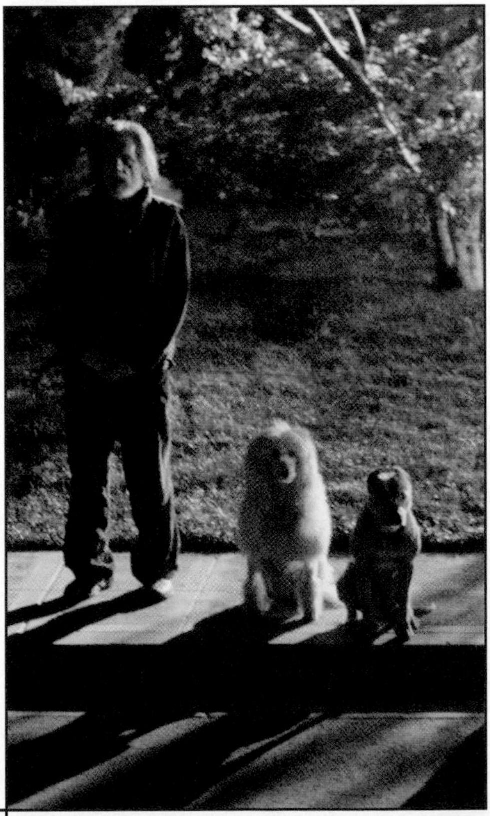

Nick Nolte brings the dogs.

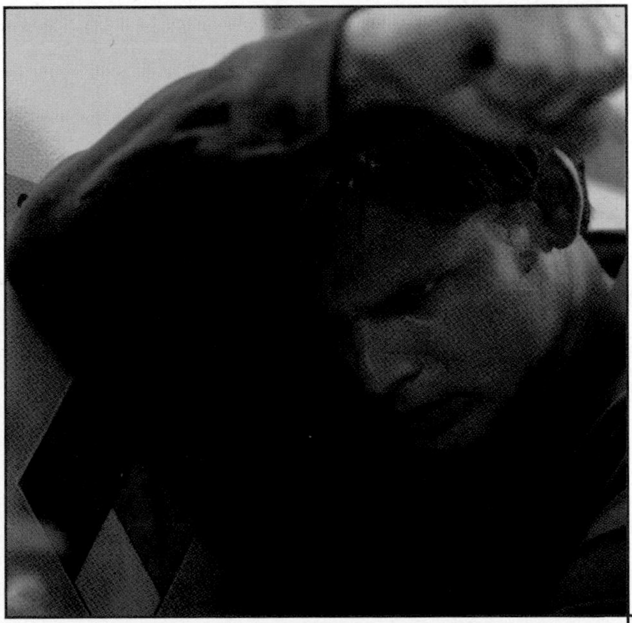

Eric Bana brings a near-manic intensity to the part of Bruce Banner.

Yin-yang Ang

Of course, you don't need to tell director Ang Lee how to use characters, no matter what language they speak or how they're created. He has character-building skills out the yin-yang — which only makes sense, because directors don't get any yin-yangier than Ang Lee.

Ang Lee treats contradictions like they're Twinkies. He scarfs 'em right down. In Ang Lee's world, English drawing-room comedies, kung-fu movies, buddy pics, period epics and high-budget action-adventures not only co-exist, they hang out with more style than the cast of *Friends*.

If you figure it takes a bipolar director to make a movie of the Incredible Hulk, Ang Lee is your man. He studied filmmaking at New York University, where he worked on *Joe's Bed-Stuy Barbershop: We Cut Heads*, the prophetic student film of that other Lee, named Spike. While Lee-comma-Spike quickly went on from that film to make *Do the Right Thing*, play Mars Blackmon and make a nuisance of himself at Knicks games, Lee-comma-Ang spent the first six years writing screenplays, which only sounds leisurely to those unfamiliar with the gone-in-60-seconds pace at which Lee works.

The Taiwan-meets-New-York coming-of-age film *Pushing Hands* (1992) was Lee's directorial debut, and was quickly followed by the Mandarin-language *Eat Drink Man Woman* and the veddy British *Sense and Sensibility*. (What do the two movies have in common? You can't understand what the characters are saying in either one.) They were succeeded in short order by the dark, contemporary American domestic drama *The Ice Storm* and the Civil War movie *Race with the Devil* — which features, of all people, Jewel. (What do *The Ice Storm, Race with the Devil* and *Spider-Man* have in common? Answer: Jewel. WRONG! Answer: Tobey Maguire.)

All those movies, good as they were, were just the warm-ups for Lee's 2000 kung-fu dreamscape epic, *Crouching Tiger, Hidden Dragon*. As delicate as kenji on rice paper and as sharply rendered as Sapporo steel, *Crouching Tiger* established a new film genre — call it the martial-art film — at the same time it established itself as one of a kind. (Think that's easy? Name another.) With a minimum of pre-release fanfare but word-of-mouth that spread like Subway franchises, *CTHD* became the highest-grossing foreign-language film in American film history, scoring 14 Oscar nominations and 16 British Academy Award nominations

Art imitating life: Ang Lee was able to convey the physical and mental fatigue generated by Bruce Banner's high-test dual personality in part by putting the actors through a grueling shooting schedule.

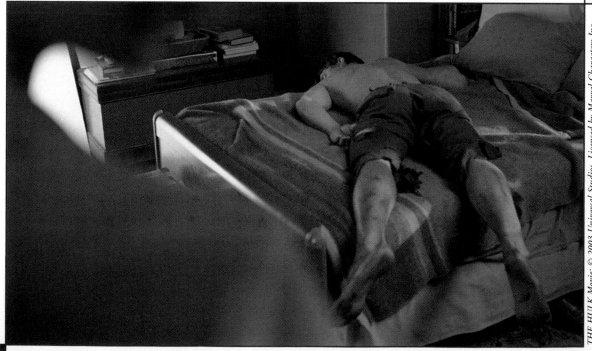

Everywhere to run, nowhere to hide: The CGI Hulk at full speed.

that turned into four Oscars, four British Academy Awards and a really cool line of action toys.

Not resting on his laurels by any means, Lee hopped into the Asian action-film genre, or something like it, for 2001's *The Hire*. Depending on who you talk to, *The Hire* is either the future of Internet marketing or one heck of a series of short promotional films made for BMW by some of the world's finest directors — and Madonna's husband, too. Either way, *The Hire* is something special and very good.

The five films in each "series" of *The Hire* feature Clive Owen as The Driver, who carts famous customers to their destinations in various models of BMW while being pursued by baddies like paparazzi, hit people, exes, fans and Audi dealers. It's like being a soccer mom with less drama and fewer empty juice boxes to clean up at the end.

The Hire does a great job of showing off BMWs; Lee's bit, called *Chosen*, does a great job of showing off his skills as a director. Without giving too much away, Lee's piece involves the safe passage of a young Tibetan child (a baby Dalai?) with mystical qualities. A lot like a 325i, when you get down to it. Hey, the line between advertising and movies is vaguer than an election promise. Ignore the fact that *The Hire* is a super-slick six-minute ad, and enjoy it for its virtues. It's the anti-Ritalin. It's like drinking adrenaline mixed with Mr. Green. It's damn good fun.

None of these movies really prepared Lee for a movie like *Hulk*. Or maybe all of them did. Maybe Ang Lee made *Hulk* by taking a dash of the family drama from *The Ice Storm* and *The Wedding Banquet*, mixing in a half-cup of the delicacy of *Sense and Sensibility*, adding two sticks of action from *Crouching Tiger, Hidden Dragon*, throwing in a generous dash of commercialism from *The Hire*, and serving it shaken, not stirred.

That's not far off. You can find hints of *Hulk*'s essential claustrophobia in *Pushing Hands* and *The Ice Storm*. The war scenes in *Race with the Devil* are eons removed from the battle scenes in *Hulk*, but the choreography and pacing (not to mention the feeling of uncontrolled chaos) are much, much closer. The relationship between Betty and Bruce could have come out of any of Lee's movies, which start with a single relationship and work outward from there. And *Crouching Tiger*'s contribution might be the most important: the stubbornly nonlinear plot, which spins tighter and tighter around its core like a tetherball on a pole.

The debts *Hulk* owes to Universal's classic horror films are obvious, but ultimately deceptive. With Ang Lee, you're never sure of the source of the inspiration, but the inspiration is always right there. You want a distinctive movie, a movie with style, a movie that wrings every last drop of movieness from its script, a movie that can turn like Tony Hawk in a halfpipe? Have Ang Lee direct it.

How can you tell Eric Bana was the right choice for the role of Bruce Banner? Check out the eyes. It's all there.

Bana, not banal

The remainder of the cast that isn't a .wav file and a couple of JPEGs follows the leader. (The leader of the film and not the Leader, thank goodness. One toilet-scrubber-turned-arch-villain with a high-rise head is plenty.) It starts from the top, with Australian comedian Eric Bana's everything-you-always-dreamed-of-and-then-some portrayal of the haunted, hunted Bruce Banner.

An Australian comic playing Bruce Banner? What's next? The Wiggles playing the Rolling Stones and lip-synching "Sympathy for the Devil"? And Eric WHO? Not so fast. Eric Bana is a comedian by trade — but like a lot of comedians, he's turned into a very talented actor who can immerse himself in a role. Think Robert DeNiro for the Subaru Impreza WRX generation.

And as far as "Eric WHO?" goes, Eric Bana has been in the top five of most search engines' most-searched-upon phrases since late last fall. So there.

After a rapid-fire decade that took him from behind the bar at Melbourne's Castle Hotel to the end-of-the-century Logie (pronounced "loogie") Awards, where he was voted Australia's Most Popular Comedy Performer, Bana burst — and we mean burst — on the international scene in 2000 with his scarifying yet blackly comedic portrayal of Aussie mass murderer, author and cult hero Mark "Chopper" Read in *Chopper*. Bana gained 30 pounds, sported a nasty Fu Manchu and some bitchin' tattoos, and nailed the part. Absolutely nailed it. His Chopper Read will keep you up at night better than a Mountain Dew nightcap chased with half a pound of M&Ms.

From playing a Chopper to riding in one, Bana then landed a key role in the wall-to-wall wartime thriller *Black Hawk Down*

(2001). In that film, Bana showed he could play in an amped-up big-screen actioner, and that he could play American — just the prerequisites for playing Bruce Banner.

Maybe it's flop sweat that gives a comedian like Bana the ability to really play scared, to give his audience the unmistakable feeling of his heart trying to dig its way out of his chest with a teaspoon. Whatever gets him there, Bana gets there. He takes the part of Bruce Banner and runs with it all the way to Perth and back. The tension and intensity that come with being the human side of a ticking time bomb aren't just conveyed; they're FedExed. It's the sort of performance that wins Oscars in the sort of movie that doesn't get Best Actor awards. Darn shame, too.

"This has obviously gone beyond my wildest dreams," Bana said in one interview. "Sam Elliot, Nick Nolte, Jennifer Connelly, Ang Lee — could you be surrounded by better people? It's great being the weakest link."

Bana proves it doesn't hurt to be a comedian at heart to play Bruce Banner, and it's okay if you're not a household name. Movies like *Hulk* make household names. Just ask Tobey Maguire and Hugh Jackman.

Glenn Talbot recoils in terror, and with pretty good reason. There's a lesson in this: Stay out of dark rooms when there's a Hulk afoot and you're a jerk.

Jennifer Connelly has made an Oscar-winning career out of playing the beautiful wives of talented-but-disturbed husbands.

Jennifer Rocketeer

It seems like forever since Disney made its ill-fated leap into the comic-book-based-superhero-movie rapids with *The Rocketeer*. The movie was dashingly made and promised instant stardom and then some for its attractive young stars, Billy Campbell and Jennifer Connolly. But the instant stardom took more than a decade to arrive — and when it did, *The Rocketeer* had nothing to do with it. For Campbell, it was the lead opposite Sela Ward on TV's *Once and Again*; for Connolly, it was supporting Russell Crowe's tour-de-force performance in *A Beautiful Mind*.

For Connolly, the irony was sweet: Crowe's performance was the engine that powered *A Beautiful Mind* to the Best Picture Oscar; she looked beautiful, aged well and hung on for dear life. But when the Oscars were awarded for acting, Connolly went home with the Best Supporting Actress statuette, and Crowe went home empty-handed.

The Oscar for *A Beautiful Mind* was the reward for more than 15 years of hard work and increasingly complex screen roles that took her from having to rescue her brother from David Bowie's clutches in *Labyrinth* to hanging around the edges of *Mulholland Falls* (where she first worked with *Hulk* co-star Nick Nolte); playing an out-of-hope junkie in *Requiem for a Dream*; and portraying the wife of another famously disturbed genius, painter Jackson Pollock, in Ed Harris' biopic *Pollock*.

By portraying Betty Ross in *Hulk*, Connolly has run her string of wives/girl-friends-of-disturbed-geniuses roles to three. She has the furrowed-brow, I-wish-I-could-climb-inside-his-brain-with-a-monkey-wrench look cold. Should acting jobs ever dry up, she can always find work as the poster person for the Love Conquers All League. Look on the bright side, though: If she hangs on for the movie adaptation of *The Ultimates*, she can have dinner with Freddie Prinze Jr.

Rich Man, Poor Man, sick, sick man

If he were a football player — and he was — the cliché best describing Nick Nolte would be, "He leaves it all out on the field." As Bruce Banner's father, occasionally beautiful mind David Banner, Nolte has plenty to leave out there and no shortage of field. It's a sort of over-the-top part that Nolte, in his infinite wisdom, leaves just this side of the top. It's the only way.

If it seems like there's no part Nick Nolte can't play, it's because there's no part Nolte *hasn't* played. After getting kicked out of Arizona State for bad grades, Nolte spent almost a decade and a half on the plate-and-a-play dinner-theater circuit, landing bit parts in B movies, never coming close to even a medium-sized break. That changed in 1974 when at the tender age of 36 he landed one of the twin leads opposite Peter Strauss in the barrier-breaking miniseries *Rich Man, Poor Man*. Given his up-from-the-wrong-side-of-the-tracks entry into big-time acting, you can guess which man Nolte played. And based on the fact that Peter Strauss isn't starring in *Hulk* and hasn't won an Oscar, you can guess which role turned out to be the plum.

Once he cracked the big time, Nolte didn't turn back. He scored plum roles in *The Deep* (1977), *North Dallas Forty* (1979), *Down and Out in Beverly Hills* (1986), *The Prince of Tides* (1991), *Mulholland Falls* (1996), *Affliction* (1997) and *The Thin Red Line* (1998) — aging a little less than gracefully but retaining every ounce of his screen-holding power, like the acting version of Neil Young.

Constantly delivering the unexpected, underplaying where a lesser actor would slather on the ham and bombast, Nolte makes David Banner the sort of father no normal child would ever want to have. He gives a sort of evil a sort of scruffy, down-at-heel look. And that's the point, isn't it?

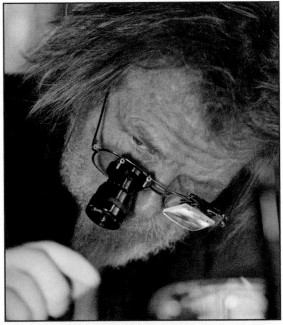

A touch of Neil Young, a touch of Jerry Garcia: Nick Nolte gets deep inside the role of David Banner.

Elliot: Western thunderstorm

It takes a great actor to give the character of Gen. Thunderbolt Ross more dimensions than a Shrinky Dink, and Sam Elliot is a great actor. What a coincidence.

Usually associated with cowboy films, Elliot always brings a touch of humanity to the most out-there parts — not that

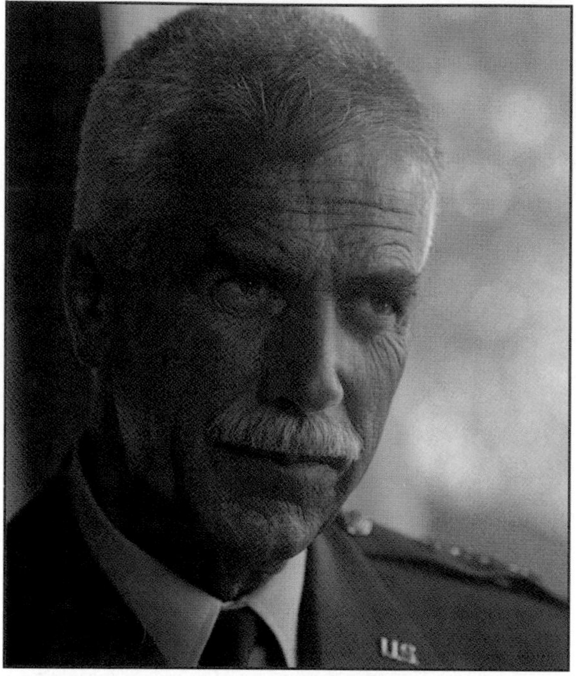

Elliott gets many of those. Most of the time, Elliot gets the parts that a guy who made his big-screen debut in *Butch Cassidy and the Sundance Kid* should get, and he does 'em up proud. He's what Gary Cooper would be if he were still around and married to the girl who drove off with Dustin Hoffman in *The Graduate* (Katherine Ross, also Mrs. Sam Elliot). Since the big-screen western has gone the way of the passenger pigeon, Elliot has done most of his cow-pokin' on TV, where he's appeared on miniseries and made-for-TV movies like *The Sacketts* (1977), *I Will Fight No More Forever* (1981), *The Shadow Riders* (1982), *Houston: The Legend of Texas* (1986), *Conagher* (1991) and *The Desperate Trail* (1995).

If you think it's overcasting having an actor of Elliot's stature play Thunderbolt Ross, you haven't seen the movie yet. To start with, Elliot has the one thing most necessary to play Thunderbolt Ross: a whopping big mustache. After that, any acting skills are gravy. Fortunately, Ross has plenty of gravy to ladle on a surprisingly meaty role. (Sorry.) Besides, there's no such thing as overcasting with Sam Elliot. He can make any role look good.

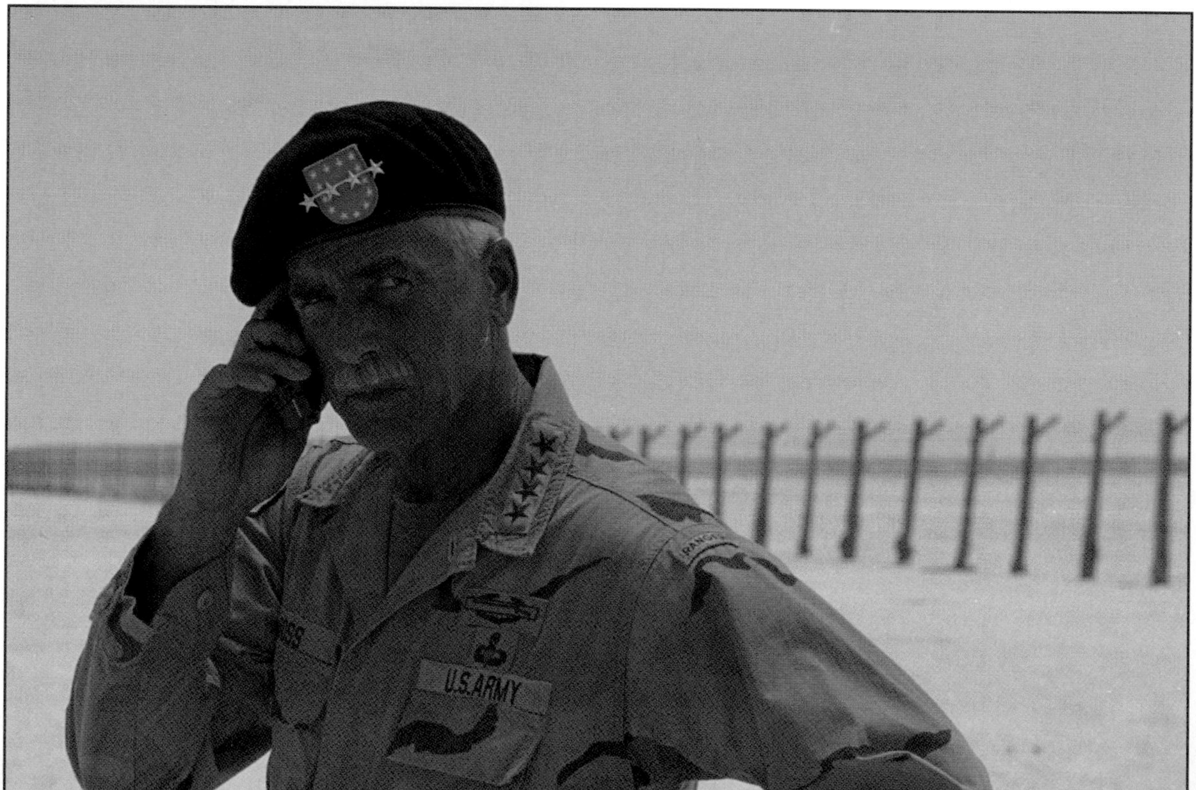
U.S.ARMY

Sam Elliot's Thunderbolt Ross is eons removed from Stan Lee's one-dimensional bluster-bag.

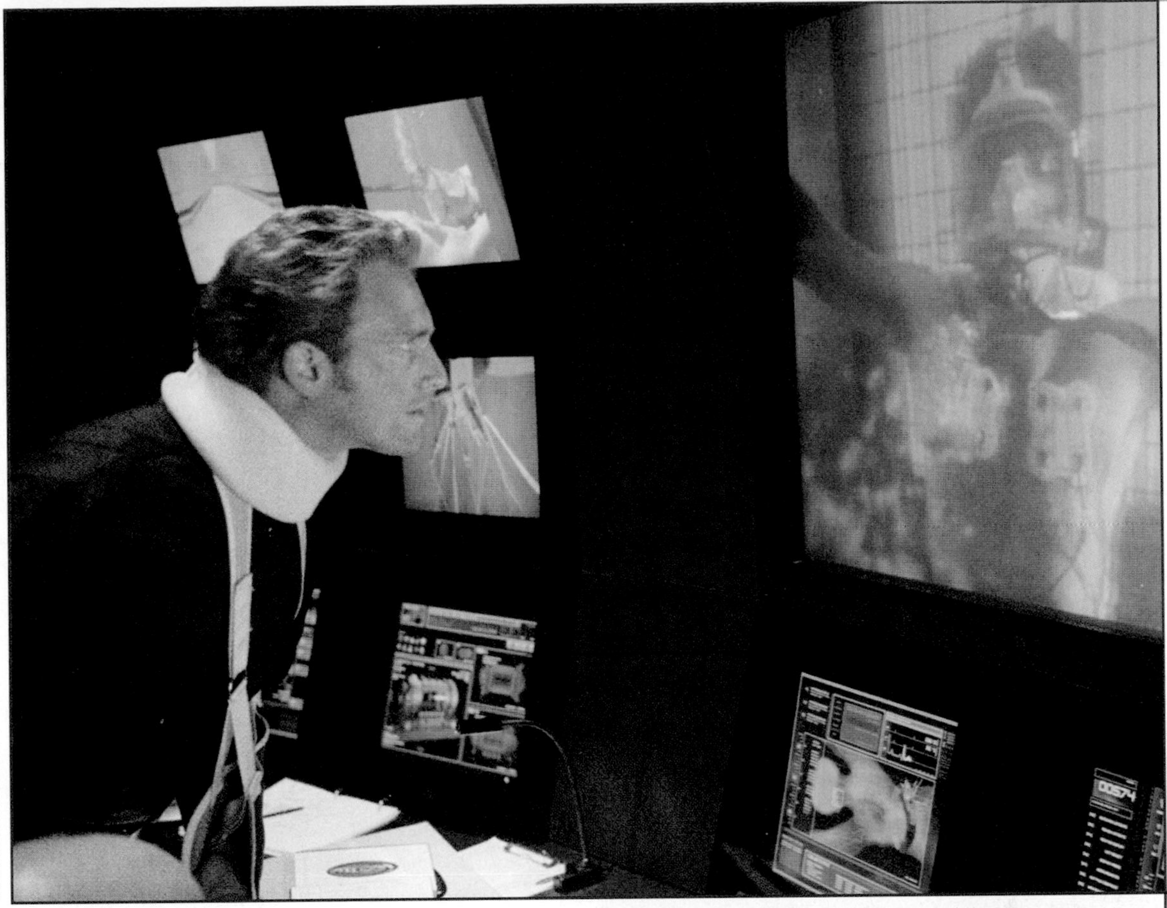

Josh Lucas has raised fuming and fretting to an art form.

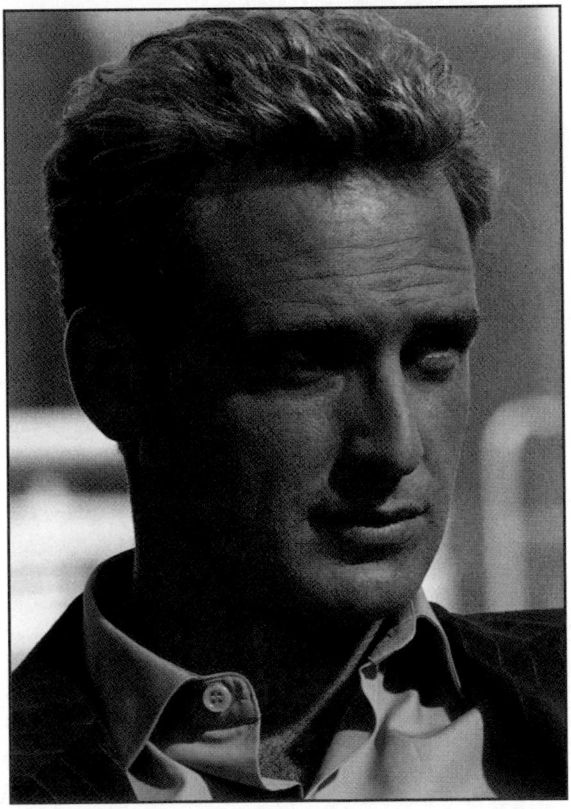

Josh Lucas: Major major

Maybe it's typecasting. Or maybe it's perfect casting. Casting Josh Lucas as Maj. Glenn Talbot, the pigheaded-but-patriotic rival for the affections of Betty Ross, puts the movies' best player of unsympathetic handsome-guy roles smack-dab in his element.

A veteran of family-TV dramas like *Life Goes On* and *Snowy River: The McGregor Saga*, Lucas' first big-screen role provided no tip-off as to his future career direction: He played one of the crash-stranded rugby players in the film of Piers Paul Read's *Alive*. It wasn't until he played the cad in *Restless* (filmed in 1998; released in 2000) that Lucas found his niche. And what a niche: The pal of a serial killer in *American Psycho* (2000); the sleaze ball older lover in *The Deep End* (2001); the smart-aleck rival of John Nash in *A Beautiful Mind* (2001), where he first worked with *Hulk* co-star Jennifer Connelly; and the cast-aside husband of Southern-belle-turned-socialite Reese Witherspoon in *Sweet Home Alabama* (2002). If you're looking for someone to frown, fume and fret — and maybe get it in the end — Lucas is your first-call guy. And the producers of *Hulk* made the call.

Putting the 'Marvel' in films

It's tempting to look at *Hulk* in a vacuum, though it's hard to eat popcorn there. But *Hulk* is just one of a series of Marvel Comics-based movies masterminded by Marvel Studios head Avi Arad. The series launched with *X-Men* in 2000; picked up a major head of steam with *Spider-Man* in 2002; and really kicks into overdrive in 2003, with sexiest-man-alive Ben Affleck as *Daredevil*, followed by *Hulk* and *X2* (with more Halle Berry as Storm — yum!).

Just for the record, Marvel makes more money on movies than it does on comic books. *Blade* grossed $70 million; *X-Men* hauled in $170 million, and *Spider-Man*'s total gross was more than $403 million. Marvel doesn't get it all, but it gets enough. And while it's way more than tempting to look at *Hulk* as a bald money grab, Marvel Studios chief Avi Arad insists it's a whole lot more. "The world is realizing that comics are good literature," Arad told *Newsweek*, and there's a shortage of fresh good literature for the screen. That's why every election year brings forth a new version of *Romeo and Juliet.*

To Marvel's credit, this isn't an assembly-line movie operation where the only thing that changes is what blows up. Each movie released has a strong identity: *X-Men* is the action-adventure team-up flick, the most effects-heavy and superficial, the best

summer movie of the bunch; *Spider-Man* is livelier, breezier, a little more concerned with character and personality but not afraid to take you web-swingin' when the opportunity arises. *Daredevil* is half darkness and grit, and half the irrepressible charm of Ben Affleck. It's a movie as sleek as its protagonist, close to the comic but condensed and streamlined.

Hulk is the darkest and most psychological of the bunch. Is it the best? It's the most grown-up, the most complex. It's the movie that benefits the most from repeated viewings. At the same time, it has some of the most pulse-pounding, out-of-this-world action you'll find in any of the Marvel movies.

And who knows? A decade from now, when the Marvel movies have pushed aside James Bond as the films everyone waits for to kick off their summer and/or holiday season, *Hulk* may be seen as the movie that took the franchise to another level, like *Goldfinger*. It may be the movie that spun off sequels and sub-sequels, taking viewers ever farther into the tortured contradictions that are at the heart of the Hulk. Or maybe it'll be one and done, with nothing much more than one heck of a DVD to show for the combined efforts of the very talented principals involved.

However it shakes out, it'll shake out big. With the Hulk, there's no other way.

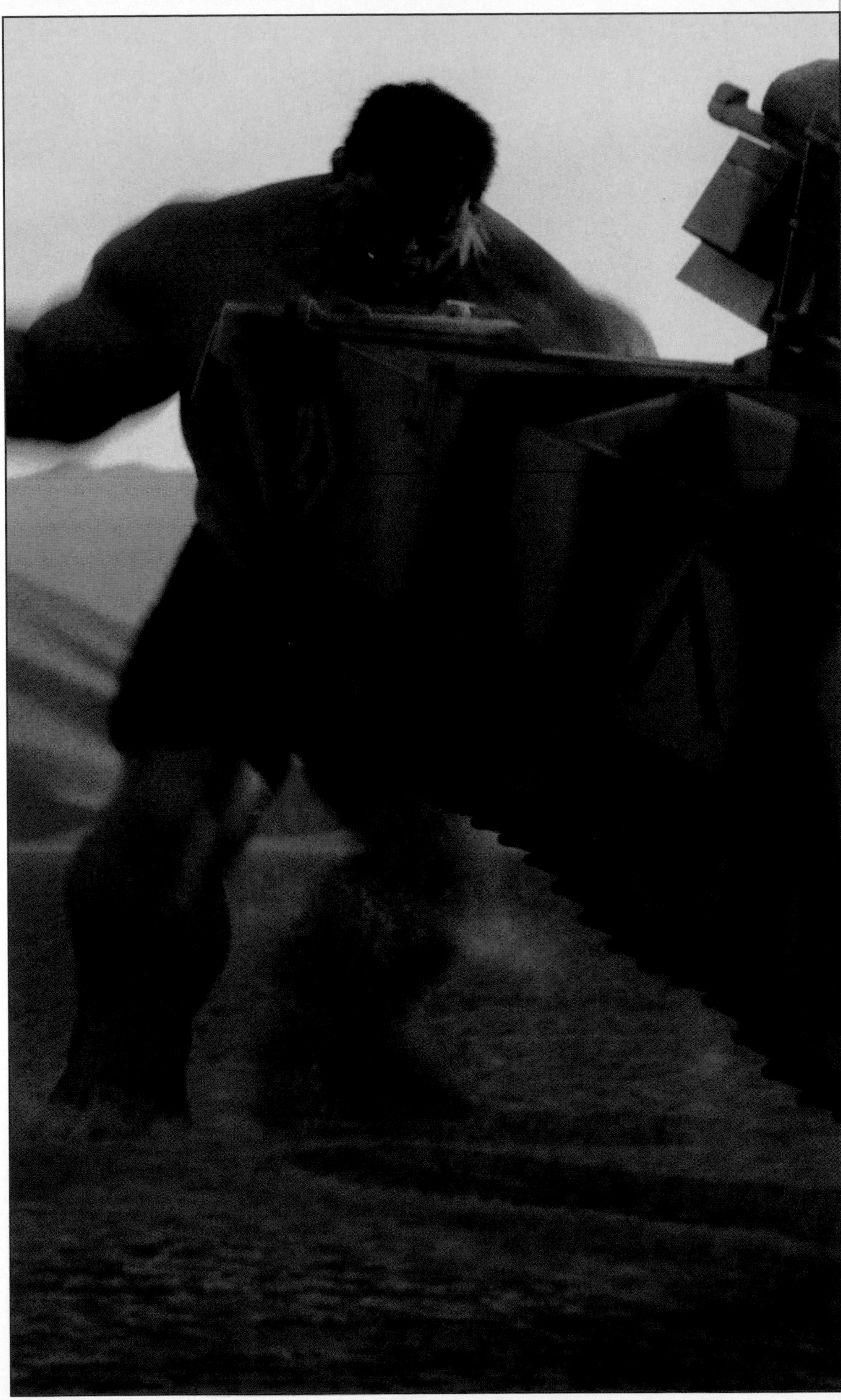

Psychological thrillers can get violent, too: The Hulk totals a tank.

Chapter Seven

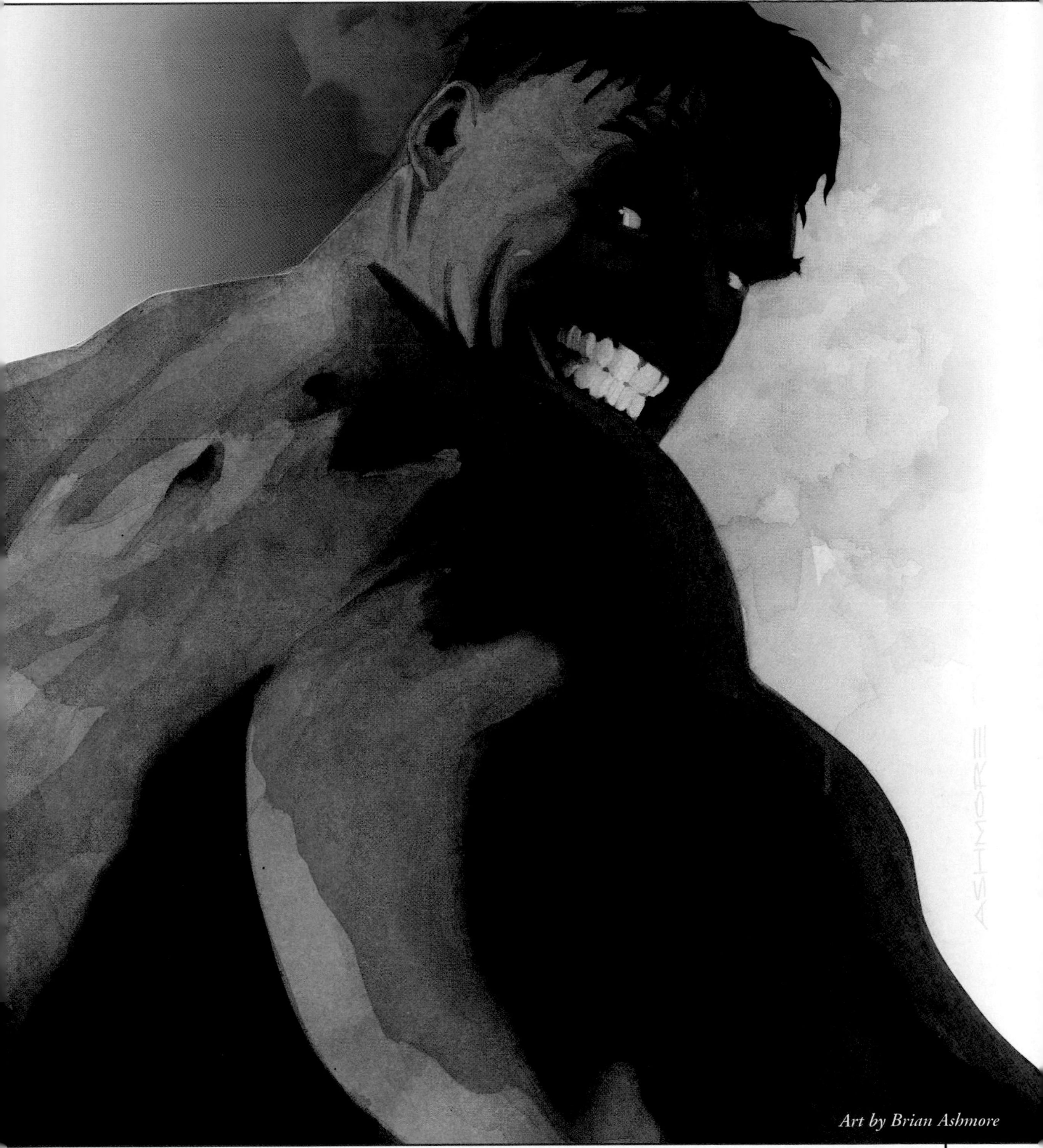
ASHMORE

Art by Brian Ashmore

GREEN DAY

The Hulk commands the spotlight — again!

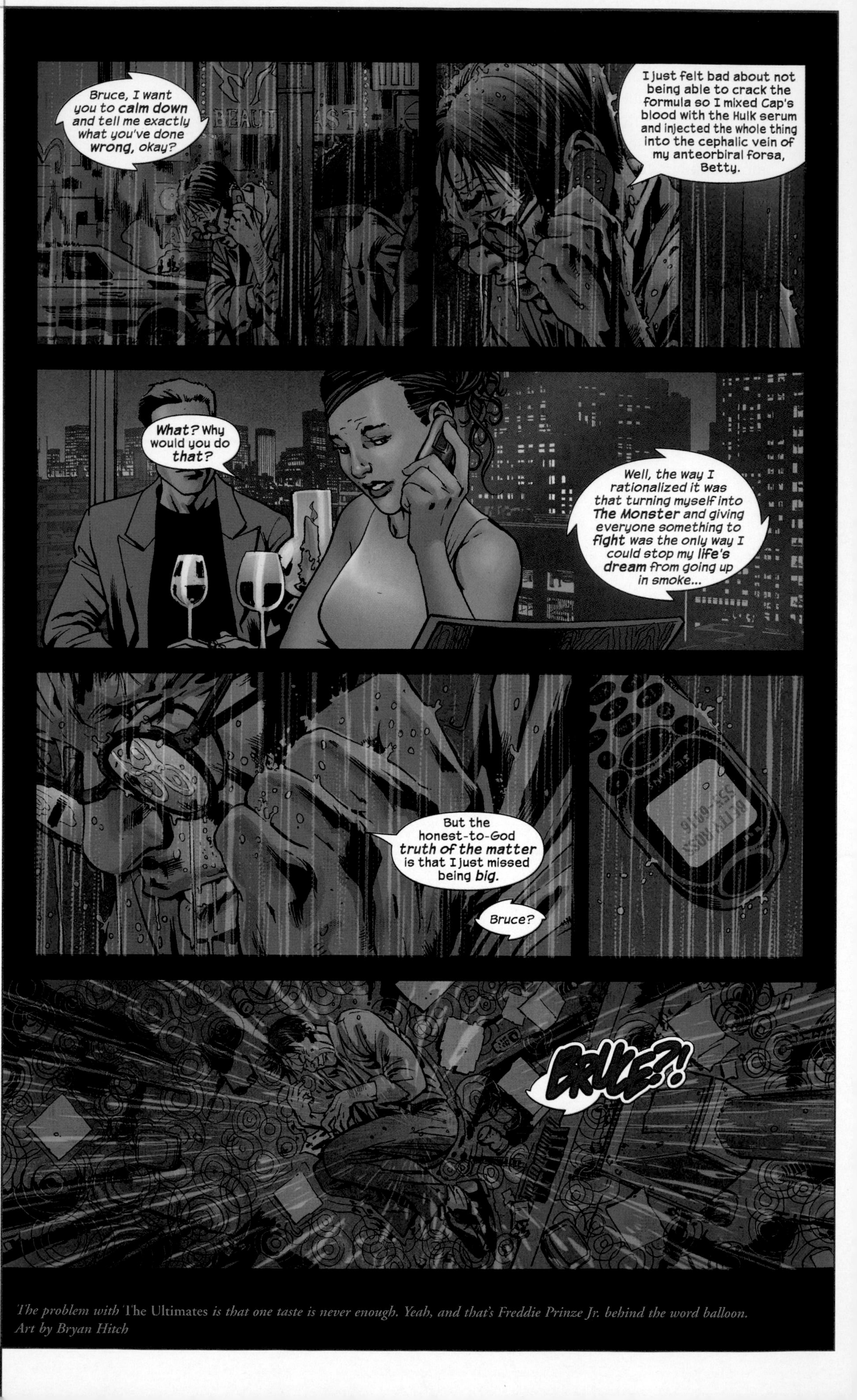

Bruce, I want you to calm down and tell me exactly what you've done wrong, okay?
I just felt bad about not being able to crack the formula so I mixed Cap's blood with the Hulk serum and injected the whole thing into the cephalic vein of my anteorbiral forsa, Betty.
What? Why would you do that?
Well, the way I rationalized it was that turning myself into The Monster and giving everyone something to fight was the only way I could stop my life's dream from going up in smoke...
But the honest-to-God truth of the matter is that I just missed being big.
Bruce?
BRUCE?!

The problem with The Ultimates *is that one taste is never enough. Yeah, and that's Freddie Prinze Jr. behind the word balloon. Art by Bryan Hitch*

With the Hulk, getting there has never been half the fun. The transformation of Bruce Banner into the Incredible Hulk is one of those necessary evils that comics occasionally require for a character's raison d'etre to hang together no matter how tattered — like those purple pants that shred at the ends but never come off.

Taking it one step farther, it's not even the transformation of Bruce Banner into the Hulk that's the problem. The problem is Bruce Banner.

Bruce Banner is the only alter-ego in comics to have gone through the North Korean version of the Dale Carnegie course. Instead of Peter Parker's youthful exuberance, Matt Murdock's intensity, Tony Stark's boozy insouciance or Jennifer Walters' looks, Bruce Banner has a problem. As a well-rounded individual, he projects slightly less well than the Unibomber. And he's a *protagonist*?

Here's an example of Banner at his best: In *The Ultimates #5*, Bruce Banner shoots up with Hulk-flavored Snapple because he can't handle rejection — from his ex-wife, no less — and can't face the fact that it's way past over. After a slam-bang wrecking ball featuring the Hulk vs. the best the Marvel Universe can throw at him (including — and hold your hand over your heart when you say it, mateys — Captain America), Banner winds up naked in the rubble of a couple blocks of prime Manhattan real estate.

The brilliance of the **Banner** *mini-series is that it's successfully built around this one mad scientist who gets really* **mad.**

Art by Stuart Immonen

He's no farther ahead than he was before he Hulked out. He still doesn't have the girl — and the girl doesn't even have Freddie Prinze Jr. The only difference between then and now is that a couple dozen one-bedroom lofts are off rent control.

Thankfully, the new *Incredible Hulk* books feature a Bruce Banner that's a little more capable of handling what's being thrown at him — even if there's a limit to parental control of the Hulk, and there probably always will be. The plot lines that put Banner in control of the Hulk ultimately fizzled. They had to. Without the instability, the Hulk's just another superhero who controls his transformations. Last anyone checked, the world wasn't clamoring for another quick-change artist. It's the volatility that sets him apart, and that applies to Kurt Cobain, Sean Penn, Pete Townsend, Jackson Pollock and antifreeze filtered through bread as well as it applies to the Hulk.

Sort of in control or totally out of control, Banner's gotta be in the picture. Think what would happen if there wasn't a Bruce Banner, if Bruce Banner had simply ceased to exist after that fateful moment when he clotheslined Rick Jones into a drainage ditch and took all the gamma radiation without tossing the leftovers into a Tupperware. Without Bruce Banner, there'd just be a big green guy doing the Teaberry Shuffle on major metropolitan areas and making like an American Godzilla for the benefit of the local armed forces, who really didn't need all those tanks anyway. If a situation called for a brilliant nuclear physicist, too bad. Unless Domino's delivers a free nuclear scientist with the purchase of a large pepperoni, all the Hulk could do is make like Samson while the Leader takes over the free world — and the pay world, too.

Maybe the best idea would be for the Hulk to be TiVo'd, so you could immediately skip the pathetic-loser Banner stuff and the messy psychological spills, and just have nothing but end-to-end Hulking, with all the plot twists left intact.

Actually, you can have that right now. It's called *reading the good parts*.

One of the best things about

Is there an Incredible Hulk deep within every pathetic loser? Hopefully not. Art by Richard Corben

books in general and comics in particular is they come with a built-in search function. You like the part where Bruce Banner jabs the *Ancient Mariner*-spouting baddie with a syringe of Hulk blood and he blows up like the Inflatable Spleen? Turn to that page; read it again. You like the issue where he lands in an idyllic Victorian town where everyone treats him like he's totally normal, only none of it exists? Buy a copy of *Incredible Hulk #147* and read it.

The brilliance of the *Banner* mini series is that it's successfully built around this one mad scientist who gets really *mad*. The brilliance of the new and improved *Incredible Hulk* comics is that they keep the madness real, tuck it under the surface, imply violence when full-blown fight scenes are expected and take the plot from 0 to 60 in five seconds flat so that the only time for navel-gazing is on the recoil from the whiplash. The brilliance of *The Ultimates* is that the pathetic loser Banner is such a pathetic loser that it's ... uh, pathetic. And the brilliance of the *Hulk* movie is that it makes the mad scientist easier to understand, if not exactly easy to love. Jennifer Connelly gets props from the Tammy Wynette Appreciation Society for standing by her man no matter what, though sometimes you get the feeling she might have been better off with one of Eric Bana's previous characters, the mass murderer and folk hero Chopper Read.

So when you figure most Hulk stories have a dysfunctional protagonist who changes into a really strong, even more dysfunctional protagonist, why has the comic survived for 40 years, and why is it as popular now as it's ever been?

Having Ang Lee direct your movie doesn't hurt. Having Eric Bana, Jennifer Connolly and Nick Nolte star in Ang Lee's movie doesn't hurt. Having Bruce Jones write your comic is a good move. Slapping

Comic artists love drawing the Hulk for a couple reasons: the Hulk-outs, the action, the fights, the musculature and the opportunities to experiment with perspective. Art by Scott Kolins

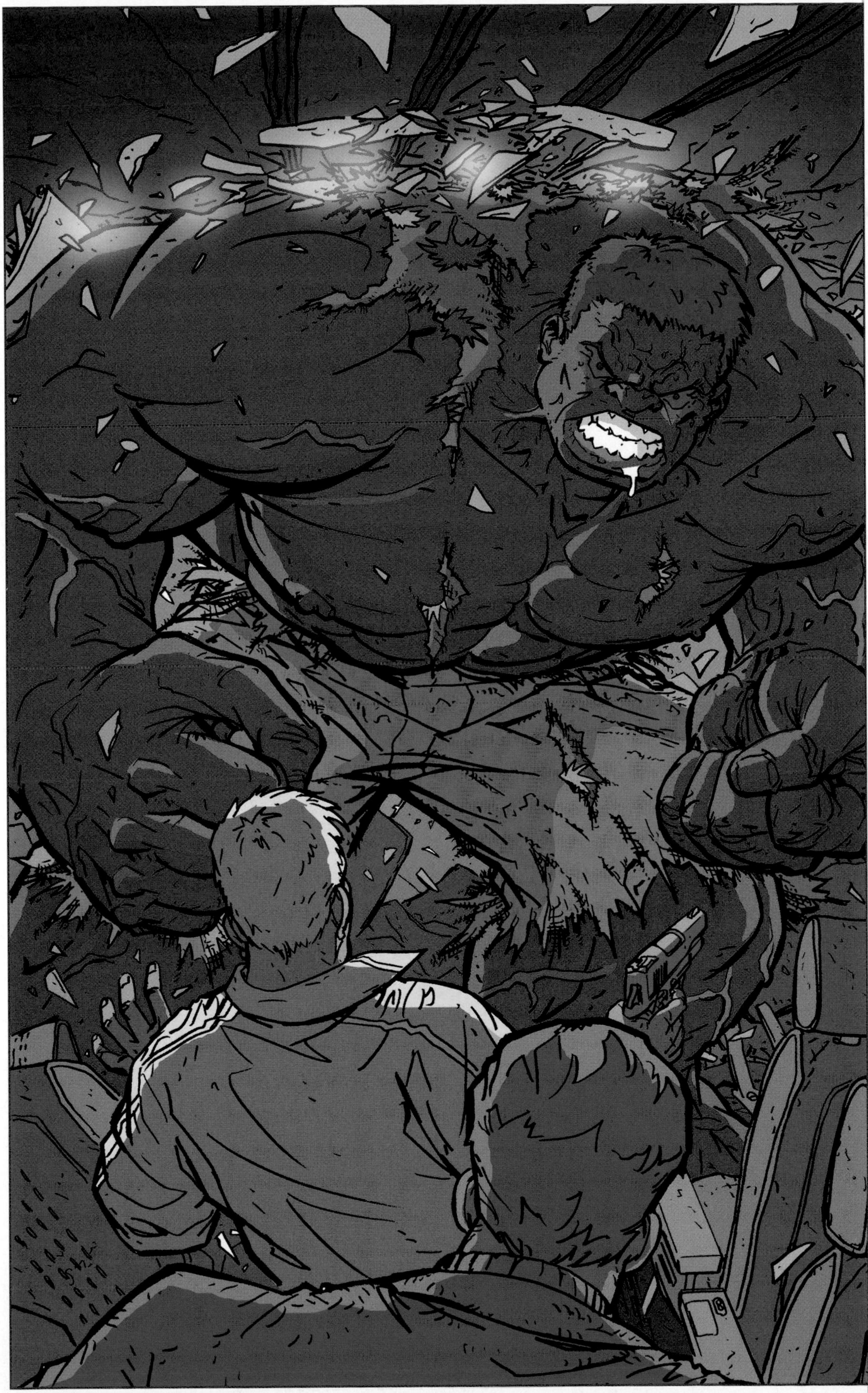

on Kaare Andrews covers is shrewd. But none of that would matter if there wasn't *something* about the Hulk that struck a chord, no matter how dissonant, in a lot of souls.

A good answer is the answer that kick-started this book 10,000 words ago: We all get a little green sometimes. Stan Lee understood that; that's why one of his first Hulks came out only when Bruce Banner

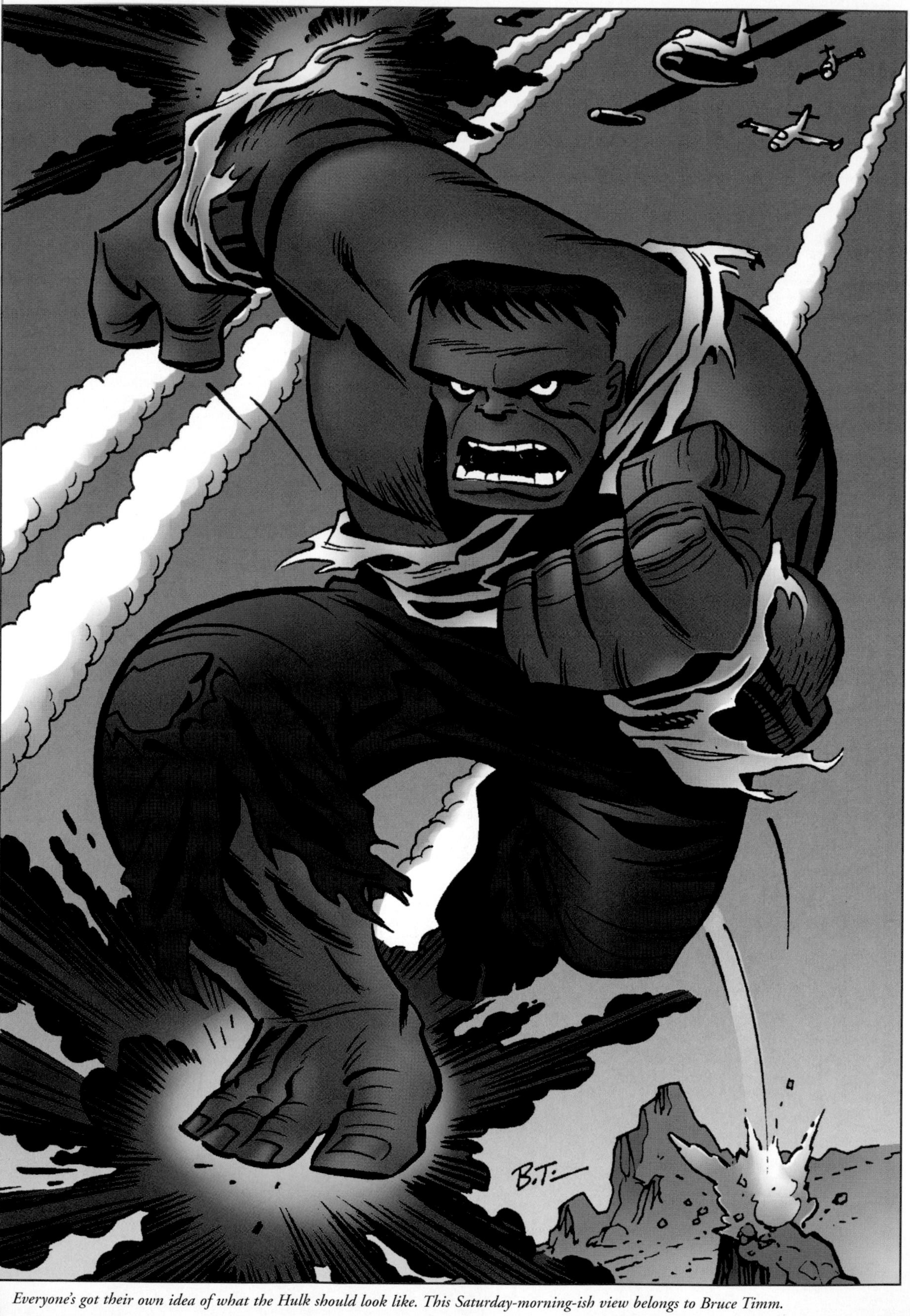
B.T.

 Everyone's got their own idea of what the Hulk should look like. This Saturday-morning-ish view belongs to Bruce Timm.

slept. The only way that message could have been clearer is if Banner's head opened up and the Hulk walked out. The Hulk did what Bruce Banner may have wanted but never could bring himself to do. That's at the heart of everything from Johnny Knoxville to suicide bombings to the Girl Scout lady who embezzles $40,000 from the cookie fund because she's always wanted to see Iceland.

The Hulk rose from a time when successful people were supposed to have problems — or rather, were supposed to have an analyst to tell their problems to. If they didn't have problems, the analyst would provide some — the same way a Holiday Inn will loan you a toothbrush if you leave yours at home. The problems may be a little long in the sleeves, but if you wrap the sleeves around you and buckle them in back no one will notice. The Incredible Hulk was superhero psychoanalysis — not the superhero soap opera the book once promised, but the next best thing. It took a shrink's archetypal problems — an unhappy childhood, repressed urges, dark and violent thoughts, a lack of understanding, a lack of appreciation, paranoia — and made them Bruce Banner's problems. Only the solutions weren't classic shrink stuff. They were a whole lot more direct, and a lot more satisfying.

Just like a navy-blue double-breasted suit, good psychodrama never goes out of style. People will always read about other people more screwed up than themselves who have an even tougher time dealing with their problems. That's superhero ground the Hulk has all to himself and will probably always have all to himself. (In the interest of editorial accuracy, it should be noted that Batman, among others, has cruised this neighborhood from time to time. His approach is darker and different, but remember this is a Marvel book. Don't look for any endorsements of AOL comics here.) It doesn't make the Hulk a good fit with other superheroes, it doesn't always make him an easy read, and it sometimes encourages his writers to get carried away.

The problems with psychodramas and dark suits is that sometimes you have to wear them on August days in West Texas while standing on the tarmac of Amarillo International waiting for the Under-

Bruce Banner *looks like he'll be on the run for a while in the comics — and as long as* ***Bruce Jones, John Romita Jr., Kaare Andrews*** *and company keep on doing what they're doing, the stories promise plenty of* ***snap*** *and* ***dazzle.***

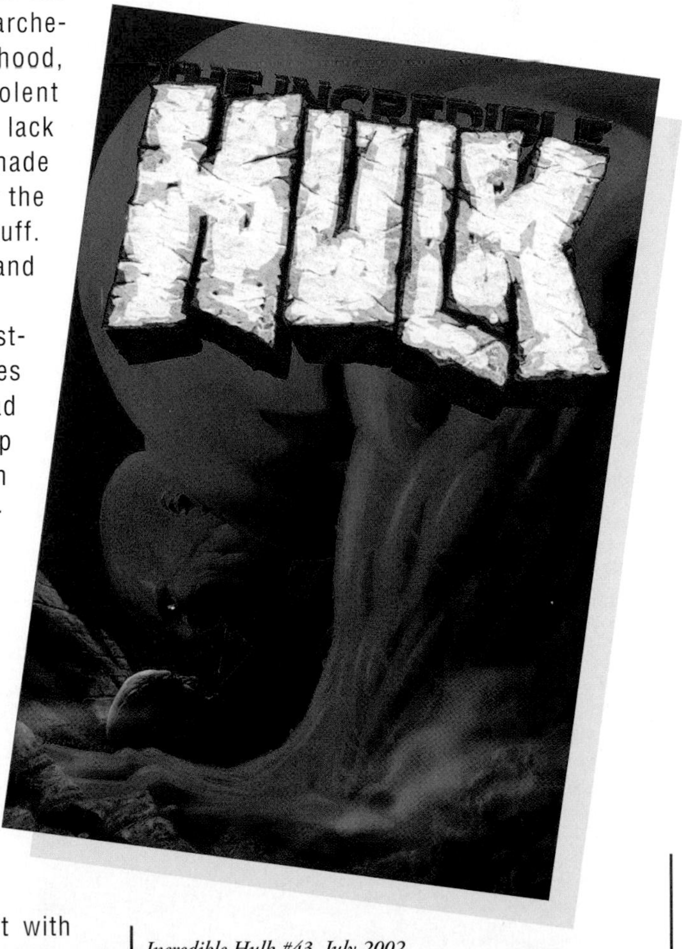
THE INCREDIBLE
HULK

Incredible Hulk #43, July 2002

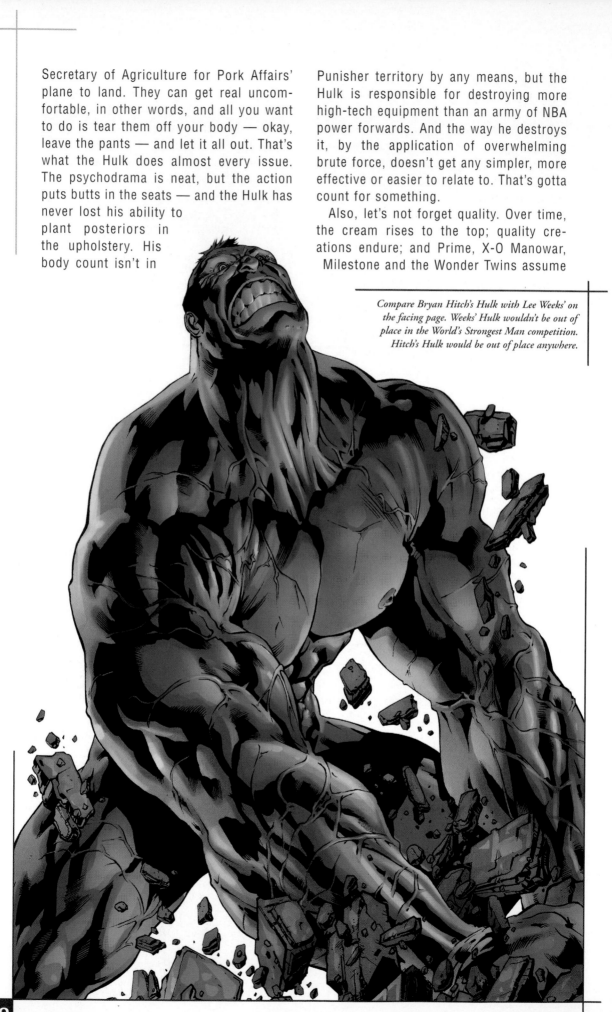

Secretary of Agriculture for Pork Affairs' plane to land. They can get real uncomfortable, in other words, and all you want to do is tear them off your body — okay, leave the pants — and let it all out. That's what the Hulk does almost every issue. The psychodrama is neat, but the action puts butts in the seats — and the Hulk has never lost his ability to plant posteriors in the upholstery. His body count isn't in Punisher territory by any means, but the Hulk is responsible for destroying more high-tech equipment than an army of NBA power forwards. And the way he destroys it, by the application of overwhelming brute force, doesn't get any simpler, more effective or easier to relate to. That's gotta count for something.

Also, let's not forget quality. Over time, the cream rises to the top; quality creations endure; and Prime, X-O Manowar, Milestone and the Wonder Twins assume

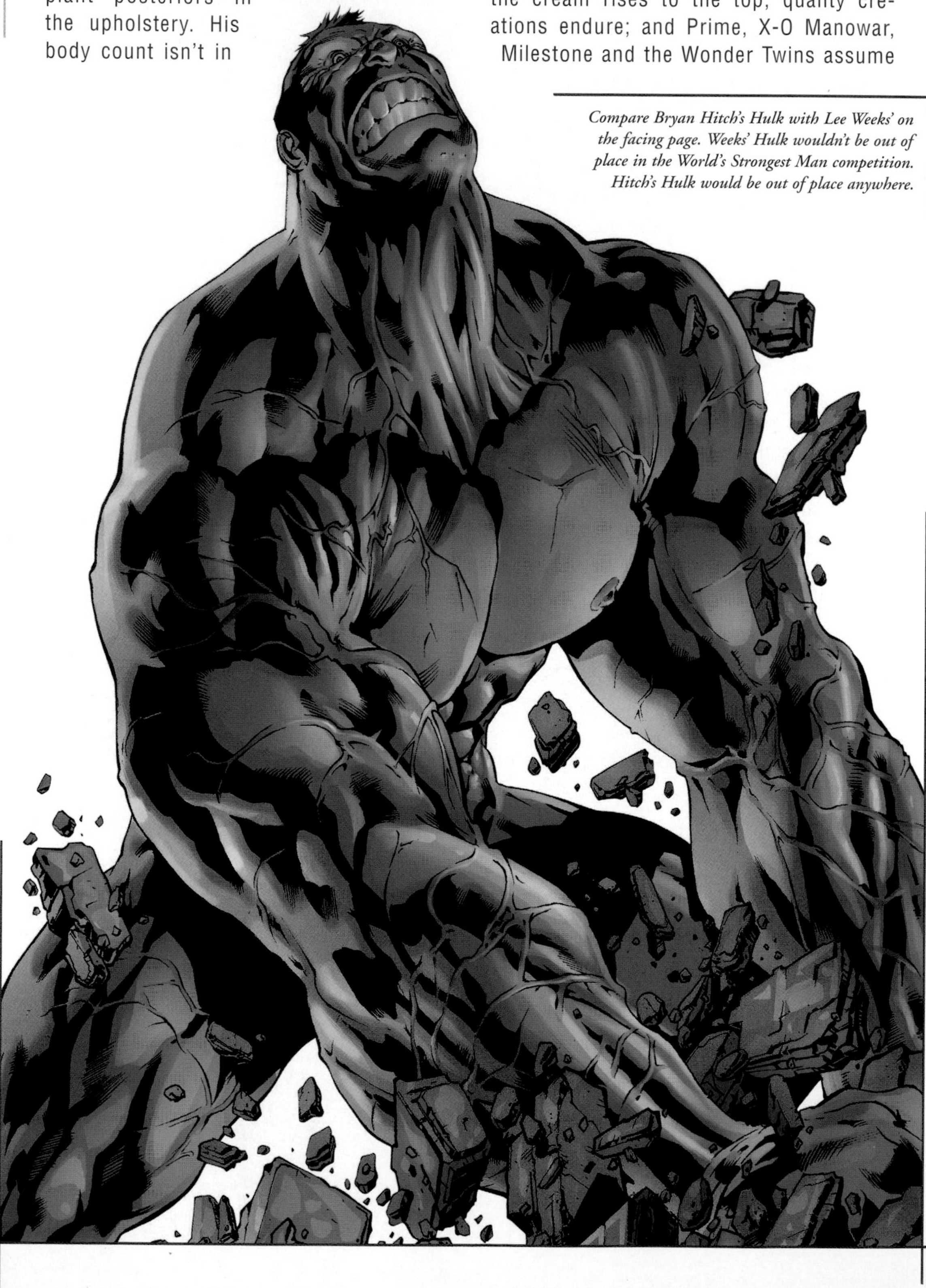

Compare Bryan Hitch's Hulk with Lee Weeks' on the facing page. Weeks' Hulk wouldn't be out of place in the World's Strongest Man competition. Hitch's Hulk would be out of place anywhere.

their rightful seats on the bench. Give comics fans their due: They recognize good art and quality writing, and the Hulk has provided plenty of both to its readers, regardless of whether that reader is a comics-are-my-life-how-could-they-not-be-yours? classic fanboy or a 12-year-old kid leafing through the comics at Jerry's Deluxe Barber Shop waiting to have the last flattop in junior high refreshed. A good story with good pictures hooks the casual reader and satisfies the fan. It's a simple equation that's too often forgotten in the comics biz. But it was top-of-mind in the beginning, and it's right there now.

The future for *Incredible Hulk* appears bright. Bruce Banner looks like he'll be on the run for a while in the comics — and as long as Bruce Jones, John Romita Jr., Kaare Andrews and company keep on doing what they're doing, the stories promise plenty of snap and dazzle. *Hulk: Gray* looks enthralling; the Loeb-Sale creative team has never delivered anything that's less than readable, and their chromatic tiptoe through the comic universe's tulips has the earmarks of something bigger and more significant. And *The Ultimates* are certainly ultimate in one regard: They're the ultimate product of their time and place. These are *the* comics of the double-naught decade, full of pop-culture references and superheroes that look like Samuel L. Jackson. They may seem quaint in 2010, but 2010's a long way off.

The movie is sure to spawn something, even if it's a recasting of the old Hulk TV series. Marvel movies are made like Marvel comics, with a big fight close to the end and at least half the plot lines left unresolved. As movie properties, Marvel characters have barely had their surfaces scratched — and if that sounds like a veiled suggestion that a Hulk sequel is coming, okay.

Heroclix are still hotter than the Kalahari, and the whiz kids at WizKids are taking extreme pains to make sure they stay that way. Hulk toys have room to grow, but it's only a matter of time before the latest generation of kids realizes the

Hulk makes Triple H look like Hello Kitty.

The inevitable conclusion is that the Hulk is built to last. He can't be destroyed, he can't be killed off, and he can't be irretrievably screwed up. But Stan Lee could have told you that, almost 40 years ago.

Art by Lee Weeks

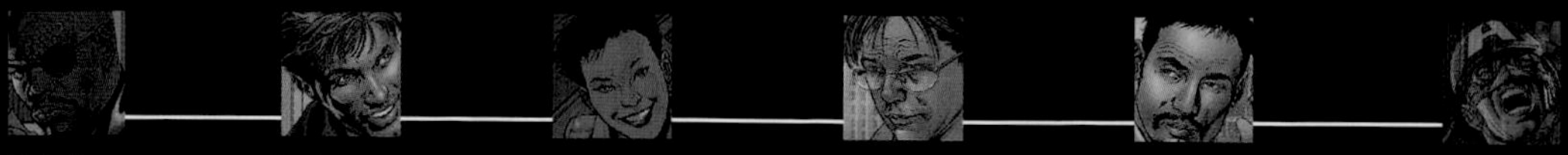

Nick Fury | Hank Pym | Janet Pym | Bruce Banner | Tony Stark | Captain America

PREVIOUSLY IN THE ULTIMATES:

The world is changing. Crime is becoming super-crime. Terrorism is becoming super-terrorism. Humans are becoming super-humans. Heroes are becoming superheroes.

With the backing of the U.S. Government, General Nick Fury and S.H.I.E.L.D. have assembled a team of super-powered beings to address any potential threat this new world may now face: THE ULTIMATES! Captain America, the Super-Soldier who will lead the team; The Iron Man, the personal weapons system of billionaire Tony Stark; Giant Man, able to grow to sixty feet tall; the Wasp; able to shrink to an inch and fly; and Dr. Bruce Banner, the scientist whose experiments led him to transform into the rampaging Hulk,; they are the superhuman task force created to safeguard mankind in these uncertain times.

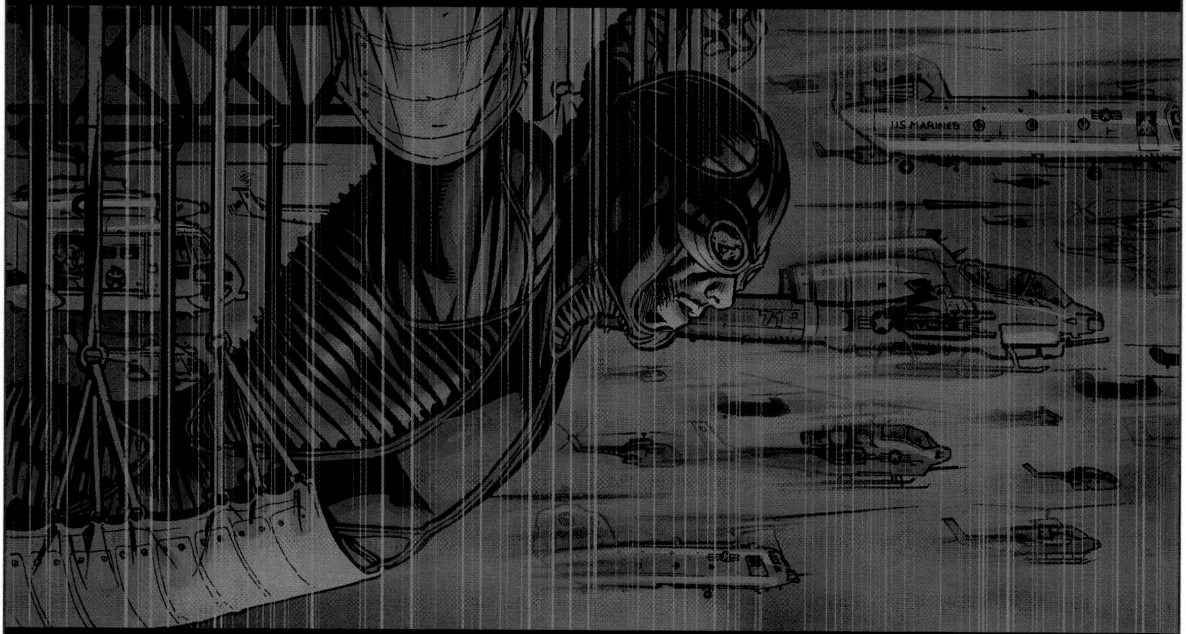
US MARINES

While the other Ultimates members seem to be adjusting to their new roles on the team, Bruce Banner continues to sink further into depression. Once head of the revived Super-Soldier program, he has since been demoted. Banner and fiancée Betty Ross are going through a trial separation. He was belittled by Thor, the self-proclaimed Son of Odin, whom he tried to recruit for the team. And after being insulted by his own teammates, Banner has taken all the abuse he can stand; he mainlines a large dosage of his Hulk serum mixed with Captain America's own Super-Soldier blood.

The Ultimates now have their first mission: Stop The Hulk before he destroys New York!

Stan Lee presents:

THE ULTIMATES

Mark Millar

Bryan Hitch   Andrew Currie

Paul Mounts   Chris Eliopoulos   C.B. Cebulski   Brian Smith   Ralph Macchio

Joe Quesada   Bill Jemas

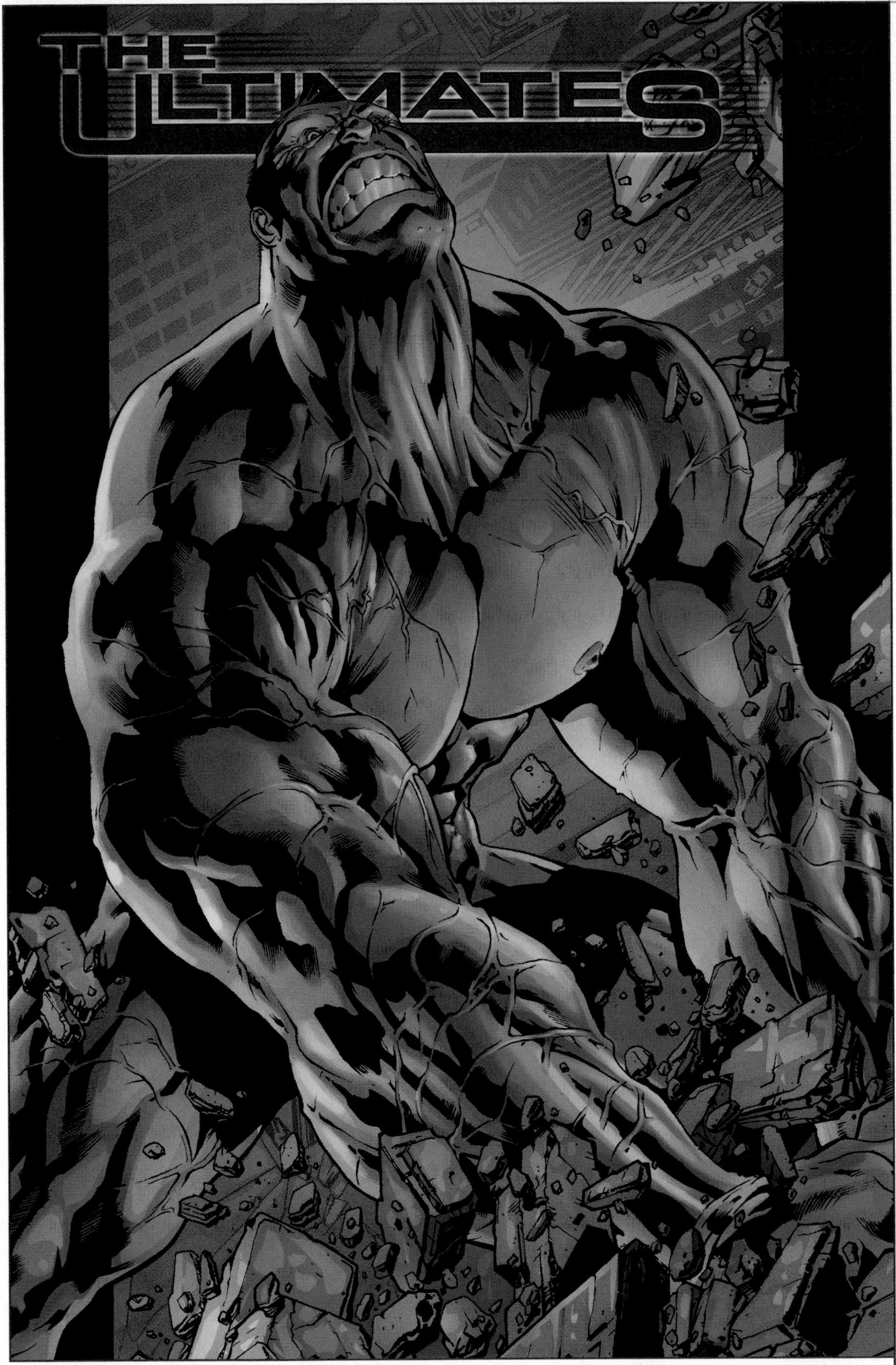
THE ULTIMATES
5

The Ultimates #5

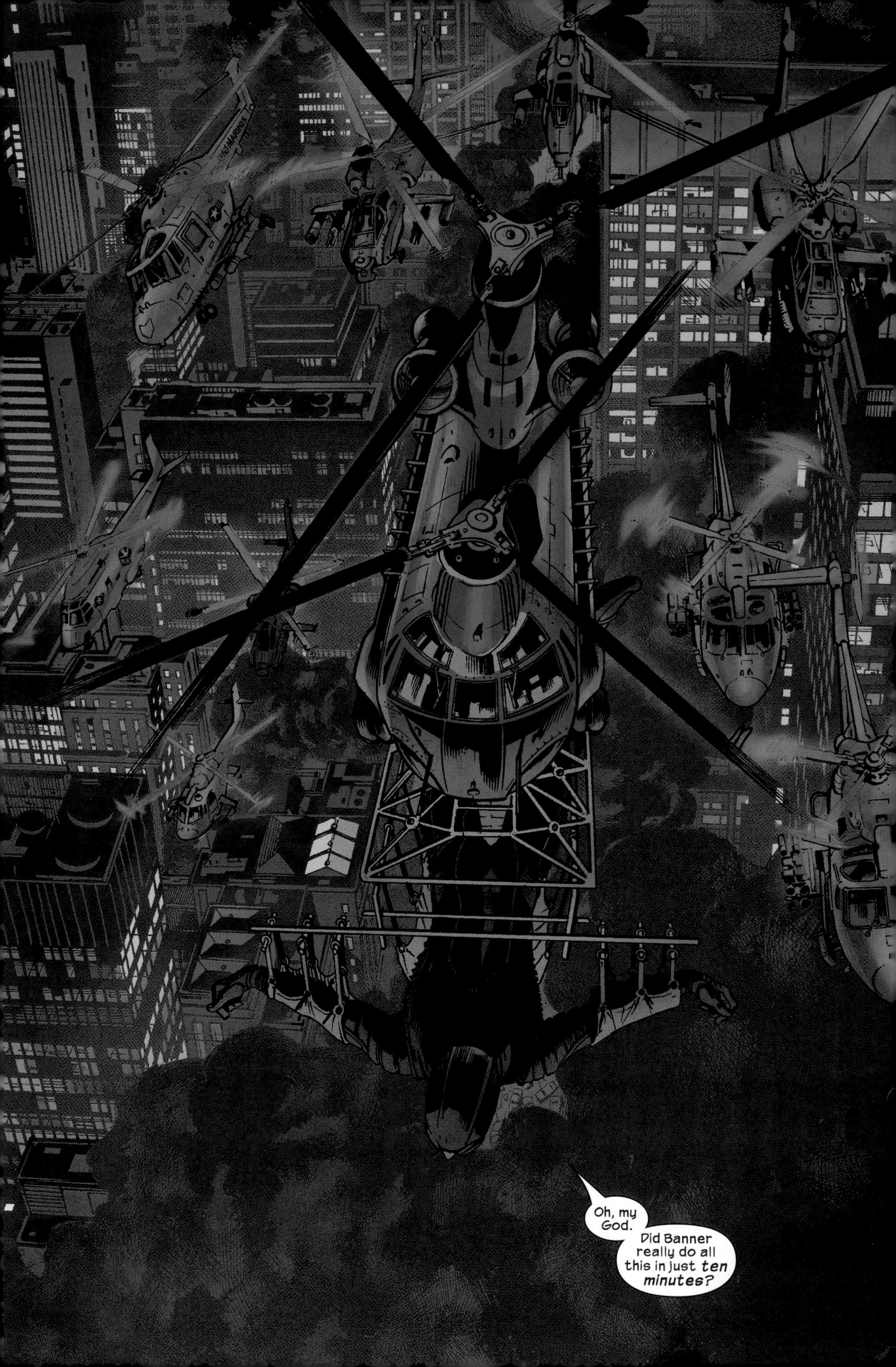
Oh, my God.
Did Banner really do all this in just *ten minutes*?

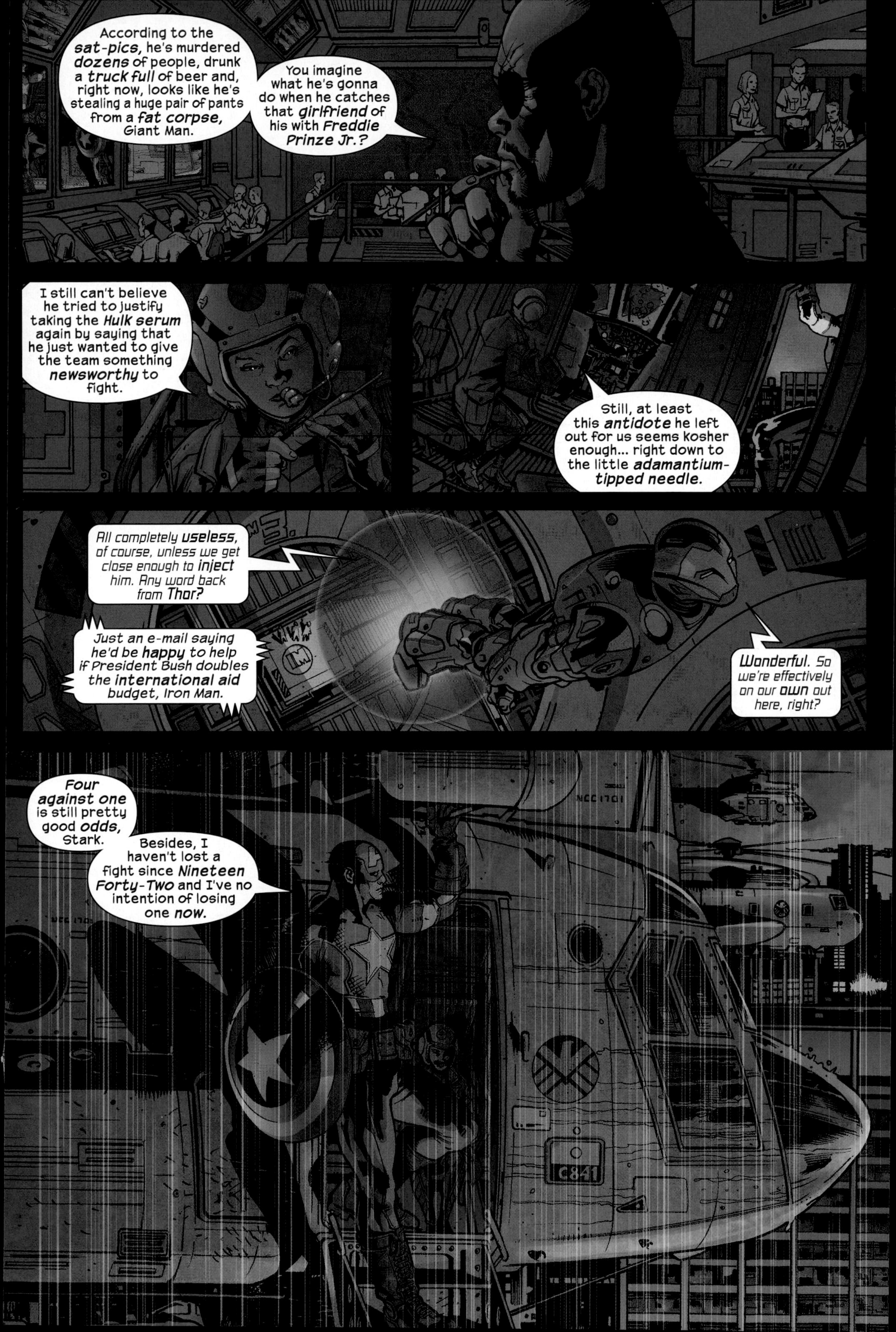

According to the sat-pics, he's murdered dozens of people, drunk a truck full of beer and, right now, looks like he's stealing a huge pair of pants from a fat corpse, Giant Man.
You imagine what he's gonna do when he catches that girlfriend of his with Freddie Prinze Jr.?
I still can't believe he tried to justify taking the Hulk serum again by saying that he just wanted to give the team something newsworthy to fight.
Still, at least this antidote he left out for us seems kosher enough... right down to the little adamantium-tipped needle.
All completely useless, of course, unless we get close enough to inject him. Any word back from Thor?
Just an e-mail saying he'd be happy to help if President Bush doubles the international aid budget, Iron Man.
Wonderful. So we're effectively on our own out here, right?
Four against one is still pretty good odds, Stark.
Besides, I haven't lost a fight since Nineteen Forty-Two and I've no intention of losing one now.
NCC 1701
C841

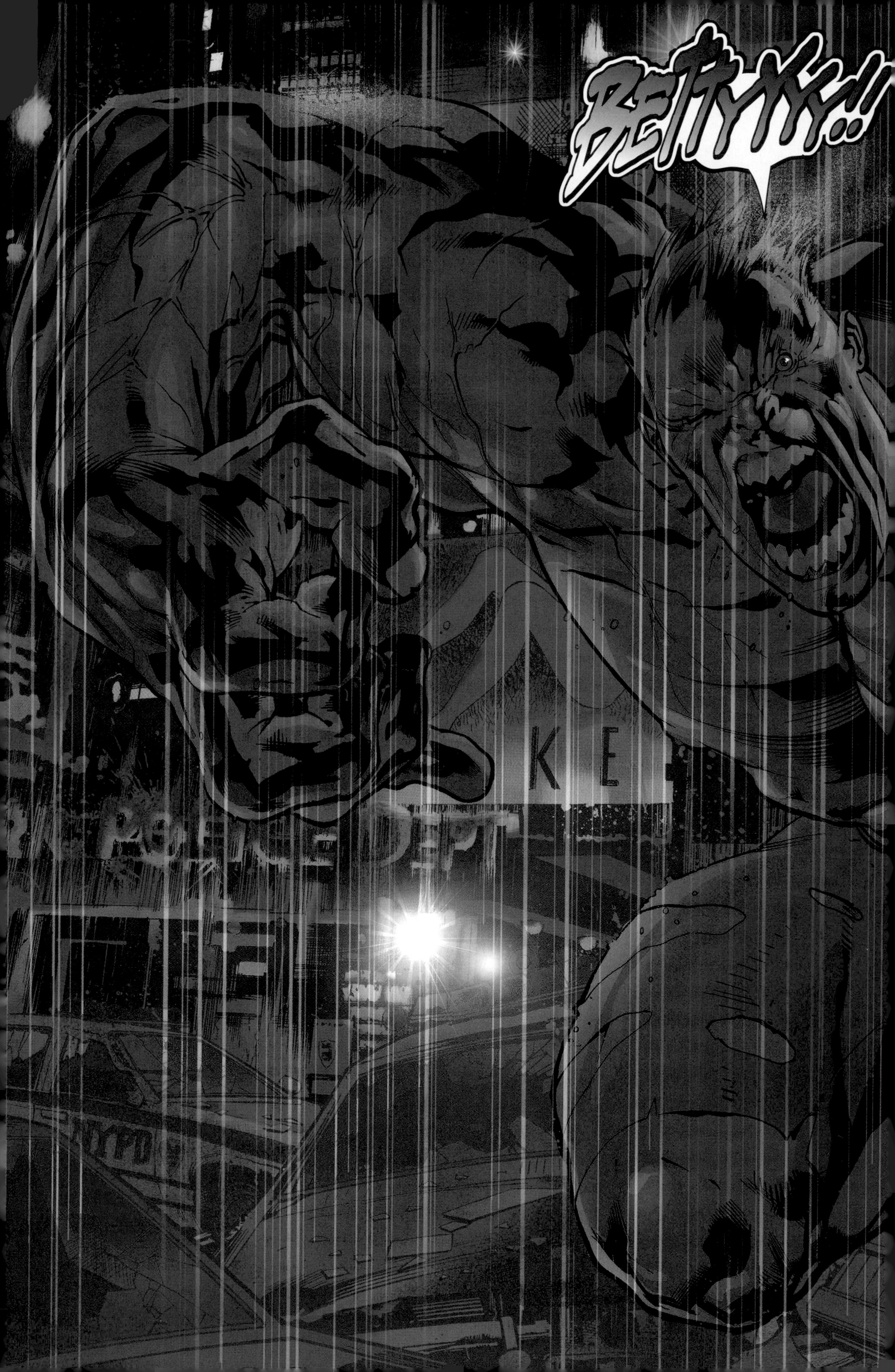
BETTYYY!!

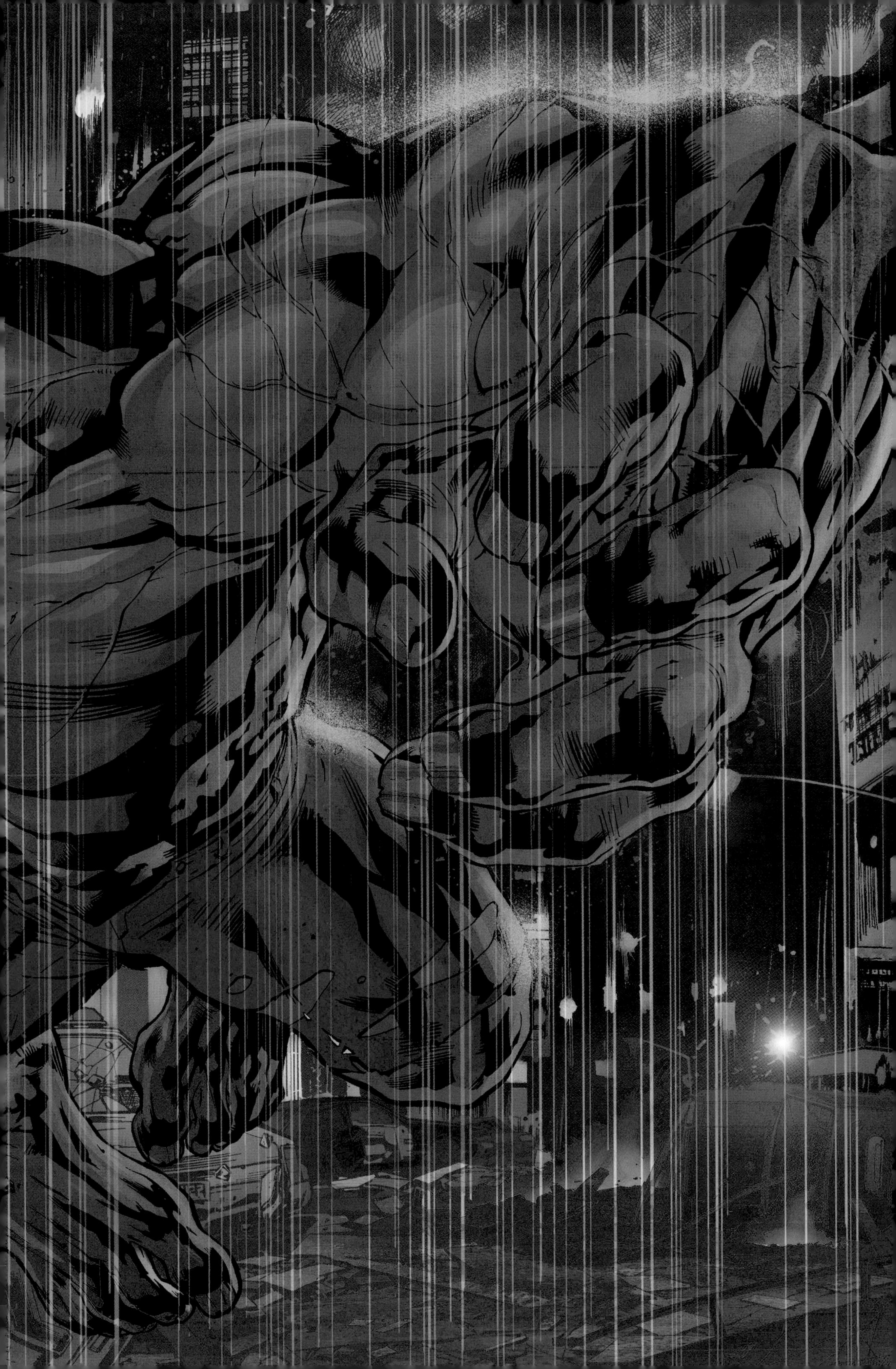

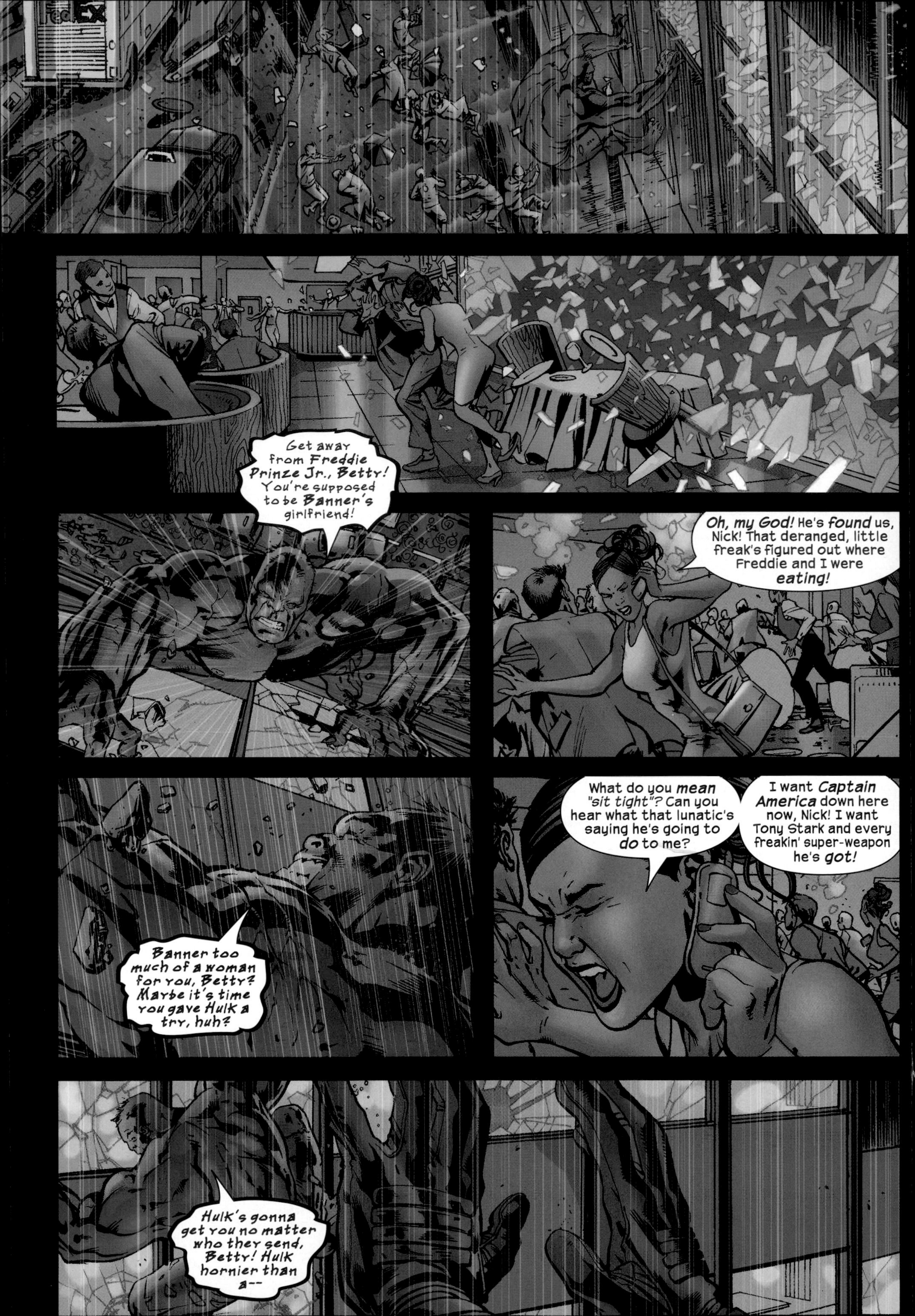

Get away from Freddie Prinze Jr., Betty! You're supposed to be Banner's girlfriend!
Oh, my God! He's found us, Nick! That deranged, little freak's figured out where Freddie and I were eating!
Banner too much of a woman for you, Betty? Maybe it's time you gave Hulk a try, huh?
What do you mean "sit tight"? Can you hear what that lunatic's saying he's going to do to me?
I want Captain America down here now, Nick! I want Tony Stark and every freakin' super-weapon he's got!
Hulk's gonna get you no matter who they send, Betty! Hulk hornier than a--

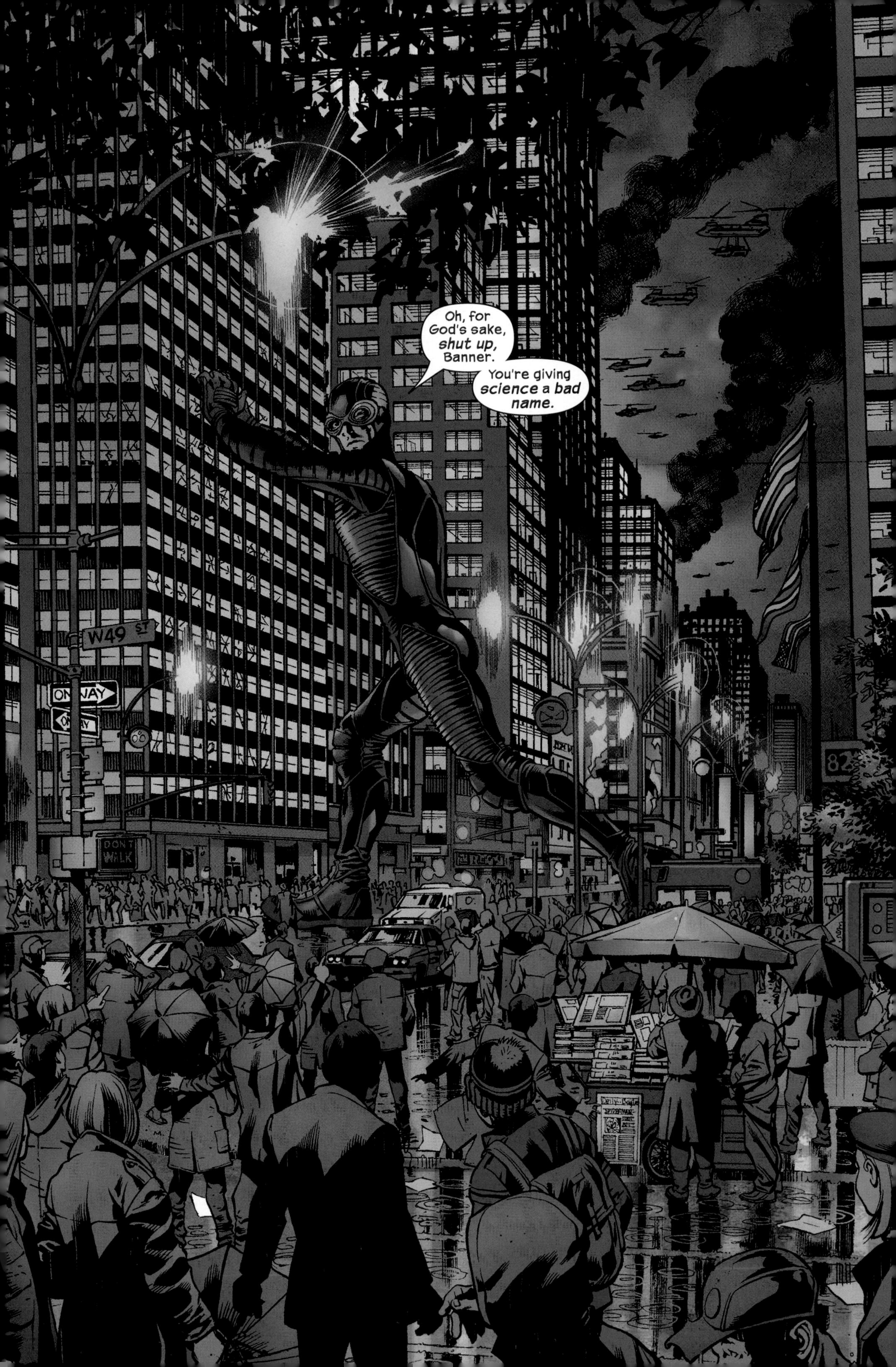
Oh, for God's sake, shut up, Banner.
You're giving science a bad name.
W49 ST
ONE WAY
DON'T WALK

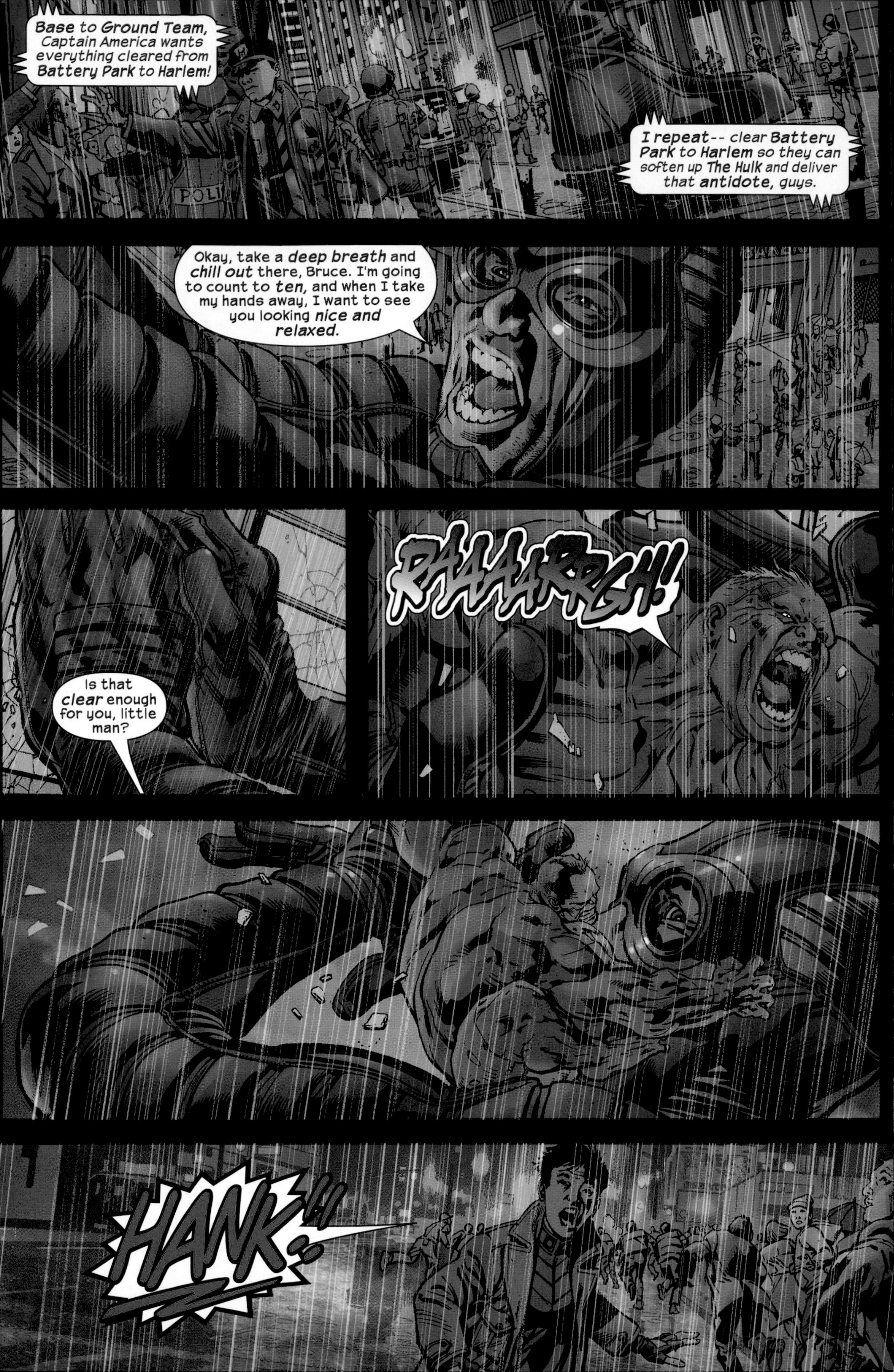
Base to Ground Team, Captain America wants everything cleared from Battery Park to Harlem!
I repeat-- clear Battery Park to Harlem so they can soften up The Hulk and deliver that antidote, guys.
Okay, take a deep breath and chill out there, Bruce. I'm going to count to ten, and when I take my hands away, I want to see you looking nice and relaxed.
Is that clear enough for you, little man?
RAAARRGH!
HANK!!

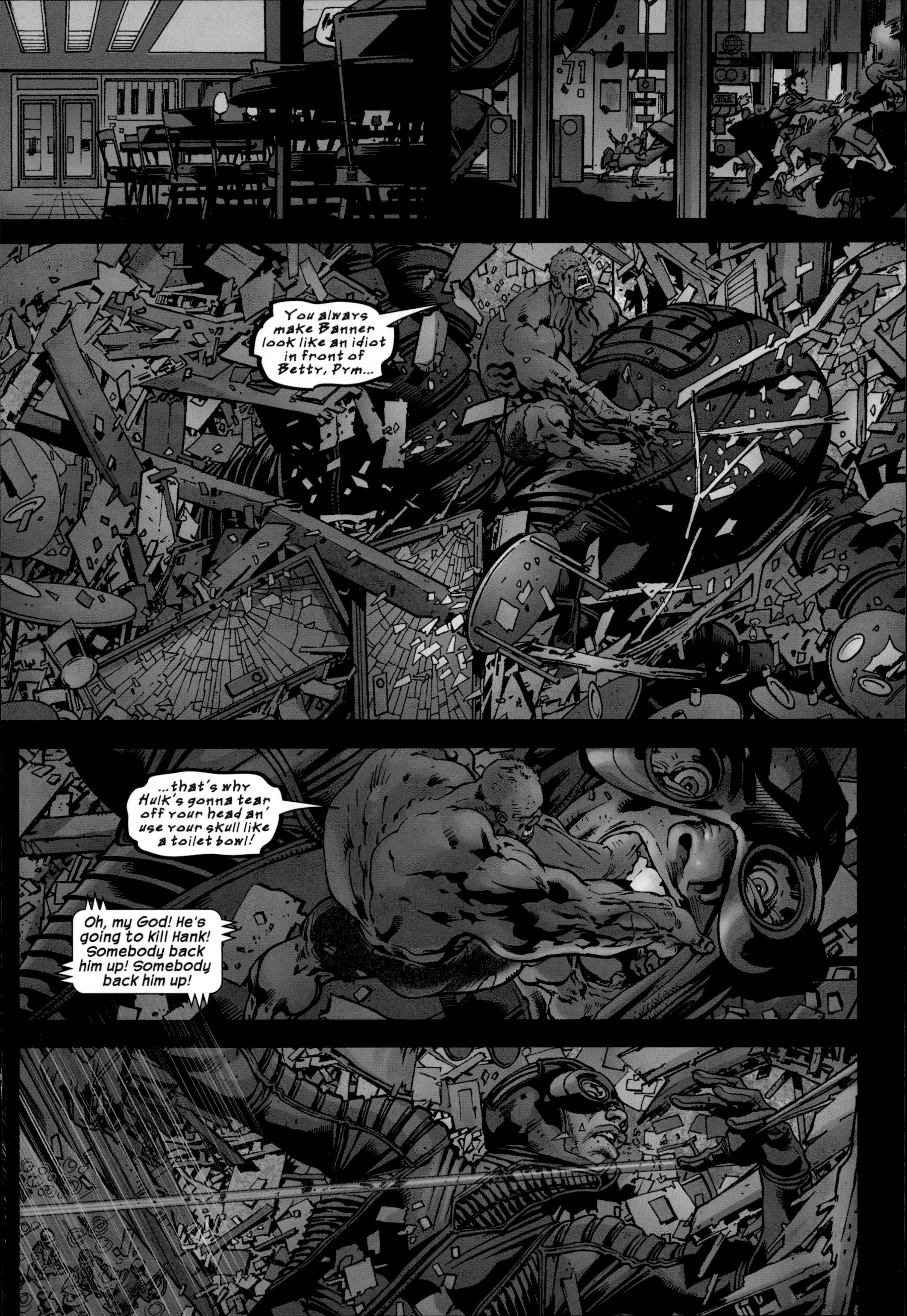
You always make Banner look like an idiot in front of Betty, Pym...
...that's why Hulk's gonna tear off your head an' use your skull like a toilet bowl!
Oh, my God! He's going to kill Hank! Somebody back him up! Somebody back him up!

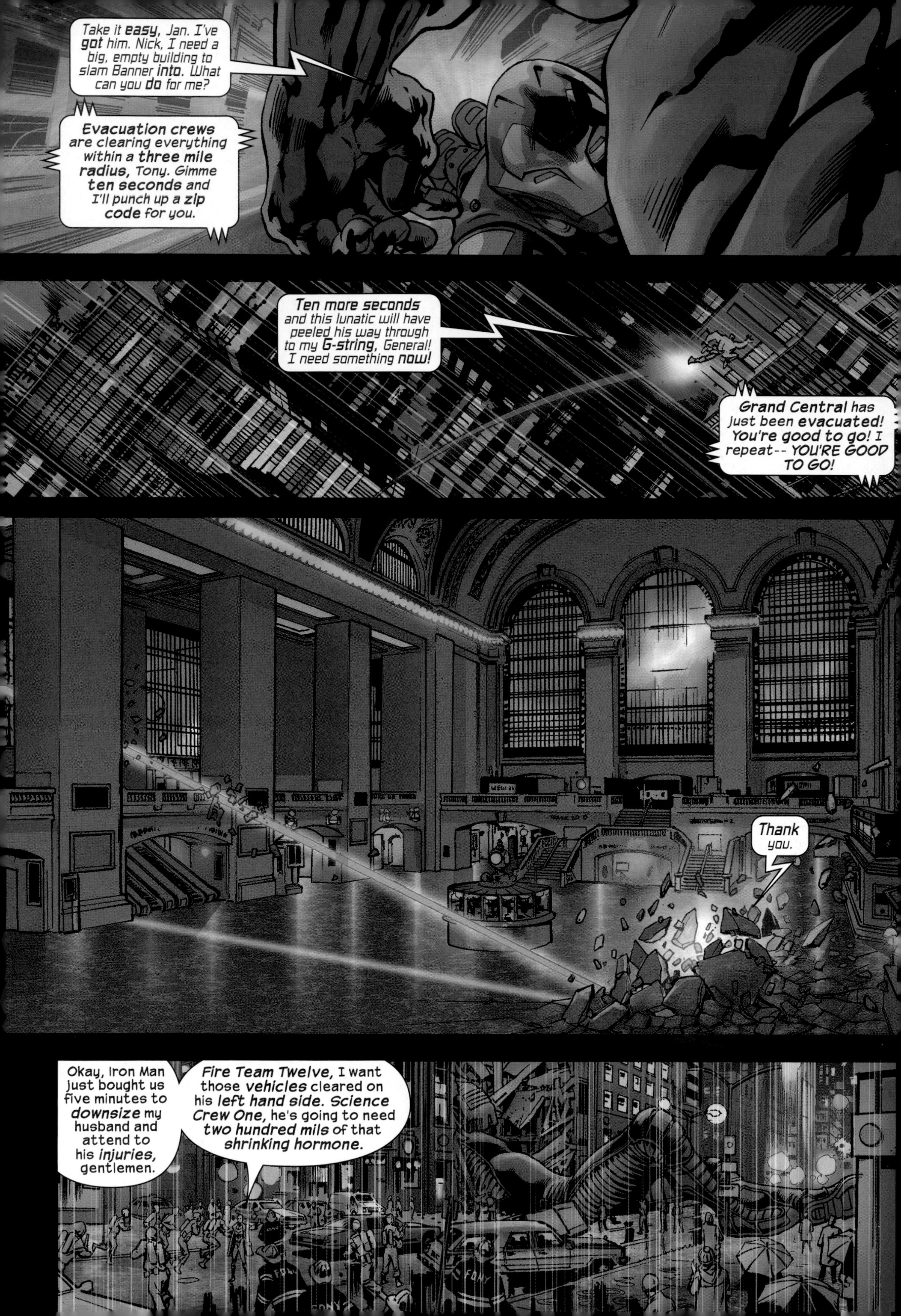
Take it easy, Jan. I've got him. Nick, I need a big, empty building to slam Banner into. What can you do for me?
Evacuation crews are clearing everything within a three mile radius, Tony. Gimme ten seconds and I'll punch up a zip code for you.
Ten more seconds and this lunatic will have peeled his way through to my G-string, General! I need something now!
Grand Central has just been evacuated! You're good to go! I repeat-- YOU'RE GOOD TO GO!
Thank you.
Okay, Iron Man just bought us five minutes to downsize my husband and attend to his injuries, gentlemen.
Fire Team Twelve, I want those vehicles cleared on his left hand side. Science Crew One, he's going to need two hundred mils of that shrinking hormone.

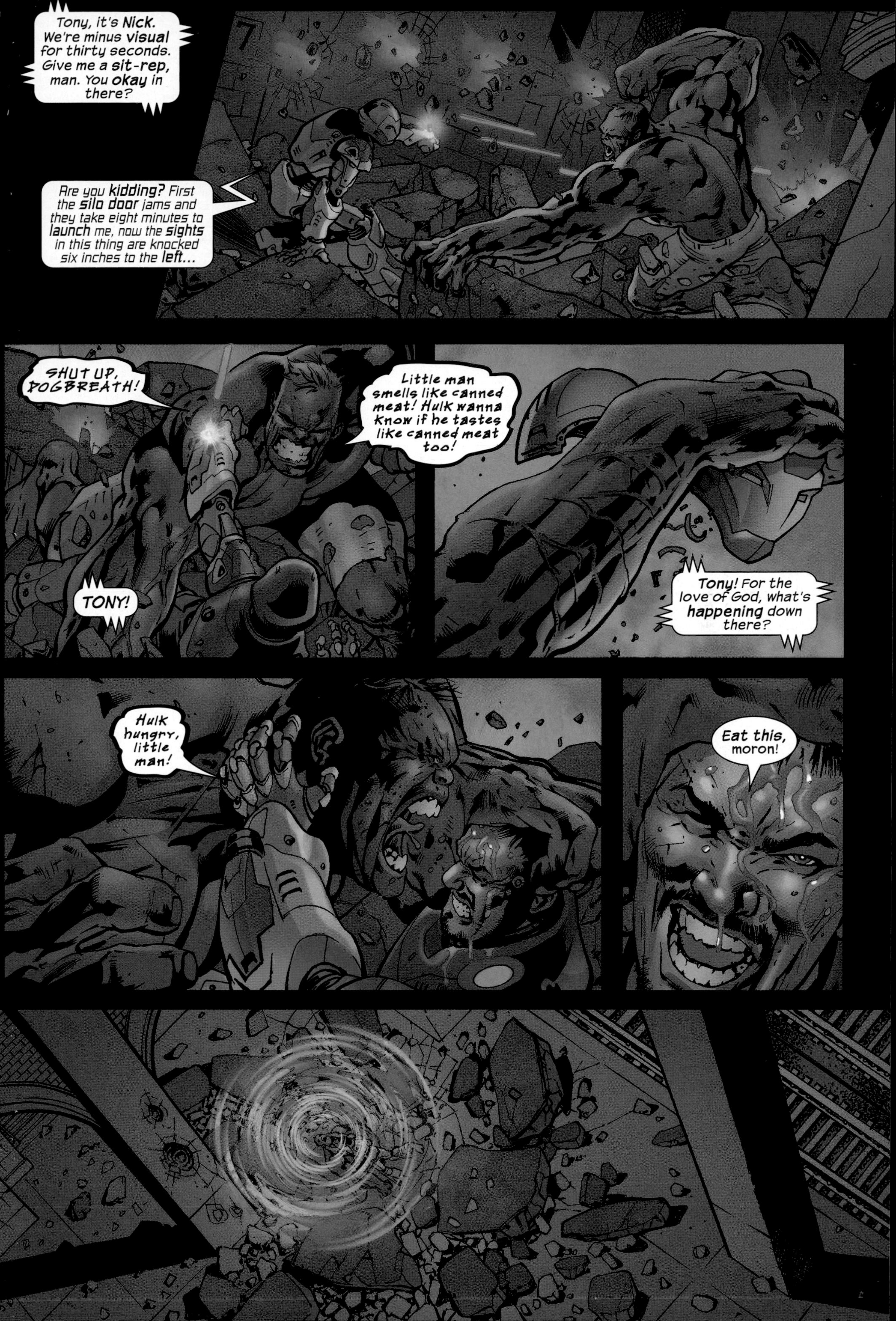

Tony, it's Nick. We're minus visual for thirty seconds. Give me a sit-rep, man. You okay in there?
Are you kidding? First the silo door jams and they take eight minutes to launch me, now the sights in this thing are knocked six inches to the left...
SHUT UP, DOGBREATH!
Little man smells like canned meat! Hulk wanna know if he tastes like canned meat too!
TONY!
Tony! For the love of God, what's happening down there?
Hulk hungry, little man!
Eat this, moron!

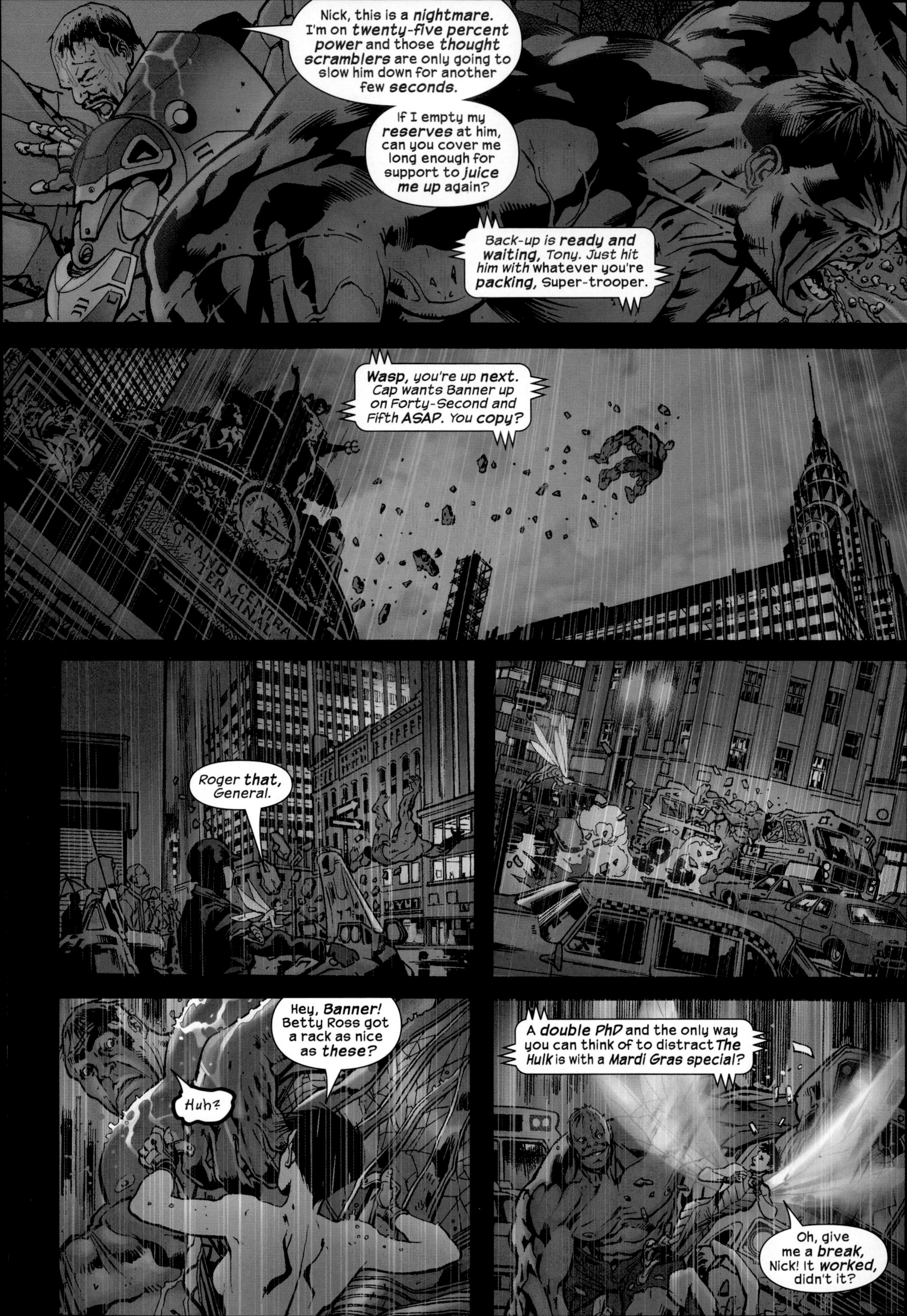
Nick, this is a nightmare. I'm on twenty-five percent power and those thought scramblers are only going to slow him down for another few seconds.
If I empty my reserves at him, can you cover me long enough for support to juice me up again?
Back-up is ready and waiting, Tony. Just hit him with whatever you're packing, Super-trooper.
Wasp, you're up next. Cap wants Banner up on Forty-Second and Fifth ASAP. You copy?
GRAND CENTRAL TERMINAL
Roger that, General.
Hey, Banner! Betty Ross got a rack as nice as these?
Huh?
A double PhD and the only way you can think of to distract The Hulk is with a Mardi Gras special?
Oh, give me a break, Nick! It worked, didn't it?

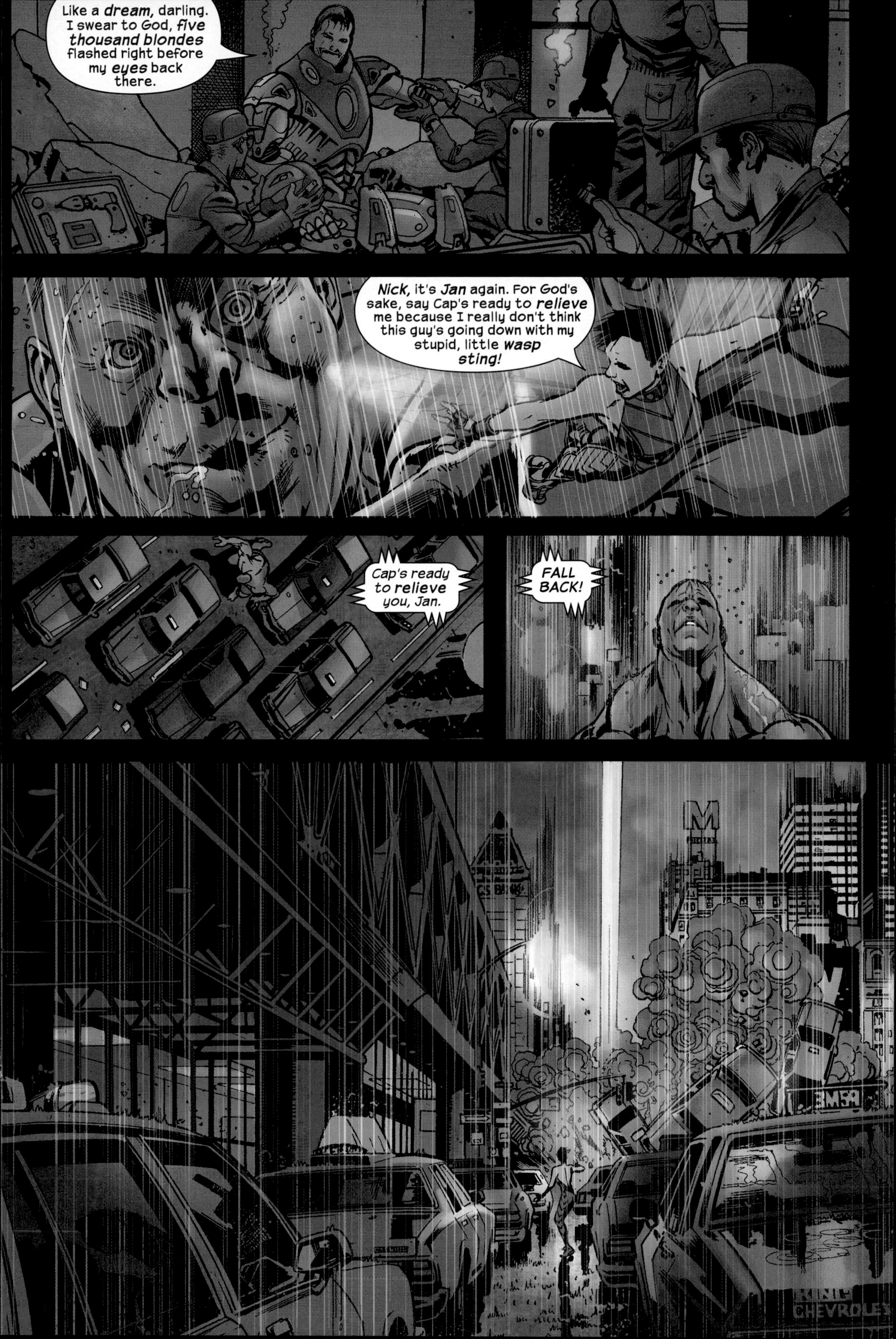
Like a *dream*, darling. I swear to God, *five thousand blondes* flashed right before my *eyes* back there.
Nick, it's *Jan* again. For God's sake, say Cap's ready to *relieve* me because I really don't think this guy's going down with my stupid, little *wasp sting!*
Cap's ready to *relieve* you, Jan.
FALL BACK!
CHEVROLET

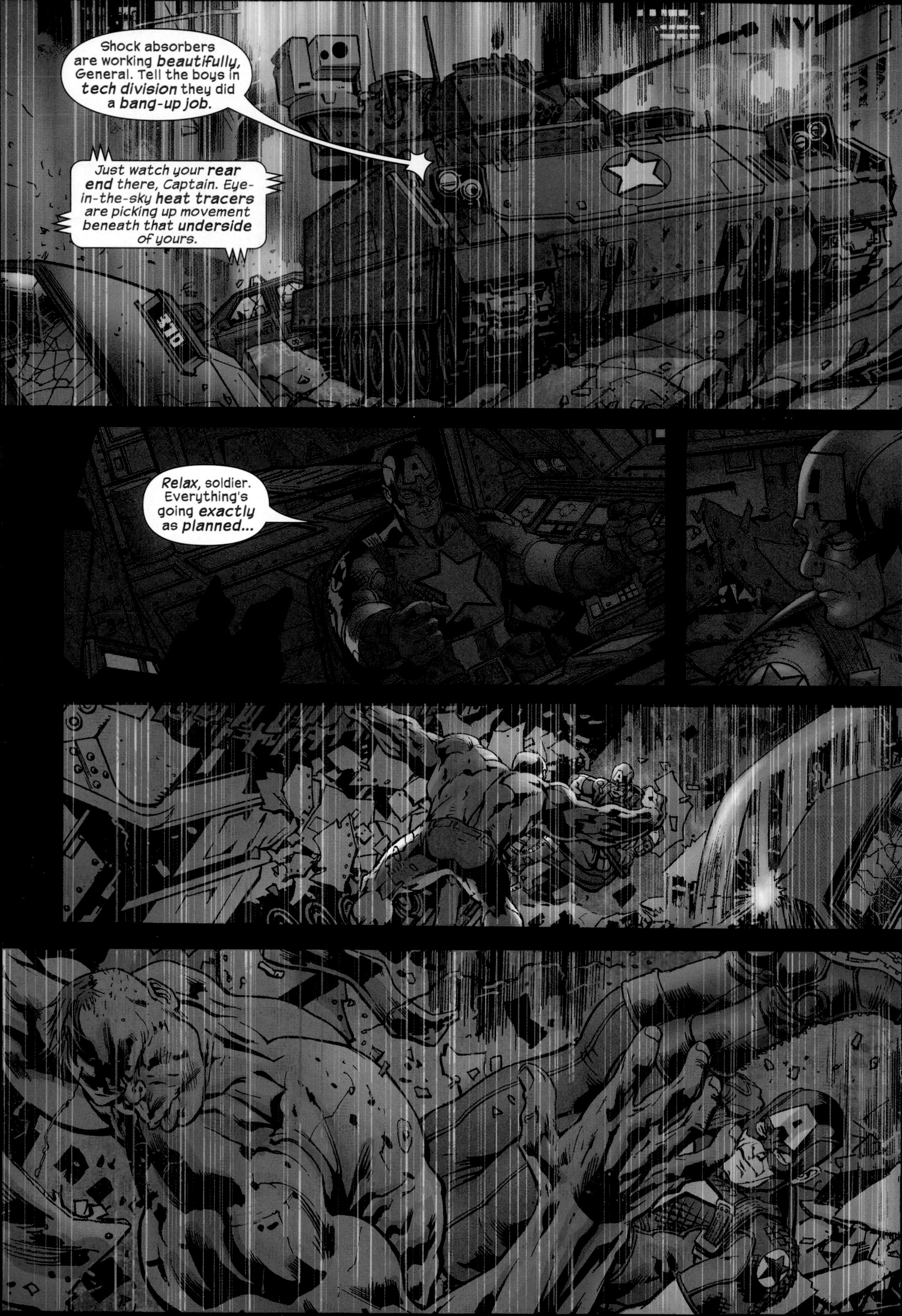
Shock absorbers are working beautifully, General. Tell the boys in tech division they did a bang-up job.
Just watch your rear end there, Captain. Eye-in-the-sky heat tracers are picking up movement beneath that underside of yours.
Relax, soldier. Everything's going exactly as planned...

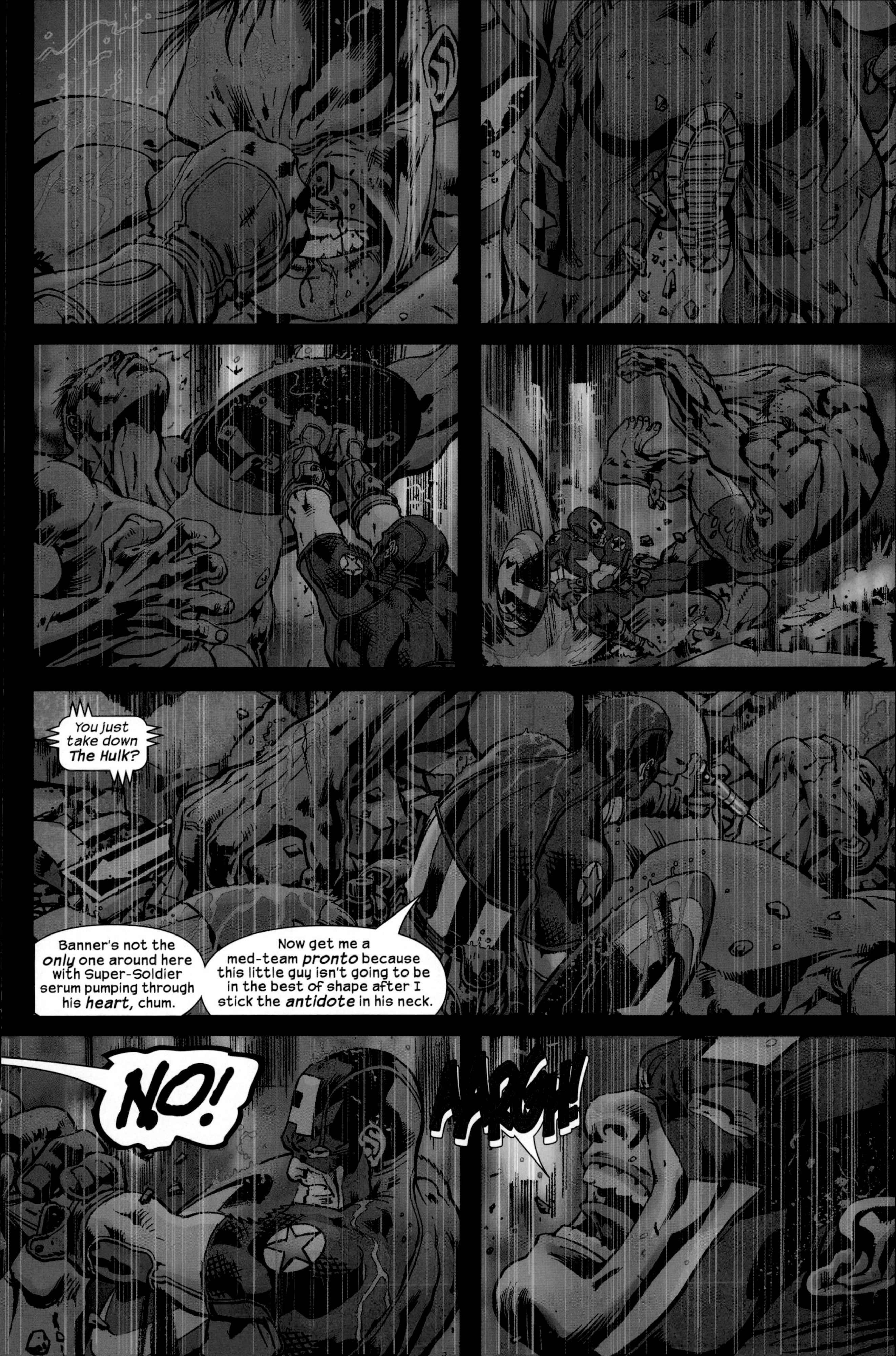
You just take down The Hulk?
Banner's not the only one around here with Super-Soldier serum pumping through his heart, chum.
Now get me a med-team pronto because this little guy isn't going to be in the best of shape after I stick the antidote in his neck.
NO!
AARGH!

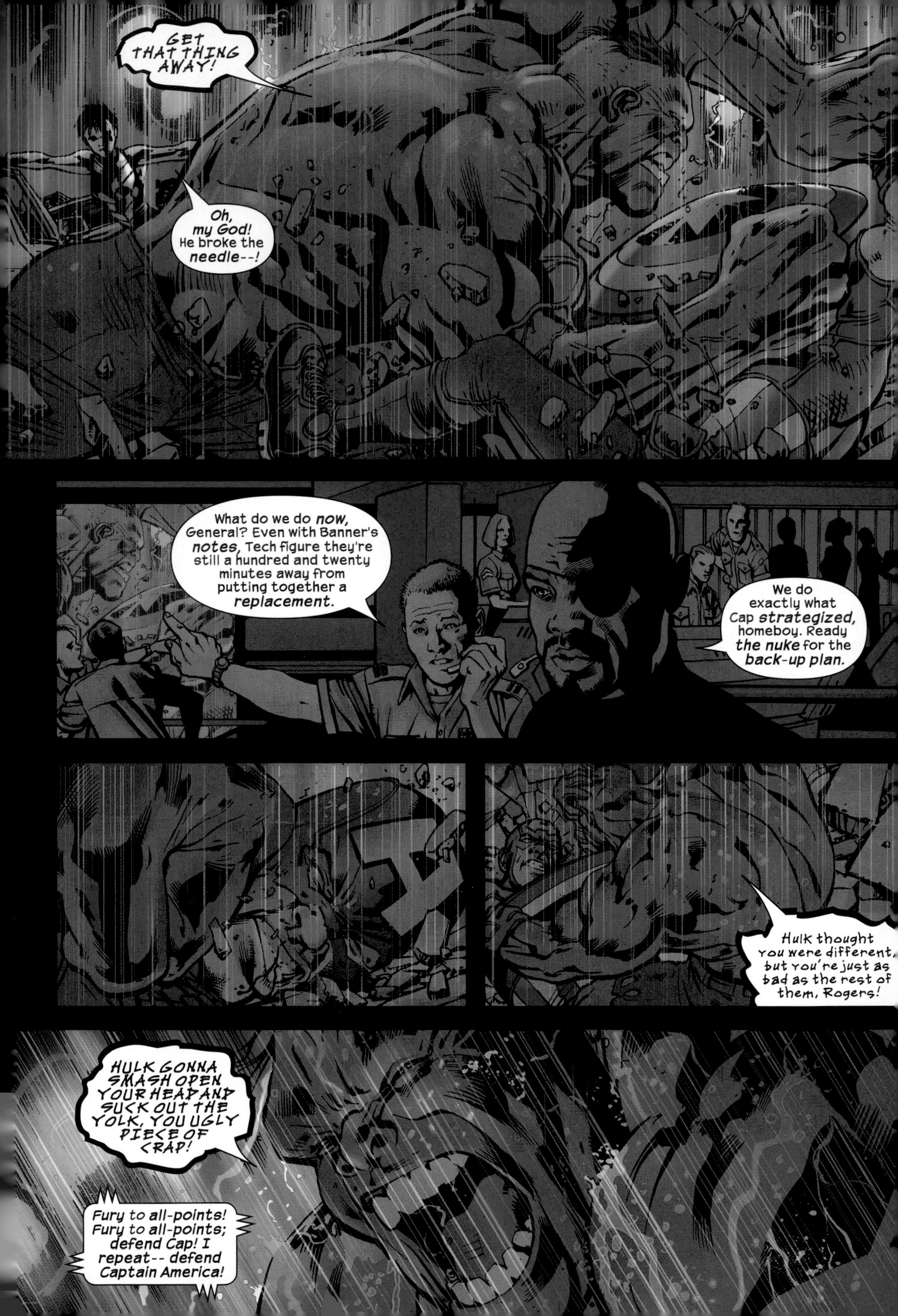
GET THAT THING AWAY!
Oh, my God! He broke the needle--!
What do we do now, General? Even with Banner's notes, Tech figure they're still a hundred and twenty minutes away from putting together a replacement.
We do exactly what Cap strategized, homeboy. Ready the nuke for the back-up plan.
Hulk thought you were different, but you're just as bad as the rest of them, Rogers!
HULK GONNA SMASH OPEN YOUR HEAD AND SUCK OUT THE YOLK, YOU UGLY PIECE OF CRAP!
Fury to all-points! Fury to all-points; defend Cap! I repeat-- defend Captain America!

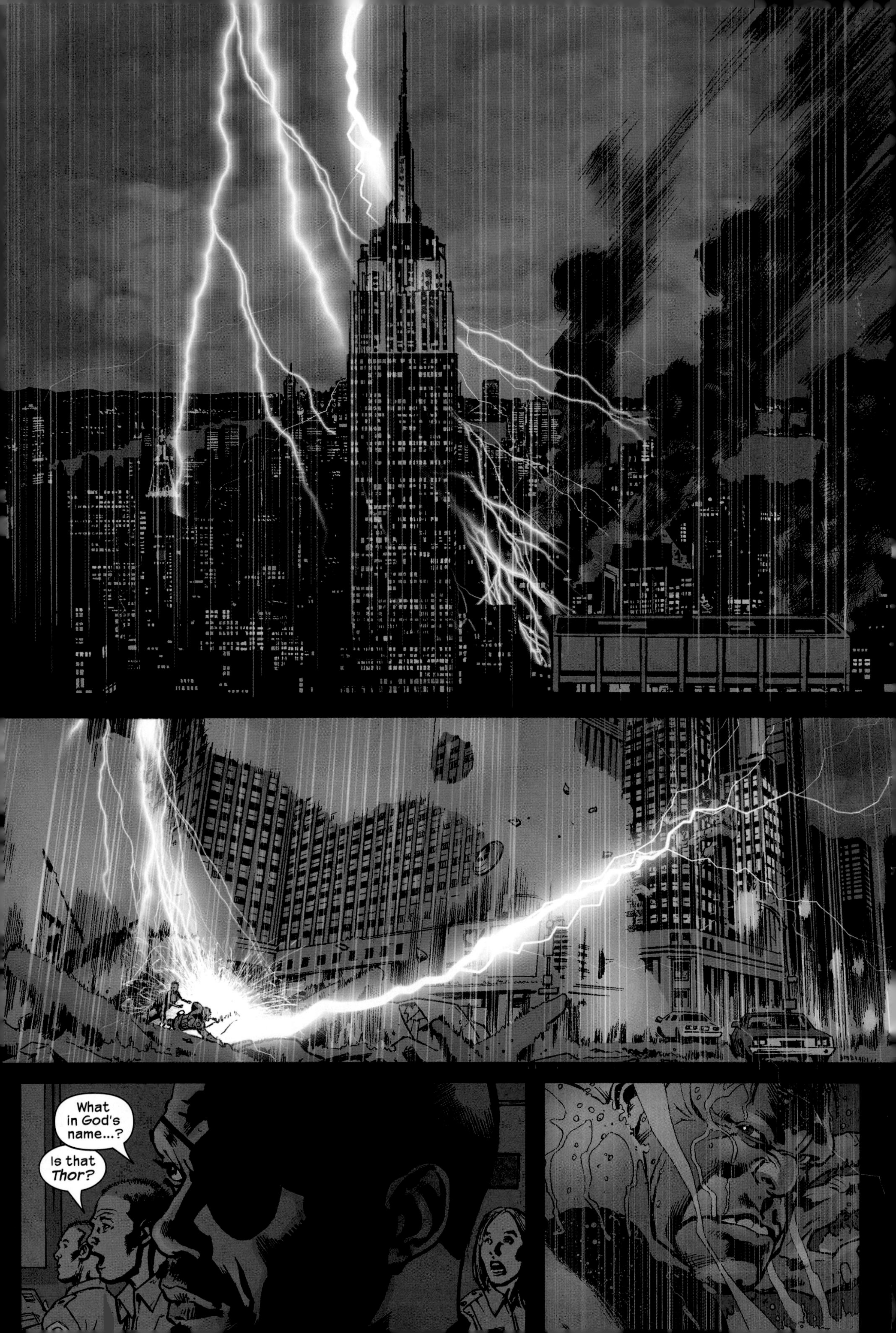
What in God's name...?
Is that Thor?

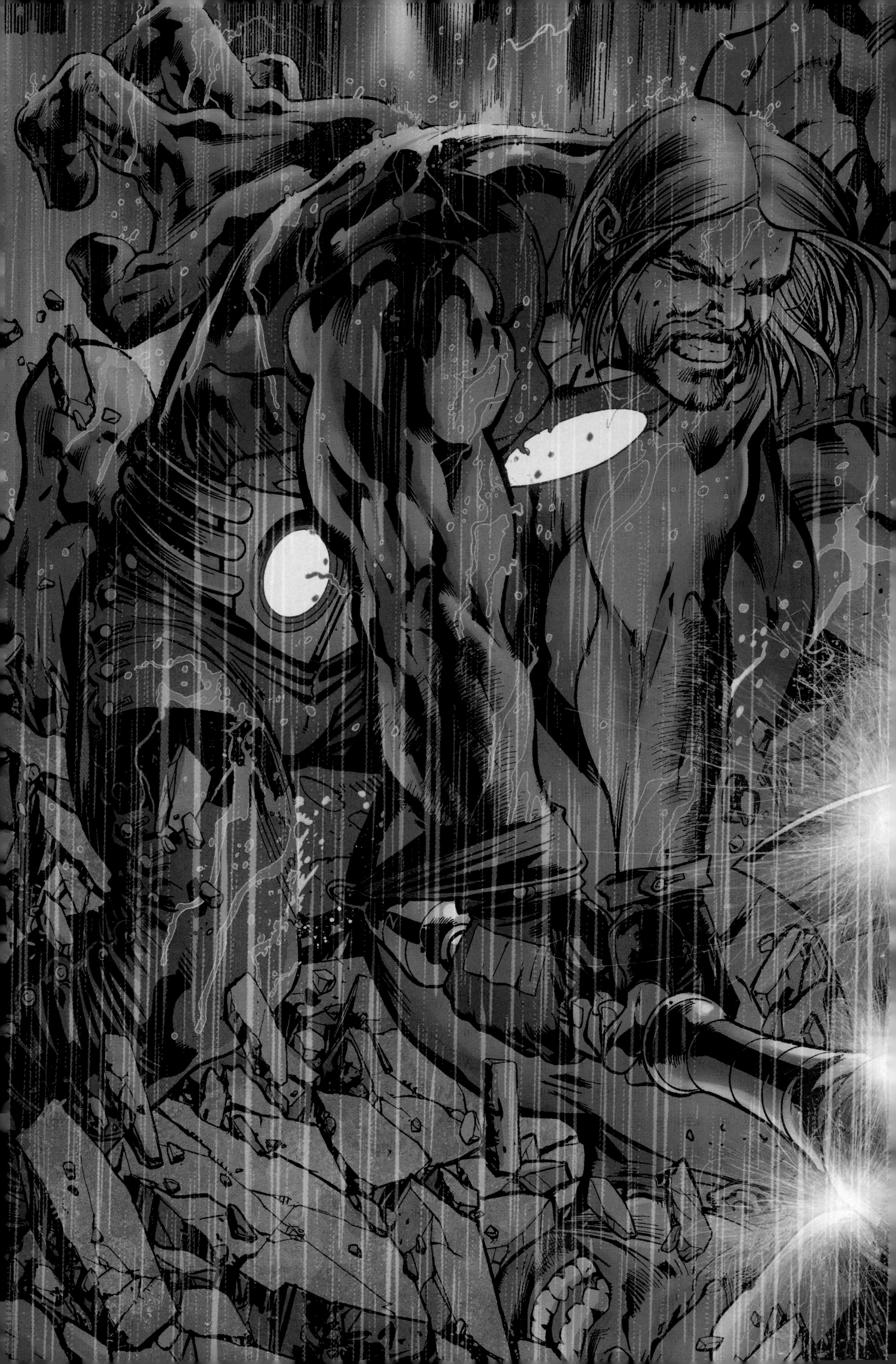

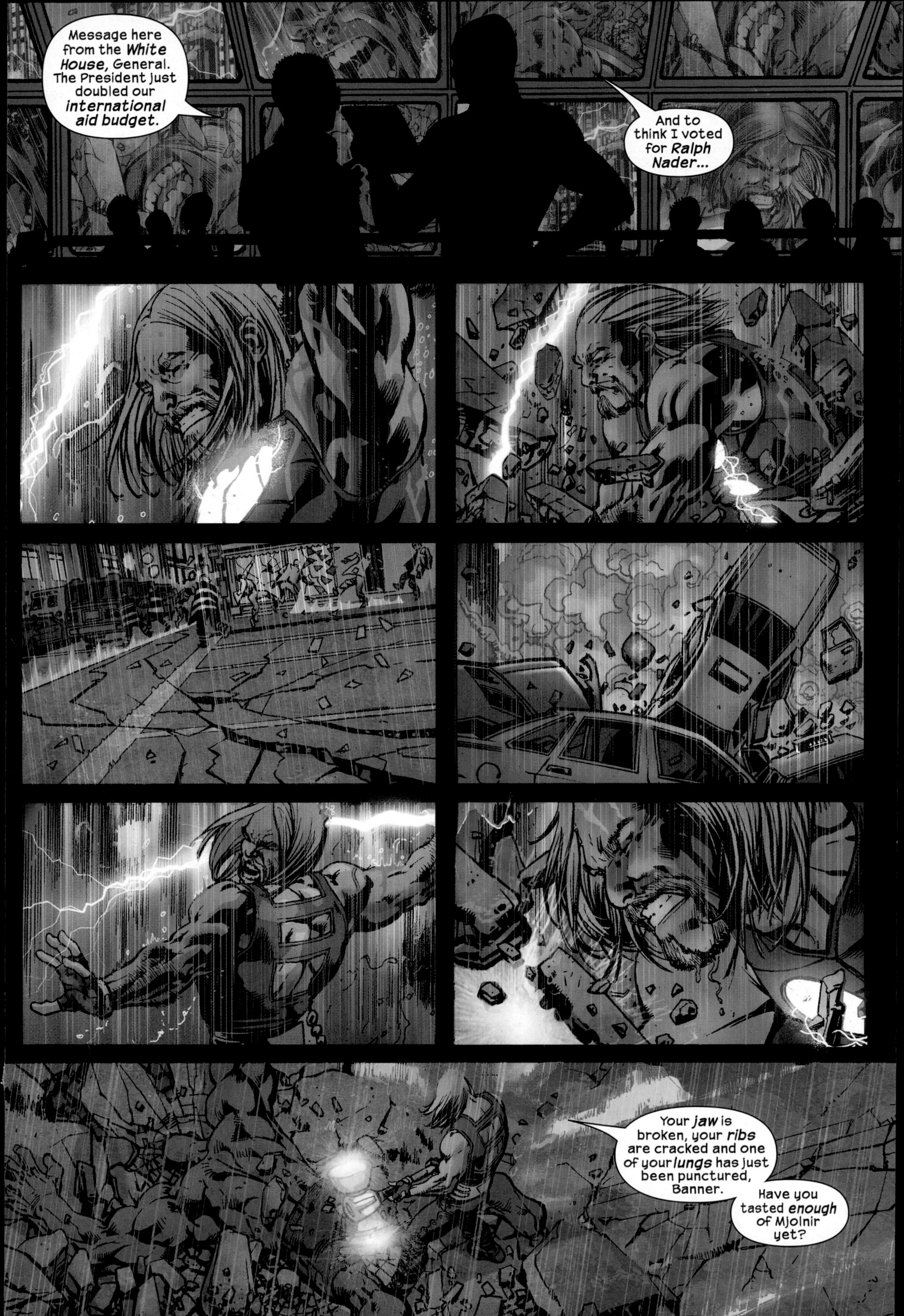
Message here from the White House, General. The President just doubled our international aid budget.
And to think I voted for Ralph Nader...
Your jaw is broken, your ribs are cracked and one of your lungs has just been punctured, Banner.
Have you tasted enough of Mjolnir yet?

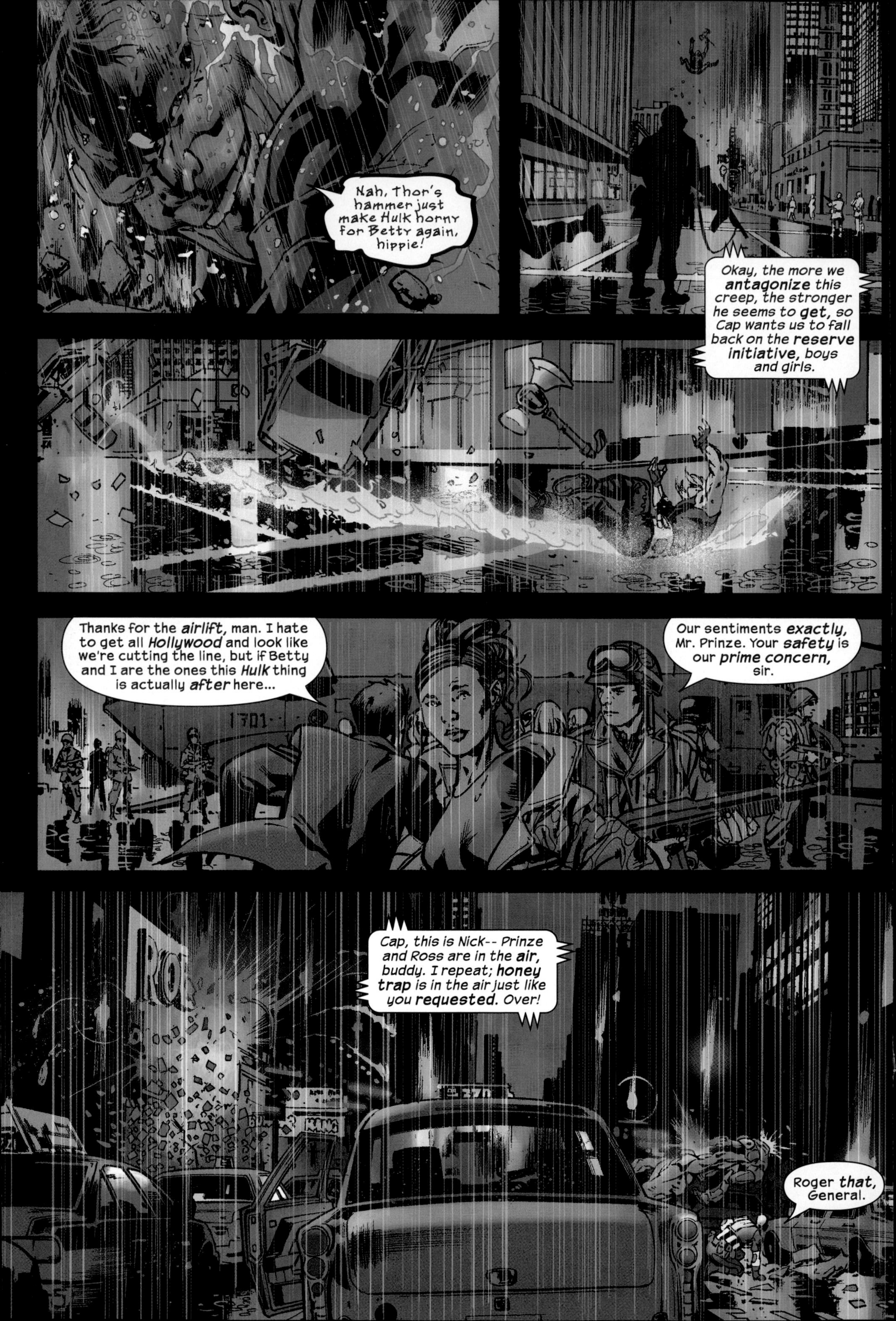
Nah, Thor's hammer just make Hulk horny for Betty again, hippie!
Okay, the more we antagonize this creep, the stronger he seems to get, so Cap wants us to fall back on the reserve initiative, boys and girls.
Thanks for the airlift, man. I hate to get all Hollywood and look like we're cutting the line, but if Betty and I are the ones this Hulk thing is actually after here...
Our sentiments exactly, Mr. Prinze. Your safety is our prime concern, sir.
Cap, this is Nick-- Prinze and Ross are in the air, buddy. I repeat; honey trap is in the air just like you requested. Over!
Roger that, General.

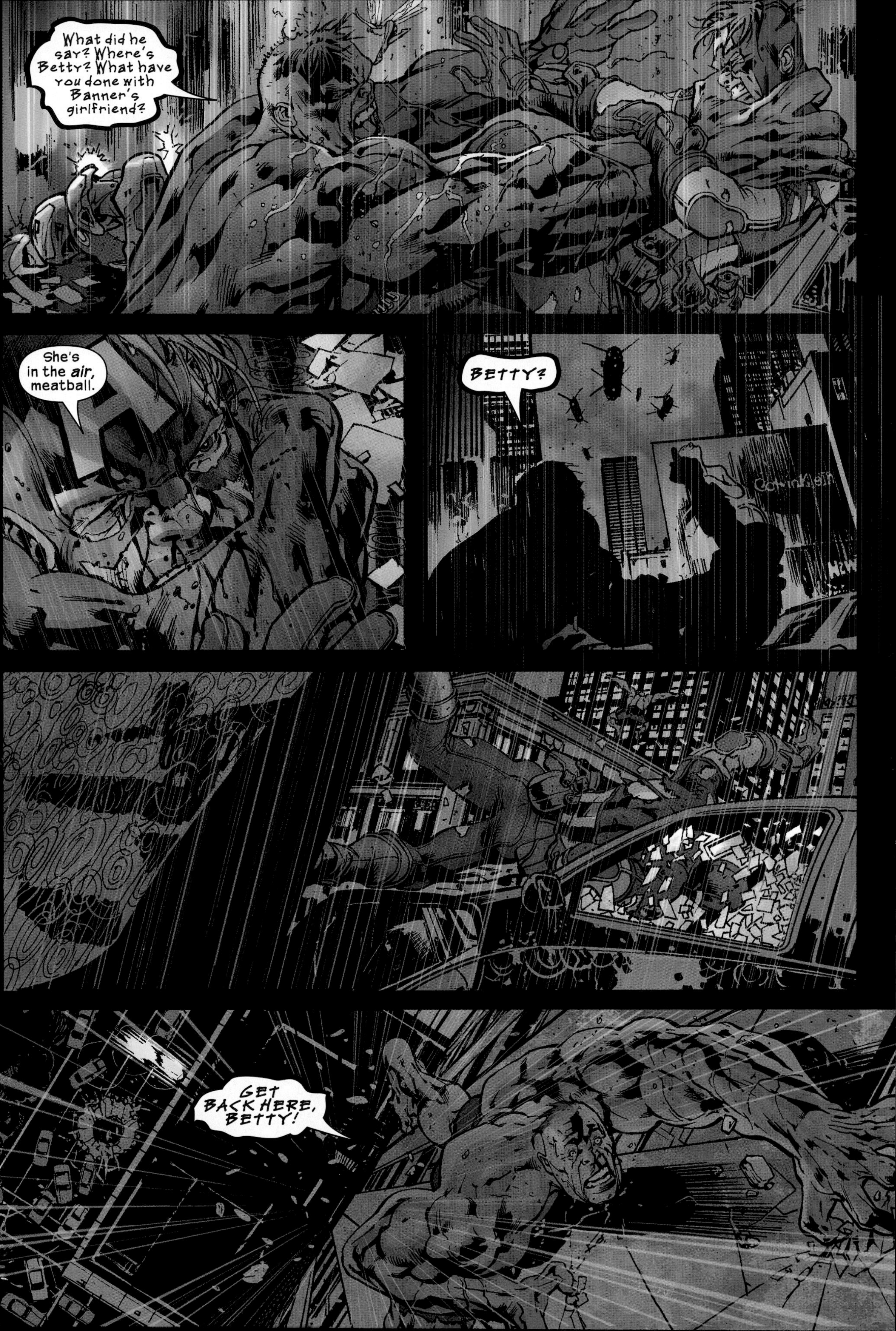
What did he say? Where's Betty? What have you done with Banner's girlfriend?
She's in the *air*, meatball.
BETTY?
GET BACK HERE, BETTY!

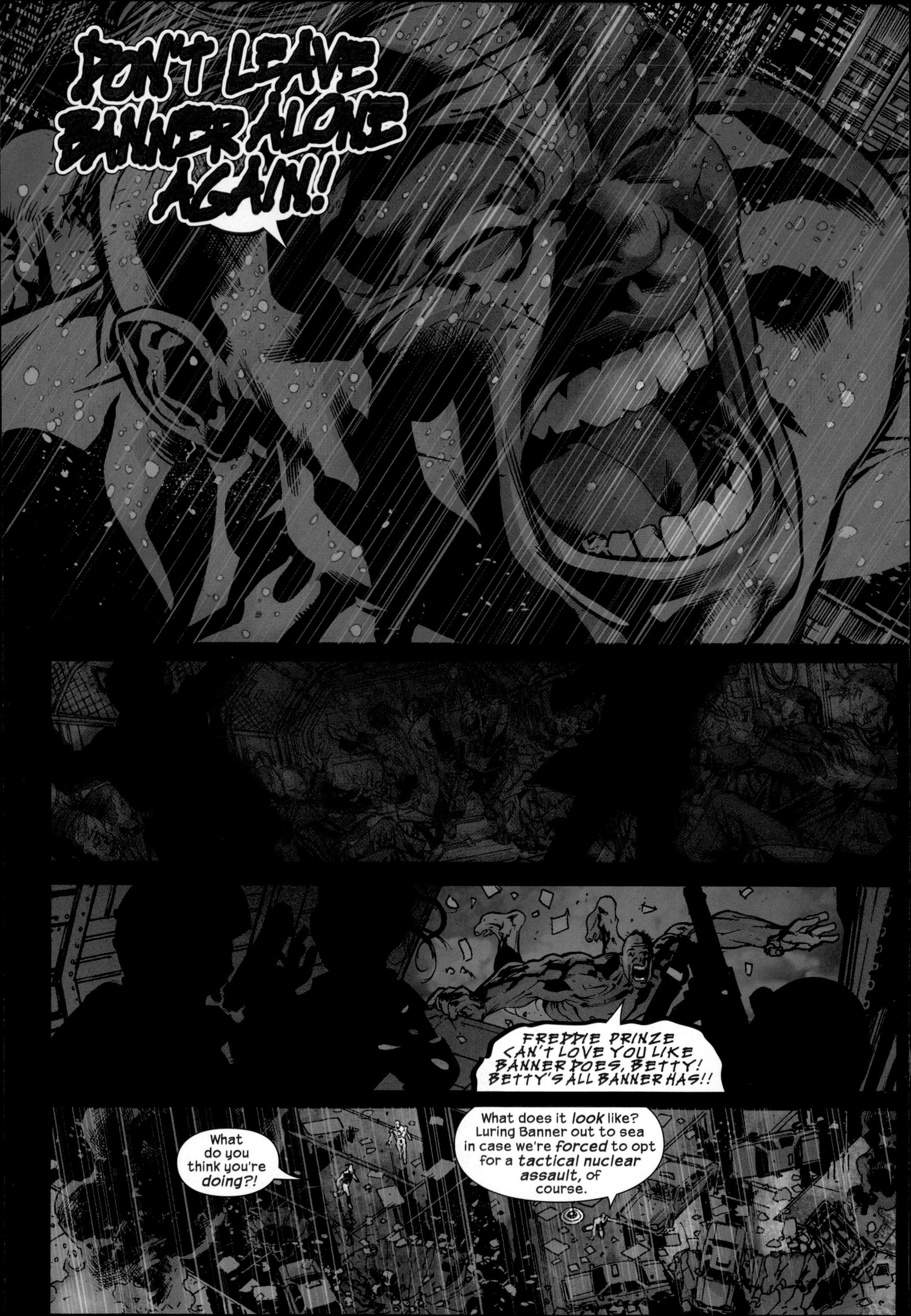
DON'T LEAVE BANNER ALONE AGAIN!
FREDDIE PRINZE CAN'T LOVE YOU LIKE BANNER DOES, BETTY! BETTY'S ALL BANNER HAS!!
What do you think you're *doing*?!
What does it *look* like? Luring Banner out to sea in case we're *forced* to opt for a *tactical nuclear assault*, of course.

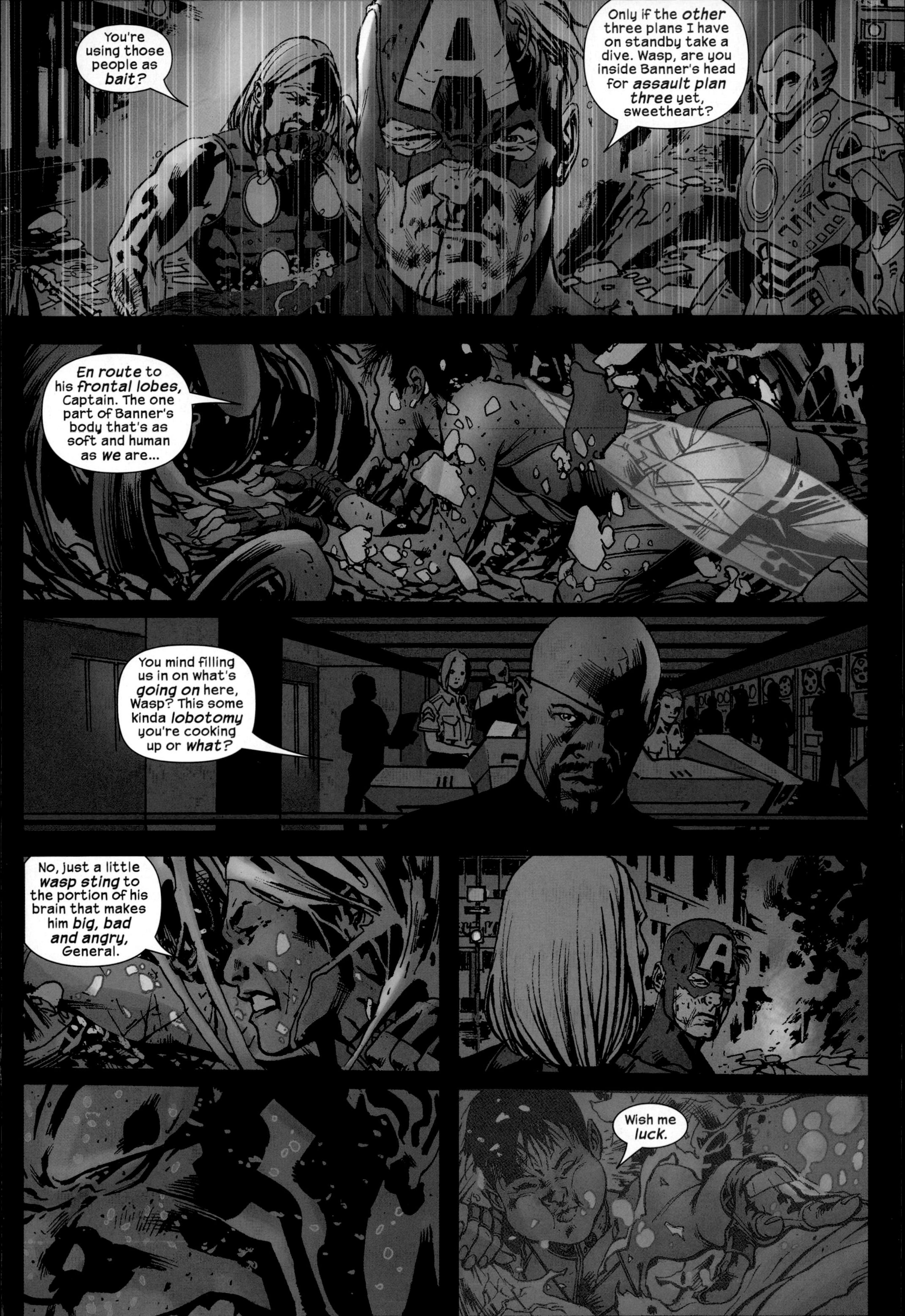
You're using those people as *bait?*
Only if the *other* three plans I have on standby take a dive. Wasp, are you inside Banner's head for *assault plan three* yet, sweetheart?
En route to his *frontal lobes,* Captain. The one part of Banner's body that's as soft and human as *we* are...
You mind filling us in on what's *going on* here, Wasp? This some kinda *lobotomy* you're cooking up or *what?*
No, just a little *wasp sting* to the portion of his brain that makes him *big, bad and angry,* General.
Wish me *luck.*

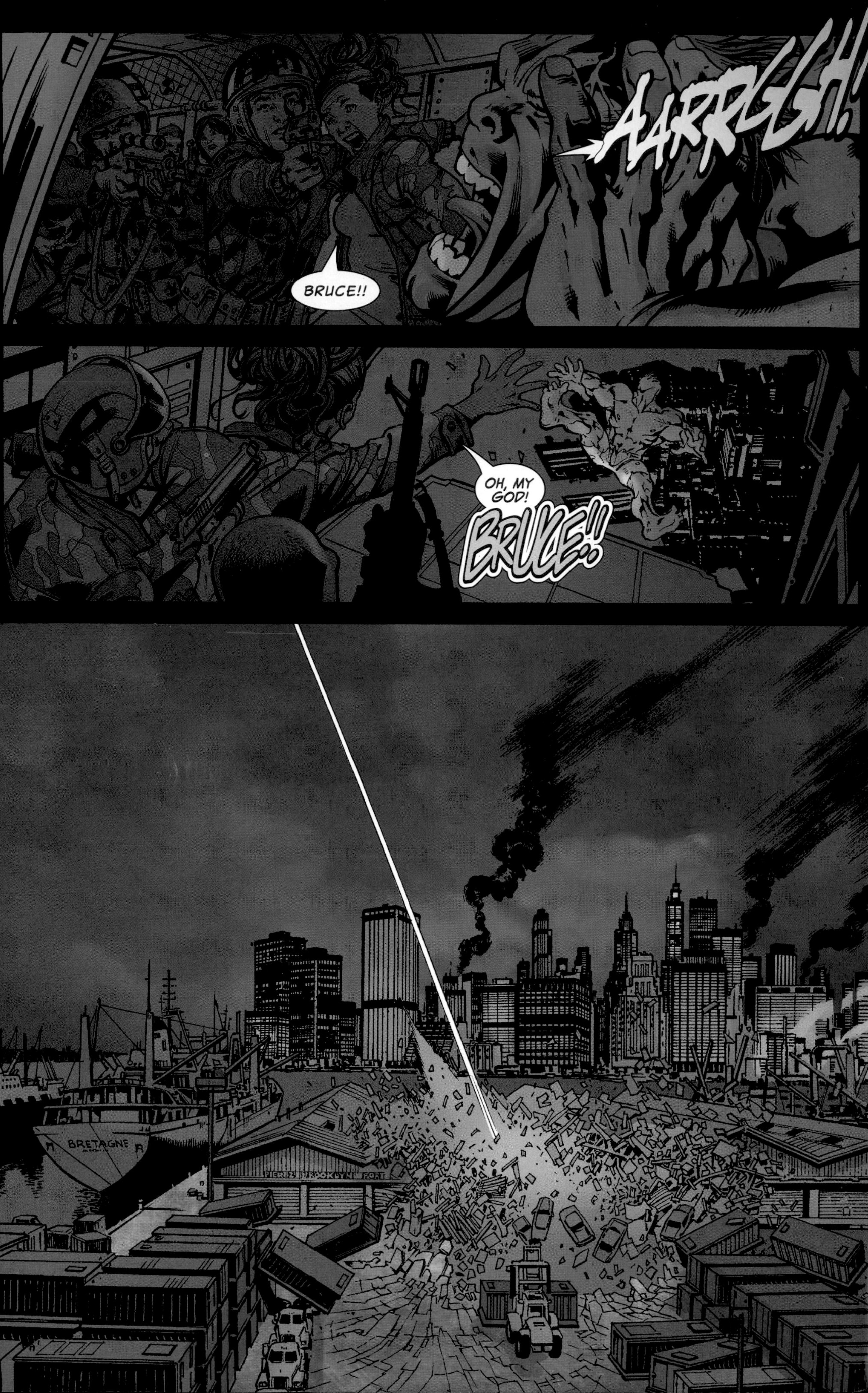
AARRGH!!
BRUCE!!
OH, MY GOD!
BRUCE!!
BRETAGNE
PIER 2 BROOKLYN PORT

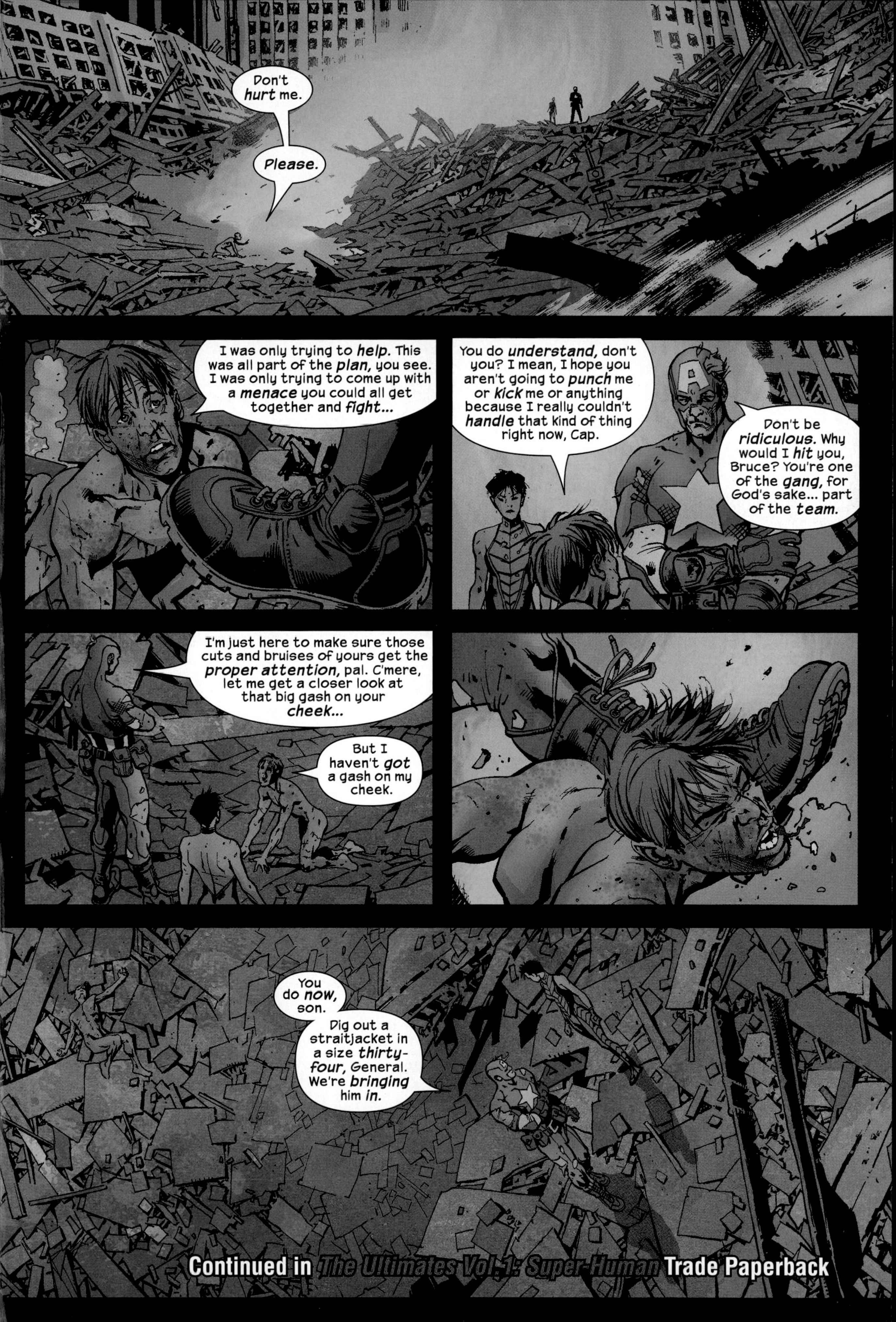

Don't hurt me.
Please.
I was only trying to help. This was all part of the plan, you see. I was only trying to come up with a menace you could all get together and fight...
You do understand, don't you? I mean, I hope you aren't going to punch me or kick me or anything because I really couldn't handle that kind of thing right now, Cap.
Don't be ridiculous. Why would I hit you, Bruce? You're one of the gang, for God's sake... part of the team.
I'm just here to make sure those cuts and bruises of yours get the proper attention, pal. C'mere, let me get a closer look at that big gash on your cheek...
But I haven't got a gash on my cheek.
You do now, son.
Dig out a straitjacket in a size thirty-four, General. We're bringing him in.

Continued in *The Ultimates Vol. 1: Super-Human* Trade Paperback

Abomination 29, 40, 43, 44, 117, 121, 123
Absorbing Man 32, 45, 87, 121
Alonso, Axel 108, 111-114
Andrews, Kaare.....................34, 35, 107, 110, 111, 178, 179, 181
Ant-Man/Giant-Man 17, 30, 35
Arad, Avi 159, 170
Avengers 17, 20, 28, 30, 31, 33, 80
Azzarello, Brian 125
Bana, Eric 13, 156, 159-162, 164,165, 167, 176
Banner (Comic Book) 31, 108, 109, 119, 125, 176
Banner, David (Movie Father) 32, 90, 155, 167
Beast-Man.................................45
Bixby, Bill 14, 23, 27, 89, 91-94, 96, 98-101
Black Bolt and the Inhumans 42, 45
Blade 170
Boomerang 42, 46
Bride of the Incredible Hulk 96, 98
Buscema, John 122
Byrne, John................................119, 123
Captain America 17, 26, 28, 35, 84, 103, 119, 121, 175
Chameleon 41, 43, 46
Colvin, Jack................................92, 94, 100
Connolly, Jennifer 156, 160, 161, 164-166, 169, 176
Corben, Richard 109, 124, 125, 176
Daredevil (Movie) 170
Daredevil/Matt Murdock 17, 22, 26, 96, 120, 175
David, Peter................................125
Death of the Incredible Hulk 96, 97
Deodato Jr., Mike 112, 121
Ditko, Steve...............................35, 122
Dr. Doom 20, 38, 43
Eisner, Will 26, 112
Elliot, Sam.................................29, 161, 165, 168
Fang, General 43, 46
Fantastic Four 17, 18, 26, 45, 75, 80, 116, 121
Ferrigno, Lou..............................15, 23, 37, 76, 89, 90, 92, 94-97, 99, 100,
....102-105, 161
Fury, Nick 17, 18, 26
Galactus 22, 38
Galaxy Master 45
Gargoyle 103
Garney, Ron 44, 124
Goodman, Martin 26
Green Goblin..............................38
Hercules 42, 46, 47
High Evolutionary 45
Hitch, Bryan 124, 180
Hulk (Comic Book) 18, 21, 28, 115, 116, 118, 123
Hulk (Movie) 15, 21, 22, 86, 87, 121, 155-157, 163,
....166, 167, 169, 170, 176
Hulk: Gray 35, 124, 181
Hulk: The Movie (Video Game)....83
Human Torch (Golden Age) 17
Immonen, Stuart.........................15, 16, 35, 46, 112-114, 175
Incredible Hulk (Cartoon) 103
Incredible Hulk (Comic Book)......16, 18, 27, 31, 32, 35, 76, 90, 108-111,
....114-119, 121, 123-125, 175, 176, 179, 181
Incredible Hulk (TV Show) 90, 92, 94, 96, 98
Incredible Hulk and She-Hulk 103
Incredible Hulk Returns 96
Incredible Hulk: Pantheon Saga ..83
Iron Man/Tony Stark 17, 30, 41, 45, 103, 120, 175
Jameson, J. Jonah 19
Jemas, Bill.................................108, 109, 125
Johnson, Kenneth.......................90-92
Jones, Bruce 35, 108, 112-114, 116, 176, 179, 181
Jones, Rick 19, 31, 91, 103, 123, 175
Kane, Gil 122

Keown, Dale 3, 25, 36, 37, 39, 80, 124, 125
Kieth, Sam..................................37, 124, 125
King Arkham 41
Kirby, Jack..................................16, 17, 19, 23, 26, 28, 32, 35, 37,
....112, 120, 122, 124, 157
Leader 20, 38-41, 43, 78, 103, 108, 122, 164, 176
Lee, Ang 12, 83, 87, 121, 154-157, 162, 163, 165, 176
Lee, Stan 12, 15, 17, 18, 20, 23, 26, 28, 32, 35, 36,
....79, 82, 90, 91, 96, 108, 112, 115, 122,
....157, 168, 178, 181
Loeb, Jeph 124, 181
Loki 45
Lord of the Living Lightning 45
Lucas, Josh................................31, 156, 160, 165, 169
Magneto 20
Mandarin...................................43, 45
McFarlane, Todd 124
McGee, Jack..............................91, 92, 99
Metal Master 43, 46
Millar, Mark 35
Mole Men 91
Mr. Fantastic 82
Namor the Sub-Mariner 17, 18, 46, 47, 103, 121, 123
Nolte, Nick.................................154, 155, 161, 165-167, 176
Parker, Aunt May 20
Professor X 20
Punisher 180
Puppet Master............................42, 45, 47, 121
Quesada, Joe 82, 108
Red Skull...................................38
Rhino..43, 46, 47, 119
Richards, Sue 81
Romita Jr., John 11, 23, 35, 112, 124, 179, 181
Ross, Betty 20, 27, 29, 31, 35, 44, 91, 103, 123, 155,
....156, 160, 166, 169
Ross, Gen. Thunderbolt 19, 20, 27, 29, 40, 91, 103, 108, 109, 154,
....155, 168
Sale, Tim 35, 124, 181
Samson, Doc 31, 34, 77, 103, 109, 119
Sandman....................................42, 45
Severin, Marie.............................32, 121, 122
She-Hulk/Jennifer Walters 20, 31, 33, 103, 175
Sienkiewicz, Bill..........................1, 82
Silver Surfer 41
Simon, Joe 26
Spider-Man (Movie) 86, 162, 170
Spider-Man/Peter Parker 16, 17, 19, 22, 26, 32, 36, 45, 78, 83, 103,
....114, 116, 120, 175
Storm 170
Talbot, Glenn.............................20, 27, 29, 31, 103, 155, 156, 160, 165, 169
Tales to Astonish (Comic Book) ..19, 21, 26, 31, 32, 38, 47, 116, 118,
....121, 123
Thing 18, 121
Thor..17, 26, 30, 32, 35, 36, 45, 96
Timm, Bruce 30, 178
Trial of the Incredible Hulk 96, 97
Trimpe, Herb..............................31, 32, 37, 109, 111, 122
Tyrannus 44, 46, 94
Ultimates, The 29, 35, 114, 119, 124-125, 166, 174-
....176, 181
Wasp 30, 35
Watson, Mary Jane 20
Weeks, Lee 35, 112, 180, 181
Wolverine 116, 119
X-Men 17, 26, 32, 83, 84, 114, 116
X-Men (Movie) 170
X2 170
Zaxon, Dr. Konard......................46